August and Marie Krogh

August and Marie Krogh

LIVES IN SCIENCE

Bodil Schmidt-Nielsen, Dr. Odont, Dr. phil.
*Professor Emeritus and Adjunct Professor,
Department of Physiology, University of Florida*

New York   Oxford
AMERICAN PHYSIOLOGICAL SOCIETY   1995

Oxford University Press

Oxford   New York   Toronto
Delhi   Bombay   Calcutta   Madras   Karachi
Kuala Lumpur   Singapore   Hong Kong   Tokyo
Nairobi   Dar es Salaam   Cape Town
Melbourne   Auckland   Madrid

and associated companies in
Berlin   Ibadan

Copyright © 1995 by the American Physiological Society

Published for the American Physiological Society by Oxford University Press, Inc.,
198 Madison Avenue, New York, New York 10016

Oxford is a registered trademark of Oxford University Press

All rights reserved. No part of this publication may be reproduced,
stored in a retrieval system, or transmitted, in any form or by any means,
electronic, mechanical, photocopying, recording, or otherwise,
without the prior permission of Oxford University Press.

Library of Congress Cataloging-in-Publication Data
Schmidt-Nielsen, Bodil.
August and Marie Krogh : lives in science
by Bodil Schmidt-Nielsen.
p.   cm. Includes index.
ISBN 0-19-509099-3
1. Krogh, August, 1874–1949.
2. Krogh, Marie, 1874–1943.
3. Physiologists—Denmark—Biography.
I. Title.
QP26.K76S35   1995   591.1′092—dc20
[B]   94-20655

9 8 7 6 5 4 3 2 1

Printed in the United States of America
on acid-free paper

Preface

When my father August Krogh died in 1949, I was with him in Denmark. My stay in Denmark was prolonged for another two months due to a concussion I sustained in an automobile accident, which occurred shortly after his death. It was then that I became familiar with the extensive material of biographical value which my father had left. Due to the pride and interest August took in his family, the material was very rich, consisting of family letters going back to his mother's birth in 1842, his own letters to his mother, father and siblings, between his siblings, between himself and my mother as well as his children. It included correspondence with his colleagues, university matters, Marie Krogh's letters, numerous notes and manuscripts, books, and scientific papers.

It became clear that I was the one to write the biography because I was a physiologist. In addition, I spoke and wrote English as well as Danish and I very much wanted to undertake the project. My brother, Erik, was to inherit the material, but he was not inclined to undertake such a major job and he as well as Torkel Weis-Fogh (my father's scientific assistant) encouraged me to write the biography.

It seems an awfully long time between making the decision and finishing the work. I began immediately after having had the material shipped to Duke University, but soon found that it was impossible to combine such a major undertaking with my other work (research, teaching, and taking care of my three children). My resolve was undiminished, but I had to put the writing on hold until my life became less complicated, which did not happen until after I retired. Weis-Fogh and I deposited the material in the Danish Royal Library in Copenhagen in 1964. During the intervening years, I continued to collect material of biographical significance. Then in 1987 the work began in earnest, but before I could start writing I had to copy all of the material we had deposited in the Danish Royal Library.

Writing the book has been an absorbing and deeply rewarding undertaking. In studying my father's and mother's writings and correspondence, I have come to admire them even more than I had before. As my mind filled with what I read and then wrote, my parents came vividly alive at all the various stages of their enormously productive lives. I have been asked if I learned things about them that I did not know before. I certainly did, but the image of these two people who were my parents did not change, only the depth of understanding. I also arrived at the sobering realization that many thoughts, beliefs, and ideas that I had believed were original to me have come to me through what my parents taught me when I was a child.

Gainesville, Fla.   B. S.-N.
July 1994

Acknowledgments

In this undertaking I have had a great deal of help and encouragement. In copying the files from the Royal Library in Copenhagen, my grandniece Maria Krogh Nielsen assisted me and Librarian Troels Lauring of Nordisk Insulin Laboratory kindly completed the task. All of it is now in my home in Gainesville, Florida. It is said that nothing is written until someone has read it. The first one to read my draft, encourage me and make small corrections was always my patient and beloved husband, Roger Chagnon. Next came my excellent editor Miss Susan Williams who helped get the Danish out of my English, then came my "two professors," Dr. Thomas Maren and Dr. Arthur Otis. I had told Tom Maren that I needed a critical audience. He suggested forming a small committee consisting of himself and Dr. Otis. During the years that I have been writing I regularly brought my pages to them. We would have lunch together while they read the next installment of the Krogh saga. I cannot thank these two friends enough for their never failing encouragement and kind suggestions. I have also regularly sent my manuscript to my family in Denmark, who have helped me with suggestions and more material and to Dr. Erik Hohwü Christensen in Sweden. Dr. Christensen's review of my chapter on exercise was very helpful. Dr. Michael Bliss kindly reviewed the chapter on insulin and Dr. Hans Ussing the isotope chapter. My former teacher and lifelong friend, Else Rahbek, was always willing to help me contact people in Denmark or find material I needed.

When I had almost finished, Dr. John West recommended the manuscript to the American Physiology History Section and to Oxford University Press, for which I am grateful.

The last and least-pleasant part has been to condense my manuscript. I was told by the publisher it had to be shortened by about a third but given no specific guidelines for what to take out. An excellent editor in New York, Ms. Beverly Pennachini, has been sufficiently tough-minded to help me take out the less essential material.

Contents

Chronology   xi

Introduction   3

1. Ancestry   5
2. Childhood in Grenaa (1874–1890)   10
3. School Years in Aarhus (1891–1893)   17
4. Becoming a Zoologist (1893–1895)   22
5. Becoming a Physiologist (1895–1899)   32
6. The Beginning of Zoophysiology (1899–1904)   44
7. August and Marie (1904)   60
8. Marriage and the Seegen Prize (1904–1906)   71
9. The Oxygen Secretion Controversy (1906–1910)   78
10. The Zoophysiological Laboratory and the Beginning of Exercise Physiology (1910–1916)   95
11. Capillaries and the Nobel Prize (1916–1922)   112
12. The Insulin Story (1922–1925)   126
13. The Happiest Years (1923–1938)   139
14. Capillary Function and the Contractility Controversy (1923–1936)   154
15. New Fields of Investigation (1928–1943)   163
16. Exercise Physiology (1918–1944)   173
17. The Introduction of Isotopes (1935–1944)   185
18. Dark Clouds (1938–1944)   193
19. Exile in Sweden (1944–1945)   209
20. The Private Laboratory in Gentofte (1945–1947)   218
21. Last Scientific Work (1945–1949)   229

Epilogue   239
Notes and References   241
August Krogh's Publications   261
Index   277

August Krogh Family Tree

Christen Christiansen Krogh (1720–1786) — **Maren Brick** (1743–?)

Children:
- **Christian Christensen** (1770–1837) Braenore-Frorup branch
- **Peter** (1773–1846) Haderslev branch
- **Jacob Andersen** (1775–1815)
- **Niels Mygind** (1778–1857) Korsor branch
- **Andreas** (1781–1858) Brewer branch
- **Marie Brick** (1788–1847)
- **Jens** (1784–1854) Skovgaard branch

Christsigne (Sine) (1809–1876) — **Johann Dreckmann** (1799–1843)

Andreas Lauritz (1816–1881) — **Bolette de Baes**

Jacob Emil (1822–1902) — **Freda Fischer** (1821–1910)

Marenline (Line) (1814–1867) — **Hans Detlef Krogh**

Marie Magdalene Bolette (Mimi) Dreckmann (1842–1927) — **Andreas Viggo Ditlev** (1848–1925)

Jacob Emil (1849–1933) another brother, 4 sisters

Schack August Steenberg (1874–1949) — **Birte Marie Jorgensen** (1874–1943)

Edel Christiene (1878–1950) (married 1 son, 1 daughter)

Frida Christiane (1882–1922) — **Johan Dreckmann** (1880–1955)

Inger Marie (Misse) (1885–1952) (married, 2 daughters)

Erik Viggo (1908–1958) — **Karen Hjort** (1914–)

Ellen Rigmor (1913–) — **Einar Ljunghusen**

Jacob Emil (1876–1950) — **Sofie Larsen**

Johan (1918–)

Agnes Helga (1917–) — **Christer Wernstedt** (?–1946)

Bodil Mimi (1918–) — **Knut Schmidt-Nielsen** (1915–)

Children:
- **Inger Marie** (1940–)
- **Ellen** (1944–)
- **Bodil** (1939–)
- **Bjorn** (1942–)
- **Bo** (1948–)
- **Lars** (1939–)
- **Christer** (1945–)
- **Astrid** (1941–)
- **Bent Krogh** (1944–)
- **Bodil Mimi** (1947–1984)

Chronology

1874	August Krogh born November 15 in Grenaa, Denmark.
1889–90	Voluntary apprentice of Danish Navy on the inspection boat *Hauch*.
1893	Artium (Entrance examination for the university) from Aarhus Cathedral school
1895	Preparatory examination for medicine, University of Copenhagen.
1899	Magister conference, University of Copenhagen. Scientific assistance in Christian Bohr's laboratory.
1902	First trip to Greenland to study atmospheric CO_2.
1903	Doctoral degree, Dr. phil.
1905	Marriage to Marie Jørgensen (born December 25, 1874)
1906	Seegen Prize.
1907	Marie gets her medical degree.
1908	August and Marie study in Greenland. Erik Viggo Krogh is born.
1910	Establishment of Zoophysiological Laboratory in Ny Vestergade. Publication of "the seven small devils."
1913	Ellen Rigmor Krogh is born.
1914	Marie's doctoral degree, Dr. med.
1916	Professor of zoophysiology.
1917	Agnes Helga Krogh is born.
1918	Bodil Mimi Krogh is born.
1920	Nobel Prize physiology or medicine.
1921	Honorary Dr. jur., University of Edinburgh.
1922	Silliman Lectures at Yale University.
1923	Starts insulin production in Denmark.
1928	Establishment of the Rockefeller Institute in Copenhagen.
1935	Honorary Dr. med., University of Budapest.
1936	Honorary Dr. sc., Harvard University. Honorary Dr. med., University of Lund.
1938	Honorary Dr. sc., Rutgers University.
1943	Marie dies March 25.

1944–45	Exile in Sweden.
1945	Establishment of private laboratory in Gentofte. Baly Medal. Croonian Lecture.
1946	Honorary Dr. phil., University of Oslo.
1949	Resignation from the Danish Royal Academy of Sciences. Dies September 13, in his house in Gentofte.

August and Marie Krogh

Introduction

> It must be a mistake, there is no Danish professor with that name.

On October 28, 1920, August Krogh and his wife, Marie, were seated at a banquet in the University of Copenhagen ceremonial hall, where the annual University Fest was in progress. The famous surgeon, Professor Thorkil Rowsing, was concluding his first year as university rector (president). Seated at the head table wearing the rector's chain, the Golden Rowsing, as he was called, was in an expansive mood. Candlelight reflected from the gold chain and from decorations on the chests of the distinguished faculty.

Rowsing had made the university celebration in 1920 unusually festive in order to appease the faculty. Great tension had prevailed in Denmark during the year as a result of the elections, which were to determine how much of southern Jutland (Schleswig) should be returned to Denmark following the end of World War I. By accepting the post as minister of education, Rowsing had angered the faculty. The cabinet lasted only a few days, but bad feelings toward Rowsing prevailed, because the faculty felt that the rector should not have mixed university affairs with politics. Now, however, the mood was improving in the festive surroundings.

Entering the hall, a journalist found her way among the seated guests, men in white ties and tails, women in long formal gowns. She found August Krogh and handed him a telegram. Soon several more reporters appeared. They approached the medical faculty and asked for Professor Krogh, who had just won the Nobel Prize for physiology or medicine. "It must be a mistake, there is no Danish professor with that name" was the answer. Eventually, it became clear that there was a Krogh on the science faculty and that he had indeed won an undivided Nobel Prize. Rowsing rose and gave a brilliant speech in Krogh's honor, but nobody could find Krogh. He had read the telegram, exclaiming, "That cannot be true." Shortly after he and Marie left unnoticed. Knowing that within half an hour the news would spread to all present, he wished to avoid the embarrassment of being celebrated.[1]

In the newsrooms of the five daily newspapers there was great confusion. Telegrams had arrived from Stockholm, but who was this August Krogh that nobody knew? How could reporters write about him for the morning papers when the only information they could find was his name and address in the telephone directory?[1]

Not a man to seek the limelight, August Krogh was unknown to the general public. However, he had made his mark in international scientific circles as early as 1906 when he won the Seegen Prize for his work on free nitrogen excretion, and again in 1910 when he and Marie published a series of papers proving that oxygen is not secreted but diffuses through the lung epithelium. The excellence and ingenuity of his continued work in metabolism, exercise physiology, and animal physiology had gained him a steadily growing reputation among his colleagues in Europe and in the United States. The Nobel Prize was awarded for his latest work, which dealt with the delivery of oxygen to the tissues and the regulation of capillary blood flow in muscle tissue during rest and work.

As the highest of honors that can be bestowed on a scientist, the Nobel Prize elevates the recipient to the uppermost layers of the scientific elite. The public demands that follow often put a damper on the prizewinner's scientific creativity. Not so for Krogh; he was to continue his remarkable scientific career for almost three decades. In addition to his studies of the physiology of circulation and exercise, he pioneered in several new fields: dissolved organic substances as food for aquatic animals, osmotic regulation in animals, transport of ions and water through biological membranes, isotopes in biological research, and, last, the physiology of insect flight. In the meantime he started insulin production in Denmark. After his death in 1949, his friend and colleague at Harvard University, Eugene Landis, wrote:

> It is rare enough that a scientist sheds light on an area which nature has kept secret and then during his lifetime, sees that area illuminate in turn every corner of physiology and medicine. It is rarer still that one man can contribute concurrently almost as much to several other biological fields as well. That meanwhile he should develop in addition a large school of devoted students who loved the man even more, if possible, than they venerated the scientist, spells the highest form of genius.[2]

1

Ancestry

> This, the devil take me, can't go on any longer.

Born November 15, 1874, in the small town of Grenaa on the Jutland peninsula of Denmark, August was the first-born child of the young shipbuilder Viggo Krogh and his wife Mimi. The couple had moved to Grenaa with Mimi's mother when they married in 1873.

Viggo and Mimi were first cousins (marriages between cousins were common) and their mutual grandfather was the Copenhagen brewer Andreas Krogh, born 1780 in Slesvig.

Andreas Krogh, founder of the "Brewer" branch of the Krogh family, had one younger and four older brothers. When his father, Christen, died, Andreas was only five years old and his mother had difficulties making ends meet. At a young age Andreas was sent out to herd cattle and when he was twelve, became a baker's apprentice. The baker liked him, found him intelligent and lively and often invited him into his living room to play *dam* (an old-fashioned checkers game). Andreas, however, understood that baking could not lead to a great future. Therefore, in 1800, he packed his knapsack and started out for Copenhagen where his younger brother Jens was working as a quartermaster in the army. When Jens received him coldly, Andreas apprenticed himself to a brewer. Andreas, who was frugal and a hard worker, saved his money and after some years Jens suggested that the two go into business together and rent a brewery, They rented one in Trompeter Street and went to work.[1]

In 1807, during the Napoleonic Wars, Copenhagen was bombarded by the British. The English had demanded that Denmark enter into an alliance with England, which the Danish Crown Prince was quite willing to do; however, when they also demanded that Denmark hand over the entire Dano-Norwegian navy in pawn for the duration of "the present situation," the Crown Prince refused. Under General Wellesley (later Duke of Wellington), Zealand was invaded when the thirty-thousand-man English artillery forces took up position outside Copenhagen. The city, surrounded by old defense ramparts, had at that time a population of 100,000. A final note demanding the surrender of the Danish fleet was dispatched by the English commander to the commandant of Copenhagen. The demand was not met so the bombardment of Copenhagen began.[2]

For the next three days bombs rained down on Copenhagen, where Andreas and Jens were busy day and night putting out the many fires to protect their brewery. After the third night without sleep, Andreas, who was the one of the two who could think best, said to Jens, "This, the devil take me, can't go on any longer." They hitched up the wagon with all four horses and drove through the gate to Amager where a kind farmer took them in. The next day, unable to stay away from their beloved brewery, Andreas and Jens walked back to Copenhagen.[1] Just as they went through Amager gate, they saw the spire of the Church of Our Lady, glowing red in flames, twisting one-half turn around in the strong heat before it fell.[2,3] In horror and disbelief they continued on to Trompeter Street, where they found their brewery relatively unharmed. Cannonballs had fallen into the courtyard but had caused little damage.[1] Later, after the fire, Andreas bought a burned-out lot in Nybro Street, facing Frederiksholms Canal, where he built his own brewery. A cannonball from the yard was built into the wall of the brewery in Nybro Street and remains there today.

The bombardment had lasted from half past seven on Wednesday evening until five o'clock on Saturday evening, when General Peymann finally gave up and sent negotiators to the English camp. Three hundred buildings had been destroyed and 1,600 badly damaged. Of the civilians, 1,600 men, women and children lost their lives and 4,000 were seriously injured.[2] But Andreas and Jens went to work brewing beer for the thirsty inhabitants of Copenhagen. Andreas's foresight in saving the wagon and the horses also paid off. The brothers made good money on the cleanup and rebuilding of Copenhagen that soon followed.[1]

Denmark's economy suffered severely from the loss of the fleet and trade following the country's seven-year war with England and from the separation from Norway, which was forced into union with Sweden.[2] In spite of all this, the two brewers made money. Jens, however, soon tired of brewing and left, so Andreas built his own brewery, to which he added beautiful, stately apartments facing the canal. These he rented to wealthy people, among them the theologian Professor Hermansen, who became a close friend of the family.

In 1808 Andreas proposed to Marie Brick, daughter of an aquavit distiller in Adelgade. The wedding date was set, but Andreas talked his fiancée into getting her birth certificate a few days earlier. Then having procured a royal marriage license, he invited her out for a carriage ride, but instead drove straight to Frederiksberg, where they were married. Great consternation ensued in Adelgade when Marie's parents found out. Andreas, like the Kroghs of later generations, hated the traditional wedding festivities and did what he could to avoid them.

Marie was a beautiful woman with large brown eyes, tall forehead,

Ancestry

and thick brown hair.[3] Four children were born to Andreas and Marie Krogh. The first, Christsigne Marie Elisabeth (Sine) Krogh, was born in 1809. Next came daughter Marenline Petrine (Line), and two sons, Andreas Lauritz and Jacob Emil.

In 1839 thirty-year-old Sine married Johann Dreckmann, who had just been appointed customs officer in Wansbeck on Holstein's southern border. Dreckmann was very eager and conscientious in his position. When he was received in audience to thank the king of Denmark for the appointment, the king patted him on the shoulder and said, "Well, can he now take good care of my customs border?"[3]

A handsome man with dark curly hair and brown eyes, Dreckmann was born November 7, 1799, and it was said in the family that he was part Gypsy. The couple had only one child, Marie Magdalene, nicknamed Mimi. In 1843, when Mimi was only one and a half years old, Johann Dreckmann died from tuberculosis following a long illness. Before he died he asked Sine to promise him never to spoil Mimi. Sine and Mimi became very close and remained together for the rest of Sine's life, even after Mimi married. As was customary for the time, Mimi was brought up firmly and sternly but also with great love. A determined and authoritative lady, Sine needed only to look at her little daughter sternly or reproachfully and Mimi knew precisely how far she dared go and what was expected of her.[3]

Mimi's childhood was spent partly in Copenhagen, where Sine and Mimi moved in with Sine's father after her mother's untimely death. Before his wife died, Andreas Krogh made the unusual decision that his two daughters should inherit equal shares of his fortune. (According to Danish law of the time, sons should inherit twice as much as daughters.) Thus Sine was well off for the rest of her life. When Mimi was ten years old, she and her mother moved to Slesvig where Mimi got an excellent education and became fluent in several languages. She had a happy, carefree childhood in relative luxury. After the 1864 war in which Denmark lost Slesvig to Germany, the situation in Slesvig became intolerable and Sine moved with Mimi back to Zealand. It was then that the twenty-two-year-old Mimi became reacquainted with her sixteen-year-old cousin, Viggo Detlev Krogh—called Viggo—son of Sine's younger brother, Jacob Krogh, proprietor of Voxstrup Farm. Viggo had been an apprentice in shipbuilding in Elsinore. Viggo was eager to learn and on Sundays went to the Massmanske School where he received not only honorable mention, but later both the small and large silver medals for his industry and ability. In Sine and Mimi's home, where he became a frequent guest, Mimi taught him German and English, and the two started to write each other in English.

In 1871 Mimi and Viggo became engaged and two years later they were finally married. The voluminous letters between them show their tremendous love and respect for each other.[4] They were both deeply religious. Mimi was light-hearted and full of humor, while Viggo was somewhat moody. Having had a happy and eventful childhood and adolescence, Mimi saw the light side of every situation. In contrast, Viggo's childhood had not been happy due to his father's complex nature and fierce temper.

At the time of the engagement, Viggo, striving to become independent in his field of shipbuilding, had moved to Frederikshavn where he was working for shipbuilder Valdemar Buhl. During the summer of 1871 Viggo was in charge of building a harbor on the island Læsø. He succeeded against many odds, such as great storms, which made him feel God's helping hand was always with him. Following completion of the harbor, Viggo had risen to become shipyard foreman and Buhl's top employee. In letters to Mimi he expressed his dearest hope that Buhl would make him a partner in the shipyard.

During Christmas vacation, when Viggo was back in Copenhagen to be with his beloved "little Mimi" and on Voxstrup Farm with his parents, Buhl apparently decided not to take a business partner. Instead he wished to make his firm "Buhl and Son" within twenty years.

Seeing his hopes dashed and reconsidering his options, Viggo sought advice from his father and Mr. Rohman in Elsinore, his former master and valued friend. In Copenhagen, Burmeister had recently started construction of iron ships. (In 1872 Burmeister and Wain founded their machine and shipbuilding company.) Jacob went to Burmeister for advice, hoping that Burmeister could give Viggo a position. Burmeister made it clear that the future lay in the construction of iron steamships and that the age of wooden ships was nearing its end. He could not definitely promise Viggo a position but advised him to learn more about iron ship construction and come back. Still waiting for Rohman's opinion, Viggo hesitated. Finally, in early March the long-awaited letter came. Yes, Rohman felt that now was the time for Viggo to go abroad and learn as much as possible about his trade before he opened his own business.

This settled it. Viggo made up his mind to leave for Glasgow to study the construction of iron ships at John Elders and Company. In April of 1872 he left, and Mimi, who had tried her best to be brave, for once lost her self-restraint and cried bitterly on the way home.

In Scotland, Viggo worked hard to learn the trade. Opportunity to study theory was scant and the pay was small (fifteen shillings a week). In August 1872 he wrote Mimi that his real desire was to obtain a position at the newly founded Burmeister and Wain Company. Even though he would not be independent, he and Mimi would be able to manage for a while on what he could earn plus the money Mimi would have from her mother.

Jacob had followed his son's career with keen interest and love. When Mimi asked him to go talk with Burmeister again, he gladly did it, but found that Burmeister could barely remember his earlier suggestion that the young Krogh, after his training in Scotland, should seek a

Ancestry

position at Burmeister and Wain. This time Burmeister gave a vague promise saying "maybe" there could be a job, but inferior to the one he had previously suggested.

After this somewhat discouraging conversation, Jacob and Sine had several long discussions, deciding they would jointly provide the capital for Viggo to return to Denmark and start his own shipyard for building wooden ships. (To start a shipyard for the construction of iron ships would be financially prohibitive.)

Viggo quickly made up his mind to return to Denmark, a little sad that his dreams again had come to naught, but grateful for the new opportunity to start his own shipyard. There followed a time of intense activity. Viggo looked over the situation in Aarhus, but found the harbor unsuitable for his plans. He particularly wanted to repair wooden ships that had been shipwrecked and wanted a place where they might come for repairs. Grenaa seemed a more logical place, if only the new harbor would become a reality. From newspaper articles, this seemed to be happening.[4]

Since 1812 the harbor had been three kilometers from the center of town on the shore of the Kattegat, the sea dividing Jutland and Sweden. In 1868 the Harbor Commission wrote the county commission that the harbor was unsatisfactory, too small and too shallow, considering its increasing importance for fishing. The County Commission agreed and directed a request to the Department of Interior Affairs. Thus, in October 1872 when Viggo arrived in Grenaa the situation looked promising.[5] Eager to prove himself worthy of the trust of his relatives and the citizens of Grenaa, Viggo now worked incessantly to get his shipyard underway. On October 22, he was at Voxstrup Farm to look at lumber with his father. He also bought wood in several parts of the country, rented a room at the harbor, and hired men to start construction of a schooner with the intention of selling shares in the vessel. Grenaa dignitaries encouraged him.

In spite of the many hopeful signs, all was not well, because harbor negotiations dragged on with the powerful Consul Momme's opposition to the harbor construction. In the year that followed his arrival in Grenaa, Viggo barely had time to visit Mimi. Even over Christmas he had to stay in Grenaa to work. Back in Copenhagen Mimi and Sine continued the preparations for the wedding while following his difficulties and progress with keen interest and letters of encouragement.

Finally on October 16, 1873, the wedding took place in beautiful sunshine in the old Frederiksberg church where brewer Andreas Krogh had married Marie Brick in 1808. The same evening the young couple sailed to Grenaa, while Sine followed later.[3]

2

Childhood in Grenaa (1874–1890)

> As happy as your father and I were that Sunday morning November 15th, 31 years ago and how we thanked God for this great gift, you cannot understand now, but you will probably learn to understand it later.

Life in the new Grenaa home seems to have been idyllic. They lived in a beautiful house purchased by Sine and Mimi on a visit to Grenaa. In the early morning Mimi picked strawberries and asparagus and in the afternoon she sat in the garden with her mother while Marie, the maid they brought with them from Copenhagen, served them tea. Viggo worked diligently at the harbor, building his first schooner.

On November 15, 1874, Mimi bore a son whom they named Schack August Steenberg after their friend and family physician, Dr. Steenberg, who attended the birth. Mimi, who had broken her weak knee two weeks earlier, was confined to bed. She had been gravely ill and they feared for her life.[1] (Since early childhood she had tuberculosis in her knee.) But, as usual, she was in high spirits despite the pain. Years later Mimi wrote in her birthday letter to the newly married August, "As happy as your father and I were that Sunday morning November 15th, 31 years ago and how we thanked God for this great gift, you cannot understand now, but you will probably learn to understand it later."[2]

Two weeks after August's birth, Viggo launched his first schooner. Sine spent much time with her little grandson, and taught him to speak at an early age. August's younger brother Johan has written about those early years in Grenaa: "Our young parents were, it seems, very happy in their marriage because they loved each other deeply and were well suited for one another in character as well as in their way of thinking. . . . The first years in Grenaa they had Grandmother Dreckmann with them and she shared their sorrows and happiness. Grandmother was very fond of the little August and taught him poems. . . . He was a healthy and intelligent little fellow and gave his parents and his grandmother much happiness.[3]

When Viggo went over his accounts after the completion of the first schooner he realized that most of his capital was used up. Even so he started building a second schooner. On September 11, 1876, Sine Dreckmann, who had often been sick in the past few years, died from cancer. The last night before she died she called Viggo to her bedside and said, "Dear Viggo, I have been deeply worried about your's and Mimi's future here in Grenaa, but a tranquility and peace, such as I have never known before, has now descended upon my soul and I *know* now that the future will turn out well for you two in this town."[4]

When Sine died, Mimi was pregnant. Her second son, Emil, was born December 19, 1876. It was a difficult time for the young couple. Viggo, who used to walk the long way to and from his shipyard each day, now stayed there for days at a time working on the second schooner. He did not even come home for August's second birthday. Half a year after Sine's death, a brewery on Lillegade came up for sale. After many discussions Viggo bought the brewery from the owner, Caspar Seiling, using the inheritance from Sine as a down payment.[4]

By this time the large house at Lillegade 50 had already been sold to Burgomaster Krabbe. (The building has since been known as the Burgomaster House. A plaque on the building tells that August Krogh was born there.)

Viggo's new business, Djursland Brewery, gradually became a large enterprise, supplying the town and a large part of the surrounding area with beer. It was at times profitable, but the demands of the growing family were great and the couple always had to save money to the utmost. Viggo eventually sold the brewery in 1908 after several meager years, due to increasing competition from the larger Danish breweries such as Carlsberg, Tuborg, and others.

Viggo and Mimi had six children: (the name by which they were called is given in italics): Schack *August* Steenberg, November 15, 1874; Jacob *Emil* Andreas, December 19, 1876; *Edel* Christine, August 27, 1878; *Johan* Dreckmann, November 6, 1880; *Frida* Christiane, December 22, 1882; Inger Marie *(Misse)*, December 27, 1885. The brewery was the childhood home for August and his siblings. The children, as was customary then, were never spoiled by their parents and were often spanked for minor trespasses, even as toddlers. But they were greatly loved and cared for and Mimi thought of every detail concerning their upbringing and welfare, as is evident from her many letters to her children. Mimi writes to the six-year-old August during his visit to Viggo's parents in Copenhagen:

> Hope you are well and behave properly at your grandparents! I miss you very much but I shall be comforted when I learn that all is well with you. I was home alone today and yesterday as your father went to Himmelbjerget on Friday. The little ones are well. I send greetings to you from Mrs. Momme and Mrs. Krabbe. I am sending your new boots, four new pocket handkerchiefs, three collars, and a boot buttoner. Now you must be a neat, good boy, help yourself, and take good care of your

own things. Wash your face, your hands, neck, and ears so that they are really clean, and remember to button all your buttons, also the suspenders. If there is something you cannot do, then ask Hansine to help you; the good girl has done that before. Your dear little Aunt Anna will probably help you write a short letter to me. You can ask her to line the writing paper as I used to do and you are permitted to write with a pencil. Don't forget your evening prayer which I know you can do yourself.[5]

August answered:

Today I wish to tell you that I am well here in Copenhagen, and I walk and play a great deal each day. Grandmother has given me a small cannon that I shoot in Frederiksberg Park. I remember your instructions, dear Mother, and Grandfather and Grandmother are well satisfied with me. Greet father and the little ones, lovingly from your little August.[6]

A few months before he died, August himself wrote a short note about his childhood in Grenaa:

I cannot say that I felt close to the life in Grenaa. I only had few close friends of my age and most of them died in their childhood. It is my impression that also my parents felt somewhat isolated. My memories are concerned mostly with home, school and the surrounding nature. . . . I remember a great deal about the brewery where I grew up, situated between Lillegade, Nedergade and Storegade. . . . Much was found that made a deep impression on me, among other things a large number of wild boars' teeth. I remember particularly the asparagus beds that were like a forest for a small boy. A yearly returning feast was the treatment of the beer barrels. The old layer of pitch was melted and burned off by means of long, red-hot irons. With intervals the pitch caught fire and a flame several meters long rushed with a howl out of the reserve opening. At last when the barrel was sufficiently warm, melted pitch was poured in, the barrel tightly closed and then rocked and rolled so that the pitch covered the entire inner surface. It became one of my privileges that at that occasion I could get new pitch for my electrical machine. For some years father burned malt for home brewing. This was done over a wood fire and for that he brought large stumps rather cheaply because they were so hard to split. Father used to blow them apart with small charges of gunpowder in drill holes and became quite an expert at it. We followed the procedure with a mixture of fear and delight.[7]

To harden her children against diseases, Mimi frequently, sometimes daily, gave them cold baths in the early morning. Taking turns, they stood in a tub while she pressed a large sponge soaked in icy fresh or salt water against their shivering small bodies. Salt water for this purpose was brought back from Grenaa harbor when the wagon delivered beer to the waterfront. Their bedrooms had no heat and August remembered from his boyhood how he, before he could wash himself on winter mornings, had to break the ice on his water jug with the rock-hard frozen sponge. As a small boy August did not always like the cold water, but when he grew up, cold morning showers in the winter and early morning swims in the sea in the summer became lifelong habits.

In many respects, August was, from the beginning, quite different from his siblings. He steered toward his goals seemingly without hesitation and demonstrated marked and surprising ingenuity from a very young age. When he and his brothers skated on their father's ponds, August made a sail so that he could glide with great speed over large areas. To his brothers' amusement, he also practiced tacking with his sail on the ice. Later, he helped his brothers and sisters with their schoolwork and taught them mathematics.

Sometime before he entered school, August's parents noticed that he was left-handed. As was the custom in those days, he was forced to wear a stiff glove on his left hand for an entire year. For a while his left hand was almost useless, but later on he became ambidextrous. At age six when August was ready for school, Mimi wrote to a friend: "August reads almost too fluently, as he often skips the punctuation from pure eagerness. We have started German, geography, and arithmetic. Next fall, God willing, I shall hand him over to the school in good shape. Then he must take care of his own learning."[8]

School for August was easy, but he was generally considered by fellow students as well as teachers to be lazy. When he was engaged he told his fiancée: "That was partly true as I hardly ever studied my lessons. I was far more interested in collecting and studying animals, as well as doing physical experiments. I often felt very guilty because of this, but Nilsson [Carl Nilsson, a teacher August thought highly of] came to my rescue. Unafraid, he explained that I did well by being lazy in this way. He helped me with books, gave much good advice and taught me to read thoughtfully and critically." Together with Nilsson he took apart a telescope he had been given for his confirmation, "studying how each lens functioned, both separately and together. We discovered among other things that the eyepiece could function as a small microscope. Before long, I had made a holder from wood and studied everything within my reach under my microscope."[9]

August's interest in insects was not limited to collecting and identifying them. He would also spend hours watching their behavior in nature. He knew them so well that years later when he studied zoology at the university, he could determine the identity of some of them from his childhood memories. August read his father's book *Naturkræfterne* and performed experiments, creating his own instruments from material he could gather or buy in Grenaa. He learned to use whatever was at hand and often had to improvise, a practice serving him well when he began his scientific work.

The person who had the greatest influence on August as a young boy and particularly during his studies at the university was Viggo's best friend, the zoologist William Sørensen. Uncle William (as Viggo's children called him) spent every summer vacation at the brewery in Grenaa (except during a stay in South America), and as August grew up a deep friendship and mutual respect developed between them. Many of August's choices in the path he was to follow can be traced to the example set by his "uncle" William. Later August wrote: "Frequently, as a boy I have followed him on nature walks. He showed me how the spider worked on its web, how the heart was beating in a transparent larvae and numerous other things, always in such a way that it became a personal experience, something I personally could see and understand. William Sørensen had an ability . . . to ask and to answer in such a way that his listeners understood that there was a problem that had to be carefully considered."[10] Sørensen had a great fund of knowledge but freely admitted what he did not know, "I know that I'm neither politician or journalist. I don't have to know everything between heaven and earth." Years later August did likewise; when asked about something he didn't know, he said, "I don't know, I am as ignorant as a piglet."

Born in Hyllested, near Grenaa, William grew up in Esbønderup on Zealand where his father was a preacher.[11] In his highly intellectual home, he received a good education. As Esbønderup was near Voxstrup Farm, William and Viggo, who were the same age, became close friends in early childhood. Because they appear to have had such different characters, it seems strange that they could appreciate each other so much. While Viggo was deeply religious, William was agnostic. Viggo rarely spoke or wrote unkindly or critically of others, while William engaged in often vicious polemics. He was intensely critical of anyone in any profession who did not live up to his own high standards of honesty, integrity, and excellence in performance. Perhaps it was because Viggo did live up to these standards that William admired and loved him.

In the fall of 1866, William moved to Copenhagen to begin his studies in the introductory courses to medicine (philosophy, chemistry, botany, and zoology) at the University of Copenhagen. In 1867 William wrote and explained to Viggo his plan to study zoology: "As you know, I had more or less decided to study medicine, but you also know that all along I have had a greater inclination toward zoology."[12] There were very few positions available for zoologists and only under the luckiest conditions could he hope to obtain one. By choosing zoology he faced a financially uncertain future. Only if he had the ability to become a first-rate scientist could he hope to make it in this field. Marriage would have to be put off for many years.

Twenty-five years later, August followed the same pattern: Much against his father's wishes he chose zoology after he had finished the introductory courses to medicine. It was an uncertain future but it was August's calling and he intended to become a scientist.

William, having finished his studies in 1873 with a magister conference (similar to a master's degree) in zoology, taught at various schools in Copenhagen. In 1884 he earned a doctorate degree (Dr. phil.) for his work "The sound organs in fishes, a physiological and comparative study." Although Sørensen became well-known and highly regarded for his scientific work, particularly his studies of spiders, he never obtained a position at the University of Copenhagen and had to scratch out a living as a substitute teacher.[11] This was not due to lack of quality in his work but rather to his biting wit and criticism, which earned him a reputation as the enfant terrible of Danish zoology. Thus, he wrote three polemic books full of often deserved, scathing criticism of several well-known university professors. He despised plagiarism and any other form of scientific dishonesty and felt compelled to expose it, regardless of the consequences to himself.

At the unveiling of a monument on William Sørensen's grave, August said: What particularly characterized him as a scientist was his incorruptible honesty both with regards to his own work and that of others before him."[10] Also in this respect August was to follow Sørensen's example. On the monument August had inscribed W. S.'s own motto: "Ultimately, everything depends on character."

When August was fourteen years old and confirmed in the cathedral in Grenaa, he had finished the local *realskole* (grade school). Because he was still too young to enter the Aarhus Cathedral School (the Latin school), he joined the navy as an apprentice with his parents' approval. At the time he even thought that he might become a navy officer. In late February 1889 Viggo and August sailed for Copenhagen, and on March 1 August had his vision and hearing tested by the navy doctor on board the ship *Zealand* that served as a military barrack. August was in great spirits and looked forward to some time in Copenhagen before he started his service aboard the surveying ship *Hauch*. "There will be two weeks' vacation in Copenhagen before I go on board. I plan to go to museums and the zoological garden and in general to see Copenhagen." He felt quite grown up and signed his letters "Your old boy August."[13]

A week after his arrival, however, he received his orders so he donned his uniform and started training on the *Zealand*. August and the other young apprentices were well trained. The food was good and the butter was excellent and plentiful; in fact, they received so much that they gave part of their ration away. August found the officers and petty officers kind and friendly. He and the other apprentices trained as orderlies, practiced shooting with carbines and studied seamanship. At the end of March he boarded the *Hauch*.

The *Hauch* crisscrossed the Danish waters numerous times, affording August visits to the Buhls in Frederikshavn and his family in Grenaa as well as Læsø, Copenhagen, Anholt, and Bornholm. He made friends with the other young apprentices and, in general, enjoyed his life on board.

In July the ship went to Hesselø and on into Issefjord and Roskildefjord. Many years later August bought a house in Lynæs on Issefjord where he sailed with his family and friends.

Wherever they landed, August had orders from his mother to look up friends and relatives. He did this dutifully and reported to his mother. But he also enjoyed the interesting sights on land. On Bornholm he copied a Latin text from a stone tablet. In Elsinore he went to Kronborg Castle and looked at "the paintings, the church, and the view." On several occasions, the *Hauch* took on royal visitors such as Prince Valdemar and one of the princesses, "We took a little trip in the sound (Øresund) with Princess Marie. She particularly liked a kind of seaweed that floated on the surface, so we fished up a whole basket of it for her to use as decorations. That kind of seaweed (bladderweed) has henceforth been dubbed 'Princess Marie grass.' "[14]

3

School Years in Aarhus (1891–1893)

> The blueprint for obtaining happiness can be expressed in one word—work!

Although August loved the sea, a love he maintained throughout life, it became clear to him that he wished to study at the university. However, he had to wait until after he was sixteen before he was permitted to take the *preliminær examen,* allowing him to enter Aarhus Cathedral School.

To study for the examination, August moved to Aarhus during spring 1891 to take the necessary courses. He stayed with his Aunt Frida (Viggo's sister) and her husband Johannes Christian Vøhtz, a gynecologist. From August's letters to his mother, it is clear that he was very serious about his studies. "I study Latin each day with the others but have not had private lessons in May. I am as far as the other students and expect to pass the examination with good grades." But he was longing for his home and the family. "I get three days off for the Pentecostal vacation. . . . I hope the little boat is in order so that I can go sailing, which I long for terribly."[1] To satisfy his longing for animals he set up an aquarium with salamanders, tadpoles, and a water spider in his room. "My water spider, which is very beautiful, has discovered that it does not pay to build a house since the other animals tear it down. Instead, it has taken up residence in an empty snail shell, where it lives quite comfortably. In the back of the aquarium there is a small grassy island, where the salamanders can land and breathe air."[1] As the written examination of a difficult Latin essay drew near, August admitted to a little nervousness, but added with characteristic self-assurance, "yet I don't have any particular fear for the outcome."[2] He apparently passed the examination with fine results.

Following a good summer at home in Grenaa, sailing, helping in the brewery, and enjoying the company of his parents, brothers, and sisters, August went back to Aarhus for his first year in the Cathedral School. Again, he lived with the Vøhtzes while their son Georg, five years younger than August, stayed at the brewery in Grenaa. August liked his teachers and soon found a friend by the name of Birck. Typically, social status was of no importance to August and his parents:

> He is the son of a shoemaker Birck in Ryes Street and he is a kind and friendly fellow, well liked by teachers and classmates. The worst is that Aunt Frida does not approve of my association with him. The other day she said she wished I would find a friend socially more equal to them. She also said some less than favorable things about Birck's parents, about whom I know nothing, as I have only visited Birck in his own room. Among other things she said that she *had heard* that they argue and that their home is not neat. But *I* don't know what to believe because my Birck has no propensity for arguing and it would be a shame to accuse him of lack of neatness. His room has been an example of order when I have visited. Indeed, the first time I was there I felt so ashamed of my own disorder the first thing I did when I came home was to thoroughly straighten up my room. And ever since I have kept it as neat as I possibly can.[3]

August added that he would like to bring Birck home with him during the fall vacation so that Mimi could evaluate him herself, a request that Mimi promptly granted.

August made several friends in school with whom he visited museums or had dinner. Each week he borrowed a book from the library and shared his excitement over them with his mother. He found Hauch's *Charles de la Bussiere* one of the best books he had ever read, and read the entire book twice during a weekend. His Aunt Frida gave him two canaries that she had tired of. August, however, liked them and found them "sweet."[4]

In November 1891, he told his mother that his French essays were improving and he expected a better grade than last. In Danish essays he expected a pretty good grade and a very good grade in mathematics. However, there were problems in the Vøhtz household:

> Do tell me what is happening with the beer sales, what you think about your new linoleum and if you have received a request from Aunt Frida not to give Georg *øllebrød* [alebread—a special Danish soup cooked from sweet ale and water-soaked stale rye bread. In the Krogh home in Grenaa this was the standard breakfast dish]. He must have complained bitterly about it in his letters because every night while we were eating, Aunt Frida and Uncle Christian lamented over the "poor" boy. Probably to get even, Aunt Frida decided the servants, Gerda, and I should have oatmeal porridge every other evening. For this no one is happier than I since oatmeal porridge is an excellent dish.[5]

This disagreement with the Vøhtz relatives may have been the reason that August soon moved to Højskole Hjemmet (the folk high school home). In the meantime August was not wasting his time on these minor problems but was pursuing his interest in biology, "Apropos my birthday, just in case you and Father should plan to give me something, then I humbly request money, preferably a *tokrone* [two-krone piece].

School Years in Aarhus 19

At a watchmaker's here, I have seen a lovely little pocket microscope that enlarges 50 times and costs only four kroner and 25 øre."[5]

August now had enough time to begin tutoring in mathematics. His first student, Bagger, apparently was giving him problems and he was glad to be rid of him. In May he wrote his mother:

> I have several good things to tell you. Shortly after Easter a man who was studying privately for the *fjerde klasse hoved examen* [examination] came to stay at Højskole Hjemmet and I accepted him as a mathematics pupil. I teach him one hour daily and receive 50 øre per hour, thus, I earn 12 Kr. per month. In addition, it is pure pleasure to teach him because he is highly intelligent and works hard. Granted there is quite an age difference between us since he is 20 and I am only 17, but that does not bother us.
>
> I got rid of Bagger in a rather peculiar way. He felt that I, after showing him how the problems should be solved, should also check and recalculate them. But I thought the time could be used better and that I had already spent too much time on him.[6]

When Bagger then complained to Birck, August decided that he had had enough and was well pleased to be through with the fellow. On that same day, the school principal asked August to give daily lessons in mathematics and Latin to a first grade student for which he would earn five kroner per month.

The yearly examinations lasted through June and July. August made top grades and was eager to hear what his parents thought of them. He apparently came out as the best in the class, for at the beginning of the following school year he was Skolens Duks (the best in the school).

Back in school the following September, in 1892, August missed his family: "I'm greatly longing to hear from you and to get my wish I'm writing you first."[7] He had also written four pages to his brother Emil and was rather proud of that. There was cholera in Aarhus, but August's greatest concern was that the disease might interfere with his studies: "I shall not speak about the cholera, which is a favorite subject here in town, partly because it is probably over and partly because it is likely that you know as much about the cases as I do. There was some talk about closing the school but fortunately that did not materialize. It would have been very unpleasant to interrupt the work now that we have a good start on it, particularly since we would have to work so much harder afterwards."[7]

When asked to join a school society called Heimdal, the forever frugal August declined because he was saving for a bicycle. When the landlord wanted to raise the rent, August was decisive: "Saturday the landlord told me that he intended to raise the rent by 5 Kr/month. I answered only with a gesture of regret, but later decided that under those circumstances it would be better to shake the dust of Højskole Hjemmet off my feet and search for another, less expensive paradise."[8] In a letter of October 7, 1892 he had good news: To start with the most important, I have been given free education for this academic year, as you can see in the enclosed document from the principal. This writing is directly worth 146 Kr. and indirectly maybe just as much. Probably at Christmas I will receive the Nissen stipend and 80 Kr. at the examination if my grades are good, but there is no reason that they shouldn't be."[9]

In spite of some battles with his teachers and occasionally his health, August continued to do well in school. When he had written a theme he was proud of, he sent it to his mother or took it to show his parents. An essay showing much of August's philosophy and attitude toward life was found among his mother's papers. The required subject of the theme was an old Danish proverb, *Enhver er sin egen lykkes smed* (Each person is the forger of his own happiness). "Speaking of happiness," August started, "two entirely different concepts come to mind. The first is immediate or material happiness or the happiness of having enough of the good things that this earth offers. These include not only gold and possessions but also position in the society, prestige, etc. The second is the happiness that comes from having a good conscience in knowing that one has done one's duty as far as it is within one's own power to do so."

August wrote that these two ways of understanding this proverb also provide a blueprint for obtaining material happiness and for obtaining true happiness.

> For those who wish to obtain the first, once in your life there will come a moment when happiness will present itself to you. You must act quickly without hesitation or caution. "One has to strike while the iron is hot." If you delay, happiness will pass you by and you may never see it again. . . . However, the proverb also provides another blueprint for obtaining happiness that can be expressed in one word—Work. "Each person is the forger of his own happiness" means that with persistent diligence and effort anyone can become happy.

He goes on to explain that this road to happiness may be hard and difficult and that many people may give up. But it is not impossible as some people would argue. "True, it is difficult to keep going, difficult to continue work without listening to the tempting voice of desire, but impossible it is not." This is what his friend Uncle William had done and this was what he intended to do. There was no doubt in the eighteen-year-old August's mind that, "by using work as the way to happiness, not only can we be sure of obtaining the happiness that the knowledge of having done our duty can bring, but also, in almost all cases, it will bring temporal happiness and comfort."[10]

As the end of the term approached, August was more occupied with his own upcoming examinations and he confided to his mother that he was aiming for *Udmærkelse* (highest grades). As usual before and dur-

School Years in Aarhus 21

ing a major examination, he became quite ill and wrote on May 26, 1893: "I have a cold as bad as a bacteria that has lived for two weeks in the brewery drain. But since I have it as a cough and a sore throat, I don't need handkerchiefs. Wednesday, I was outright sick with headache and nausea and went to bed, but fortunately both went away during the night."[11]

August finished his examinations with the expected high grades and graduated with artium in mathematics-science[12] at the end of June 1893. During his years in Aarhus he had made two important decisions that he did not tell his mother. He had decided to become a scientist and he had made up his mind to resign from *den danske folkekirke* (the national church). Overexposed to religion during their childhood, August and his brothers did not share their parents' faith.

4

Becoming a Zoologist (1893–1895)

> Whatever I study and whatever I become I will cultivate natural history as long as there is any possibility for it, simply because I have to.

In September of 1893 August matriculated at the University of Copenhagen for the medical preparatory examination. He wrote his mother:

> I presently go to lectures in philosophy, botany, chemistry, physics, and zoology. I have been told that by taking the medical preparatory examination I will not have to take physics and chemistry for my final university degree. When I have completed these studies, I can spend all of my time on mathematics and astronomy. In return, I have to study botany and zoology; but I would very likely have done that anyway because of my interest in these subjects.[1]

He took up residence in Copenhagen, finding room and board at a Miss Klingsey's home in Gothers Street. The first person August looked up in Copenhagen was Uncle William. We can be reasonably certain that during discussions with Sørensen, August made up his mind to study for the medical preparatory examination, not because it included physics and chemistry, but rather because it included botany and zoology. After settling into his new routine of attending lectures and studying, August became a regular Sunday visitor in Uncle William's home. Sunday afternoons he would walk to Frederiksberg to have dinner with the family and stay into the evening. Frequently, during the fall, the two friends went mushroom hunting in the vicinity of Copenhagen.

In December 1893 August wrote his mother, "Uncle William has a great deal of work due to a terrible fight currently raging within zoological circles concerning the cover for the breathing holes in dung beetle larvae [the spiracles of scarab larvae], but, together with Dr. Meinert, he feels chances are excellent the combat will end in victory for himself."[2] To August's practical parents these controversies must have appeared rather peculiar and farfetched and they contributed to Viggo's view of zoology as a useless field. To Sørensen, however, the young

Krogh gradually became his best and most valued friend and colleague, with whom he discussed the many controversies in detail in which he, Sørensen, became involved. According to Sørensen's son, the two, who in some ways were very different, also had much in common. "The two scientists had the same upright character and were moved by the same idealism with respect to the fight for what they saw as the truth. Thus in spite of their great age difference, a friendship of the most ideal character with deep mutual personal affection developed between them."[3] Sørensen, like Krogh, was an agnostic and neither of the two were musical. To both music was nothing more than unpleasant noise.

When August visited the Sørensens, he would play with their children and read to them. The Sørensen family lived in an apartment on a modest side street to Gammel Kongevej. The building was rather large with a stately entrance hall and broad staircase, while the other buildings on the street were smaller and far more modest. The rooms were large with high ceilings. They were lighted by kerosene lamps which usually burned in all the rooms so the Sørensens would not have to carry the lamps around. The home gradually became crowded with many strong-minded children; because the Sørensens were more liberal in their upbringing than was customary then, it was not a quiet home. Sørensen's study was the most crowded of all. The walls were covered with bookcases and when these became full more bookcases were placed in the hall and then in the dining room which also served as the family room. Used books ended up on the dining room table, chairs, or any other place, so chairs had to be cleared for visitors.

In November 1893, when his sixteen-year-old sister Edel came to Copenhagen, August took time off to visit friends and family with her. His Aunt Inger gave them theater tickets and August liked a play by Shakespeare, "where particularly Olaf Poulsen played heavenly." On another night he was less enthusiastic. "We were in the theater again and saw 'The Only Fault' and the opera 'Jolanthe' both of which in my opinion were rather boring, but that may be because my former teacher Lund (that beast!) succeeded in completely killing the little interest I had for romantic drama."[4]

As the weather got colder, Miss Klingsey, wondering why Krogh did not heat his room, gave him a thermometer for his birthday, "to induce me to light a fire in my stove. So far though she has not succeeded!"[4] In the next letter to his mother, "You ask why I do not light a fire! Naturally, because I do not find it cold. When the thermometer shows 10° [Reaumur—corresponds to 12.5°C or 54.5°F] it seems to me sufficient and so far that is what it has been."[2] He celebrated his nineteenth birthday quietly, having hot chocolate with Miss Klingsey and the other boarder, Mr. Hildebrandt, and later visiting his friend Axel Schlambusch.

In the spring, August laboriously worked his way through a five hundred-page book on anthropology written in French. To aid him in his studies he asked that his brother Johan dig up some parts of skeletons at the ruin of an old cloister in the vicinity of Grenaa. In April 1894 he wrote:

> I have now finished the part of zoology that I had decided to read this semester (birds, reptiles, and fish) and have started seriously with botany. Each day I spend an hour in the botanical garden, taking many branches and flowers home to study them more closely. All in all I spend two to three hours on botany daily and if I cannot learn it that way then botany must be a peculiar subject or I a peculiar idiot. I do not plan to interrupt my study of zoology, *but only to stop reading it for the examination*.[5]

To study philosophy he had borrowed a number of books at the Royal Library but forgot to read them. He had to hurry and make the notes he needed before the books were recalled by the library, "but it goes slowly as they are so confounded dull."[5] August's lack of interest in philosophy worried his mother and in his next letter he had to reassure her that he had no problem with the subject as he found it very easy (as simple as mathematics!).

As spring progressed August spent most of his spare time botanizing in the beautiful countryside, sometimes finding very rare plants. One trip took him with his tent to Esbønderup, Voxstrup Farm and the north coast of Zealand where he looked out over the water to see if he could see Djursland (the peninsula where Grenaa is situated). He found many plants and also collected spiders for Sørensen.

During spring Mr. Hildebrandt, who had not been well, became gravely ill. He rallied briefly, but died in the middle of May. August, who found him to be "a fine human being," was profoundly saddened. Miss Klingsey considered moving after the summer vacation because the apartment was too big for her with only one boarder.[6]

The baptism of Sørensen's youngest child, Ingrid, took place in Frederiksberg Church in May followed by a reception and dinner at the Sørensen home. August was godfather and Mimi had requested a detailed description of the party. On the first of June, while August was writing his mother, he was interrupted by Uncle William, who suddenly showed up with a champignon he had found in the botanical garden and told August to find some more and bring them to his house next Sunday. Uncle William was too busy himself because he was on his way to the Society for Natural History to convince them not to make Lector (associate professor) J. E. V. Boaz a member of the council. Sørensen was accusing Boaz of having stolen the results of a German scientist and published them as his own. August continued his account of the party telling how he got out of giving the toast for the child as Mrs. Leshley (a friend of Sørensen's family) volunteered. Later in the evening, following many glasses of wine, he and Mrs. Leshley agreed that zoology was not at all a bad subject to study.[7]

Following still another botanical excursion and an examination on June 6, August was ready to pack his clothes and numerous books to return to Grenaa for summer vacation. As usual August was delighted to go home and hoped to spend time with his family. But he must also have worried about the upcoming discussions with his father concerning his choice of study which was now clearly zoology.

There is no record of the ensuing discussions which took place during the summer. Not daring to confront his father directly, August wrote him a letter and left it on his desk.

> Dear Father, since I know that I express myself far better in writing than orally, and, furthermore, since by weighing the arguments and writing them down, I can include all considerations and points of view, I have decided to present to you the, to me, all-important question concerning my career direction. It is my hope to be able to remove at least some of your objections concerning zoology. It must be the purpose of my education to be able to support myself and also become as useful and happy a member of the society as possible. What direction should my education then take to achieve this goal? To answer this question it is necessary to take into consideration my overall mental and physical traits as well as the special abilities and desires I may have. So far, this has been the case since my education until now has proceeded in the most advantageous direction for me. From where I am now I can choose various directions, so the question is which way should I go? With my mathematical artium, I can study the following important areas: engineering, medicine, mathematics, physics, and natural history. Of these, I believe that we agree to exclude the first two, of which one would bring me into a practical occupation that would neither suit me, nor satisfy me, while the other, medicine, actually is an abomination to me, and furthermore because of the large number of medical students is a very uncertain occupation. What is left is mathematics, physics, and natural history. These could, except for natural history which I shall return to, only lead to a position as teacher in a Latin school.[8]

In great detail he went on to discuss the various fields. He felt he was already overqualified to become a teacher, "Furthermore, a position as a teacher in a grade school is far from enviable. The pay is low, at least far less than in the Latin school and there is no pension except at the few public schools." Viggo was hoping that August would become a school principal, but August felt there was no reason he would succeed:

> For this one needs talent for business, administration, and last but not least capital, three things of which I possess less than nothing. . . . You may feel that I am underestimating my abilities for progress in practical situations. I have often and carefully contemplated this area. However, it is impossible for me to see myself in a practical endeavor or something similar, when I consider the difficulties I experience in expressing myself, yes, how hard it has been for me to overcome my inability to start even the simplest conversation with strangers, and with what embarrassment I have always done it. Often from pure

embarrassment and shyness I have omitted the simplest acts of politeness. In the fortunately few parties in which I have participated I have moved with a feeling of being forced. It took me three months before I got together with classmates other than Birck, and a full year before I associated with any students from the other classes; and I have now studied a whole year at the university without getting to know more than two other students. Therefore, I cannot possibly believe I am suited for such a position.

In the same letter August discussed the possibilities open to him if he studied mathematics or physics. He felt that he would have to teach these subjects in a Latin school but stated there was keen competition for the few openings at the schools. About the possibilities if he studied mathematics he was quite negative, adding:

It is for sure that I don't have any particular gift for mathematics, even though it is easier for me to learn the elementary mathematics than it is for most. There is, therefore, no reason to assume that I should excel in such a way that my possibilities are better than those of others. Concerning my interest in mathematics, then, I am now aware that it interests me considerably less than I thought earlier. Mathematics interests me while I am working with it but, if I may say so, it does not exert any attractive influence upon me.

August had always shown an interest in physics, but as in mathematics there were too many students for the available openings. The previous year, four new students in physics entered the university and that was a low number. He then states, "Physics is more interesting to me than mathematics, and I think that I have a good talent for it. Yet it does not interest me sufficiently that by itself it could satisfy me in the long run."

Finally on the ninth page he arrives at natural history.

In natural history there are as in the other subjects, two examinations: magister conference and the qualifying examination for a teaching career [candidatus magisterii or cand. mag]. Of these, magister conference has one major, zoology or botany, with minors in mineralogy, geology, physics, and chemistry. The teacher's examination has three majors, zoology, botany, and geography. The minors are physics and chemistry which are not required for either examination if one has passed the medical preliminary examination. The magister conference is really a scientific examination. To pass it significant knowledge is required including a thorough familiarity with all branches of the major, without neglecting the minors. Facility with languages (Latin, French, English, and German) is necessary, as most of the textbooks are written in foreign languages. For the teachers examination a certain specific knowledge is required, but it does not have to be particularly deep or far-reaching. However, because it demands a great deal of memorization, the study takes the same amount of time as the magister conference. The magister conference examination, consisting primarily of a written thesis for which six weeks are allowed, is more a measure of maturity.[8]

During the first three years the studies for the two types of studies would be the same,

> and after that it would surely be clear if I am suited for the scientific direction and the decision can be made accordingly. Without being immodest, I can, however, say that it is possible, even likely, that I am suited for scientific work. About my abilities and talent I will only say that Uncle William says that they are good, and since he said it while trying to talk me out of studying zoology, I have no reason to believe that he exaggerated.
>
> And now my interest! Yes, that is the terrible dilemma, because on this point that to me is the main point, I am unable to explain myself so that you can understand my feelings. When I say that I cannot live without zoology that is, of course, an exaggeration, and when I say that I will not live without zoology, then you can look at it as a whim, and when I persist, as stubbornness, and yet both statements are essentially correct. Whatever I study and whatever I become I will cultivate natural history as long as there is any possibility for it, simply because I have to. You must believe my word if you can because such cannot be proven.[8]

Viggo gave in and August, grateful and much relieved, returned to Copenhagen in September 1894 to finish his studies for the medical preparatory exam. From there he wrote to his mother, "Most of all I am happy and grateful that Father has given me permission to follow my inclination, yes I dare say, my call, and I ask Father to be assured that I shall not forget his well-founded warnings that accompanied the permission, but endeavor to avoid the dangers they pointed out.[9]

August studied hard. His old friend Birck, who had dropped out of school in Aarhus, was now in Copenhagen and asked August to prepare him for the artium by giving him private lessons in math, physics, and French. August was not particularly pleased with the prospect, partly because Birck was a lazy student and partly because August already had a full schedule of twenty-four lectures a week. In addition to this he had what he called his private studies which involved reading a three-volume geology text in English. However, he gave in to Birck for the sake of old friendship and because the ten kroner per month he would earn were to August a considerable sum of money. As it turned out Birck got his private lessons, but in the end failed to pay.

At the time August's best and closest friend was a medical student, Valdemar Sørensen (not a relative of William Sørensen). Valdemar and August shared the same intellectual curiosity and spent much of their spare time together on walks or visiting at home.

Following the habit begun the previous academic year, August visited Uncle William's home every Sunday, sometimes in the company of Valdemar Sørensen. He helped W. S. dissect fish to establish the function of the swimbladder, or rather to disprove the hydrostatic theory of two Englishmen, Bridge and Haddon. Actually, the hydrostatic theory was correct, but August did not yet know that. He played with the children and read to them, staying late into the evening to discuss with his friend after the children went to bed.

August had no interest at all in visiting his mother's friends and flatly refused being introduced to young ladies. He was, however, deeply interested in and spared no trouble for his siblings. His eighteen-year-old brother Emil had made up his mind (and gotten his parents' permission) to continue as a seaman. When Emil was out at sea during bad storms, August worried about him. Whenever Emil was in Copenhagen between ships, August had him stay in his own small room and rearranged his furniture so that Emil could be comfortable. When Emil had to show up at 5:30 in the morning to load a ship, August bought an alarm clock out of his meager allowance and then had to wake up at the same time as Emil even though he himself lost sleep. August also cared about his fourteen-year-old brother Johan who was still at home and in grade school. Having taught Johan mathematics, he expected him to do well in school. In spring of 1895 he told him to aim for the highest grades (*Udmærkelse*) and explained to him how he should plan his time carefully when he studied for the final exam.

In February, a few weeks after his return from the Christmas vacation in Grenaa, August had moved from Miss Klingsey's to a new room in Webers Street. His new landlady brought him tea in the morning and straightened his room daily, but he had to get his own food. It was cheaper than his previous room and August wrote home that now he needed only forty kroner per month for all of his expenses instead of the fifty-five kroner while staying with Miss Klingsey.

It was bitter cold and the room was impossible to heat. He could not get the temperature up above 45°–47°F. To keep warm August had to stay in bed while studying. For the first time in many years he was not plagued by a stomach pain and he had a voracious appetite, but food was expensive. He went out for dinner and walked daily several kilometers to a rooming house near the round tower where he could get his dinner for thirty-eight øre. For breakfast he made himself oatmeal porridge but in February his lunch and evening meals consisted mostly of rye bread, either plain or with powdered sugar. So he wrote his mother: "I am very well and eat about one and a half times as much as in the last couple of years and since my stomach does not complain it feels good. . . . Could you sent me some of what you have of meat dishes in the house such as meatballs that I can use as lunch meat, because these kinds of things are too expensive here. Such goodies as pancakes would also be appreciated."[10] His mother was glad to send the food but his father objected to the demands and felt that August wanted to indulge himself. To this August answered: "I don't wish to indulge myself, I have never been a gourmand before and have not become one now. I just felt that I could save Father from expenses because it seemed obvious to me that I should not have to live exclusively on plain bread or bread with powdered sugar, and also that it is considerably less expensive to have lunch meat sent from home instead of buying it here where it is very expensive."[11]

In late April, August became increasingly busy studying for the upcoming exam. Finding lectures a waste of time, he reduced the number he attended. He had a special knack for physics, but he worried about how he would perform in chemistry. It was typical of him that memorization did not come to him easily, while his intuitive understanding of the laws of physics was highly developed. He learned botany and zoology by studying plants and animals directly. Although he was sure he would do well, as usual he started having stomach trouble as the examination approached.[12] The stomach problem remained with him most of his life. (He probably suffered from an ulcer although this was never mentioned in our home.)

In early June, August had adopted his new work schedule, "I start reading at 6:30 and continue until 10, have my lunch and rest until 11, begin again and study until 3 p.m. when I go for dinner and walk until 5 p.m., and finally I study from 5 to 8 and from 9 to 11:30 p.m."[14] For the examinations the students had to appear in formal attire (white tie). August did not own tails and had to find someone who could lend them to him, which was a real problem. He finally tried to borrow his Uncle Emil's as he had for his artium. The family, however, had misgivings, believing he might ruin it during the exam in practical chemistry. August, finding the misunderstanding preposterous, wrote his mother: "I must admit that I am surprised that your confidence in the intelligence of our university professors, the academic cabinet and the high cabinet is even less than mine which is not particularly great. However, one can do even a rogue wrong; fortunately they are not so impractical, that they would demand that we meet in white tie to stand for 8 hours and mess with acids and alkali and other strong substances."[13]

Already before the exam August made elaborate plans for his summer vacation:

> When I get home! Yes, then a great deal shall be done, and, even though two months is a long time, I doubt that I shall be able to do most of what I plan to do. First of all, I shall botanize, partly alone and partly together with Valdemar. We plan to crisscross Djursland at least twice. Then I shall be a mechanical engineer, try the steamer, and also construct various instruments that I need. Furthermore, I wish to sail and to teach Valdemar how to handle the oars, helm, and sails. Hopefully, father can be moved to lend us the boat for a couple of shorter and longer excursions. I believe Valdemar learns easily and besides he is strong as a bear, so I promise myself the best results. In addition, I must dissect half a dozen frogs to learn their inner anatomy in detail. I must act as censor at the grade school, I have to give Edel a course

in math, and finally, I should have time to be lazy and rest after the exhausting examination.[12]

At home in Grenaa his two youngest sisters Misse and Frida looked forward to August's visits as always, but feared the return of the very selfish and mean Emil. As Misse wrote August many years later:

> From the time I was barely four years old I have a few clear memories of you and Johan as loving older brothers in whom I could confide and who often went out of your way to please your little sisters. From the time I grew older these memories are more complete and my confidence in your brotherly love and fairness became the firm foundation for my existence. About Emil, I don't remember anything from when I was little probably because he already then hated small children and therefore did not bother with us. My first memory of Emil stems from when I was eight and Emil, who must have been 17, returned from sea. You, August, had written telling Frida and me what a great and happy event it would be for us when Emil came home. But we were bitterly disappointed. Emil teased us without mercy and used all kinds of ship's boy tricks on us. He twisted our arms until we shrieked from pain. Then father's thunderous voice would be heard from the office, "can't you stop that racket?" and Frida and I were ordered out of the room, while Emil stood there and gloated. . . . No we did not look forward to Emil's visits, and if all our three brothers had been like him Frida and I would have had a miserable childhood. But we were so lucky that Johan always was a dear brother with whom we had lots of fun and we looked forward to your visits as to a celebration. You were never too big or superior to play with us, teach us something exciting, and open our eyes for new interests. Christmas was not Christmas if you did not come home to be the center that joined the family together and gave the season cheerfulness and radiance.[14]

August finished his examinations with the highest grades, and made a successful tent trip to Bornholm with Valdemar Sørensen before he returned to his summer vacation in Grenaa. Back home in Grenaa he had a wonderful time as usual. For his experiments, August taught his little sister Misse to collect and grow larvae to ship to Copenhagen when he needed them. August in return wrote her interesting letters and sent her rewards. When she stopped the winter she turned seventeen, as a final price for the good work she had done for him, August gave her a brand-new illustrated English dictionary, a gift she greatly coveted.[14]

In Grenaa, August's family consisted not only of his parents and siblings but also his Uncle Emil, a bachelor, who ran the brewery together with his brother Viggo. His two grandparents (Viggo's parents, Jacob and Frida Krogh) also lived in Grenaa. Jacob had lost a great deal of his money in a bad speculation. He suffered from bouts of temper which put him in a mental hospital for two years (1887–89), but was otherwise a warm-hearted and kind man. During the time that Jacob was in the hospital, his wife Frida moved to Grenaa and now both of them lived in a little house on Lillegade across from the brewery. August was fond of his relatives in Grenaa and enjoyed his summer vacation. Before he returned to Copenhagen to continue his studies, his grandfather Jacob gave him the large sum of five hundred kroner.

5

Becoming a Physiologist (1895–1899)

> "It is my intention to qualify myself for acceptance in Professor Bohr's physiological laboratory after Christmas. This I very much desire, partly because physiology, in my opinion, is the most interesting field and partly because Professor Bohr is an especially capable and intelligent man."

Returning to Copenhagen in September 1895, August finally began his studies for a magister conference in zoology. Now William Sørensen, far ahead of his colleagues in understanding the importance of physiology for zoology, recommended that Krogh take a physiology course in addition to his regular studies. Physiology was not taught within the Naturhistorisk Fakultet (the Mathematics–Natural Science Department), but in the Medical School, where Christian Bohr was professor of physiology. The first lecture Krogh attended became decisive for his future. Bohr lectured on methods for determining the quantity of blood and blood gasses in the body. The quantitative treatment of the subject and the physical principles involved appealed enormously to the young Krogh.

On September 16, 1895, August wrote his mother:

> I am now rather busy with physiology and particularly with anatomy and plan to get up full steam this week. As I have already told you I am engaged in three types of anatomy; namely, plant anatomy, anatomy of selected animals, and human anatomy. The first two kinds are primarily practical, the latter theoretical. The anatomical laboratory exercises on selected animals started with frogs today, and Dr. Bergh was quite complimentary on my preparation of blood vessels. Since I have never before dissected out blood vessels I dare conclude from this that I am not clumsy at dissection, a fact which pleases me all the more as I had anticipated it as being very difficult.[1]

Characteristically, he learned far more from doing than from listening to lectures or from reading. A few weeks into the course, he wrote:

> The practical dissection exercises interest me greatly and judging from what I have experienced so far it appears that I can become a rather

competent anatomist. I have therefore decided to continue dissection on my own after the laboratory exercises are over at Christmas. Undoubtedly, it will make my studies easier and almost eliminate the necessity of reading two heavy volumes for the examination, and besides it will prove useful later in my (possible) scientific studies.[2]

For the dissections as well as his private experiments he needed a better microscope. He would not have dreamed of spending the large sum of money his grandfather had given him for this purpose, but things worked out to his advantage. When he planned to seek a stipend for books, his parents and Uncle William told him that he was not eligible because he was the owner of five hundred kroner. Happily, August decided to go all out and spend the entire sum on a Seibert compound microscope, a drawing instrument (he was also taking private drawing lessons), and a Zeiss dissection microscope. Uncle William agreed with August's choice of instruments and Viggo agreed to the purchase. Steering straight toward his goal of becoming a scientist and thinking of his future publications, August made up his mind to master English and began to write his mother in that language. His first attempts were pretty bad (not nearly as good as his parents were when they wrote to each other in English) but with time he improved. Indeed, fellow scientists have told me that my father's scientific papers are written in such clear and concise English that they use them not only for their content but as examples of good English writing for their students. "My dear mother," August wrote in English for the first time in December 1895, "If you will permit it I think in future to write to you in the English language, I am if I ever shall be an author of zoology obliged to be able to write a foreign language, and among the three the German, the French and the English, I have selected the latter." He went on to explain that, "French is too difficult to learn and the German I will not for national causes write." Because of the wars with Germany and the bad treatment of the Danes south of the border he, as did his parents, harbored strong anti-German sentiments. August had also read a paper by H. J. Hansen sharply criticizing Danish scientists for publishing in German. "He shows how this is very dangerous to our nationality, how it leads particularly our youth, to an uncritical admiration of German science and German spirit, which is not at all very admirable."[3]

His mother wrote back suggesting that he could improve his English by reading English novels as she had done. She also corrected his mistakes and suggested that he might have written the letter in haste. This was not the case, said August; it had taken him four hours, but he had not written any English since the third grade and he didn't have an English dictionary. Continuing to write several letters in English for the next five months, August's ability slowly improved.

In fall 1896 August finally admitted his deep interest in physiology to his parents. In September he wrote:

I am deeply buried in loads of the most interesting work. Every day I am in town for lectures and laboratory exercises without stop from 9–3 or 4 p.m. Fortunately it is mostly laboratories because the lectures are not particularly interesting or stimulating. In the afternoon from 5 to 8, I mostly study physiology or do physiological experiments on frogs. Through this, it is my intention to qualify myself for acceptance in Professor Bohr's physiological laboratory after Christmas. This I very much desire, partly because physiology in my opinion is the most interesting field and partly because Professor Bohr is an especially capable and intelligent man.[4]

Christian Bohr was born in 1855 and died from a heart attack in 1911, barely fifty-six years old. Interested in science and natural history from childhood, he studied medicine at the University of Copenhagen. Following his medical school graduation, he became an assistant to the famous Danish physiologist P. L. Panum. Bohr soon became known as an astute, independent, and penetrating thinker with a special understanding of physics. He became a Doctor of Medicine in 1880 and continued his studies in physiology with Carl Ludwig in Leipzig in 1881 and again in 1883. In 1886, the thirty-one-year-old Bohr succeeded Panum as professor of physiology at the University of Copenhagen. His earliest research in Ludwig's laboratory dealt with the effect of electrical stimulations on muscle contraction (shape and height of the tetanus curve).[5]

It was not until 1883 that Bohr became interested in blood gases, but from then on he devoted all of his energy to these problems. He published a number of papers on solubility of gases in various fluids as well as their "invasion" coefficients.[6] In the 1890s he published work on oxygen absorption in distilled water and in hemoglobin solutions, which he had started in Leipzig.[7] It was these studies that had caught the interest of the young Krogh from the first of Bohr's lectures he attended in 1895. Having much to learn, however, it would be another year before he could take up physiology seriously.

As planned, August carried out his physiological studies during the fall semester of 1896, and upon his return from Christmas vacation went to Bohr. "I have talked with Professor Bohr," August wrote. "He did not think that the problems he was working on at the moment were suited for me to start on, so he recommended that I wait until next semester. Consequently, I shall now try to get as much work behind me as possible so that, in the next semester, I can go in for physiology with even greater zeal."[8]

In fall 1897 he wrote: "My work is going well. I have studied hard (among other things a scientific work of more than 1000 pages in English) and I have overcome, I believe, most of the difficulties in my study of the mechanism of stomatas in plants. A famous German has been engaged in this problem earlier. His work is some physically impossible nonsense, but it has been generally acknowledged and has been accepted by Professor Warming with enthusiasm. It shall be a great delight to prove it wrong."[9]

In the following letter he tells about the start in Bohr's laboratory. Again, he is carefully planning his future leaving as much time as possible for scientific studies:

> I really don't have time to write this letter, because I have started to work in the physiological laboratory. That is something that takes time, especially because I, through Professor Bohr's extreme kindness, have been excused from participating to any degree in the elementary course for the medical students. Instead, I will receive individual instruction, and as soon as possible start working on my own. I go to the laboratory Tuesday, Wednesday, and Friday from 12 to 5 or 6. In addition, I have a great deal of reading to do at home in this connection (that is really what I should be doing now). Naturally, it is impossible for me to spend all this time and effort, in addition to the experiments I am doing here at home, and not have my work for the exam suffer. There is no doubt, however, that this arrangement makes me read more. By seriously weighing my knowledge and the demand for the exam, I have reached the conclusion that I can take it easy (i.e. work on other things) until next summer vacation in 1898. After that I shall put everything aside and exclusively (or almost exclusively) feed my brain with the barely nourishing, unappetizing, and poorly digestible porridge of exam studies. When this stuffing has lasted about a year, I will undoubtedly (as other Strassburger geese) in fall 1899 or at the latest in spring 1900 be able to present my scientific liver for inspection by the competent authorities and be reasonably sure to have it declared admissible. During summer 1900 I shall play soldier, if I am not lucky enough to be rejected. While that is going on I can assail consistorium with applications for residence and Smith's Candidatstipendium [stipend for graduates]. The chances are good that I can get both—if I don't become disliked by the authorities.
>
> These are my future prospects, (it wasn't my intention to write about them) but now I shall enjoy my freedom while I have it and try to learn to work and think for myself and do both well.[10]

During the academic year 1895–96, August lived in a rented room with his brother Emil. He continued to see a great deal of his fellow student Valdemar Sørensen. Together the two friends went on tent trips to Tisvilde in September 1895, where they got caught in a rainstorm and spent the night in the best room of Asserbo Castle. August added that the room had only three walls and no roof. They picked so many chanterelles that they had enough to dry for the winter—a delicious supplement to August's diet. In May 1896 the two friends went on a tent trip to Skaraliden in Scania (a section of southern Sweden that is, as August wrote, "one of the most beautiful places in Scandinavia"), Odensjön, and Kullen. They also dissected a number of animals together in Grenaa and in Copenhagen.

During early summer 1896, August took a biological course in Frederikshavn and had little time to write his mother, because he was so busy. During the following academic year August became even busier. He saw his friend and fellow student Axel Raphael-Petersen, but Valdemar Sørensen was busy with hospital duties and they saw less and less of each other. In May 1897 August wrote:

> I believe I am losing Valdemar Sørensen. I could say with a citation: "The continuous dinner party has swallowed him." Anyway I think he spends most of his spare time on parties and card games. He visits me only when he wants to borrow money, and several times I have tried without luck to find him at home. The only one I now see is Axel Raphael. Even though our natures are quite different, we agree on many things and enjoy each other's company. I can thank him—and him alone—for awakening my dormant interest in literature and art. On the other hand, I have not been without value for his mental growth. We take trips together as he wishes to get to know the Danish flora and we visit back and forth talking until late at night. The other night it was so late that we could see the sunrise as we walked on Frederiksberg hill, which gave us great pleasure.[11]

What had happened was that Valdemar had become more friendly with Emil than with August. Emil, far less serious-minded than August, gladly took time off for the pleasures life offered. Raphael went with August on a trip to Møen that spring (1897) but it turned out miserably because it rained all the time.[12]

During these busy years August had a continuing and often painful dialogue about religion with his mother. While he worked harder and became increasingly isolated during the winter of 1896–97, his mother worried about his happiness and that he was removing himself from God. She also felt that he was too proud of himself. Time and again August had to explain his own feelings about science and religion. In November 1896 he wrote:

> I do not believe that I am particularly clever and astute, but I must most firmly insist on one thing: If I, in earnest, intend to do scientific research then it is my imperative duty not to accept anything on other's authority, but instead always to demand the reasons for any opinions and, as far as possible, test them myself. By following this road, there is, of course, no guarantee that absolute certainty can be reached or that mistakes can be avoided, but it is the only road that is scientifically legitimate.
>
> On the other hand, I am not as far removed from Christianity as you seem to assume according to your letter. But I don't wish to elaborate any further, however, because it will take me years of study and reflection before my standpoint becomes distinct and clarified. . . .
>
> I will end by thanking you and father for praying for me. I know that you do not doubt that it is neither because of bad feelings nor, as

it is sometimes expressed, because of hatred for God, that I have removed myself somewhat from Christianity as it is normally accepted, but only because like you, I seek the truth.[13]

A year later, a few days after his birthday, August wrote:

Thank you for your long and wonderful letter for my birthday. It is a long time since anything has made me so happy. You are absolutely right when you say that we both agree that the love and trust between us is unchanged. Also that love, love for people and love for truth, is all-important and life's main cornerstone. I have often had the feeling that I may seem cold and unsympathetic toward the sorrows and happiness of others and sometimes it worries me, but I comfort myself: you two know that it is not so. My very few friends surely know too, and that will have to do for me.[14]

But Mimi was not reassured with respect to his religion and again August answered her as honestly and completely as he could, before concluding:

In your last letter you sincerely beg of me to seek the truth (i.e. God). I think I can honestly say that I do that according to my ability, even though I do not think I can find it within the narrow frame of the Lutheran church's dogmas. . . . There is no reason for you to be deeply worried about me. You do not share the barbaric and revolting "hell and devil" faith of the missionaries according to whom the God would be a tyrant more cruel than even the meanest of people. For you, too, God is infinitely loving, wanting happiness for all his creatures. Toward such a God I have no fears.[15]

In fall 1897, when August had started work in Bohr's laboratory, he had moved into his new unfurnished apartment and Emil now lived by himself. August was pleased with his landlord and was busy making the room functional and cozy. He asked his mother for cushions for his wicker chair and advice on buying material for a table cover since he had "no idea about such things." Then he added, "As you see I have started to acquire a sense of coziness and orderliness that I lacked in the past. I believe that Raphael's good example is the reason for this."[9] For his birthday in November, August received the usual gifts, a roasted goose and other good things to eat from home.

My birthday went as follows: In the morning as usual I rushed out into the city to do my work. At noon I found time to get home to read the letters I knew would be there, but after that I again had to get out until 6 p.m. When I came home I had a delicious piece of goose, sat down to read, waiting for something to happen and it did. At nine o'clock Raphael, Valdemar Sørensen, and Herluf Christensen all came and we spent a most enjoyable evening in high spirit while we drank the bottle of port wine that Johan so generously had given me. . . . Having no wine glasses, and to make the whole thing properly scientific, we used four of my test tubes as drinking vessels.[14]

In Bohr's laboratory, however, all was not to August's liking. He was in good spirit, nevertheless, and confident that his time would come: "About my life in general there is not much to say; I diligently go to the laboratory; but I don't feel I get as much out of it as I should and as I had expected. Professor Bohr currently has one of his unapproachable periods, but hopefully that will soon be over. Once I really get the contact, I think I can show him that the time he spends on me is not wasted."[14]

August was not disappointed because soon after that he and Bohr started doing experiments together and in early February 1898 he was in full swing in the laboratory. Bohr wished to study the respiration through skin in various animals. August became busy constructing and setting up a very complicated apparatus for determining the relationship between oxygen uptake and CO_2 production in snails, frogs, and fishes. August now worked even harder than before. He often slept poorly and had nightmares, but he reassured his mother: "I have felt extremely well ever since I came back and got over the cold. My stomach has not complained. . . . My spirit is good and I think that I can feel in my work that my head is getting clearer, my judgment sharper and more alert, and my energy greater."[16]

As spring approached, the long hours he spent in the laboratory began to take their toll. He was lonely. He was no longer getting visits from his friends: he never talked to anybody except on Sundays at Uncle William's house. Now engaged to be married, Raphael was busy himself. August went out to catch frogs alone but did not enjoy it. At the same time his parents, particularly his father, continued to reproach him for having left God. Time and again August had to explain to his parents that he was seeking the truth just as they were. When August joined Studenter Samfundet (Student Society) for more contact with other young people, his father objected that the group was ungodly and, therefore, not good for him. In Studenter Samfundet he met Norwegian playwright Henrik Ibsen at a white tie gala, (Ibsen disliked speaking so he did not give a talk) and he heard a talk by Emile Zola which upset his parents, because they felt Zola, an anarchist and agnostic, was a bad influence. Also, the novelists he read (such as Jonas Lie) were criticized. August bravely defended his own opinions.

In his loneliness, in spite of the criticism, the letters from home became all-important to him. For weeks he waited for letters. Coming home from the laboratory he would run up the stairs every evening thinking that now there had to be a letter for him:

> I have as you know, this spring, and particularly the last month and a half, only spoken with other people on Sundays and sometimes Saturday evenings in the society, and you will therefore understand that it is a particular pleasure to receive letters. Naturally, it is good for me to get used to being alone, as it can be expected that in the future I will

be even more alone than I am now. I don't doubt that I can adjust to it without much trouble, but it does take a little time and apparently I am still not fully adjusted.[17]

In a later letter in answer to his mother's worried questions, he explained, "When I assume that I will be more lonesome in the future, then it is a simple deduction from premises that are not certain, but likely: (1) my friends will sooner or later leave Copenhagen, (2) I will not make new friends."[18] His premises turned out to be wrong as he made several new friends in the coming year and had, for him, a rather lively social life. He probably was much influenced by William Sørensen, who with his sarcastic writings had lost much goodwill in zoological circles. Sørensen had been very lonely in his youth as he was unable to marry and support a wife until he was in his forties. Because of August's fierce loyalty and devotion to Sørensen, he, too, lost some friends, such as Dr. Bergh, with whom he had unpleasant arguments because Bergh was offended by the writings of Sørensen and because August did not admire Bergh's viewpoints. The well-known botanist Professor Eugene Warming did not look with kindness on the young Krogh, a fact that Krogh himself took rather lightly.

The experiments with Bohr proceeded well, gradually focusing on the skin and lung respiration of frogs. August managed to continue his experiments at home on sap rising in plants and on the function of plant stomata. At the end of May 1898 he gave a seminar on his findings. Warming had organized scientific seminars at his home one evening each month for the natural history students and some of the older botanists. Because August felt that the botanists had the wrong opinion on sap rising, he decided to use one of these meetings to present his criticism and results. Warming agreed to let him speak. "Since late in March," August wrote, "I have been busy studying the long-winded literature on this subject in preparation for my lecture, which ought to combine sufficient sharpness and clarity with the mildest and least provocative form. I succeeded almost too well. I had expected some resistance to my opinions and a lively discussion to follow, but Dr. Johansen, who was invited by Warming as the expert in the field, agreed with me without reservations, abandoning his previous views."[19]

Professor Bohr, who attended the meeting, was so impressed with Krogh that the next day he asked Krogh to continue at his laboratory following his final examination and offered him a position as scientific assistant. With great pleasure August accepted the offer, which would assure his future economically and also provide him the best possible opportunity for continuing his investigations.

August stayed in Copenhagen late into the summer of 1898 as Bohr wished to carry the investigation on frogs to such a conclusion that the results could be published. The following spring at a dinner party at the Bohrs, while August was deep in exam studies, Bohr told him that he planned to publish the results. How serious August was about not using the German language for his scientific publication is evident from his letters. To his mother he wrote:

> I received the unpleasant news that Bohr plans to publish in German our study of lung and skin respiration in frogs. I did not voice my objection, but having mulled it over for a couple of days I wrote a letter that I let Uncle William see and improve, which gave it a very humble form. I asked Bohr not to use my name as a coauthor as you can see of the enclosed copy. I have on the advice of Uncle William given the reason that you and father would strongly disapprove of me publishing in German, an opinion I actually share to a high degree. I have not yet had an answer but hope that Bohr simply honors my request, even though it is a small disappointment that I don't get "my name in the literature."[20]

To Bohr he wrote:

> Honorable Professor Bohr, Following careful consideration I ask you not to include my name as coauthor on the investigation of the lung and skin respiration in frogs. What brings me to this is first of all, that all along and especially now that the publication is at hand, I have felt that my part of the work aside from the purely mechanical experimentation, is too small to warrant that I become coauthor. I shall be totally satisfied with being acknowledged as the one who carried out the experiments. Furthermore, I must add that I believe that my parents would not be pleased were my first publication to be published in German.[21]

Bohr obliged and published the paper without Krogh's name.

According to his well-laid plan, August began cramming for his exams in fall 1898. One evening shortly before he began, while sitting in the botanical laboratory working on the plant stomata, Professor Warming came in and asked, "Well, how is it coming?" "Thank you, very well," said August as he turned toward Warming, "but I am planning to quit studying." Then he paused while Warming stiffened. Here was one of the best students he had ever met and he planned to give up his studies, but August continued, "and start reading for the exam."[22]

Having found two fellow students with whom to study, August was not as lonely as he had anticipated. He rearranged his room to make it more comfortable for studying, got rid of the bed so that he had only the chaise longue and he now started what became a lifelong habit of taking cold showers every morning. Standing in a tub he could give himself a shower with a sponge. He did this to harden himself against the very frequent colds he had.

As usual August followed a rigid schedule: "Get up at 10 a.m. and arrive at the library at 11. Make my own dinner between 3 and 5 and work again at the library until 8. Then I go home and eat my evening meal and at 10–11 after a reasonable rest I begin reading again until 2 in the morning."[23]

His arduous studies were occasionally interrupted by pleasant visits. Through Raphael he became familiar with the writer Jeppe Aakjær and was later invited to his house. He also got to know and like the writer Hjalmar Bergstrøm. About his studies he wrote: "One day is very much like the other, I am forced to keep my thoughts tethered to the textbooks' monotonous grassy field to bring them to the required condition of fattening prior to slaughter."[24] He went to the theater every other week and he and his fellow students started a discussion group called Collegium Politicum. He was intensely occupied by the politics of his time and deeply disturbed by the tyrannical treatment of the Finns by the Russians.

When August finally finished his library studies in January 1899 he had to admit that he had profited considerably from them even though it had been a "confounded dull" existence with days on end without any human contact.

To his great relief August was disqualified for military service (probably due to his bad posture). In February he received an invitation to a white tie dinner party at Professor Bohr's home in Bredgade. To his father he wrote: "Of news I can tell you that on Tuesday I received a dinner invitation from Bohr. . . . Even though I do not overlook the importance of this invitation, because among other things it means that I am now among 'the promising young scientists,' I cannot say that I take unmixed pleasure in it. As is well known, I am least of all a party-goer."[25]

The guests at Bohr's party, aside from a few younger physiologists, were all among those considered the most important university professors. The front of their elegant dress coats were covered with *ordner* (medals and decorations) galore. "However I remained imperturbed," wrote August, "by the learned society and the numerous decorations shown off to such a degree."[26] One professor did not exhibit a single decoration. He looked great, thought the young August, and he made up his mind then and there never to accept any decorations.

On Sundays he helped his friend William Sørensen, who was finishing one of his scathingly critical and satirical attacks on the zoologist Japetus Steenstrup. August helped Sørensen with the mailing of the reprints. What is surprising is that August, as well as Sørensen, believed that the paper would help Sørensen to obtain a position. At first there were no comments from Steenstrup, but then a protest was published in the Danish newspaper *Politiken,* signed by nineteen zoologists, botanists (including Professor Warming), geologists, and politicians. No counter-arguments were given but the anger was vehement. August's loyalty to Sørensen and his part in helping him did not go unnoticed and he acquired some powerful enemies in the faculty.

In April, August sent in his application requesting permission to submit himself to the examinations. In this connection he had to make a series of visits to the various professors to show the list of literature he had read: "Jungersen was very pleased with what I had read in zoology. Warming, however, was extremely displeased with the botany. On closer examination it became clear that he had very few objections of any substance. I was given three papers that I had to read. The rest of the list he accepted as it was. It was not unknown to me, that he did not take kindly to me, so I am taking his dissatisfaction with me on this occasion rather lightly."[27] Later in April he wrote:

> I have been informed that the faculty has nothing against that I submit myself to the magister conference examinations. I have made a small test of my knowledge in botany and mineralogy by answering some written tests. Since they came out highly satisfactory, I look forward to the exam with complete composure. I am reasonably sure that even if Boas should become professor, and I therefore could expect that both he and Warming would do everything in their power to prevent me from getting the exam, their attempts will fail miserably.[27]

The magister conference examinations started at the end of May with a major thesis on the subject "Structure and function of the lungs and air sacks of birds."[28] While writing the thesis, he took time out to write a loving letter for his mother's birthday: "Little mother, you know how much I care for you, and that I deeply desire to see you happy now and always. True, we disagree in many things and probably many of my opinions do not make you happy. But you know, it is not because I wish to give you sorrow that I follow the road I do, but because it is the only passable road I see for my thoughts. You yourself have faith that the one who honestly seeks truth will find it in the end."[29]

When he had finished writing and still had time left over, August set up experiments at the Physiological Laboratory to answer some questions, "to which the existing literature did not have sufficient answers. It will be something unprecedented that my thesis will include independent research. Furthermore, my paper will be different from most others in that it contains a thorough critical examination of the papers on which it is based."[30] (Forty years later, he gave his student Erik Zeuthen the identical problem for his magister conference thesis and, when Zeuthen had finished, showed him his own handwritten thesis.)

In fall 1899 the rest of the written and oral examinations took place. They went very well, except for the botanical examination by Warming, which was "very unpleasant because it was based entirely on memorization."

At last, the twenty-five-year-old August Krogh had completed his formal education. He and his friends celebrated by going down to the "Bodega," where they emptied a few glasses while assuring each other of their friendship and respect. On Sunday, August wandered around in the forest with Raphael and his fiancée, ending up in August's room discussing the arts until late in the night. "It was like a refreshing bath after the tedious, spiritless exam studies."[31]

6

The Beginning of Zoophysiology (1899–1904)

> The lecture shall be a kind of program declaration, designed to show what I understand by *Zoophysiology* [comparative physiology] and that this is an independent and—so far—very neglected science, which can be pursued to great advantage.

The future now looked bright. August had a position in Bohr's laboratory and would soon have a regular salary. In November 1899 he received a document from Viggo advising him that his education since he was eighteen years old had cost his parents DKr 3,309.25. This sum was to be considered an advance on his inheritance. The financial agreement that August had with his parents was very complete and included the cost of having his laundry done in Grenaa by his mother. But now even that would be charged directly. Back home in Grenaa finances were tight as Viggo was fighting to keep his business afloat. August tried to be as helpful to his father as he could. When a law to tax beer sales was proposed, August spent hours listening to the parliamentary debates and reporting them in detail to his father. To help his father brew beer, he designed and constructed an alarm-thermometer to wake Viggo when the temperature of the mash fell below a certain level.

With the variable and, at times, uncertain income from the brewery, Viggo paid for his sons' education, but not for his three daughters. Thus, after they finished school, August's sisters were sent out to earn livings as governesses in wealthy families.

In October 1899, as soon as his examinations were over, August went to Bohr's laboratory in Bredgade, where to his amazement he found that the laboratory rooms were being renovated and all of the instruments removed. He did not find Bohr, but Mrs. Bohr told him that Bohr was longing for him. The next day, Bohr informed him that the renovation would last until after New Year's, but that he would be on the payroll from November 1. In the meantime, he could do some drawings. "Thus, I will have loads of spare time and hope to bring my own experiments very far during that period. In the near future, I shall start on my be-

The Beginning of Zoophysiology

loved mosquito larvae and try to bring the work to a conclusion during the winter. Furthermore, I plan to read and write so much English that I can do my papers on these animals in that language."[1]

August was able to start immediately on English, translating zoology texts from English to Danish and then back to English to check the accuracy of his translations. He could not start his experiments right away because he was waiting for some instruments. Furthermore, for the rest of October, August had his brother Johan as his guest and the two made several visits to friends and various professors. He wrote to Mimi:

> This does not mean that I have been lazy, to the contrary, I have done a great deal in the service of the laboratory. I have the satisfaction that Professor Bohr regularly approves of my dispositions and suggestions. The other day, he said that he wished to leave as much as possible of the design and organization of the laboratory to me and give me a free hand to do it. I don't believe it is common to talk like this to a young man coming directly from his exam with a theoretical education. Now it will be up to me to see to it that he does not regret it. In this regard, it will prove useful that I have always had my eyes open for technical problems and machine construction of all kinds.[2]

It was indeed August's unusual ability to design instruments and apparatus that served him so well during his long career. He now took up the problems of constructing instruments for Bohr's laboratory.

Sometime during the fall of 1899 August had become an active member of the Society for the Protection of the Defenseless. This society helped unwed mothers by placing their children in foster homes. During 1900, August, in spite of his busy schedule in Bohr's laboratory, did a great deal of work for the society. He enlisted his mother's help in finding suitable foster homes for the children in Grenaa. Many of the letters between Mimi and August during that time dealt with the arrangements they made concerning the children, their mothers, and the foster families.

At the end of January the laboratory was finally finished and the experimental studies could begin. The work in Bohr's laboratory centered on the problems of respiration. In particular, Bohr was interested in the transport of oxygen from the lungs to the blood.

At the middle of the nineteenth century most physiologists believed that all transport through living membranes followed simple physical laws. Gradually it was realized that this model could not hold for some organs, such as the kidneys, intestine, and various glands, and that vital forces had to be involved. For the lungs, the generally accepted opinion at the time was based on the physical theory, namely that gases such as oxygen and CO_2 diffuse passively across the lung epithelium: oxygen from a higher oxygen tension in the alveolar air to a lower tension in the lung capillaries, and CO_2 in the opposite direction from a higher CO_2 tension in the lung capillaries to a lower tension in the alveolar air.

In 1870 the eminent Leipzig physiologist Carl Ludwig was the first to suggest that oxygen may be actively secreted by the lung epithelium. This led to a debate with his rival in Bonn, Eduard Pflüger, who claimed that diffusion was sufficient.[3] The question was unresolved because the available techniques were not sufficiently accurate to answer the question. However, in 1887 Bohr came to agree with Ludwig. In 1890 he attempted to test the hypotheses. He wrote, "All in all, my experiments have confirmed that the lung tissue plays an active role in the transport of gases, whereby the function of the lung must be regarded as that of a gland. At least as far as oxygen is concerned, this viewpoint does not agree with the present opinion, which is generally accepted in physiology."[4]

In England, John Scott Haldane became interested in Bohr's papers, and in 1891 he and his coworker James Lorraine Smith came to Bohr's laboratory to study his methods. In a paper published in 1896, Haldane and Smith claimed to have measured tensions of oxygen and CO_2 in the arterial blood and in the alveolar air favoring Bohr's conclusion that oxygen as well as CO_2 are secreted.[3]

When Krogh started working with Bohr he probably did not fully share Bohr's opinion. He was more inclined to believe the physical theory as he read it in contemporary textbooks. He went to work for Bohr determined to find the truth by making the most accurate measurements possible to settle the questions Bohr had raised.

Bohr's and Krogh's interests coincided in that both wanted to study gas transport in many organisms. The study on frog respiration that Krogh had carried out during 1898 was, as Krogh had requested, published by Bohr alone. Bohr concluded from the results that respiration in frogs take place through the skin as well as through the lungs. The finding that the metabolism remained unchanged even when lung respiration was prevented indicated to him that both lung and skin respiration were active.

Bohr had also been interested in the swimbladders of fishes, because oxygen apparently is secreted into the swimbladders. What Krogh was doing in his room (his "private studies") was studying the hydrostatic function of the closed air bladders present in the tracheal system of *corethra* larvae (a species of mosquito). He could show that these air bladders appeared to be analogous to—and served the same function as—the swim bladders in fish. They, too, regulated the density (mass/volume) of the animals making it possible for the larvae to maintain their position in the water column. When the pressure was increased and the air in the air sacs compressed, the larvae sank to the bottom. Soon the volume of the air in the air sacs returned to normal, however, and the larvae rose again.

At the time, Krogh assumed that the mechanism was the same as in fishes, i.e. that the volume of air was restored by secretion of oxygen into the tracheal bladders. This is what he later suggested to his audience when he presented his results at Biologisk Selskab (the Biological Society).[5] But as his work progressed he felt that it would be incomplete without accurate determinations of the gas composition in the tiny air bladders. Therefore, he did not publish the work until 1911, after he had returned to the problem. This time he constructed the necessary instruments to analyze the small air bubbles (0.03 mm^3). As it turned out, the air bubbles did not contain oxygen but mostly nitrogen. Krogh now showed that the air bubbles are formed when fluid is absorbed from the tracheal bladders. When pressure is increased and the air in the tracheal bladders is compressed, fluid reenters. Readjustment is accomplished through reabsorption of this fluid and diffusion of gas into the space from the surrounding tissue.[6]

When Krogh told Bohr in fall 1900 about some of his experiments on *corethra* larvae, the professor suggested that he should do them in the laboratory and let the laboratory pay for the expenses. With great pleasure, Krogh accepted the offer. Now he worked in Bohr's laboratory from nine in the morning until midnight, leaving only for a few hours in the afternoon to get his dinner. When he wanted to practice bicycling he had to do it after midnight.[7]

In the laboratory Krogh became well acquainted with Bohr's two other assistants, Dr. Karl A. Hasselbalch[8] and Dr. Vilhelm Maar. Maar later became a professor of medical history. Maar and Krogh shared an interest in the famous Danish scientist Niels Stensen (known as Nicolaus Steno; 1638–1686), and the two decided to work together on a Danish translation of some of Steno's Latin papers. Maar also told Krogh about England. "Yesterday I had a long talk with Dr. Maar . . . he has spent a long time in England and what he told me caused me to make the firm decision that I will try get over there for about a month next summer."[7] Maar and Krogh soon started on the translation of the work *De solido intra solidum naturaliter contento dissertationis prodromus* (Preliminary account of a dissertation concerning solids naturally contained within solids). This is a famous work showing for the first time that what appear to be animal parts imbedded in rocks actually are fossils from earlier species.[9]

More work was piled on Krogh, when Bohr invited him to become a member of the Biological Society and give three lectures during the coming winter. In addition, he was asked to take over the job of writing for an international catalog on natural science literature to be published in January. "It will be my job to summarize (in English) everything that is published in Denmark of zoology, human anatomy, physiology, experimental psychology, and some other minor subjects."[10]

With all he had to do, August worked relentlessly. "It is natural enough that I don't notice the passing of time. One day rolls around like the next, and I cannot keep count of them. I observe by certain outer signs when it is Sunday, and when I have made that observation I stop working at three and hurry out to Uncle William."[11]

On November 8, 1900, he gave his first talk before the Biological Society on the role of turgor pressure in plants and the opening mechanism of plant stomata. He gave a physical explanation for how the increased turgor pressure in the guard cells would cause the stomata to open.[12] It was exceedingly well received and he was asked to repeat it before the Natural History Society (Naturhistorisk Forening), but something strange happened to him. "The lecture did not go as well as at the Biological Society because I—for no reason that I can understand—was very nervous."[13] In the same letter, August had become argumentative and answered his mother's usual questions about religion and the Bible in an uncharacteristically harsh and hurtful way. Another highly noticeable change about the letter is the handwriting. The flowing style had abruptly changed to a cramped and uneven penmanship and the letters were almost vertical. In the next letter, written after his unhappy and worried mother had complained and told him that he had changed—and not for the better—he wrote:

> You wrote the other day that this is a sad life-style for a young man. There is nothing that can be done about it. My self-preservation instinct tells me that this is the way for me at least for the time being. If I don't work at the utmost limit of my capacity, it is utterly impossible for me to tolerate existence. And the reason? About that I shall keep quiet. There is no use talking about it; it would pain me too much. As early as last summer, you have noticed and were uneasy about the change in me. I am so sorry. I can only assure you that I am doing what I can to return to my usual self.[14]

There may have been several reasons for the change in August. He may have had a love affair during the spring of 1900, which had ended. August had no intention and was in no position to marry before he could support a wife. His dearest friend Uncle William had been in the same unhappy position when he was young. Another reason could have been overwork. Later on in 1903, when August continued to work too hard, he himself contributed his "strange attacks of nervousness" to overwork. Years later he told his children that for a period during his youth he suffered from overextending himself through his work, and he promised himself never to do it again. However, there may well have been another cause for his bad temper and nervous attacks and that is mercury poisoning.

The apparatus that August used for his mosquito larvae studies

> consisted of two cylindrical glass bulbs connected by a long rubber tube and containing enough mercury to fill one of the bulbs. The other vessel, which could be closed at the top by a piece of rubber tubing and screw clip, was completely filled with water and one or more larvae

The Beginning of Zoophysiology

put in. The screw clip was then closed, and the pressure in the water could now be varied and measured simply by raising and lowering the mercury bulb and reading off the difference in level."[6]

As August conducted the experiments in his own living quarters between 1897 and 1900, mercury must have frequently spilled on the floor. Thus, he was exposed to mercury vapor in his own room as well as in the laboratory. Around the turn of the century no one worried about mercury poisoning. Even as late as the early 1930s, I clearly recall the apparatus for cleaning mercury in the corner of my father's laboratory with spilled mercury droplets everywhere. On an old-fashioned wooden floor, drops of mercury collect in the cracks between the floorboards and become smaller and smaller as the mercury gradually disperses. This process greatly increases the amount of mercury vapor in the room, because evaporation from the droplets increases in direct proportion to the free surface area of mercury. Not only did he sleep in a room filled with mercury vapor, but mercury was used in all the gas-analysis apparatus in Bohr's laboratory.

As his hectic work schedule continued, so did the change that had come over August. One day in March 1901, while working in the laboratory, he became acutely ill with headache, dizziness, and repeated vomiting. The symptoms he described in his letter to his mother are identical to the symptoms suffered in 1937 by two young physiologists in August's laboratory accidentally exposed to acute mercury poisoning.[15]

"Fortunately I was surrounded by physicians," August wrote, "and they took such good care of me with ether and Antifebrin, that an hour later I was reasonably well and could go home." At home he slept for thirteen hours and rested for four more.

> I usually get such an attack about once a year; but this time, it was undeniably unusually violent. It is probably because I have worked under great time pressure during the last few days. It is the talk I have to present that takes so much time, mostly because the decision was made so suddenly. Professor Bohr asked me last Thursday if I knew anybody that would give a talk (he is the chairman and has to produce the speakers.) . . . I offered to do two lectures even though I had planned them for next year.
>
> It is a matter of considerable importance to me, because the lecture shall be a kind of program declaration, designed to show what I understand by Zoophysiology (comparative physiology) and that this is an independent and—so far—very neglected science, which can be pursued to great advantage.[16]

The lectures presented March 14 and 28, 1901, dealt with hydrostatic relationships in the animal kingdom.[7] He explained the various mechanisms used by animals to keep themselves afloat in the water without active movements. It was the first time Krogh presented what is now called comparative physiologic studies. In spite of his illness, the two lectures were great successes.

I know that the first has interested many people and has been the subject of discussions among zoologists and botanists for several days. I have not heard anything about the other yet, mostly because I have not spoken with anybody, but I believe the audience liked it. The demonstrations that I showed during the lecture were enthusiastically received. I showed some experiments of the effects of changing pressures on goldfish and my old experiments with mosquito larvae. To make them visible for everybody, I enclosed them in a flat glass box inside a sciopticon [a projection instrument], and the living larvae could be seen foot-long on a large white screen. Since they are transparent, all the inner organs are visible and they looked magnificent. Of course the experiments succeeded, the only disadvantage was that the larvae became restless from the concentrated electric light. For effect only, following the lecture, I placed a batch of microscopic crustaceans in the glass box with some very hungry larvae so that the whole cribble-crabble took place in clear view of the audience.[17]

In May 1901, August was planning his trip to London where he intended to stay five weeks. He bought a new gray suit and had his old one repaired. He also took time out for a long bicycle ride in the country. As usual he had to test himself to the utmost. He rode south from Copenhagen as fast as he could (30 km/hour). "It was all perfectly wonderful," he told his mother in her birthday letter, "and was accompanied by a feeling of physical lightness and unbounded freedom that I have not felt for a very long time."[18]

Arriving in London, August noticed to his dismay that he did not understand much of the spoken English, but he liked London. "The city is bigger than Copenhagen, but one does not feel cramped because the houses are lower, the streets much wider and open squares with large flower beds are numerous. In addition there are large, fully accessible parks." The life in the streets was freer than in Copenhagen, with troupes of entertainers, acrobats, and pantomimes performing in the middle of some streets. As his English improved, he started talking with workers in the street.[19]

Awed by Westminster Abbey, he wrote:

> That is a place I shall never forget. Memorial after memorial, some of great beauty, over England's great men, politicians, war heroes, scientists, artists and philanthropists. On many, a list of their many deeds are given, but on the greatest only the years of birth and death are shown. I found the place where Newton, Herschel and Darwin are buried and for a long time I stood contemplating the simple stones covering their graves. On Newton's it says in Latin, "here rests what is mortal of Isaac Newton." My general impression of England and the English is that the cultural level is considerably higher than it is at home.[19]

Visiting the National Gallery twice, he commented later: "For the first time, I became fully aware of the great masters in all their splendor.

I have particularly enjoyed a series of pictures by Murillo and some by Greuze."[20]

For a while August studied seven hours daily in the magnificent British Museum Reading Room. But he also paid several visits to colleagues. On visits it was customary to wear a formal black suit and a silk top hat, but because of the great heat in London in those July days he could dispense with the "uniform."[20] "I have visited a professor in physiology, [Ernest H.] Starling, whose laboratory I saw and where I attended a very interesting vivisection. I did not find another professor, Vaughan Harley, at home but shall meet him tomorrow in his laboratory." Being particularly anxious to meet John Scott Haldane, August traveled to Oxford.

Early in January 1902, August and Maar had finished the Steno translation and the Carlsberg Foundation had granted them a six-hundred-kroner honorarium. August finished the introduction and the following week the printing had started. Now he received another tempting proposition:

> The other day I received a letter from my friend the botanist M. Porsild, who urged me to participate in an expedition to Greenland with him next summer. I found the plan most agreeable, considering that it undoubtedly will be very good for my health and that I probably can justify taking such a (relative) vacation for half a year. I presented the plan to my friends, all of whom fully sanctioned it. I decided to accept when Professor Bohr also agreed, provided my dissertation is reasonably completed before I leave. Now I have sent the necessary application to the commission for Greenland investigations. According to the plan, I shall leave for Godhavn with one of the trading vessels by the end of April and from there on to Nugsuak peninsula north of Disko. From there we travel by "umiak" [a sealskin boat rowed by Eskimo women; the men use kayaks] south along the west coast of Disko. We travel by water one-half to one day at a time and then stay ashore for several days. We will take several trips into the mountains over the ice to study possible valleys in the island's interior. On the entire trip we shall sleep in sleeping bags and tents. And we will live partly from hunting and fishing though primarily from canned food. We return to Godhavn in about three months and hopefully we will be back in Copenhagen in October.[21]

Before he could leave, August worked as hard as he could writing his dissertation and designing instruments for his trip. He and Emil had time for a short Easter vacation in Grenaa to see his parents before he left. The Steno translation was published in the middle of April, and August sent his father a copy. He had finished most of his dissertation by then.

On Saturday, April 26, 1902, August boarded the sailing vessel *Peru* after working late Friday and Saturday nights to finish the instruments for the trip. On Sunday morning at seven the vessel was towed out into the middle of the Øresund [the strait between Copenhagen and Sweden] and the sail hoisted, but the wind died and the ship lay still in the Øresund. With a favorable wind on Tuesday they finally got out of the Øresund and were soon in the North Sea off Norway's coast. For the next eight weeks the vessel, totally unfit to tack against wind, made very slow progress. August observed: "It is a sad situation that no one on board except the passengers are interested in a fast trip. The captain himself would rather that the trip takes a long time. He acts accordingly, sails with the smallest sails and lies to as soon as he can find an excuse."[22]

Due to the rough sea, August was unable to do analysis and experiments. He limited himself to taking samples of plankton and measuring temperature and salt content of the seawater. Between Porsild and August, however, there was enough to read. Having several volumes of the English weekly journal *Nature*, Porsild "issued" one each day, but when the weather was particularly bad and spirits low, a special edition appeared.

On June 18 after fifty-three days at sea, while stranded across from the Sukkertoppen headland of southwestern Greenland the Danish steamer *Godthaab* appeared. *Peru*'s passengers boarded for a visit and the captain promised to help them. *Godthaab* towed *Peru* for a day and let her loose a hundred kilometers south of Holsteinborg. It took Peru two more days in dense fog to reach Egesminde. In Egesminde they were well received and stayed up all night. The next evening in dense fog they continued in two fully loaded umiaks toward Godhavn. But with the Greenlanders' good sense of direction they reached Hundeeiland where the crew of one of the umiaks lived. They slept briefly and continued a few hours later. Again they were delayed because of fog, high wind, and rough sea but finally reached Godhavn July 1. Here they had to reorganize and reduce their gear working with only one hand, while killing mosquitoes with the other. All was soon done and the expedition proceeded by umiak along the coast of Disko.

The expedition was successful and resulted in three publications. Two very important papers were published in English by Krogh in 1904 in *Meddelelser om Grønland* (Communications on Greenland): "The Tension of Carbonic Acid in Natural Waters and especially in the Sea," and "The Abnormal CO_2-Percentage in the Air in Greenland and the General Relations between Atmospheric and Oceanic Carbonic Acid (CO_2)."[23] In the first paper he wrote:

> In the summer of 1902 I accompanied my friend Mr. Porsild on an expedition to the island of Disko on the west-coast of Greenland, under the auspices of the Danish Commission for the Geological and Geographic Investigation of Greenland. I intended to study the respiratory exchange of the organisms of the Arctic Sea, and in order to do so I constructed an apparatus according to the principles mentioned above

for the determination of the dissolved gasses. At the same time I had in view the determination of the tensions in the surface-water of the sea and especially ascertaining as to whether the carbonic acid [CO_2] was really in equilibrium with the atmosphere. The results I attained with regard to the last-mentioned question appeared to me to be so interesting that I devoted most of my time to it during my stay in Greenland, and I have, since my return, pursued it further.[23]

In 1896 the well-known Swedish physicist Svante August Arrhenius proposed what is now called the greenhouse effect. He postulated that the surface temperature of the earth depended to a large extent on the heat-absorbing power of the atmospheric CO_2. Through a consideration of the overall balance of CO_2 in water and air, August wanted to find out if atmospheric CO_2 was constant, rising, or falling. Measuring CO_2 tension in air and oceanic waters around the island of Disko and in the North Atlantic, he found that the CO_2 percentage in the Greenland air was on the average much higher than that of the southern part of the earth. He suggested, "This phenomenon cannot be explained by any enhanced production of CO_2 from the land (the island of Disko), but may possibly be due to a liberation of the gas from the sea, such as will take place if bottom-waters, possessing a high tension, should rise to the surface." Hence, "The CO_2-tension of the ocean surface often differs from that of the atmosphere and may cause considerable absorption or elimination of the gas."

Theoretical considerations and calculations of production and removal of CO_2 from the earth's atmosphere led him to conclude that the burning of coal was the major factor:

> The combustion of coal by man is an ever increasing factor that has in recent years reached very considerable magnitude. . . . The world's production of coal amounted in 1902 to 700 million tons giving by combustion 2.6×10^9 tons of carbonic acid or rather more than 1/1000 of the quantity present in the atmosphere. In the geological insignificant period of 1000 years the percentage of carbonic acid could therefore be doubled by this course alone, if other factors remained unchanged.[23]

Through further calculations, however, he concluded correctly that the ocean acts as a regulator by taking up or giving off CO_2, "The action of the ocean will retard and diminish any influence upon the climate which the variations of the percentage of CO_2 in the atmosphere might exercise."[23]

On the return trip across the Atlantic, August analyzed samples of surface water and air finding the percentage to be higher in the air than in the water, "By a comparison between the average CO_2-tension of the ocean-surface and the percentage of the gas in the atmosphere, it will be possible to ascertain whether the latter is increasing or decreasing or perhaps stationary. The evidence now available points toward the first of these alternatives, but it is not sufficient to decide the question."[23]

While in Greenland, August learned to pilot an eskimo kayak (made of sealskin and whale bones), which he undoubtedly used while collecting samples. He liked it so much that he brought one back to Denmark and was still using it almost twenty years later.

August returned to Denmark by steamer in October 1902 and went straight to Grenaa to visit his parents. Unfortunately, there is no record of what he told his parents and friends upon his return. Coming back to Copenhagen in early October, he was soon in full swing at the laboratory working on his dissertation and a couple of small papers.

Having long been interested in the oxygen-carrying capacity of blood, Bohr wished to measure the effect of carbon dioxide on oxygen binding by hemoglobin. To make these measurements Krogh invented and constructed a new apparatus for measuring the oxygen binding of blood at different gas tensions. In February, when he was setting up his newly constructed apparatus, he wrote, "I have had the satisfaction that my constructions seem to be highly successful."[24] The study, in collaboration with Hasselbalch and Bohr, showed that increasing CO_2 tension decreases the ability of hemoglobin to bind oxygen (i.e. shifts the oxygen hemoglobin binding curve to the right.) In other words, the effect of CO_2 on hemoglobin causes oxygen to be released in the tissue where it is needed for the metabolism. When the now famous paper was published in 1904 under the title "Ueber den Einfluss der Kohlensäurespannung auf die Saurstoffaufnahme in Blute," by Bohr, Hasselbalch, and Krogh, the phenomenon became known as "the Bohr effect."[25]

At home in Wiedervelt Street, August was now sharing his apartment with Valdemar Sørensen and Emil, both studying for their final exams in June. Apparently an agreement had been made that August should act as a sort of guardian for Valdemar, teaching him to study hard and improve his ways. The reason for this peculiar arrangement was that while Valdemar had been drinking he was arrested and imprisoned for alleged child molestation. The charges were dropped for lack of evidence and Valdemar was released. Emil used some of August's money to help Valdemar and a student society granted him a small monthly sum of money provided Valdemar would straighten up and complete his medical studies.[26]

At first the arrangement in Wiedervelt Street worked reasonably well. "There is not much room and the order is not the best, but it works quite well," wrote August. He added in the margin, "We always have a window open at night."[27] Apparently, Mimi, forever health conscious, had told them that this was desirable. They had a cleaning woman, but when she did not do a good job they fired her and Emil's girlfriend Sidsel came instead and cleaned the apartment. They later found a Madam Thomsen who was excellent and worked for August even after he was married.

In December 1902, grandfather Jacob died in Grenaa and August went home for the funeral. For Christmas, however, he could not find time to go home, which he later regretted because he felt so lazy that he did very little work. Instead he read English fiction and slept ten hours every night. Valdemar and he celebrated Christmas Eve at home with an excellent dinner they prepared together. Christmas Day a strong storm blew down trees all over Copenhagen and ruined windmills in the countryside. Horrible weather followed the storm contributing to August's low spirit.

In his letter of December 29, 1902, August told his mother two things that were to have great importance for the future: "The medical faculty has submitted a proposal to the department of education that the scientific assistants with the medical professors, among them Bohr, in the future shall help lecture the medical students two to three hours per week and be paid 600–1000 Kr. per year."[28] This would mean a good extra income for August starting in about one year. As it turned out it changed August's life in a way he could not have anticipated.

The second thing became important to Emil and later to his father in a significant way. A new issue of the shipping journal *Søfartstidende* had arrived for Emil. An announcement caught August's interest, "In the near future a special nautical editor will be hired. I do not know what it means but I have my thoughts about it." The special nautical editor hired would be Emil Krogh and later when Emil obtained a government position, his father, Viggo, became the editor.[28]

In February, August decided to take time off which meant *not* working every evening in addition to his hectic daytime routine. He had rewritten part of his dissertation.

> Having made some supplementary experiments in December and thought hard about the whole question, it turned out that with certainty I could suggest results of considerable importance for the understanding of respiratory physiology. As a result I rather suddenly changed my plan for the whole paper, took out all experiments with animals other than frogs and made the whole thing less zoological and considerably more physiological than was my original plan. Now I believe I have written a good and coherent physiological paper.[29]

The work he did for his dissertation involved measuring separately the respiration (the amount of oxygen taken up and the amount of CO_2 given off) through the skin and the lungs of frogs under various condition. It did not involve measuring the tension of oxygen in blood.

By comparing the surface areas, the anatomy of skin and lungs, and the effect of sectioning of nerves on oxygen uptake, he concluded: "The cutaneous absorption of oxygen cannot be regulated at all by the organism, hence I am of the opinion that with a probability almost amounting to certainty it is affected by plain physical powers—diffusion."[30]

However, as far as the lung respiration was concerned, he still agreed with Bohr and with Haldane and Smith, defending their point of view. "The supposition of the absorption of oxygen being chiefly effected by secretion and regulation of the latter through influence of the nerves reconciles the relations in the frogs lungs with those known from the air-bladder of the fishes and from the lungs of higher animals. No experimental facts pleads against this result."[30]

Both Emil and Valdemar did quite well on their final exams. With that, August's responsibility for Valdemar was over. It had not been easy. In February, August had told his mother, "He [Valdemar] has finally succeeded in destroying all faith I have had in him. I always hear dishonesty in his words and under these circumstances it is so unpleasant to be his guardian that I have given it up altogether. . . . Clearly, I am not suited for reforming anybody, and this negative knowledge may be all I have gained from the experiment."[31] In October, Valdemar became a Dutch military physician, signing up for a five-year hitch with rank of lieutenant and four thousand kroner a year, plus private practice. He apparently continued as a military doctor until around 1920 when he had to resign due to ill health. He renewed his friendship with August who visited him in the hospital. From the correspondence which ensued, it appears that Valdemar suffered from a chronic, debilitating disease, probably syphilis, contracted during his extended sea voyages. During his illness, Valdemar studied scientific developments and followed August's career with the greatest interest. The correspondence ends in 1923, presumably with Valdemar's death.

In March 1903 August went home for a short vacation and afterwards thanked his parents warmly for the lovely days with them. The galley proofs for his dissertation were waiting for him when he returned and he rushed to correct them. The following week the final printing was finished and submitted to the faculty. According to August's wish, Bohr and a plant physiologist, Professor R. Pedersen, became the official opponents.

In June 1903, while August was happily engaged in his CO_2 work, he read in the papers about an accident in which two well diggers died. One digger collapsed in the well and the other going after him suffered the same fate. The papers suggested that they had died from toxic fumes from the soil, but August, suspecting another cause, went to Fyn to investigate:

> I left Copenhagen at midnight and arrived in Odense at four in the morning from where I bicycled into the countryside. I tried lying down in the grass at a reasonable place to catch some sleep, but sleep did not come. At six-thirty, after a breakfast at an inn, I arrived at the farm where the accident had occurred. Here I met the obstacle that, for no

reason whatsoever, the owner did not permit the investigation of the well. I ended the discussion by saying that then I had to get permission through the courts, but that I would go and look at the well anyway. Fortunately, it was out in a field far from the farmhouse. At the well two men were working on setting stones and I had no difficulties with them. They fully understood the advantage of having the problem investigated, gave me all the information I needed, and helped me getting the samples of air and water from the well. . . . The well diggers told me about a well in a nearby village from which "air blows out at certain winds." Naturally I went to see it. It turned out that it was not at certain winds, but at falling barometric pressure that air blew out of the well, while at rising pressure it blew into the well. The owner, an intelligent and knowledgeable man, had discovered this peculiarity. When he gave up using the well because it was too deep, he covered it with bricks except for a small hole. Over the hole he placed a small windmill, this showed him by its direction and velocity if the barometer was falling or rising and the speed of the changes. The well actually serves as a barometer for the entire village. The explanation is quite simple and is connected to the "toxicity" of the other well. The upper layers of soil are impermeable clay, but under them, there is loose gravel that can take up enormous quantities of air and naturally more at high than at low pressure. In the air that remains for some time, the oxygen gets used up. From a new well, at falling barometric pressure, almost pure nitrogen will stream out. This is so much more dangerous because you do not notice anything wrong before losing consciousness. The analyses that I have since made have fully confirmed the opinion I already had.[32]

To make it generally known and to warn other well diggers to take proper precautions, August wrote a newspaper article about his finding and later a paper for a medical journal.[33] As his warnings were forgotten, these accidents continued to happen for many years and my father was still doing his best to educate the public to the dangers of certain wells when I was a child.

At the end of July 1903 August went to Holte. Bohr had invited him to stay with the Bohr family at their summer home for a couple of weeks. The purpose of this visit was for August to take samples of water and air in a large body of water, Fure Lake, to supplement his data from the Greenland trip on CO_2 in natural bodies of water and air. The first week the weather was sunny and calm. Spending every day from ten in the morning until late afternoon in a rowboat taking samples, August became deeply suntanned. When the weather changed the following week and became windy, Bohr rented a small steamer and joined August on board. At the end of the two weeks August had succeeded in getting all the samples he needed in Fure Lake. He still needed some more samples from Greenland and stayed in Copenhagen until the middle of August to make arrangements for a steamer leaving for Greenland to take water samples for him.

While in Holte, August received the official announcement from the university that his dissertation had been accepted.[34] Following a brief vacation in Grenaa, August returned to Copenhagen in early September. The dissertation was now bound and published (in Danish), and the defense was set for October 11. August was eager to have his parents present on the occasion. Finally having the apartment to himself, he had it painted and wallpapered. He also bought new furniture and a rug, assuring his parents that they could stay with him while in Copenhagen. During the summer, a Mrs. Leshley, a friend of Sørensen, had finished the English translation of August's dissertation. August, who by now had become quite proficient in English himself, found the translation horrible, full of misunderstandings, and the language stilted and poor. He corrected it some but it never measured up to his standards. His brother Johan helped him handwrite a clean copy for publication.

To August's enormous disappointment, Viggo and Mimi did not come for his dissertation defense. Instead they went to their minister's silver anniversary. They had great difficulties with the brewery and in addition had the financial and emotional burden of Viggo's younger brother Carl and his large family living with them for some time. Carl, who had lived in Estonia for many years, had fallen on hard times, and Viggo and Mimi worried about their uncertain future. August wrote, "It was very sad that neither you nor father could come. You would have been pleased to hear all the pretty and kind words that were addressed to me. The procedure was completely friendly since the zoologists who had challenged my thesis did not come."[35]

In spite of having finished the dissertation, August had plenty of work to do. With Emil he constructed an instrument to take soundings in the ocean, and the two were seeking government support for it. He was also writing two other papers on investigations derived from his Greenland trip.

What occupied August's thoughts the most, however, was the problems of diffusion versus secretion. A paper Krogh published shortly after the frog paper dealt with cutaneous respiration in other vertebrates. The conclusion was the same as for frogs: cutaneous respiration plays an important role and "is governed solely by the difference of tensions of the blood and the atmosphere and the permeability of the skin, in short by purely physical features."[36] Krogh had begun to suspect that oxygen transport takes place by diffusion in lungs as well as in skin. He decided to investigate the problem more thoroughly.

In November 1903, August was again bothered by the sudden resurgence of nervous attacks, which he had experienced before. He consulted a neurologist, Professor Pontopidan, who after several visits was unable to find anything wrong with August's nervous system. Professor Bohr and Dr. Maar both suggested that August take a long vacation and

The Beginning of Zoophysiology

Bohr suggested that he go to Norway and ski in Telemark. "Fortunately Pontopidan did not find this necessary. I should avoid overexertion and should exercise in fresh air, but I could continue my work as usual. In that connection I shall take every Sunday off and I shall try to take a walk, daily."[37] Taking the advice seriously, this schedule became a lifelong habit for August Krogh. Later in life he also took Saturday afternoons off to go for long walks with his brother Emil. In 1903 some of his outings consisted of going by kayak out on Fure Lake or in the Øresund to the island of Saltholm.

At the end of 1903, August was again so busy that many people told him that he was overworked, "and the same people who insist on it proceed to contradict themselves by giving me still more to do."[39] Uncle William asked August to read and comment on his *Supplement to Teachings in Natural History,* and Bohr asked him to write the paper on the effect of carbon dioxide on oxygen binding by hemoglobin (the collaborative work they had just completed). "I shall do both with pleasure, particularly the first, but they will not contribute to giving me less to do."[37] Consequently, August couldn't go home for Christmas. But feeling well and very strong he stayed in Copenhagen where he got most of his work done. The Bohrs invited him home several times as usual. He particularly appreciated New Year's Eve when he was the only guest, "I came there at ten in the evening and we had a delightful time until long after midnight. Precisely at midnight we stood up, drank champagne and wished each other a happy New Year."[38]

It is no wonder that August enjoyed the company of the highly intelligent and harmonious Bohr family. Christian Bohr, interested in helping in the women's movement, had met his future wife, the lovely Ellen Adler, when he was tutoring young adult women for the university entrance examination. They married in 1881. Now, the family had three children—Jenny, nineteen; Niels, eighteen; and Harald, sixteen. (Jenny would die relatively young, while Niels was to become the famous nuclear physicist and Harald a well-known mathematician.) In the course of the evening August and the young Miss Bohr discussed books they had read and agreed to visit museums together. "I think you see much more and get less tired when you are two," August told his mother.[38]

As spring approached August started to ease off on his work and take pleasure in other pursuits. He and Emil joined a consortium to buy a retired coast guard sailing boat, which they named *Ragna*. The consortium consisted of twenty-eight men, mostly young scientists, but included professors Bohr and Jungersen. To improve his sailing skills August studied for the pilot examination. Emil, with his extensive seamanship experience, was to be the titular owner of *Ragna*. After August and Emil had finished working on the rigging, interesting sailing trips followed. Some were rather exhausting when the weather turned bad and half of the hands on board became seasick.

7

August and Marie (1904)

> The thought that I shall not see you for two months makes me ill. I must tell you now. I care for you infinitely. Will you, do you dare follow me through life?

"When happiness presents itself to you, you must act quickly without hesitation or caution. 'One has to strike while the iron is hot.' If you delay, happiness will pass you by and you may never see it again." This is what the eighteen-year-old August wrote in 1892 in his paper on the theme "Each person is the forger of his own happiness." Now, twelve years later in spring 1904, happiness unexpectedly presented itself to August and he followed his own blueprint. During the preceding years, he had followed the other part of his blueprint for happiness—*work*.

Since the beginning of the 1904 spring semester, August had been lecturing to the medical students. Then one morning in April the laboratory exercises in physiological chemistry started, for which August had written the text. He was in a bad mood. He felt there were too many students in the group and, worse yet, one of them was a woman. In his experience women made poor physiologists and he had tried in vain not to have her in his group. That morning he tried to avoid her.[1,2] Then a miracle occurred. The serious, sincere, young woman with gentle, intelligent, brown eyes and shiny dark hair spoke to him. As August later wrote to Marie Jørgensen, "You overcame my displeasure with the first word you said and the picture of you from that day on is the most vivid in my memory."[2]

On June 9, he wrote her a note:

> Miss Marie Jørgensen, I would very much appreciate a meeting with you. Partly because I should like to hear your opinion concerning the course in physiological chemistry (since I will have the opportunity to change it, I think it is reasonable to hear the opinion of those who are using it concerning its deficiencies and possible superfluities). Partly, (and I shall not hide that it is a slightly more important motive), I should very much like to have a sensible talk with a sensible person.

Would you find it very peculiar if I suggest to you that you come and have tea with me in my apartment Tuesday at eight? I trust that you find the suggestion reasonable, but if you would care to accept it is another question."[3]

Miss Jørgensen's answer was written the same day, "I grant you the desired conversation with pleasure. Tuesday at eight, as you suggest, will suit me fine. Kind regards, yours, B. Marie Jørgensen."[4]

Who was this medical student?

Birthe Marie Jørgensen was born on Vosegaard, a farm near Husby, on the island of Fyn on Christmas Day 1874. The same age as August, she was older than the other students. Vosegaard was a copyhold farm[5] at the time Marie lived there. It belonged to Count Karl Wilhelm Adam Sigismund Wedell of Wedellsborg, who had inherited the estate from his father in 1828. The beautiful Wedellsborg estate, situated on a peninsula, included the main building with its impressive, richly decorated manor house, large forests, meadows, many churches, and some fifty copyhold farms.[6]

Marie's father Anders Jørgen Jørgensen was born September 7 1830, the son of Jørgen Hansen and Ane Margrethe Nielsdatter.[7]

Anders and his wife Ane Jørgensen had nine children, but only four survived. One after the other the children died from tuberculosis, which was rampant among the farmers. Three of Marie's younger siblings died.[8] Considering the living quarters on the farms and the lack of knowledge about the spread of tuberculosis (from cattle as well as from person to person), it is not surprising that so many died. Marie's father, Anders, was ill with tuberculosis for many years. The rooms on the farm were small, damp, and poorly ventilated. When the children were outside they were well protected against the sun, since a suntan was not considered proper. Ane used to warn her children, "You don't want to get brown on both ends like the children of the poor families."

Ane told her family that it was always the prettiest of her children that died; "they had such lovely red cheeks and clear eyes." Ane was determined that Birthe Marie (nicknamed Mie) should live. Believing that a good diet could save her child, she fed the little Mie lots of scrambled eggs, and to make it even better she put wine in the egg dish. One day when Mie was only four or five years old she disappeared. A frantic search started. For several hours everyone on the farm looked for her. At long last Mie was found in deep sleep in the hay. Having had too much wine in her scrambled eggs, she had wandered off and naturally fallen asleep.[8]

The surviving children were Margrethe, Jørgen, Kirsten, and Birthe Marie. The children were intelligent and loved to read, but Ane found it a waste of their time. To get a chance to read Kirsten had to hide in the long hay.[8] Mie, too, loved to read. When she was six years old, she burned all her dolls and started serious reading of the best Danish authors (particularly Ludvig Holberg). At the same time she made up her mind that when she grew up, she would become a doctor. She never told us why and she never told us much about her childhood. It may have been the tragedy of seeing her siblings die that made her decide, or it may also be because she had read that women could now study medicine at the University of Copenhagen for the first time.

A young woman, Nielsine Nielsen, had singlehandedly brought about the change at the university. She was a private teacher, one of the few intellectual pursuits open to women in those days. In 1873 Nielsine read in the newspaper that the ladies in America had now begun to study medicine and one had even started a practice. Nielsine, on the spot, took the solemn oath that she would overcome any obstacle and become a physician. Until that time no woman had been admitted to the University of Copenhagen. In January 1874, she submitted her application to the government Department of Culture. The time must have been ripe for this dramatic change. In October 1874 the Department of Culture voted "not to advise against that Miss Nielsen's application be granted." Only eight months later the king of Denmark, Christian IX, signed a decree permitting women to acquire academic citizenship at the University of Copenhagen. The female students were granted most of the rights of the male students, with the exception that they had no right to any academic benefits or support (such as stipends).[9]

When the King decreed that women had permission to study at the university, there were no schools or courses designed to prepare women for the university entrance exam, the artium. The first two women, entering the university in 1877, had been tutored privately. But in that same year an artium course for women was established by the well-known Nathalie Zahle. For some time already Miss Zahle had shown great initiative in women's education, but she was reluctant to start the artium course and had to be pressured into this venture. She gave in, because she realized how difficult it was for young women, particularly those without independent means, to obtain an education. She did not think that women should have equal rights with men, but accentuated that the ideal education for women was one that gave them the opportunity "to school and develop the special talents that women possess." However, Miss Zahle's school began, and in 1886 the school gained the right to graduate students for university admission.[9]

When Marie Jørgensen entered Miss Zahle's school in 1898 she was one of the oldest in her class. Due to her mother's pleading, she had reluctantly and with some resentment stayed on the farm. Not until she was twenty-four did Marie finally leave for Copenhagen to start her studies. In school, she made two special friends among her classmates. One was Paula Brønnum who later married a zoologist, Adam Bøving. She was a year older than Marie and the two formed a close friendship (which continued with Adam Bøving and his new wife, Anna, after

Paula died from tuberculosis in 1912). The other was Johanne (Jonna) Christiansen. Being eight years younger than Marie, the outspoken Jonna at first did not think much of the shy and quiet Marie. Not only did Marie Jørgensen come from a farm, but she was also "old" (twenty-four years) when she started school (personal communication 1950). With time, however, a friendship developed. They followed each other through medical school and remained friends and colleagues for the rest of Marie's life. Jonna practiced medicine in Copenhagen and was a specialist in stomach and intestinal diseases. She also published several scientific papers and discussed her research with Marie. When she came to our home to talk with my mother we could always hear her loud voice reverberating through the house.

In 1901 Marie graduated from Zahle's school with honors and began her medical studies. In 1903 she finished the medical preparatory examination. Again she made good grades and her family was proud of her. While she studied, she had a lively correspondence with Emma Jørgensen, her new sister-in-law.

The next part of her medical studies involved anatomy and physiology and thus August Krogh became her laboratory instructor. Three days after Marie first visited August, he wrote her another note suggesting a bicycle ride in the country Saturday evening. He proposed that Marie bicycle to his place after seven in the evening.[10] Again Marie accepted, and she came even though it rained hard and she got soaked. August felt terrible that he had treated her so badly,[11] but it did not worry Marie. To get wet did not hurt her in the least. After two weeks of bad weather and postponed bicycle rides Marie visited August again and in a June 28 thank-you note, she wrote that she had signed up for a trip to Møen with the student society. Paula Bøving had urged her to do so. Marie added, "Too bad that you are not going. I plan to leave for home on July 5."[12]

Promptly, August made up his mind to join the trip to Møen. Afterwards he wrote his mother about the enjoyable trip. He had not had much sleep and was very tired, but he did not mention Marie.[13] To Marie he wrote and proposed marriage on July fifth. At the time my mother died he told us children about the trip to Møen and said, "I was afraid to speak to her then, so I wrote":

> Dear Miss Jørgensen, I must thank you and again thank you for the wonderful trip. You are forever in my thoughts, I seem to hear your voice. The thought that I shall not see you for two months makes me ill. I must tell you now. I care for you infinitely. Will you, do you dare follow me through life? How terrible it is to write this on the dead paper. I would tell you face to face. You would see that my entire soul is in my words and I would read your answer in your eyes, even before I had finished speaking. Now I know nothing and I must, for a long, long time, remain torn between fear and agony.

> I am sure you are my friend and for that I am grateful, but the question is much greater. Do you love me? I fervently hope so, and yet it seems so unlikely. What can there be in me to love.
>
> The fear and the knowledge of how little I can measure up to an ideal humbles me. Do you think you will come to care for me the way I care for you? If you think so, then I shall patiently wait for your answer and not bother you more than you yourself permit. Because as far as the essential is concerned I am not humble. I will not build my house on sand, I want nothing or all.
>
> I see the difficulties looming over us and my courage falters but does not desert me. We have known each other for such a short time. You do not know my family and I do not know yours. If you can have as much confidence in me as I have in you it does not matter.
>
> My future prospects are not particularly bright. Under the best of circumstances I shall become a docent [somewhat equivalent to associate professor], but it is possible that I will have to emigrate because I am firmly determined not to tolerate any obstacles to the development of my abilities. It can possibly be difficult to follow me. But then the fact you were with me would double my strength and it would be the real happiness to fight for.
>
> You have your work and goals just as I have mine. I believe this is good. It will not be one-sided. I believe we can take each other by the hand and in many ways help one another. All difficulties can be overcome if there is the one essential ingredient, and therefore I am asking you: Do you love me as I love you? Yours, August Krogh.[14]

Mail went quickly in those days, Marie's answer was written July 6:

> It was not kind of me not to write you already yesterday, but I could not sit down and write to you about what is the most important question in my life while the entire household [in her sister's home in Copenhagen] was in an uproar because of my trip. Dear Dr. Krogh, you don't know how happy I am over the confidence you have shown me, and at the same time afraid that I may not deserve it fully. You ask if I love you. I do not know that myself; but I know that I care for you deeply, too much not to be open and honest with you. I know that you are my best friend, that I am happy when I am with you, and long for you when I don't see you. But if that is the feeling one can live on through life, I do not know, I think so, but I don't know yet.[15]

Marie suggested that they meet somewhere in Jutland during the summer. August, who had waited in great suspense, was overjoyed with her answer. "Now I am at peace and intensely happy, because you care for me, you are happy when we are together and long for me when we are not. What more can I ask? You do not know yet if it is the feeling that you can live on through life, but that will come. It is not the storm of desire that is upon us; but the feeling of deep harmony, and mutual (do I dare say it) indispensability."[16]

August arranged to travel via Fyn to Grenaa. They planned to meet on the train. He asked for a picture of Marie and he himself went to a photographer, "what I have not willingly done for many years."[16] They were planning the meeting when tragedy struck Marie's family. Her brother Jørgen's young wife Emma died in childbirth. On June 9, Marie wrote August: "Dearest friend you cannot imagine how terrible it is to see one of those closest to you die and not be able to do anything to save her. It is so unmerciful that she should die, a young healthy person that all of us wanted to keep, and who loved life and her home so dearly."[17] August answered that they would work to gain knowledge to avoid such tragedies. Marie moved in with her brother to help care for him and the fourteen-month-old boy. The newborn, who was christened Erik, was cared for temporarily by Emma's mother.

The meeting with August, postponed until after the funeral, took place on June 16 on the train between Ejby and Fredericia. Of the meeting itself there is no written record, but it resulted in their engagement and they agreed to keep their secret from the families.

The next day August wrote:

> My own, own, own, friend, I have come home now. I have been all over the old brewery, said hello to the workers and seen to the horses. I have made a firm friendship with the kittens and with my little nephew [Edel's son] who is at about the same stage of development. We were just in the middle of a game that we both enjoyed, when I suddenly had to retire to my room to tell you what you already know "how incredibly happy I am." I will not get any further than to this elementary, but extremely important fact this morning because in a moment the big bell will ring for dinner—there it is!

In the afternoon he continued the letter, telling her that he had had to stay and be shown off to the minister who came for afternoon coffee. Comparing the minister to another minister he knew, August wrote: "[He is] a couple of degrees worse with respect to unction and self-righteousness. I have a very hard time putting up with him, but I had to be shown off."

The letter continues:

> You want to know what happened after we left each other in Middelfart. First, was it very wrong of me that I stayed at the window [of the train]? Was there anybody who should not see us together? I thought there might be, but I could not let you out of my sight as long as it could be avoided. Therefore I stayed defiantly. After that I sat down in a ditch and "wept," which I might have done, but did not find sufficiently manly. Instead I went to a small inexpensive inn and got something to eat. I love such inns where one is received with simplicity and is free from professional waiter-politeness. . . . Then I walked along the beach and thought about you and about the wonderful day we have had, the first day of our life and happiness together. How clear the day was, without a cloud. They cannot all be like this, but when I hold your hand then I look just as much forward to overcome storms and difficulties of all kinds, as to enjoying our happiness in peace. I kiss

you, I hold you tight and I look into your clear eyes and say good-bye for today. But tomorrow I come again. Your August.[18]

Marie's mother Ane had for a long time thought about leaving the farm, as Marie wrote August, "because she was tired and unhappy about being alone on the farm with nobody but the hired farmhands."

> But even so she could not decide to leave the old home. But now there is the added reason that she would like to move to Jørgen and care for the little boys. Therefore, I believe she is serious this time. A mother is a peculiar sensitive and caring being: the one of her children who needs her love the most is the one closest to her heart. In the later years, when my siblings have had homes of their own, I was the recipient of her motherly care. Now I think my brother and his small children have taken first place in her heart. I don't mind giving up the place, now that I have so much more, now I have you, my own friend. You don't know how supremely happy and content I am because I feel that I own you so completely.[19]

The two were desperately longing for each other and made secret plans to meet in Randers, where Marie had to take her nephew, Anders Vagn, to the doctor. Because they did not want their families to know about the engagement their plans became ever more complicated. When Marie's brother Jørgen decided to follow her to Fredericia, August could not meet her at the train. When August's father was going to Randers to meet with some brewers the same day as August was to meet Marie there, August took a special pleasure in overcoming all the obstacles, "I shall discreetly attempt to investigate where in Randers father plans to stay and shall then find a hotel for myself. I shall find a relatively remote and obscure location because it will be good to have a rendezvous where you can find me, since I cannot go to you. In 45.5 hours we shall see each other my love."[20] In spite of all their plans, the rendezvous in Randers came to naught because the little boy's doctor was on vacation. They then planned to meet when August was going on a longer sailing trip with the cutter *Ragna*. In early August, they finally had a much too brief meeting, leaving them longing even more to be together.

In her new happiness and longing Marie felt that "never had the summer been more beautiful." Frequently, she bicycled over the dusty, sandy road to the railroad station to mail her letters to Grenaa. and sometimes when the mailman brought August's letters she asked him to wait while she wrote her answer. During the long summer days she studied pharmacology, took care of little Anders Vagn, and entertained her mother. She went on outings with her family when they drove with horse and buggy to the woods to pick wild raspberries and catch crayfish. She spent time with her niece Astrid picking gooseberries, apples, and plums in her mother's garden on Vosegaard. But all the time she was dreaming about August and looking forward to September when they would be together again. Even though she had a full schedule studying medicine, she would also be working with August in the laboratory. She planned to move away from her sister to a place closer to where August lived and closer to the university. "Then I can invite you home to me," she wrote to August. "I will not promise you tea, but an extra good cup of coffee."[21]

August in the meantime was longing as intensely as Marie. Late at night when all was calm in the brewery and the family had gone to bed, August sat on his bed and wrote Marie. He read her letters over and over again and his great love for her grew. He helped in the brewery, which he enjoyed, and he had to sit through long afternoon teas when friends or the minister came for visits. He was impatient to get back to his letters even during Uncle William's yearly visit to the brewery. In his happiness, he made friends again with his sister Edel and became particularly fond of her little son Eyvind. August asked Marie if she liked sailing, to which Marie answered that she had never sailed. She was used to a barge they poled out over the shallow water when they went bathing in the sea.[21] In the middle of August, he moved back to Copenhagen to get on with his work, while Marie had to stay on Fyn until September. On August 21 he wrote Marie:

> Thank you for the little picture of you [as a child], the more I look at it—and I look at it very often—the more I recognize you in it and it makes me happy. Friday night my brother Emil went home to Grenaa for vacation, which he sorely needs [Emil was by then editor of the shipping journal *Søfartstidende*]. I shall miss him some, but on the other hand, it is rather nice that he is not here when you arrive because then we are more safeguarded against interruptions. He usually comes to see me any time it suits him. And since he has a key to my apartment he cannot be kept out.[22]

August went on to say that they might have to tell Emil their secret, when he returned at the end of September, but that would be no problem since he trusted Emil explicitly. "I think you will like him," wrote August, "he is the one of my siblings that I care for the most." What he did not anticipate then was Emil's extreme jealousy toward Marie, which would result in Emil's refusing to visit their home for a long time after they were married. Emil's relationship to Marie never became more than polite and he continued to address her using the formal *De* rather than the familiar *Du*.

Marie returned to Copenhagen. Since she was uncomfortable with the secrecy and knew that her mother must have guessed, she wrote and told her mother about the engagement and her plans to move away from her sister Grethe and brother-in-law. Ane had noticed the frequent letters in a man's handwriting, but each time she asked where they came from, Marie refused to answer. Ane thought it was not quite proper that Marie move away from her sister, particularly now that she was engaged.[23] The following day Ane wrote again, "Yesterday I had to end my letter because the mailman came, but I had more to write about your engagement, dear Mie. I am longing to get a picture of your fiancé. I picture him in my thoughts. He is tall, but not heavy, dark haired, with a pale face after all the studying. And with all the degrees he has earned he must be over 30 years."[24] Ane's mental picture was not very close to reality. August was about six feet with a slight stoop and was very slender, almost skinny. His hair was blond and straight and his eyes blue. He wore a mustache and a goatee that he kept neatly trimmed after he had met Marie. His expressive face and the light in his eyes were his strongest features.

Mie moved to Østersø Street very close to Wiedervelt Street and they saw each other often. Marie would come over to August's apartment almost every night to study. As August's love turned into passion he told her that he could see nothing wrong in that he, in his love for her, also desired her as a woman. But Marie withdrew. Her conservative upbringing held her back and they were unable to talk with each other. Marie, deeply distressed, wrote to clear up their misunderstanding:

> You are right silence must not reign between us, not for any price. . . . You ask if it is convention and rules that hold me back, and you say that you do not have the courage to break them openly, but that they do not mean anything to you, personally; yes then I must say that to me it is quite different. What other people will say or do is of minor importance, but I could not do it for my own sake without suffering terribly. I would no longer feel that I had the right to hold my head high, because I would feel that I had betrayed the confidence that my mother most of all has the right to have in me."[25]

They did finally become lovers and resolved to marry soon; but now another question had to be cleared up before their happiness was complete. Marie wrote: "One evening, some time ago, when we talked about getting married soon you asked if it would be possible to have children soon. The quiet natural way in which you asked me made me so happy and secure, because I understood that you loved me enough to resign yourself to wait for a while so that I could keep my work." And now she reminded him of what he had written to her:

> August, once you wrote that you would not tolerate any hindrance to the development of your abilities. By that you stated how much your work means to you, and I can fully appreciate it, in every way possible I shall endeavor never to make demands on you that can hinder you in your work, rather I shall try to be of help to you to the best of my ability. I so dearly hope that you too can understand that my work also means a great deal to me. And it is not so that it means less to me now since we got to know each other, to the contrary the work means twice as much, for now I feel that I have something to work for and gain competence for. But then you must know that I am not free until I have passed the final examination and the last two years of the study

are particularly demanding. It may seem terribly egocentric of me but don't make it too difficult for me and don't make greater demands on me than I can satisfy. If you love me as I love you, as I so fervently hope you do, then I think you will understand me and help me. Forgive me because I cannot bear it if anything separates us so that I cannot be your own Mie.[26]

In early November, August wrote his father and mother about his engagement to Marie, "This letter will come as a considerable surprise, since it will tell you that I have become engaged or rather that I have been engaged for a long time to the lady whose picture I enclose." In the letter he told them that Marie's mother was a widow with a farm and that Marie was a medical student:

It is the plan that Marie will continue her studies energetically and take her examinations within the normal time. Our marriage—when we decide to get married—will be very modern, since we will each pursue our respective careers. But our studies are so closely related that we can fully understand each other's work and also on many occasions be of help to one another. I shall not write anything about how Marie is and how much I care for her because that could only be a very pale rendering of the real thing. But we plan to come to Grenaa during Christmas vacation.[27]

He added that they might think Marie was a learned lady with no domestic experience, but assured them that Marie knew how to keep house since she had done so for her sister and brother while she studied in Copenhagen. At the end of the letter he wrote:

What will you think of this step? Personally, I have always thought that it was one of the most difficult and dangerous situations one could get into, but I hope and believe that I have managed well. Even when I try to ignore the infatuation I find that we agree so closely in interests, abilities and inclinations that we can be happy together for life, and continue to love each other even more. It is our best intention that our relationship shall become as ideal and free from discord as yours. You two shall be the shining example for your August.[27]

Mimi and Viggo were overjoyed. His mother wrote:

Dearest August, that was a real surprise you gave us, and I agree with you that it is most joyful! I would have written to you right away, but I had to wait until now, five afternoon, because I was in the middle of the major house cleaning and it would be unfair to leave the maid alone with the work. All day long during my varied jobs I have thought of you and Marie, thought about all you wrote and off and on looked at the beautiful and so serious face that your beloved shows us on the picture. Many a heartfelt sigh for your happiness and welfare has arisen over there in the washhouse, while I all by myself polished the double windows. I thought you were unusually well and happy last summer and kind and friendly too, but I failed to discover the inner glow that caused it. Thank God, that it no longer looks as if you shall become a confirmed old bachelor! Under these circumstances it is twice as dear of you that you will help Inger Marie with her education.[28]

At Christmastime the couple went to Fyn to visit Marie's family. As the horse and buggy, bringing them from the train station, swung into the farmyard, Marie's mother stood in the doorway with the maid, Trine, behind her. Trine was particularly fond of Marie and wanted to meet her fiancé. But the man they saw bore no resemblance to the picture they had conjured up in their minds, "Oh my God, Ane!" said the disappointed Trine as she pulled at Ane's dress. The disappointment, however, did not last long and August was welcomed into Marie's family.[8]

During their stay August and Marie walked around the farm and along the fields, followed by Marie's jealous and snarling dog snapping at August's heels just above the shoes. The visit to Grenaa followed at New Year's. They were welcomed by the parents and by Frida, and Marie was quite overwhelmed by their kindness and love, "To be received this way far exceeded what I had expected. I did not deserve it since I had taken August from you."[29] In answer to Marie's thank-you letter Mimi reassured her and offered some advice concerning August:

> My dear little Marie, You shall not live with the thought that you have taken August from us, that is far from the way we look at it. With God's help you will give him to us in a new and better shape, that is as a good husband. It is not an old, worn out saying, that true love glorifies and enlarges the hearts, it is the eternal truth. Only by the side of a good wife does a man fully become a man, and many good abilities develop that would otherwise lie fallow. We expect all good of your union and greet it with unqualified happiness. August has a loving heart and is not afraid of sacrificing for others. I also hope that he has not acquired more peculiarities than you, with diligence and patience, can rid him of. Start picking at them gently.[30]

8

Marriage and the Seegen Prize (1904–1906)

> I lay for a long time with my eyes closed thinking about life in general and you and the experiments I shall do tomorrow in particular. And all my thoughts were either rose colored or light green.

Returning to Copenhagen from Grenaa, August and Marie made the round of visits to family and friends expected of a newly engaged couple. Marie then left for a month's stay in Lund, Sweden, for her anatomical dissection course while August continued his work in the laboratory. August was now working with a new apparatus he had built for measuring the respiratory excretion of nitrogen.

A rare opportunity had presented itself in the spring of 1904 when the Imperial Academy of Sciences in Vienna had announced that the Seegen Prize would be awarded for the best scientific study showing "whether or not free nitrogen or nitrogenous gases are excreted from the body as a normal by-product of the metabolism."[1] With the Seegen Prize came a monetary award of four thousand kroner. The prestige of winning the Seegen Prize could help August obtain a position at the University of Copenhagen and the monetary award would be most welcome since he was thinking of marriage.

Immediately following the 1904 summer vacation, August had begun constructing his complicated apparatus for the experiments. In the past, investigators had attempted to solve the problem by means of either respiration experiments or quantitative analysis of nitrogen in ingested food and fluids and in the excreta, feces, and urine. These were studies that continued over prolonged periods of time. August designed his experiments for measuring respiratory nitrogen excretion and constructed his apparatus with the utmost care because he realized that the controversy surrounding this subject stemmed from numerous sources of errors in both types of experiments. While Marie was in Lund, he worked day and night to overcome the many difficulties. "My own Mie," he wrote in January:

> It was good there was a little letter from you today. I needed some cheering-up because I have been haunted by bad luck with the experi-

ments. I did not reach a result yesterday and today when I had made everything clear to start I forgot to close a valve and sucked all the soda lye over into the pump. I had to take everything apart and start all over again. Then I wanted to introduce an improvement to prevent such reversal of the suction, but while doing this I broke the neck of the control chamber and there I am with the whole apparatus out of order. The repair and the new calibration will take all day tomorrow and maybe even more. But then I console myself a little that I can use the occasion to improve the construction, which is worth the effort. It *is* going to work.[2]

He worked all the next day and the apparatus was again in working order. He had eliminated sources of error and his calculations showed that nitrogen remained absolutely constant in his control experiments. His happiness increased when Marie came over from Lund to see him. After she left he went to the laboratory. To Mie he wrote telling her of his pleasure in finding a detailed account of his carbon dioxide papers in the latest issue of *Nature:*

> I believe that it will mean a great deal in directing the attention to these questions [CO_2 in the atmosphere and natural waters] and will induce others to do similar experiments.
>
> When I had rejoiced over this and read the rest of Nature, I felt hungry, made tea and had something to eat. Then I slept a little on the chaise longue and afterwards I lay for a long time with my eyes closed thinking about life in general and you and the experiments I shall do tomorrow in particular. And all my thoughts were either rose colored or light green. They resulted in various decisions of which this letter is one.
>
> Now you are asleep Mie, far away in an other country, and a few hours ago you were in my arms and I felt your breath and your slightest movement. But it does not matter, in my thoughts you are still with me and I believe that you are dreaming of me and smiling in your sleep. I think I will be able to stand it now until we are together again. Your August.[3]

Marie returned to Copenhagen in early February and the wedding day was set for March 24. They had rented an apartment on Petersborg Street, and Madam Thomsen, August's cleaning lady was going to work for them. Since August had long since resigned from the state church, they naturally decided on a civil wedding ceremony. This decision was almost more than Mimi and Viggo could bear. Mimi told her daughter Frida that she never expected to get relief from the sorrow and pain she felt by their decision and particularly by learning that August was no longer a member of the church, but Frida comforted her mother:

> Don't be so sad over what has happened. You know and have known for a long time how August feels about Christianity. And remembering that, it is of minor importance that he has left the church and will have a civil ceremony. Through this act he shows himself as a completely

honest person remaining true to himself. Is it not better to be honest than to feign? A wedding ceremony in God's name would mean nothing to August. To him it would be meaningless, untrue and offensive and thereby also offensive to others. According to the Bible it is better to be cold than to be lukewarm. And I believe that there is much hypocrisy sheltered by our state church. It is no more an honor to be a Christian, than it is a shame not to be one. Such notions do not apply to something of such vital importance as one's life principle. Mother, you write that you will not live to get relief from this sorrow and pain, but it is my hope that God will know how to find August even outside the church. August does not need God now, but God surely needs him and will take care of him for his own sake and for the sake of our prayers. Just as Monika lived to see her prayers heard you may experience the same. And think of Paulus who was cold before he became warm. Exactly because he was such an eager enemy he became such a great Christian. There is so much good and true and loving in August that God surely, in his own time, will bring into His service.[4]

Mimi also wrote August about her great sorrow, but she timed her letter so that it would reach them well ahead of the wedding day and not ruin it for them. To Marie's surprise her own mother Ane was also deeply disturbed.

August and Marie went ahead with their plans, but did not ask anybody to attend their wedding. The apartment was wallpapered and painted and the furniture moved in before their wedding day. Four days after the wedding, Marie wrote her mother-in-law, "We have been very busy both of us during the past week arranging our home, but it has been a happy occupation, and we now feel so comfortable and happy here by ourselves." About the wedding she wrote:

> Our wedding day was in our opinion ideal, because we had it completely to ourselves. In the morning we did our work as usual. August lectured and I had clinic. We were married at one o'clock. The ritual for the civil service has been written by the old Madvig and is beautiful. In clear and lovely words it speaks about the meaning of marriage and its foundation, love.
>
> We had lunch at Bristol following the ceremony and then we went home to our own home. There were letters from Frida and Inger Marie and some telegrams from the few people who knew the wedding date.
>
> We did not send out messages about our wedding until last night because we wanted to have time to get our home in order before the visits. Already today we have received several congratulations and pretty flowers. I shall not tell you how we have arranged our home because we prefer that you yourself come and see it before too long.[5]

The many visits started, but August and Marie continued their busy schedules. Marie had to meet at the clinic at eight and August rearranged his daily routine according to Marie's schedule. "August has his sleeping time completely disturbed because he gets up when I get up at seven in the morning, as a result he gets sleepy very early at night,"[6] Marie wrote. Mimi, who had never approved of August's late rising, wrote: "I am rather gleeful at the thought that August now rises early in the morning, not because I think it will hurt him, just the opposite! But don't tell him, then he will stay in bed just to be contrary!"[7]

Marie and August went about their private, busy lives. The work on nitrogen excretion was going well and August did experiments daily, while Marie went to clinics in the mornings and sometimes afternoons. August now woke up before Marie and saw to it that she got off on time for her clinic. Getting to the laboratory at this early hour, he discovered that he could accomplish a great deal while working undisturbed before the other people arrived.[8] Having once discovered the great advantage of an early rising followed by undisturbed work in the laboratory, August did it for the rest of his life.

During spring, August had many things to do, but worked primarily on nitrogen excretion. In his apparatus he endeavored, as he said, "to exclude by suitable construction of the details as many of the known sources of error as in any way possible, and to investigate with energy the possible existence of hitherto unknown sources of error."[1] His predecessors had always used large apparatus for animals weighing one kilogram or more. August's apparatus was constructed for small animals weighing no more than fifty grams. By reducing the size he could eliminate many sources of error. "A small apparatus is constructed entirely of glass, and it is an easy matter to submerge the whole of it in a waterbath and thereby secure a uniform temperature throughout, at the same time as the risk of undetected leakage is reduced to a minimum."

He did two series of experiments on "animals that do not eat, drink or move about, while at the same time their respiratory exchange [metabolism] can be comparatively high viz. chrysalides (pupae) of butterflies and eggs of common fowl [chick embryos]." This greatly reduced the sources of errors because they would have no intestinal bacteria. In a third series of experiments he used mice, "and even this series can, as I hope to show, lay claim to no small accuracy," he wrote in his paper.[1]

The dates in his published paper show that he worked on the butterfly pupae in the days just before and after his wedding. The experiments were highly satisfactory and showed no or minimal release of free nitrogen from the pupae. He also planned to work with reptiles; Marie asked her small nephews and nieces on Fyn to collect these for him.[9] For his work on eggs, he got Johan to secure him some laying hens and he built a suitable thermoregulated incubator for the eggs and did the experiments in early July. A similar (or possibly the same) incubator was later used in his and Marie's household during the fall semester of 1905.

August and Marie were also working together on carbon monoxide (CO) diffusion through the lungs in June of 1905 while Bohr was in England, but nothing about their findings is mentioned in their letters to Mimi. Part of their summer vacation was spent in Grenaa and part on Fyn with their respective families.

In early August, they were happily home in their own apartment, which Madam Thomsen had scrubbed and cleaned for their return. Now Marie studied for her examinations from early morning to midnight every day. Thanks to Madam Thomsen and the thermostat, Marie could work almost undisturbed. Madam Thomsen would prepare their dinner which Marie then heated in the incubator. Even August's traditional birthday goose was cooked in the incubator following browning in the oven.[10] Three years later August used this versatile incubator to save the life of their prematurely born infant son.

Meantime August was busy with lectures and laboratory exercises. By the end of September, he had almost finished his experiments with mice. "I now feel that I have found the solution to the nitrogen question. The answer is that animals do not excrete gaseous nitrogen in measurable quantities," he stated to his mother. But to make it convincing to others he still needed to do additional experiments.[11]

During his egg experiments some unexpected difficulties had surfaced, i.e. the embryos could not survive more than one or two respiration experiments of two to six hours. As usual August did not take this lightly but made every effort to understand the underlying cause. He noticed that Hasselbalch (1900) had encountered the same problem in his work with embryos which he (Hasselbalch) ascribed to toxic fumes, and that Seegen and Novak (1875) found that their animals became ill in a similar apparatus. In his own apparatus (which contained mercury in many parts) August noticed a fine yellow precipitate appearing in his combustion tube. An analysis of the precipitate revealed it to consist of mercuric oxide. Suspecting mercury vapors in his apparatus to be the cause of the high mortality of his chick embryos, August performed a simple experiment on a pigeon, which he exposed to air bubbled through mercury. He found that the pigeon became ill and showed the very same symptoms described by Seegen and Novak.[1] (There is nothing to indicate that August, even at this time, suspected that he himself had suffered from mercury poisoning a few years earlier.)

August's new knowledge also paid off in practical matters. One morning, August and Marie read in the newspaper that children in a local school fainted one after the other. The doctor who was called in declared that it was carbon monoxide (CO) poisoning from the heater, but August, according to the description in the paper, arrived at the result that it was probably not CO-poisoning. After talking with the engineer in charge of the heating system, August analyzed samples of the air in the classroom and found no CO. Now another engineer wanted to talk to August. In another school, mercury had been spilled in a space heater and the children as well as the teacher became ill. The mercury was removed but the teacher was still nervous. August was called in as a consultant to determine if the air still contained mercury vapor. He used a new, very sensitive method to determine if there was any mercury left in the classroom air. He found none and the teacher was relieved.[12]

As August began writing his paper for the Seegen Prize, he engaged his sister Misse to do the drawings of his various apparatus. She had already illustrated for his physiology lectures. "August is pleased since she draws well and accurately," wrote Marie. "All summer long August has been acting director of the laboratory while Prof. Bohr was in Africa, but now the professor has come home and has begun taking over his administrative duties."[12] In November the young couple invited Professor Bohr and his wife and daughter together with Dr. Hasselbalch for an evening party, and on August's birthday they gave the traditional goose party with Uncle William, Emil, Johan, and Misse as guests.[13]

In December, however, there was no more time for partying. Marie's big examination (part one for medical students, which included anatomy, physiology, and pharmacology) was to begin in January and the deadline for August's nitrogen paper was in the middle of that month. "Mie studies courageously from morning to night," wrote August, "even though she sometimes feels that it does not suffice compared to the vastness of the requirements. I eagerly and successfully object to such downhearted laments."[13] By the end of December, Mie felt good about her knowledge and August had almost finished writing the final copy of his paper (in longhand). True to his convictions, he had written it in English, even though it was to be submitted to the Austrian Kaiserlische Academie der Wissenshaften.

January 16, 1906, August and Marie sent a short, triumphant note to his parents. "Pharmacology 13. Thereby, it is over. Honors in all. My paper finished and at the bookbinders. Now we take a vacation. Many greetings M. and A."[14]

They celebrated by giving a party for children and parents of family and friends. But their vacation took an unexpected turn when August got the flu after he had visited Porsild to talk about Greenland. Marie took good care of him while he was ill, but had to use her rather weak authority as a medical student to keep him in bed after he started feeling better. She even had to read to him from her *Lehrbuch der innere Medicin* before he would take her advice. All August's siblings came to see him, including Emil and Sidsel.[15]

By the end of January both August and Marie were anxious to start working again. For Marie the clinical part of her studies began, while August started new experimental studies. Not much is said about these studies in the letters except that August expected much of them. There is no doubt that it was the oxygen transport through the lung epithelium that he now wished to work on, and he was constructing a new tonometer for measuring the tension of blood gases.

During the spring August and Marie wondered and worried. Would August win the Seegen Prize? First they felt sure because nobody could possibly match the accuracy of August's experiments; August declared, if anybody else won it, he would have to have reached the same result as he, because it was the only correct answer. But with time they started to worry that maybe it would be awarded to an Austrian, rather than a foreigner.[16] Then at the end of May the announcement came. It was printed in the newspapers May 31, 1906. Viggo Krogh had attended a funeral in Grenaa, when his old friend, Kruse, came and stuck his arm under Viggo's saying, "You must be congratulated today." Viggo answered, "I have no idea why I should be congratulated today." "It is written in Nationaltidende that your son has received a prize from the Scientific Society of Vienna," said Kruse. "Yes, then I must thank you," said Viggo, "because it is an international prize for 4000 Kroner." Old Kruse made big eyes and said, "Then I must congratulate you a second time, my hearty congratulations!"[17]

Viggo and Mimi were enormously pleased. Viggo continued the letter, telling August that he wished August would thank God and not become proud, not think too highly of himself, and not become lazy:

> Because it is He who has given you the ability and stamina for scientific work and a job under such good circumstances with professor Bohr in that nice laboratory. Believe it, it is often a peculiar thought and feeling for us, that we should never work our way up and that our abilities and strength are so limited. Our entire life, we have been allotted such insignificant work as brewing beer, packing bottles in crates and the like. And how many people must be content with even lower occupations. However, what keeps so many up, and even let us work with happiness and thanks, is the thought and the certainty that the loving God also gives an international prize for the humble, namely that we shall be His children with Jesus Christ."[17]

How little Viggo had understood in the past his son's efforts is illustrated by the following paragraph from Viggo's letter:

> When you had defended your doctor's thesis somebody sent me a clipping from a newspaper . . . in which they characterized your work as scientific trivia; especially because it concerned the respiration in frogs. Really, that paper had no idea what they wrote about. It is often the small things that bring great results. I believe that this last result was built on the foundation of your first studies, however insignificant it may seem to work on frogs.[17]

Marie laughed at her father-in-law's worries about August becoming lazy. He surely could not mean that; "August is already so occupied with new experiments that he would prefer not take time off for the summer vacation." Marie learned about the prize when she met August at the railroad station to go to a dinner party at the Bohrs in Rungsted. "[At the Bohrs] the news was received with great enthusiasm, and at the dinner, Professor Bohr opened a bottle of champagne for the occasion."[16]

9

The Oxygen Secretion Controversy (1906–1910)

> The absorption of oxygen and the elimination of carbon dioxide in the lungs takes place by diffusion and by diffusion alone. There is no trustworthy evidence of any regulation of this process on the part of the organism.

In his long association with William Sørensen, August had rather enjoyed the challenge arising from scientific controversies. Now, as his time in Bohr's laboratory was nearing its end, he found himself unintentionally caught in an emotionally charged scientific controversy with his own mentor. This conflict not only affected him deeply, but also was decisive in shaping his future research which in turn led to some of his most important discoveries. In an address given to the XIII International Congress of Physiological Sciences in 1929, Krogh clearly referred to this experience:

> We may fondly imagine that we are impartial seekers after truth, but with very few exceptions, to which I know I do not belong, we are influenced, and sometimes strongly, by our personal bias and we give our best thoughts to those ideas which we have to defend. Nevertheless we should of course all do our best to avoid controversy, in the sense that we should take every possible care to verify our facts and substantiate our conclusions before we publish our results.[1]

Bohr's belief that O_2 as well as CO_2 are actively secreted across the lung epithelium in opposite directions, was based on his own observations that the O_2 tension in the arterial blood was higher than in the alveolar air, and that the CO_2 tension was higher in the alveolar air than in the arterial blood. But were his measurements correct? Krogh was not convinced.

To measure gas tensions in arterial blood, Bohr had used a haematæerometer (a kind of tonometer) he developed while working in Carl Ludwig's laboratory. It was based on a principle applied first by Edouard Pflüger (modified by Ludwig) of reaching diffusion equilibrium between a small sample of air and a large sample of fluid (in this case blood).

Bohr had shown that the time required for equalization of gas tension in the blood and the air was directly proportional to the ratio of diffusion surface between air and blood (s) divided by the volume (v) of the air—s/v, or "specific surface." Bohr's haemataerometer had a rather small specific surface of 5.2,[2] but as Krogh was to show, it also had other shortcomings which rendered the measurements quite unreliable.

Before Krogh went to Greenland in 1902, he constructed a much improved tonometer, with a specific surface of 20–30, that he subsequently used to measure CO_2 tension in natural waters (see figure 11).[3] It was then that he realized the defects in Bohr's heamataerometer. In fact, in Bohr's apparatus the volume of air was relatively large (50 cm^3); and the quantities of blood that actually came in contact with the air were much too small to attain the same O_2 tension in the air as in the blood.

In January 1906, having successfully finished his work for the Seegen Prize, Krogh went to work on the O_2 secretion problem. He modified his Greenland tonometer "for determination of any gas in any fluid of which a sufficient quantity is available."[2] By using a smaller volume of air (5–15 cm^3) and a greatly increased air-fluid interface, he obtained a specific surface of about 20, and could reach complete equalization in twenty minutes.

Using the new tonometer for determining O_2 and CO_2 tension in the arterial blood, and a new, more direct method for measuring gas tension in the alveolar air, August and Marie did a series of experiments on rabbits during the summer of 1906. Their results showed that the O_2 tension in the arterial blood was always lower than in the alveolar air, while the CO_2 tension was almost identical in blood and alveolar air. Thus, the gradients were such that O_2 could enter the blood and CO_2 could leave by diffusion alone, results that *did not* support Bohr's gas secretion theory. In the first of seven papers on this subject published by August and Marie Krogh in 1910, they stated:

> The experiments described in the present paper were undertaken in the summer of 1906 with a view to investigate in greater detail than had hitherto been possible the gas-secretion supposed to take place in the lungs. The results were contrary to our expectations and the publication has been put off until now, in order that the problem might be approached in some other ways and conclusions, representing, if possible, some sort of finality in the protracted discussion of this most complicated subject, arrived at. The present paper is the first in a short series dealing with the several aspects of the problem.[4]

Why was the publication put off for so long? The reason was that Bohr, who had always been immensely kind and supportive of the young Krogh, found himself in a distressing situation: The secretion theory he had championed since 1890 appeared to be wrong.[5] For a while Bohr refused to discuss the matter with Krogh and the situation at the laboratory grew tense.[6] August continued his experiments into October 1906, but had to stop when he became busy with lectures and laboratory exercises. "It does not interest him much, but it has to be done at this time of year," wrote Marie to Mimi.[7] In the spring semester he was again working on the problem and hoping to convince Bohr.

In February 1907, August wrote to his mother,

> The experiments are going rather well. I had beautiful results of a study with turtles,[8] that I will publish right away, and I rush to get more out of them while I still have time. It has been decided that I, together with Dr. Bohr, shall undertake a major investigation which shall decisively determine the main question with respect to how the lungs function. This question has been in the forefront in this laboratory for 20 years. It has gradually become clear to the professor that with the new methods that I have developed during the past year, it is really possible to get to the bottom of the question. If everything goes as I hope, it should be a glittering conclusion to my assistantship here at the laboratory."[9]

The work that August was doing with turtles involved another testing of the secretion theory. In 1903, Maar had shown that when the vagus nerve (in the turtle) was cut on one side, the absorption of O_2 in the corresponding lung rose considerably.[10] Maar took this to indicate that the vagus nerve fibers inhibited the secretion of O_2. August himself used a similar argument in his work with frog respiration when his results were similar to those of Maar.[11] Now as he was testing this theory in turtles, he found a different explanation for the increased O_2 uptake by the lung following sectioning of the vagus. Rather than inhibit O_2 secretion, the vagus nerve constricted the blood flow to the lung.[12]

When Bohr agreed to collaborate with Krogh, he was still hoping to salvage his theory. On April 17, August wrote again about the big series of experiments about to begin. "I am now in the last phase of the preparations for the major series of experiments. The day after tomorrow we shall plunge in, I believe."[13] On April 22 a brief note about Marie's first examination and August's first experiment with Bohr: "Today first experiment, rather successful."[14] Then nothing more is mentioned about the experiments.

In preparation for the collaboration with Bohr, August had developed his ingenious "microtonometer,"[2] and methods for microanalysis of gases,[15] but communication between the two scientists broke down following their first experiment. In the microtonometer a large specific surface ($s/v = 30$) was obtained by reducing the volume of air to a tiny bubble with a diameter of only 2 mm. There were many other advantages to miniaturizing the tonometer. Not only was it easier and simpler to handle; but by increasing the speed of sampling and equalization of gas tensions, it eliminated a possible source of error suggested by Haldane and Smith in 1896. These authors pointed out that a certain amount of O_2 is used up, and a corresponding quantity of CO_2 formed in the blood itself, during the tonometry and before the blood reaches the apparatus. This may have been one of Bohr's objections to August and Marie Krogh's findings during the summer of 1906. However, by using the microtonometer inserted into a carotid artery via a T-tube, the arterial blood could come into contact with the air bubble in the microtonometer about two seconds after leaving the lungs. Krogh was able to quantify the metabolic process in blood (by using his microtonometer as a "slow" and a "fast" tonometer), and showed that metabolism was insufficient to affect his measurements. Also these results had to wait until 1910 for publication.[16]

The letters to Grenaa are few during this period, and they do not tell about the problems in the laboratory. No doubt it pained August that Bohr could not accept the facts; but he and Marie became even more determined to get at the truth and to publish the results when they were completely certain.

In March, August had the good news that his appointment as lecturer in zoophysiology was now almost certain, and he might get an institute in a street named Ny Vestergade where the university owned some old buildings. With the prospect of getting a laboratory of his own in the foreseeable future, August put the publications on hold and turned his attention to several other matters.

During spring 1907, Marie was very busy studying for her final examinations for her medical degree. In June 1907 she obtained her medical degree and applied for an internship to begin after the summer.[17] Toward the end of the summer following a family vacation, she and August took off for a scientific congress in Heidelberg, Germany. At the meeting August demonstrated his new tonometers in a talk, "Ueber die Prinzipien der exakten Respirationsversuche" (About the principles of exact respiration experiments). "My instruments seemed to give rise to considerable excitement and interest among the listeners. I had to repeat my demonstrations and explain all details so long that it was almost too much for me."[18]

The pains August took in explaining his instruments at the congress paid off in several ways. For some time he had realized the potential importance of demonstrating his instruments. Not only did he make them internationally known for their accuracy and ingenuity, but equally important, he was laying a foundation for the future support of his own scientific work. A demand for his instruments was developing within the international scientific community, beginning in 1905 when a Dr. Thoulet from France wanted to use Krogh's Greenland tonometer. At the time, Krogh arranged to have it built by a company, but he foresaw the possibility that once he had a laboratory of his own, his instruments could be built there and the profit used to support his scientific work.

When the Heidelberg congress was over, the Kroghs went to Berlin to visit Nathan Zuntz's laboratory. As early as 1867, Professor Nathan Zuntz had suggested that CO_2 is carried in the blood by virtue of some substance present in the red cells. Since then, he had made many important contributions to physiology, particularly in metabolism and respiration. Zuntz was also a proponent of the diffusion theory for the lungs.

Maybe the most important outcome of the Heidelberg congress and the visit to Zuntz was that August met Joseph Barcroft, who later came to play a very important part in the O_2 secretion controversy.

Barcroft, two years older than Krogh, came from a family of Quakers. He was a kind and happy man. He had graduated with a Bachelor of Arts in natural science from King's College in Cambridge in 1896 and was junior demonstrator of physiology at King's College at the time of their meeting. Barcroft did not have a doctoral degree. He had thought of studying medicine but contented himself with becoming a perpetual medical student. However, his outstanding research in respiratory physiology had already made him famous and had earned him several awards. He was highly regarded by Ernest H. Starling, J. Scott Haldane, and other senior physiologists. The meeting of the two men initiated the closest and dearest friendship in August's adult life. The two had much in common. Not only did their scientific interests overlap, but they also shared the same philosophies, human values, and joy in life. In a letter from August to Lady Barcroft after Barcroft's death in 1947, August wrote: "I met Barcroft in 1907 in Heidelberg and a few days later again in Zuntz's laboratory in Berlin, and the sympathy between us rapidly became very deep. I have the most vivid memory of those happy, far-off days and of the delight of old Zuntz in your husband's micro-method for oxygen in blood: 'Das ist ja für die Kliniker geradezu gefundenes Fressen' "[19]

During fall 1907, the difficulties in Bohr's laboratory began to take their toll on August. Marie was now an intern at Blegdams Hospital. In addition, she was tutoring students in physiology and, together with August, was teaching the medical students in laboratory exercises. August was overworked and the bad mood in the laboratory affected him. With the laboratory technician ill, August had to make all of the preparations for the students himself. In early October 1907, Marie wrote, "August has had a cold and is out of sorts, but I think he is getting better."[20] But August did not get better. At the end of December, Marie wrote, "During the entire fall, August has not been able to work as well as usual, possibly because he had too much to do early in the semester."[21] He was better when he was home in Grenaa to help his parents with the final sale of the brewery, and as Marie wrote in December, "When he sits home and writes he is quite well, but, whenever he has worked a day in the laboratory, he comes home with a headache."[21]

Nonetheless, August kept working. He completed two papers describing his macrotonometer and microtonometer[2] and microanalysis of gases.[16] With Marie's help he completed a physiology textbook for use by the public schools,[22] and several minor scientific investigations with resultant papers.[23] He also tried to obtain patents for two of his practical inventions, one for the thermostatic box he and Marie used to cook in, and keep their food warm, the other a gas jet that he used to light their apartment's coal stove.

Perhaps to get away from it all, he and Marie planned to study the metabolism of Eskimos in Greenland. During his stay in Greenland in 1902, August had been impressed with the large amounts of seal meat that an Eskimo could eat in a single meal. August learned (probably from his friend the botanist Morten P. Porsild) that an Eskimo can eat as much as fifteen pounds of pure meat in less than fourteen hours. (This turned out to be an exaggeration.) Since it seemed inconceivable that they could completely metabolize such a large quantity in a twenty-four-hour period August and Marie speculated that the protein taken up could be split into a nitrogenous and a non-nitrogenous part (the nitrogenous part being excreted and the other part stored in the body for later use).[24] August had discussed this with Porsild in 1906 when the Danish Arctic Station for biological research had been erected in Greenland on Disko Island, near the trading station of Godhavn.

In spring 1907 August had met Professor Francis G. Benedict, director of the Carnegie Nutrition Laboratory in Boston, who was visiting Bohr's laboratory. When August consulted with him about their Greenland plans, Benedict offered to collaborate with them by doing the extensive analysis of urine and feces. In January 1908 the Kroghs were awarded a grant from the Carlsberg Foundation for the work with the Eskimos. This made the trip possible and serious plans for the Greenland expedition could get under way. Benedict was still enthusiastic about the collaboration and a lively correspondence about the details of the plan ensued.[25]

The final plans for their investigations were as follows:

> We would go up to the Arctic Station in the spring and there erect in the open a respiration apparatus constructed beforehand and capable of accommodating two subjects. By means of this chamber we would make experiments of 4–5 days duration with determinations in two- to three-hour periods of oxygen intake and CO_2 output. The urine should be collected in similar intervals, measured and samples preserved. The subjects should be fed chiefly on seal meat, their favorite food, and samples both of food and feces collected for subsequent analyses.[24]

Departing for Greenland in April 1908 also meant leaving Bohr's laboratory where he had spent ten productive and instructive years. Upon his return from Greenland, Krogh would have an independent position. Following short farewell visits to Grenaa and Fyn, and a party for family and friends in Copenhagen, the young couple was ready for the adventure. All the instruments, metabolic chambers, glassware, and so on were packed and ready to ship, and on May 30, 1908, August and Marie sailed from Copenhagen on board the SS *Hans Egede*. As they rounded Fair Hill, Scotland, and came out into the Atlantic, the sea became very rough and almost everybody on board was seasick. On June 15 they came into Davis Strait where the sea was calmer. Then they could move around on the ship and admire the deep blue colors in the icebergs. The ship remained in Godthaab for a few days and they went ashore by motorboat. Everybody from the community who was able to walk was there to look at the newcomers with the greatest interest, while Marie returned their inspection with equal interest:

> Sunday it was sunny and calm and the Greenlanders, particularly the women, were in their finest clothes, which are very picturesque and beautiful. White or red decorated kamiks [bootees], sealskin pants, with colored skinborders and an anorak of fabric, often made of silk, velvet, or muslin bordered with wide silk ribbons. Around the hair top, they wore a colored ribbon, red for a young girl, green for a girl who had borne a child, blue for a married woman and white or black for a widow.[26]

Finally after visiting several other trading stations along the coast of Greenland, *Hans Egede* arrived in Egedesminde on June 23, 1908.

> By kayak the Arctic Station lying 50 miles northward across the Disco bay was informed, and three days later in the early morning Mr. Porsild arrived in the motorboat belonging to the Station. The same day we left for Disco. Owing to the bulk of our luggage it was necessary to load a smaller boat with some of it and take it in tow. It became very foggy during the passage and suddenly it was discovered that this boat had become filled and was on the verge of sinking. The goods were immediately transferred to the motorboat but some of our apparatus was damaged and certain pieces belonging to the respiration chamber drifted away in the mist. In the same moment, the screw of the motor boat got fouled and we lay helpless. Happily a group of small islets were not far off to leeward. These we succeeded in reaching by sail. The screw and machinery were cleared again, a depot of our apparatus was left covered with canvas and after some hour's delay we set out again for Godhavn; this time reaching our destination without further mishap. Eskimos were afterwards sent out in kayaks to search for the missing things and by good luck and accurate knowledge of the currents found them. The Danish Arctic Station distant about a mile from the trading station Godhavn—the residence of the Governor of North Greenland—consists of a small group of buildings. It is intended for biological and chiefly botanical work and not specially adapted for physiological work. It possesses, however, a small chemical laboratory

in which our gas analysis apparatus could be fitted up. The respiration chamber itself was erected near the Station on a piece of comparatively level ground. It was a small hut 2 m × 1.8 m square and 1.85 m high in front. Inside it was fitted up like a real Eskimo hut. The only furniture consisted of a broad couch of boards covered with furs. It was painted in bright colours and gaily decorated everywhere with cheap coloured pictures to keep the subjects in good spirits during their confinement. The front was covered with a tent to protect it and the gas sampling apparatus against rain. Behind the chamber were two tents of which one was used as a laboratory, while the other was to be occupied by our Eskimo assistant and interpreter and a cook to prepare the food of the subjects so far in accordance with their taste as the experimental conditions would allow. The chamber was ventilated by means of a large gas meter acting as a pump and driven by means of the water wheel . . . which proved to be an efficient and very constant motor. The Arctic Station possessed a sort of water works consisting simply of a barrel put up in a brook about 50 feet above the house. The water main from this vessel was close at hand behind the respiration chamber and provided water for the wheel. The whole of the camp had to be hedged in to protect it against the Eskimo dogs which were lurking about everywhere and whose appetite is not limited to substances generally admitted as eatable. Our chief anxiety was that they might break into the camp at night and eat the leather string connecting the waterwheel with the meter, thereby stopping ventilation. To provide against this contingency a special electric signal was put up which would ring a bell as soon as the string was torn away from the meter. The dogs never got inside the hedge but it was torn away once by a gust of wind.[24]

Following some trouble with the respiration chamber (overcome with help from the Station), August and Marie were ready to begin the experiments:

Now arose the problem of getting suitable subjects. It was arranged from the outset to experiment on two persons simultaneously because it was considered impossible to persuade any Eskimo to be alone in the chamber. We offered high wages but the Eskimos were very unwilling to accept our offers though the prospect of having only to sit quietly in a hut for four days and having all they would eat should of itself be rather tempting to them. The difficulty was that the whole affair could not avoid to appear in a rather comical light to the natives. Anybody taking part in it would be sure to be the laughing stock of the place for a long time, and the Eskimos fear being laughed at more than anything else. Fortunately Godhavn was visited for a day by the famous Arctic traveler Mr. Knud Rasmussen who understands the Eskimo language and the Eskimo mind perfectly and knew personally most of the inhabitants and possesses their confidence. He gave the natives an explanation of the object we had in view which was perhaps slightly beside the point, but which they thought they could understand and appreciate. It was something in the direction of our finding out how it came about that the Eskimos though living chiefly on meat, never become gouty like the Europeans.[24]

Knud Rasmussen succeeded in persuading the natives and the subjects started coming. The experiments could begin. The amount of work which the Kroghs had to perform during the experiments was enormous. At night, August and Marie took turns sleeping in a sleeping bag in the laboratory tent. They also made urea determinations of most of the urine samples in case some should be lost during transportation; August was busy with his gas analyses. "There are a number of other things to do that take time," wrote Marie. "For example I have quite a practice with swollen fingers and infected hands, etc. One day I had a consultation that lasted several hours and the interpreter declared that he was so tired that he 'could hardly lift his tongue!' "[27]

Among the Eskimos at the trading posts were a few who had learned to speak Danish. At the time the Kroghs were in Greenland, the botanist J. L. A. Kolderup Rosenvinge was also working at the Arctic Station. Rosenvinge prided himself on his knowledge of the Eskimo language. One day an Eskimo came to Rosenvinge's tent demanding "*saltinquaq.*" While Rosenvinge desperately looked through his dictionary, the Eskimo stood quietly looking at him, then, with utter contempt in his voice and in perfectly good Danish, he said, "Salt, you idiot." The ending added to the word *salt* signifies "a little" in the Eskimo language.[28]

While in Greenland, August and Marie became interested in the education of the Greenlanders and particularly in the availability of material written by Greenlanders in their own language. Most of the material available in the Eskimo language was translated Bible stories and stories about countries and events of little meaning to the Eskimos in their cold northern country. A Greenland newspaper, *Atuagagdliutit,* was published once a month by a peculiarly gifted native Eskimo printer, Lars Møller, but it only reached the outlying settlements once a year.[29] Upon August's return to Copenhagen, he joined Knud Rasmussen as one of several members of a literary society with the purpose of publishing books for the Greenlanders. The members of the society included Danes as well as Greenlanders. The books published by the society were mostly written in the Eskimo language, but with the understanding that more books would be available in Danish as the Greenlanders' knowledge of Danish improved.

To Benedict, Krogh wrote: "The Eskimo subjects behaved admirably and did everything they were told to do, but certain difficulties were of course met with. Habitually the Eskimos urinate only with very long and irregular intervals, and they could not be prevailed upon in this respect. Partly to obtain a copious flow of urine and partly also to keep the subjects in good spirit we gave them plenty of coffee, their favorite drink."[30]

The work in Greenland turned out to be rather strenuous, as Krogh related to Benedict:

> I thought at the beginning that two persons could easily do all the work of weighing, sampling, gas-analyzing, etc., but we soon found that we had to work exceedingly hard, both of us, to get it done. The routine employed was this: during the day from 8 a.m. to 10 p.m. my wife was present in the experimental camp administering the food, made all the weighings and samplings, and made also a series of preliminary nitrogen determinations on the urines by the Esbach-method. During the day generally from 11 to 8, I analyzed as many gas-samples as possible. At 10 p.m. I took the watch, the subjects slept generally between 10 and 6. I could also creep into a sleeping bag in the laboratory tent having arranged a system of electric signals to call me out when air sampling should be made and if anything went wrong. At 4 a.m. I utilized the tranquil hours from 4 to 6 a.m. to make the gas analyses which I wished to be especially accurate.[30]

The Kroghs left Greenland around the middle of August, arriving in Copenhagen on September 14, 1908. Marie was pregnant while she was in Greenland, and upon their return, August went to Grenaa to tell his parents the great news. "God bless you and keep you my sweet daughter-in-law," wrote the delighted Mimi, "you are much in my thoughts and I share the joy with you and August."[31]

Returning to Copenhagen, August took up the duties of his new position as temporary lecturer in zoophysiology. To teach physiology that included animal and human systems had been his intention for a long time. The textbook he completed early in 1908 was also part of this plan. He never intended or hoped to become Bohr's successor as professor of physiology on the medical faculty. What he desired was a new position in physiology within the science faculty that would bring physiology to the future science teachers in the public schools. He felt so strongly about this that later (1911), when Benedict offered him a position in Boston, he declined, stating that his present post was created for him as a consequence of the introduction of physiology into the curriculum of public schools: "I am greatly interested in this new departure and though it may seem preposterous I venture to think that it is of some importance for the ultimate success of the measure that I retain my position at least until a sufficient number of teachers have been trained. I am, so to speak, appointed to do this work, which I fear that nobody else could or would do just now and I feel that it would be a sort of treason to leave it only half done."[32]

At the time Dr. Jungersen, professor of zoology, had submitted an application to the university, "that a teaching position in zoophysiology be established at the University, a position to which Dr. phil. August Krogh must be considered the obvious candidate." It had taken nearly two years before Krogh's appointment became final. Following Jungersen's application, a committee consisting of Professors C. Bohr, C. J. Salomonson, E. Warming, H. Jungersen, and W. Johansen had been established and their report, following approval of the faculty, was sent to the Ministry of Finance. The committee pointed out that physiology had so far been taught only within the Medical School, "but anyone studying zoology meets during his studies numerous physiological problems." Zoology students wishing to study physiology had asked August Krogh to go over the material for them in a manner more useful to their specific needs, and in the spring of 1906 Krogh had obliged them by giving lectures and laboratory exercises specifically for zoology students. Thus, it was requested that a teaching position in zoöphysiology be established under the science faculty and that August Krogh be given this position.[33]

In 1908 the Ministry of Finance granted the position, but only as temporary lecturer; Jungersen's recommendation that a zoophysiological laboratory be established was not acted upon by the Ministry of Finance. Krogh was to receive a meager yearly salary of 2500 kroner for his teaching duties. Not having a laboratory was a severe blow to August, and the salary was barely enough to support his little family. The money from the Seegen Prize was gone, due to a bad loan to August's friend Axel Schlambusch.

In October 1908 August and Marie moved to a bigger apartment. They were barely settled when Marie's labor started on October 30. All during the Greenland trip she had not had a proper diet and she was exhausted after moving. On October 31 August wrote Marie's mother.

> Dear mother-in-law! I have the report to make that Mie yesterday evening between 10 and 11 has given birth to two small boys. They are about two months too early. The last of them was very tiny and died about an hour after the birth, but the first one looks as if he will make it.
>
> Nov. 1 at 3 p.m. This is how far I got yesterday afternoon when I was interrupted by difficulties with the little one. He was turning blue and would not breathe. We got him over it by bathing him. But there were several more attacks during the evening and night. We got through them all with great difficulty and since three o'clock this morning it has not been serious. He weighs a little over three and a half pounds. He can suckle a little, but there is no milk for him yet. He gets a little milk-water to drink. We are very happy with him. If only we may keep him. The birth went rather easily and lasted only from 5 to 11.[34]

During the following month August and Marie fought bravely to keep their little son alive. He could not stay warm by himself and August soon found that he could turn the thermostatic box they had for heating food into an incubator for the little boy, whom they named Erik.

But every so often for the following weeks he would stop breathing. Night after night they took turns staying awake to watch over Erik and help him through each frightening attack when his breathing would stop and he turned blue. Then one night, totally exhausted from four weeks of anxiety and lack of sleep, they gave up all hope. Erik did not breathe for fifteen minutes. Then he took one deep breath. Another fifteen minutes passed, and Erik began to breathe regularly on his own.[35] He learned to suck properly and spent a great deal of time sleeping in his mother's arms or in his little bed with three hot water bottles. Frida found that he looked like his father with his "up-standing hairdo."[36]

By Christmastime 1908, August and Marie were happy that their little Erik was alive and doing well. Affectionately, they called him "Snøblen" (the cub). August had by this time also become lecturer in physiology at the School of Dentistry. He had been greatly relieved when his Greenland samples arrived safely in Boston. He had managed to find temporary quarters in the plant physiological laboratory And in December he wrote to Benedict, "In the spring of next year I will take in hand the construction of a new gas analysis apparatus for metabolism work by which I confidently hope to be able to determine O_2 and CO_2 to 0.001% accuracy."[37]

But it troubled him that he did not have a proper laboratory and he spent hours working on proposals for a better one. In his first proposal, he applied for rooms occupied by the bacteriological laboratories in the middle building in the Ny Vestergade complex. These were well-designed laboratory rooms with all the necessary installations. The same building housed a fair-sized auditorium with room for a teaching laboratory. In April he thought he would get his laboratory, and Benedict wrote to congratulate him: "I am delighted to think that you will have a laboratory of your own. I have long felt that your work should be put on a more established basis and I am glad that the University and your Government are appreciating your scientific efforts." But the proposal was turned down, and August became busy trying to finish his and Marie's work on O_2 diffusion through the lungs. In his frustration he became disorganized and misplaced Benedict's letter with the Greenland results. When Benedict wrote that he planned to visit Krogh's laboratory, Krogh wrote back:

> I have been extremely busy in preparing for publication a series of papers on the gas exchange in the lungs and I have been very much occupied with that and some troubles about my laboratory ever since. . . .
>
> You write about reaching my laboratory. Alas: I have no laboratory, and I am rather afraid that I shall not have any. The state is very hard up for money, and parsimony is the cry on all sides. My first proposal or rather the second was friendly, considered in the department for three months and finally rejected altogether. I have since presented another, cutting down the estimated cost to the lowest possible sum,

and, I fear, beyond that. I hope that I shall have this proposal included in the supplementary bill of supply and presented to Parliament in February [1910]. If I get this through I will receive the building from the present occupant in August or September but the installation of a laboratory will necessarily take three months. If my proposal is not accepted I do not quite know what to do. I think I shall be obliged to take a year's leave and to go abroad and try to obtain a suitable post. However what may develop, you will be heartily welcome here at any time next summer, and I think that I may have something of interest to show you, even if I have no laboratory."[38]

The work the Kroghs had to do on the Eskimo data was delayed for a long time because of these and other difficulties. There was a huge amount of data and it took time to make all the calculations. The paper was finally published in 1913. The findings must have been somewhat disappointing since the Eskimos in their study did not eat as much meat as the Kroghs had been led to believe. The largest amount consumed by one male Eskimo in one day was 1,800 grams and the analysis from Benedict's laboratory showed that the meat contained a higher percentage of fat than had been anticipated. August and Marie had wanted their subjects to exercise by walking and the Eskimos were given pedometers to measure the amount of work, but the Eskimos used the pedometers as playthings instead. What the Kroghs did find was hat nitrogen excretion was somewhat delayed: "When meat was given after a diet poor in nitrogen only about 60% was excreted during the first 24 hours . . ."[24] Their conclusion that protein was retained for a certain period exceeding twenty-four hours and used later as a source of energy, was not necessarily correct. No reliable method existed for measuring urea in the blood in 1908, and therefore the Kroghs could not know to what degree blood urea concentration had been elevated.

Despite these disappointments the summer in Greenland had a profound effect on their later work. August became interested in measuring metabolic rate during exercise under well-controlled laboratory conditions. Marie had found it deeply satisfying to help the trusting and grateful Eskimos with their medical problems. The experience made her decide to continue practicing medicine after her return to Denmark.[39]

In the summer of 1909, Krogh was thinking of spending some time in England to work with Haldane. Haldane and Smith's "proof" of O_2 secretion was based on determinations made with Haldane's indirect method of calculating the arterial O_2 tension from measurements of the relative binding of CO and O_2 to hemoglobin. From his work with CO poisoning he had found that both O_2 and CO bind to the same binding site on hemoglobin and that the form of the binding curve was the same for both ligands. He deduced that he could calculate the arterial O_2

tension from the alveolar CO tension and the ratio between CO and O_2 bound to hemoglobin.

Wanting to clear up the discrepancy between Haldane's and his own findings, Krogh tested Haldane's method on rabbit blood. In April 1909, he wrote to Haldane:

> You will perceive that my results are very different from those obtained by yourself and Dr. Smith. I have tried hard to think out the causes of this discrepancy but have been unable to do so and I would venture to suggest, therefore, the undertaking of a joint investigation to clear up the problem. I have been led by a variety of experiments undertaken during the years 1906–09 to the conclusion that the gas exchange in the lungs is governed solely by diffusion and it is unnecessary to assume that any vital processes come into play (It may interest you in this connection that I have demonstrated in a series of experiments that the CO_2 tension of the arterial blood of the rabbit is in all cases almost absolutely equal to the corresponding tension in the alveoli (i.e. 0.1 to 0.3% higher).[40]

Krogh suggested that, if Haldane's time permitted, he could come to England in June and July to undertake a short series of experiments together with Haldane. He added, "I have at present no laboratory and shall not have any before next year." Haldane's cordial answer arrived shortly. He wrote that he had intended to make some experiments on rabbit blood to see if he could get the same results as Krogh, but had not found the time. Haldane continued:

> On this whole subject my mind is very open, as I have never been able to see that there is any teleological probability in favor of the active secretion theory. On the other hand the experiments published by Bohr about 18 months ago in *Physiol. Zentralblatt* seemed to give conclusive evidence that at any rate during hypercapnia produced by excess of CO_2 there is active excretion of CO_2. Do you think there is any source of fallacy in these experiments?[41]

Haldane, however, said he was unable to work with Krogh during the coming summer. The work did not get done. At the end of his paper, "On the Combination of Hæmoglobin with Mixtures of Oxygen and Carbonic Oxide," August wrote: "I have been prevented by external circumstances from making more experiments than those recorded, but it is obvious that an extended investigation of the distribution between oxygen and carbonic oxide of the haemoglobin in genuine blood from different animals must be made by experiments both in vitro and in the living body in order to clear up any uncertainty now existing."[42]

The uncertainty was never cleared up. However, in 1985 J. S. Millidge offered the following explanation for Haldane's erroneous results: "In 1938 she [a student of Haldane's, Esther Killick] examined the effect of repeated exposure to carbon monoxide using his [Haldane's] CO method. Her results seemed to show the development of oxygen secretion. But this result could be explained if there developed a difference between the in vivo and in vitro CO/O_2 affinity ratios."[43]

August and Marie stayed in Denmark working together during spring and early summer on diffusion of CO through human lungs. It was crucial "to see whether the conditions of gas diffusion in the lungs were such as to allow the necessary quantities to pass through at the tension differences which could be found. In this case and in this one only, the secretion-theory ought, in our opinion, to be abandoned," wrote August and Marie in their sixth paper on the subject.[44] Using themselves as experimental subjects they measured the rates of CO diffusion across the lung epithelium during normal and forced breathing. From these figures they could calculate the rates of diffusion for O_2 and CO_2, respectively.[44] They concluded that the diffusion constants measured were sufficiently high to allow for the necessary quantities of O_2 and CO_2 to diffuse across the lung epithelium not only during rest but also during heavy work.

During the fall, while August was busy teaching, he and Marie finished writing the papers for publication. Some of the work they had finished when Krogh was still in Bohr's laboratory, while two of the studies were done in the temporary facilities he had at the plant physiological laboratory.

On November 3, 1909, the first two of a series of seven papers reached the editor of *Skandinavishe Archiv für Physiologie,* Dr. Robert Tigerstedt. The other five papers followed shortly, with the last arriving December 5, 1909. The astonished Tigerstedt, a good friend of Bohr and Krogh, read them and sent them to be printed. On December 15 he wrote Krogh: "My good brother, permit me to ask. Does Bohr have any knowledge of your papers and their result? If not then I would be very grateful if you would let him have the parts that are already in galley proofs so that he will be informed before the papers are published."[45]

Krogh answered that he had tried to keep Bohr informed of his findings as early as 1906, but Bohr had refused to discuss the matter any further. In fact, Krogh had informed Bohr of his intensions through a long letter written in August 1909:

> Dear Professor. In the same moment as I mailed a paper to *Zentralblt. Physiol.* on CO diffusion through human lungs,[46] I received the latest number of this periodical in which I found that you had treated a related subject experimentally.[46] I regret this coincidence because it may appear to outsiders, and I fear to you, as if I have forced myself on your area of research. The fact is that since the beginning of 1906, I have been engaged in a series of experiments which led me to measure the lung diffusion. To my mind the results of these experiments made the secretion theory highly unlikely.[47]

Krogh continued the letter explaining how he had waited until he had sufficient evidence to feel absolutely certain of his conclusion.

Bohr's brief answer stated, "As I return the enclosed, I must remark that it was unknown to me before I mailed my paper for publication."[48] Apparently Bohr and Krogh were simultaneously using CO for measuring lung diffusion. Bohr, in a fifty-seven-page theoretical paper on gas diffusion through the lungs, published in 1909, ended with a strong statement in support of his secretion theory, "The carbon dioxide excretion as well as the uptake of oxygen must be regarded as secretory processes."[49]

Between them, August and Marie called their seven papers, published in 1910, "the seven small devils." Each of the papers, short and to the point, dealt with an important aspect of the problem. They were all published in English, which was at the time quite unusual for *Skandinavishe Archiv für Physiologie*.

In the seventh paper, "On the Mechanism of the Gas-Exchange in the Lungs," August Krogh discussed all of their own findings and those of their opponents. But first he paid tribute to his teacher Christian Bohr:

> I shall be obliged in the following pages to combat the views of my teacher Prof. Bohr on certain essential points and also to criticize a few of his experiments. I wish here not only to acknowledge the debt of gratitude which I, personally, owe to him but also to emphasize the fact, patent to everybody, who is familiar with the problems here discussed, that the real progress made during the past 20 years in the knowledge of processes in the lung is mainly due to his labors and to the refinement of methods which he has introduced. The theory of the lung as a gland has justified its existence and done excellent service in bringing forth facts, which will survive any theoretical construction which has been put or shall hereafter be put upon them.[50]

In what followed, August carefully discussed the methods and recalculated the results of Bohr and of Haldane and Smith, pointing out the quantitative sources of errors which led to the erroneous conclusions. Many years later he said, "In my opinion it is not quite legitimate to reject experimental results on the strength of possible sources of error. It must be shown that the errors do really exist and that they are quantitatively sufficient to explain the results."[1] This rule he followed in this as well as in all of his scientific works. His paper ended with the statement written in large bold type,

> The absorption of oxygen and the elimination of carbon dioxide in the lungs takes place by diffusion and by diffusion alone. There is no trustworthy evidence of any regulation of this process on the part of the organism.[50]

Krogh had mailed the reprints to Haldane and on February 19, 1910, Haldane thanked him. "I write to thank you for the very clear and valuable papers which you have sent me. I have read them with great pleasure, particularly as the English in which they are expressed is a model of good style and clearness. I feel very sorry now that it was not possible to arrange for you to come here and work for a short time as you proposed last summer."[51] But Haldane was not convinced. Citing an example from his own work he wrote, "We are thus driven to the conclusion that while diffusion alone is at play during rest, under normal conditions active secretory absorption occurs whenever there is want of oxygen."[51]

In June, Haldane wrote and invited the Kroghs to attend a meeting of the British Medical Association in London to take place in July. August went alone, since Marie could not leave her practice and her little son. The night before the meeting August sat alone in the hotel room writing his talk for the next day and a letter to Marie.

For August, it proved a very satisfying meeting. He demonstrated his tonometric methods and in a separate talk discussed his findings and conclusions. In the discussion Haldane restated his idea that active secretion occurs under special circumstances, but Professor Starling disagreed with Haldane and felt that most of the facts pointed to the diffusion theory as being the correct one.[52]

The trip to England had been extremely satisfying and interesting. August's friendship with Starling, Haldane, and Douglas continued for many years in spite of the scientific disagreements with Haldane. His high regard for Haldane is evident in a letter to a Danish Professor in Oxford, George Dreyer. He was curious if Haldane would get a professorship that had become vacant, and added, "I assume it could be Haldane's if he wants it, which I do not know. Even though I thoroughly disagree with Haldane on more than one point, as you know, I greatly respect his work and it would please me if he got it." In the same letter to Dreyer he added, "I am beginning to examine the CO method [Haldane's indirect method for estimating oxygen tension] and I hope to kill it completely."[53]

The oxygen secretion controversy did not end in 1910, but Krogh had succeeded in convincing most of the scientific community and had acquired several staunch supporters.

10

The Zoophysiological Laboratory and the Beginning of Exercise Physiology (1910–1916)

> I was given a small laboratory in 1910, but Lindhard had none and neither of us had any assistance. We therefore decided to work together and to study muscular physiology in my laboratory.

In January 1910, while "the seven small devils" were in press, August took off for Norway to work with the oceanographer Bjørn Helland Hansen at the Biological Station in Bergen. The previous summer August had read in the *Times* that the Arctic explorer Captain Roald Amundsen was planning an expedition on the ship *Fram* to the North pole by way of Cape Horn.[1] Amundsen, a man of enormous competence and ambition, was the first to navigate the top of the world from ocean to ocean, the Northwest Passage, in 1905. Now he had Fridjof Nansen's permission to use *Fram* for another expedition to the North Pole with the stated main objective of "a scientific study of the polar sea itself."[2] To learn oceanographic methods Amundsen had spent two months in Bergen taking a course given by Helland Hansen. Krogh wrote Amundsen to offer his help with instrumentation for gas analysis of air and seawater during the upcoming expedition. The question of rising atmospheric CO_2, which Krogh had investigated on his Greenland expedition in 1902, was still of intense interest to him, and he was eager to gather more data using his own techniques, since the methods that Nansen had used had not been satisfactory. Krogh had arrived at the conclusion that the sea is a sort of regulator for the amount of CO_2 in the atmosphere.

Amundsen had asked Helland Hansen to arrange for the oceanographic equipment for his polar expedition and gave him Krogh's letter. The outcome was that Krogh built and tested a new instrument which he shipped to Helland Hansen in Bergen in July 1909. When Amundsen's expedition was postponed for at least a year, Helland Hansen arranged for Krogh to come to Bergen in January–February 1910 to personally instruct several of the members of Amundsen's expedition.[3]

The fact of the matter was that Amundsen was far more interested in setting a spectacular record than making scientific investigations. When in September 1909 the world learned that Peary had reached the North Pole, Amundsen instantly decided to go south to attempt to beat Captain Scott to the South Pole. Except for his brother and Helland Hansen, Amundsen kept his plan secret from all involved. Not until *Fram* in September 1910 was leaving Funchal, Madeira, did he tell his men that they were going for the South Pole rather than the Arctic, but he arranged that *Fram* should sail the South Atlantic and the polar sea for oceanographic studies during his own attempt to reach the South Pole.[2]

In January 1910 some of the men going on Amundsen's expedition were learning oceanographic techniques at the biological station in Bergen. Leaving Marie and his little son Erik behind in Copenhagen, August traveled by train to Bergen on January 18, 1910. Two days later, he finally arrived in Bergen where it was bitter cold with snow and ice. Before trying his instruments in a motorboat, he gave a course in their use for Helland Hansen, a German oceanographer Dr. Schröer, a marine lieutenant named Gjertsen, and a Russian named Kutchin. All learned rather quickly, which pleased August. Gjertsen and Kutchin later joined the Amundsen expedition and remained on board *Fram* for the oceanographic studies during Amundsen's trip to the South Pole.[2]

What came out of the experiments? I have found no account of Krogh's tonometer being used on the *Fram* expedition in the South Atlantic. Helland Hansen tried to use the tonometer on an expedition with *Fram* to the North Atlantic during June and July 1910. He wrote Krogh that he did not succeed in making the gas analyses, because there was too much to do (they were measuring temperature and salinity) and because the instrument broke.[3] Apparently there was also another reason: during the trip Helland Hansen suffered frostbite of his fingers and lost finger-joints on both hands. Later, however, Helland Hansen described Krogh's methods in his book on oceanography.

While August was enjoying the work in Norway, Marie made up her mind to inquire about the laboratory for which August had been fighting so long. In his most recent proposal he had given up on the good laboratory rooms in the middle building and was asking for the front building and the basement in the middle building. There was still no promise that August would get the building he wanted. Gathering up her courage, Marie went to the ministry for church and education. A bit uncertain if she should speak to the department chief first or take on the minister directly, she decided on the minister:

> It was rather easy and straightforward. He was maybe a little surprised at first. I said that it might surprise him that I showed up. But he said he knew you were away. I said that it meant so much to you to get this laboratory (he remembered that it was about Ny Vestergade), since you otherwise saw no other way than to go to a foreign country, because you had no place where you could work, etc.

Furthermore, I said that we would be sorry to leave, because also economically it would be difficult since I was a doctor and could earn some money here, while it might not be possible in another country. "So you are a doctor?" "Yes," I said, "and it is essential to get the appropriation for the laboratory on this year's budget." He wrote something down on a piece of paper and said, "Well now we must get serious about it." With that the audience was over.[4]

Marie now enlisted August's brother Emil to keep her informed about further developments. Since early 1908, Emil had been department chief in the Ministry for Trade and Shipping.

Marie's diplomacy worked wonders. Only four days later she was told that the minister and several others had been to Ny Vestergade to look at the buildings and that they took it for granted that August Krogh would get the front building. The state geologist Victor Madsen had also arrived; he too wanted the front building and was rather angry when he learned that he would not get it. August was delighted but told Marie not to get her hopes up, and pressed her to come to Norway with Erik and the Bøvings for a vacation in the beautiful mountains after he had finished his work. But Marie had to decline. There was still much to be done and she was running from office to office seeing to it that the appropriation would be made the same year and that sufficient money would be granted for the remodeling of the laboratory and their new official residence. In Norway, August spent several days on the motorboat in Sognefjord testing his instruments with Helland Hansen. The instruments worked well and August got orders for no less than five complete sets.[5]

True to his word, the minister for church and education, M. B. C. Nielsen, sent his proposal to the Finance Committee of the lower house on February 23, 1910. Emphasizing how modest Dr. Krogh had been in his request, he strongly emphasized the desirability of providing a laboratory "so that the University in full measure can benefit from Dr. Krogh's outstanding abilities."[6]

In May 1910, the sum for the laboratory (ten thousand kroner for remodeling and three thousand kroner annually for its operation, including the caretaker's salary, was voted by the lower and upper house of the Danish Parliament. "I can feel assured that at last I shall have a place of my own to work in," August wrote to Benedict.[7] In June the building was vacated and the remodeling of the laboratories and apartment could finally begin.

The front building in Ny Vestergade 11 is a beautiful old house, once the home of a wealthy family. Now, the ground floor was to house an apartment for the caretaker and, more importantly, the large workshop where Krogh's instruments would be built for his own laboratory and for sale to others. The income from these sales substantially supported the scientific work. The caretaker, Møller, would also serve as the only laboratory assistant and machinist. Later, as the sale of his apparatus to other scientists increased, Krogh could afford more machinists to build his instruments.

The second floor, which had formerly been the spacious living quarters for Professor Carl J. Salomonsen, was converted into several laboratories. Marie got her own private laboratory next to August's and also a consultation room. In those years Marie's income from a private practice was essential for the Kroghs, because August's salary as a temporary university lecturer was low. The third, floor, under the eaves, (previously the servants' quarters) became the Kroghs' living quarters. The rooms were heated with coal-fired stoves. Across the courtyard, in the so-called middle building, Krogh got the basement for animal rooms and so forth, and in the courtyard behind the middle building Krogh was delighted to find a little pond he could use for his frogs.

On September 1, they officially moved. The uncertainty of the past two years was over. August had his own institute proudly named the UNIVERSITETETS DYREFYSIOLOGISKE LABORATORIUM (University Zoophysiological Laboratory). As soon as the laboratory was in order, the experimental work went into high gear, marking the beginning of an immensely productive period in August's life.

Having the apartment right above his laboratory, August could maximize the use of his time. As he had done since he was a very young man, he scheduled his time precisely and efficiently. Experiments in progress could be supervised or samples taken at all hours, day or night, by going downstairs to the laboratory. He did not, however, forget the lesson he had learned as a young man in Bohr's laboratory and was careful not to overwork himself to the point of exhaustion. On weekends he took time off for his family and long walks.

His weekday schedule, as far back as I can remember, was probably already set then: Rising before seven, he put on his slippers and old dressing gown and went downstairs to his laboratory. There he worked, totally undisturbed for a couple of hours. Nobody, not even Marie, was permitted to disturb him during these hours. At nine he went back upstairs where he showered, shaved, dressed, and enjoyed a quiet breakfast with Marie while he read his mail. Work in the laboratory officially started at ten o'clock and lasted until five. At ten o'clock he greeted his coworkers and assistants with a friendly handshake. At twelve he returned to the apartment for lunch with his family. The discussions at lunch and dinner mostly centered on physiological problems. Visitors to the laboratory were often invited to lunch or dinner with the family. Anyone wishing to call on him was told to see him between five and six. This had the advantage that it could not drag out too long because dinner was served at exactly six. If he did not show up at dinnertime, one of the children was sent to announce that dinner was served. Following dinner and coffee with the family in the living room, August spent the evening hours writing papers and letters, and discussing the work with Marie. At eleven they went to bed.

The most serious work he probably did during the night and early morning hours through a process which he later called "visual thinking":

> In 1896 I began in my small student's room serious experimentation on the hydrostatics of corethra larvae. As part of this study I developed methods for gas analysis under the microscope, but nothing was published until many years later. It was, I believe, in the course of this research that I became conscious of my own experimental and constructive methods. A considerable part of my work was done in bed during the night when I would try to visualize the processes studied and the experiments to be carried out. I found that I could visualize fairly complicated apparatus and all details of their working. The constructive ideas would come, apparently, out of nowhere, but the visionary examination of them was a conscious and rational affair. I never made, and even now never make, drawings, not even rough sketches, until the construction of an apparatus was complete, because I found that a drawing would hamper the free flow of ideas and bind me down to that particular solution of the problem. I believe that the work was often going on unconsciously and during sleep, because I would wake up with an apparently new idea, which was then immediately worked up and put to all kinds of imaginary tests. It goes without saying that the final practical test often showed that something had been overlooked and that the matter failed to behave the way I had imagined. Because the imagination had been quite clear and definite each such failure taught me a lesson which stuck.[8]

The first study, completed and submitted for publication in November 1910 from the new laboratory, was the work referred to above, on the hydrostatic regulation of the air bladders in mosquito larvae.[9] The results showed that oxygen is not secreted into the bladders, as Krogh had previously suggested, but instead fluid is reabsorbed from the bladders, when the larvae readjust to increased hydrostatic pressure. He may have put off even this publication because the findings did not agree with Bohr's hypothesis. But now he was free to publish it.

Krogh's major scientific achievements during the next several years, were in exercise physiology in collaboration with Johannes Lindhard and the work on capillary physiology which would bring him the Nobel Prize. Simultaneously he worked on several comparative physiological problems. In all of these studies his primary interest was the "Call for Oxygen," that is the organism's demand for oxygen for internal combustion, which liberates energy essential for the life processes. The process results in that oxygen disappears and is replaced by CO_2 and water. At the time it was known that the process differs from combustion outside the body but nothing was known about the intermediary steps of metabolic processes.

Krogh turned his attention to the demands placed on the organism when muscles are working and the Call for Oxygen is greatly increased.

How does oxygen reach the sites of combustion and how is this process regulated?

Before his laboratory was ready, August had made plans for his friend Lindhard to join him. "I was given a small laboratory in 1910, but Lindhard had none and neither of us had any assistance. We therefore decided to work together and to study muscular physiology in my laboratory."[10] Jens Peter Johannes Lindhard was born in 1870 and got his medical degree in 1898. He had the same fighting spirit as William Sørensen, and Krogh had taken a liking to him because of his strong dedication to science:

> He was irresistibly attracted to science. He was the first of three physicians I have known, who gave up a profitable practice for the opportunity to do scientific work. The only possibility he could find in 1906 was to join the Danish expedition to North Greenland. On account of this he came to the Physiological Laboratory to discuss his plans and receive advice and instructions on how to carry them out.[11]

Lindhard studied the effect of the Arctic conditions and particularly the effects of the changing light on human physiology. In 1908 he got a position at the laboratory of the Finsen Light Institute where Hasselbalch was chief. In 1909 he was made temporary lecturer in the theory of gymnastics at the University of Copenhagen.

> How much Lindhard knew about the theoretical foundation for gymnastics I do not know. But it is certain that he soon found out that it did not exist and that the practice of gymnastics was built upon speculations and empirical knowledge. He determined to make this fact clear and also to try to improve on the knowledge. Through this he came into a fight not only with leading men in gymnastics but also with the University.[11]

The Krogh-Lindhard collaboration, which marks the birth of exercise physiology in the Scandinavian countries, was to continue until Krogh got the Nobel Prize in 1920. By that time Lindhard had his own laboratory and Krogh became occupied with other problems. However, collaboration was renewed around 1930 and lasted until Lindhard retired in 1936 (see chapter 16).

At first they set out to study the regulation of respiration and blood circulation that take place during and just after muscular work. Later they studied the value of fat and carbohydrate as sources of muscular energy (chapter 16). A solid foundation had to be laid for accurate measurements of work load and respiratory exchange. To measure muscular work performed, Krogh constructed the bicycle ergometer. Benedict and Carpenter (1909) had constructed a stationary bicycle, using magnets for resistance. The work done was measured from the strength of current employed for actuating the magnets. When Krogh found that this method was not accurate, he changed the design by not using fixed magnets, but instead keeping the magnets in place by means of weights with which he could weigh the magnitude of the work directly.[12] Benedict tested the new ergometer in a calorimeter and became so impressed with its accuracy that he himself ordered several for his own laboratory. Krogh's bicycle ergometer is still in use.

For measuring oxygen consumption, Krogh designed a new "tilting" spirometer ("vippespirometer") made of very thin aluminum that turned on knife edges rather than moving up and down in water.[12] The two investigators devoted several studies to the alveolar air composition during rest and muscular work and the regulation of respiration during the initial phases of muscular work.[13]

Krogh and Lindhard experimented on themselves, on Marie and on a fourteen-year-old boy. Sitting on the bicycle ergometer, breathing through valves, they measured the oxygen uptake before and during heavy muscular work. Finding a very sudden, five- to six-fold rise in oxygen uptake at the onset of work, they speculated that the blood flow through the lungs must have increased to the same degree. To measure the blood flow through the lungs (equal to cardiac output) during rest and work, they modified a method first introduced by Bornstein (see description below).

Measurements of cardiac output started with Fick in 1870, later Zuntz and Hageman in 1898, and Markoff, Müller, and Zuntz in 1911. The latter used a nitrous oxide method. The method Krogh and Lindhard devised gave far more accurate results than previous methods. Bornstein had washed out the lungs with pure oxygen and determined the blood flow from the amount of nitrogen released into the lungs. But Krogh found this method to be inaccurate. Instead his subjects breathed in a mixture of air and nitrous oxide and the blood flow was determined from the amount of nitrous oxide that disappeared from the alveolar air in a short period (6–26 seconds). As suspected the heart pumped blood much faster during muscular work than during rest and at the same time the oxygen available in the blood was used to a greater extent.[14]

Krogh pored over Tigersted's papers to understand the new phenomenon. How did the heart increase its output? And how was the blood directed so as to supply the working muscles with oxygen? He reasoned (from the literature) that in addition to an increase in heart rate the rate of right ventricular filling also had to increase through an increase in venous supply of blood.[15] But how did the supply of blood increase? From a careful study of the literature, he concluded that during muscular work, blood is directed away from the portal system (the vasculature of liver, spleen, intestine, and stomach) to the working muscles.[16] In 1912 Krogh published three papers on these subjects and in 1913 Krogh and Lindhard published three more papers on their methods and other findings. His thinking about the blood supply to the working muscles gradually led Krogh to his insight and discoveries of the physiology of capillaries.

The great productivity of Krogh's laboratory from 1910 to 1915 included far more than exercise physiology and gas diffusion in the lungs. Several young collaborators were doing a number of comparative physiological studies involving respiratory mechanisms in insects, and effects of temperature on metabolic rate and embryonic development. Experimental animals included insects, fish, frogs, and mammals.

In insects, oxygen does not reach the tissue via capillaries, but by diffusing through air-filled rigid tubes. The tracheae, as these tubes are called, have chitinous (chitin is a hard, horny substance) walls that give them their rigidity. The tracheal system consists of extremely long and narrow tubes opening to the outside through the spiracles. They end in thin tracheoles which run directly into the muscle fibers. They seemed poorly adapted for rapid and complete renewal of the gases. In some insects there were respiratory movements and tracheal sacs; in others, none. In 1913 August studied grasshoppers during rest and after work and analyzed the air in the leg tracheae. To increase the oxygen consumption by the grasshoppers, August and Marie chased them across the lawn and found the oxygen tension in the tracheae to be considerably reduced.[17] In 1920, the year he was awarded the Nobel Prize, August published three more papers on tracheal respiration showing that because diffusion of oxygen in air is hundreds of thousands of times faster than in fluids the exchange in the tracheae is sufficiently rapid to supply the tissue with oxygen at the rate at which it is used (chapter 20).

At the same time a young man named Richard Ege worked in Krogh's laboratory on a number of problems of hydrostatic relations and respiratory functions in aquatic insects. Ege showed that these insects carry air bubbles down into the water when they dive and use this air for respiration. As the oxygen in the air bubble is used, it is renewed by diffusion from the surrounding water.[18]

Krogh's studies on the influence of temperature on metabolic rate in frog, goldfish, and dog showed that "the influence of temperature on the metabolism of an animal is regular and constant and can be expressed in a definite curve, which is not a straight line and cannot be expressed by Arrhenius' formula or the rule of van't Hoff."[19]

As a result of his publications Krogh was invited to write a book, *The Respiratory Exchange of Animals and Man,* for a series of biochemical monographs published in England.[20] As he wrote in the preface, "The relations between the respiratory exchange and functional activity have been excluded from the scope of the present monograph, which deals therefore with one very limited problem only: the quantitative aspect of the catabolic activity of the living animal." In other words, the book dealt with the metabolism of animals during rest and the various internal factors affecting the metabolic rate. An extensive review of the literature, the book surveyed his own work as well as that of several other investigators.

While Krogh was reviewing and recalculating data on the relationship between body size and metabolic rate he became convinced of the correctness of the so-called surface law (first proposed by Max Rubner in 1883), which states that the standard metabolic rate in animals of different body size is roughly proportional to the body surface area. Treating Benedict's data statistically (which was rare in those days), Krogh arrived at the opposite conclusion from Benedict, who had stated in a paper (1915) that there is no close relationship between body size and metabolism and particularly deprecated the use of the surface law as a basis for the comparison. Because Benedict was his friend, Krogh could not avoid the issue and he wrote him a long letter:

> By the closer study of those papers I have been forced to recognize, however, that I must disagree with you on certain points, which I think to be of importance and I have expressed myself accordingly in the monograph. I want to write you directly about this matter because I feel sure that you will accept my criticism and suggestion in the same spirit of desire to further our common science in which they are written. My main point is that you do not get as much out of your splendid material as you could, and make your papers very difficult to read because you do not treat the figures statistically. It is practically impossible to get at the true significance of a long series of determinations by mere inspection.[21]

Krogh himself had started using statistical treatment of his data around 1913. Benedict, slightly offended but always a gentleman, reacted well. He wrote a six-page letter explaining his position. He agreed with Krogh that "we do not get all that is possible from our material, I would not for one moment differ." But, he stated, "it is beyond human possibility for a man to conduct experimental investigations on a scale that is going on in our laboratory and at the same time devote his *entire* time to a literary consideration of the results." He went on to say: "I have frequently stated that in an ordinary University physiological laboratory a privat-docent with an assistant would make a few experiments and then on this write a doctor's dissertation. Such form of experimentation we may not indulge in and while we have an unusually large number of experiments I must say that I have never seen the time when we had too much available data."[22]

These statements show in nutshell the difference between Benedict's and Krogh's approaches to science. In 1929, while attending a meeting in America, Krogh wrote, "Too many experiments are done and too few thoughts are bestowed upon them.[23] He himself was sparing in the number of experiments he carried out, and he found it useless when investigators did fifty identical experiments showing exactly the same phenomenon, where fewer more crucial experiments under differing experimental conditions would have told a more complete story. What he demanded of his own experiments was the highest degree of accuracy possible. When using a method or instrument designed by others, he invariably modified it so that the accuracy was greatly increased. Even though he was constantly designing new instruments he never used them for the sake of gathering data with the new tool. He used them solely to solve specific questions raised in his mind.

Later in the same letter Benedict wrote:

> I should differ with you strongly that it is impossible to get at the true significance of such a long series of determinations by inspection and by graphical plotting. . . . Of all the scientists, physiologists and medical writers have been the last to seriously consider the statistical treatment, and on my numerous trips to Europe I have conferred with various writers on this very point. The consensus of opinion has seemed to be that the statistical treatment would not receive the appreciation and would not be as well understood by physicians and medical men in general as our present method of handling.[22]

Benedict did not hear from Krogh right away but wrote a kind and amiable letter to Krogh in September. Benedict was trying to get a trained statistician and one of the first places he wanted to visit was Krogh's laboratory. However, Lindhard, who was less than diplomatic in dealing with scientific controversies, published a paper in which he openly and rather viciously criticized Benedict's work. Benedict became incensed and outraged. Lindhard's paper had been published from the Finsen Institute where Hasselbalch was director, and Benedict asked Krogh if he should write Hasselbalch and complain.

Benedict wrote, "To me it is infinitely preferable to carry out discussions of this nature in private correspondence than to enter into journalistic polemics."[24] Krogh himself, probably because of Marie's influence, had early realized the uselessness of journalistic polemics. During his student years he had made enemies when his loyalty to William Sørensen forced him to take sides in a public debate. When Sørensen died in 1916, Krogh, in his obituary, wrote that Sørensen's polemical writings unfortunately had not had the effect that he had intended.[25] He was now close to losing Benedict's friendship because of his loyalty to Lindhard and his own dedication to absolute honesty in scientific matters.

He talked the matter over with Marie and wrote a long, tactful, and carefully worded letter to Benedict. He did not say that he disagreed with Lindhard but told Benedict that Lindhard was one of his nearest and dearest friends. "I well know that Lindhard is apt to be somewhat rash in his utterances and does not carefully choose his words so as to avoid giving offense. In fact, he is so keen about the problem at hand that he never starts to think about the susceptibilities of the people whose work he is discussing."[26] He dissuaded Benedict from writing

Hasselbalch, noting that Hasselbalch had nothing to do with it. He emphasized that each person was responsible for what he wrote and had the freedom to express himself in his own way. In fact, in sharp contrast to the practice in the United States, in Denmark neither the director of a laboratory nor the editor of a journal interfered with how a scientific paper was written. This was hard for Benedict to accept, but from the correspondence it appears that in the long run his friendship and admiration for Krogh remained undiminished.

Krogh also had to go to bat for Lindhard in other ways. Lindhard's position as lecturer and in 1920 as professor belonged under the medical faculty, while his teaching and scientific work was within the science faculty. Lindhard with Krogh's strong support tried again and again to change this awkward position. In February 1920, Krogh had prepared a long speech on Lindhard's many qualifications and reasons why he should belong to the science faculty, which he wanted to present in the faculty council. He started by saying: "Although I rarely speak in this faculty, I feel that in this case it is a duty from which I cannot shrink. I must therefore ask for your patience to listen to a rather lengthy report," but the faculty did not want to listen to his report, particularly not a written statement. This so angered Krogh that he went home and wrote the faculty council a letter in which he asked permission to be free from participating in the meetings. He stated, "Since I can only think of partaking in the conference, when I have prepared statements in advance, it is impossible for me to imagine that my presence at the meetings can be of any use whatsoever to the faculty."[27] With the letter he included his prepared statement concerning Lindhard. His deep anger may also have been prompted by the callous way in which he had been refused a rent-free apartment a month earlier.

The battle apparently was won and Lindhard became professor in the Science School. His first laboratory was a large room under the auditorium in Studiestræde.

While August was busy working with Lindhard, Marie was busy with her little boy, her new home, family matters, helping August, her own scientific work, and her medical practice. In 1925 after her work had won widespread recognition, she wrote, "Women who wish to bear children and take care of their well-being and upbringing, can, of course, not direct their full energy toward other tasks. There will even be periods while the children are small when these other tasks must be treated in a rather stepmotherly fashion." But to the question if women with children should give up their work, she answered with a resounding no. If a woman had studied for a specific calling, she should definitely not give it up because of children. It might be necessary temporarily to interrupt or modify her schedule, but it should only be done in such a way that she could resume her work as soon as the children were old enough. This would be more satisfying and enriching for the mother, and would thereby benefit the children.[28]

Marie felt well during her second pregnancy. When labor started on January 29, 1911, Marie's friend and colleague the female gynecologist, Dr. Eli Møller, was called to Ny Vestergade. But all was not well. Complications arose because the baby was in the breech position, and after the protracted labor he was stillborn. August and Marie mourned deeply.

As always in August's life he sought and found his peace of mind in intense work. But the disappointment in never getting a healthy son stayed with him. Erik, though greatly loved by his parents, was often ill and had suffered permanent damage from his premature birth. Another deep sorrow hit Marie when her best friend from her school days at Zahle's, Paula Bøving, died of tuberculosis in 1912. The Kroghs had become very close to the Bøvings and August had shown high regard for Adam Bøving's work. (August and William Sørensen were the two official opponents at Adam Bøving's dissertation). Shortly after Paula's death, Adam Bøving emigrated to America, where he found work at the Smithsonian Institution in Washington, D.C.

Marie continued her work. She was at long last getting together the unwieldy material from the Greenland expedition with all the data that Benedict had provided. The paper was published in 1913.[29] She was also working on a major study that was to be her doctoral dissertation, "The Diffusion of Gasses through the Lungs of Man."[30] What she wanted to investigate was if the rate of diffusion of oxygen under all possible conditions was sufficient to supply the organism with oxygen. Christian Bohr had died in 1911 from a heart attack. But the belief in oxygen secretion was kept alive by Haldane and his collaborators. Marie's work followed the publication (1913) of Douglas, Haldane, Henderson, and Schneider's results of their investigations carried out at high altitude on Pikes Peak in Colorado.[31] The group had reached the conclusion that under the conditions of low oxygen pressure at high altitude the lungs function as a gland and secrete oxygen. Marie doubted their conclusions because their description of the physical condition of the subjects indicated extreme lack of oxygen, which clearly contradicted their measurements and conclusions that the arterial oxygen tension was quite high due to oxygen secretion across the lung epithelium. J. S. Haldane had used his indirect carbon monoxide method for measuring oxygen tension in arterial blood, the same method that August had found suspect for many years.

Marie used the techniques she and August had worked out for estimating oxygen diffusion in human lungs (from measurements of carbon monoxide diffusion) and she used the new methods worked out by Krogh and Lindhard, and by herself. In addition to herself and August, she worked on a number of subjects such as August's two brothers (August's brother Johan was home from Chile for a visit), his father, her patients, and several others. Her subjects were studied during rest and during heavy muscular work. She arrived at the conclusion that diffusion was sufficient to explain gas exchange between alveolar air and blood under any conditions, including low oxygen pressure, heavy work, or respiratory illness.[30] Marie used the method to prove a point; she did not use the technique clinically, and she could not know that her method, thirty-five years later, would be found to be a useful technique for defining the diffusion characteristics of the alveolar membrane in health and disease.

What makes the carbon monoxide diffusion method so useful is that it is not necessary to measure the CO tension in the blood because the binding of CO to hemoglobin is so complete that the tension in the blood is negligible and can be ignored. Therefore, the tension difference between alveolar air and blood can be taken as equal to the tension in the alveoli. As told by Julius Comroe in 1977, Marie's method (published in English in 1915) was essentially forgotten or unused until 1950. "In that year, I was asked to be Editor of a "methods volume" on Pulmonary Function Tests. I designated one chapter 'Gas-Blood Diffusion'." Comroe asked Seymour Kety to write this chapter. Kety strongly advocated the use of Marie Krogh's CO method, which avoids the necessity for obtaining mixed venous blood. The CO method became particularly useful after Robert Forster in 1950 devised a new infrared analysis for CO requiring less time and care than the original method.[32]

Marie's paper still did not convince Haldane, and as late as 1920 Joseph Barcroft found it necessary to prove or disprove oxygen secretion at simulated high altitudes. Barcroft began subjecting himself to increasing oxygen deprivation in a chamber. He measured his alveolar oxygen tension under various conditions and took blood samples directly from his radial artery. In the last part of his stay in the chamber, the oxygen pressure was only 84 mm Hg, corresponding to that of an altitude of 18,000 ft. above sea level. Barcroft further simulated the conditions Haldane's group had experienced at Pikes Peak by increasing the humidity and by doing heavy work on a bicycle ergometer. The dramatic moment came with the drawing of the sample of arterial blood. Barcroft saw that it was very dark, a strong indication of low oxygen tension in the blood (normal oxygenated arterial blood is bright red). Analysis of the arterial blood and the alveolar air confirmed the results: *no* evidence of oxygen secretion! On February 21 Barcroft reported his findings to the meeting of the Physiological Society. Haldane, still unconvinced, raised the objection that no adequate acclimatization had developed under laboratory conditions.[33] In his 1935 book on respiration, he was still promoting his secretion theory.[34]

On May 24, 1914, Marie defended her doctoral thesis and became the fourth Danish woman to earn a doctoral (scientific) degree in medicine (Dr. med.). The official opponents, Professors Valdemar Henriques and Johannes Bock, discussed at great length the equations Marie had used, and Henriques said there was nothing new in Marie's work that Christian Bohr had not already shown. But Marie skillfully defended herself and so impressed the audience with her mathematical know-how, that the reporter for one of the newspapers wrote that only once did one of the opponents "score," but Marie prevented him from taking advantage of it as she immediately admitted her error. Sitting in the front row in the packed auditorium, August from time to time sent Marie encouraging smiles. Present in the audience were the three women who had earned their doctorates in medicine before Marie Krogh (Eli Møller, Johanne Christiansen, and Hedvig Reinhard), and also the courageous woman, who through her action, had opened the university to women, the physician Dr. N. M. Nielsen.[35]

By the time Marie had earned her doctorate, she was the mother of two children. Her healthy little girl, born February 1, 1913, was named Ellen Rigmor. Since early in 1909 August's parents had lived in Copenhagen. After the brewery was sold, August and Marie could no longer vacation in Grenaa. For a few years Marie went to Fyn to visit her family during the summer, but with two children the time had come for the young Kroghs to get a summer house of their own. They bought a lot covered with heather and wildflowers bordering a beautiful white sand beach on Køge Bay in the small village of Solrød, south of Copenhagen. It could be reached by bicycle from Copenhagen or by train and horse and buggy from the train station. To better design the house, August constructed a complete scale model.

In summer 1914 the Solrød house was ready and the Kroghs moved in, but their stay was not long. The summer started with ominous news when Archduke Francis Ferdinand, heir to the Habsburg Monarchy of the Austro-Hungarian Kingdom, was murdered by a Serb nationalist.[36] When Germany declared war on Russia the first day of August, the Kroghs considered it too dangerous to stay at Køge Bay, where mines were being laid by the Germans and their U-boats controlled the waters. The Krogh family fled to Fyn to stay with Marie's brother Jørgen Jørgensen. Two days later August returned to Copenhagen. The Danish government was on high alert expecting a German invasion at any time. Jørgen, who was now a judge, was kept informed of the events by telephone. "There are guards", wrote Marie, "posted along the coasts to report the possible landing of troops, in which case the railroads can be made useless. The ferries carry dynamite to blow up the bridge heads to prevent passage (across the sounds.)"[37] Thus, the connection between Zealand and Fyn could be interrupted any time. When England declared war on Germany, on August 4, 1914, Jørgensen's office was ordered by the ministry of war to keep watch by the telephone day and night in case of general mobilization. The sounds of canon fire at sea filled the air on August 6. The following day rumors circulated in Copenhagen that the English Navy had won a decisive victory at Dogger

Bank. On August 8 messages reached Jørgensen's office to discontinue the telephone watch.[38]

Denmark, the other Scandinavian countries, and Holland succeeded in remaining neutral throughout the war. Because the English Navy dominated the seas, in spite of the danger from German U-boats, trade with England continued. Mail service also continued between the Scandinavian countries, England, and the United States. August and Marie could continue their work while their friends and colleagues in England were occupied and distracted by the war. J. Scott Haldane was close to the war efforts. His older brother, Lord Richard Burdon Haldane secretary of war since 1905, had an enormous influence on the outcome of the war. It was he who had modernized the British army by initiating and bringing to fruition a series of reforms unparalleled in the Army's history.[36] March 1915, Douglas wrote: "When I left Haldane in October last he admitted that he was quite unable to concentrate on work, and I was certainly in the same condition. So were we all, in fact. After all, when you are up against the biggest thing in history, one's ordinary occupations seem quite tame and rather futile. So alveolar "airs" etc. have for the time being been given up."[39]

As the war went on, few of the physiologists in England were able to pursue their studies. Starling was doing some work for which he needed hirudin, which Krogh was able to send him at the time of the sinking of the *Lusitania* by the Germans. Krogh wrote:

> Though we in our country are accustomed to German callousness and disregard for other people's rights and having witnessed through many years their prosecution of our countrymen in North Slesvig their conduct during this war has nevertheless been a shocking revelation to us and their exploit against *Lusitania* has filled us with deep horror. Though most of our newspapers are always very cautious and avoid as far as possible anything that might be construed as offensive toward Germany, and I fear they have good reason to do so, in this case the condemnation has been universal and outspoken.[40]

Preoccupied with the war, Starling wrote, "The average Englishman at present would like to see all newspapers suppressed and all politicians hung." He ended the letter with, "No victory will be of any use that does not mean absolute annihilation of the Prussian power—and that implies going on to the bitter end—at the expense of half our men."[41] A short time later Starling joined the war efforts in the Hygiene Department of the Royal Army Medical College. R. H. A. Plimmer, to whom Krogh sent the manuscript of his book in May 1915, was equally outraged by the sinking of the *Lusitania* and wrote, "No one has any doubt that we are fighting with barbarians." Plimmer hoped that Krogh had a second copy of his book as the manuscript might well be lost in the North Sea.

The attack on the *Lusitania,* a passenger ship, profoundly changed attitudes in the neutral countries, including Denmark, where prior to it, many unscrupulous businessmen were helping defeat the British blockade of Germany by increasing their import from America and secretly exporting to Germany. The general outrage caused by the event had a sobering effect, and by mid-1916, export to Germany had largely been curtailed.[36]

In Denmark, money for the university and for scientific work was hard to obtain. While August's reputation abroad had continued to rise and many visitors came to his laboratory, he had had no luck in getting a better salary or getting his apartment properly repaired. In 1914 Marie was seeking a hospital position to help defray their expenses. Three years in a row (1911–13) before it was finally granted, August had applied for money from the state for a scientific assistant to work in his laboratory. Fortunately, the Carlsberg Foundation was more generous in granting the Kroghs support for their scientific work. Repeatedly, August applied to the state for money for repairs of the apartment, which was in bad shape. In 1914 his request was finally granted, but he was reminded that in the future he would have to pay for any repairs. Year after year he asked if he could have the apartment rent-free, as was customary for many university professors.[42] This was denied. The last time it was denied, January 15, 1920, Krogh was told that, in fact, he had paid too little rent for many years and his rent would now be raised, retroactively, and the money deducted from his salary.[43]

In April 1915 Krogh sent an application to the Ministry for Church and Education that his position as a temporary lecturer be upgraded to an extraordinary professorship. Pointing to the fact that zoophysiology had now become an integral part of the curriculum with the result that his teaching duties were the same as those of a full professor, he stated that he was too busy to supplement his income through other activities.

> In this regard it should also be mentioned that the laboratory is increasingly being visited by foreigners who wish to learn the new methods that have been developed in this laboratory. For obvious reasons, I have not felt that I could refuse these visits. They have not only resulted in a considerable amount of extra work, which I had to do personally until I was recently granted an assistant, but also in perceptible expenses for representation.

Supplementing his application with a long series of publications from his laboratory, of which he was justifiably proud, he added: "It is not up to me to express an opinion on the value of these publications, but I dare believe that they testify to the fact that a considerable amount of hard work has been done here. Furthermore, several more papers will be published during the summer."[44]

Luckily the application was favorably reviewed and recommended by the academic council and a new position, professor of zoophysiology, was created for August in 1916. That same year another Dane who had distinguished himself as an outstanding scientist, Niels Bohr, son of Christian Bohr, became professor in theoretical physics at the University of Copenhagen.[45]

11

Capillaries and the Nobel Prize (1916–1922)

> It seemed to me clear that there might be some mechanism regulating the conditions of supply [of oxygen]. With constant conditions the facilities for transport must either be ridiculously out of proportion to the requirements of the muscles during rest or ridiculously inadequate to meet their needs during heavy work.

Krogh's interest in capillaries was a natural consequence of his interest in oxygen and metabolism. Essential for energy production, oxygen must reach all living cells. He knew that it diffuses across the lung epithelium and becomes bound to hemoglobin in the blood in the lung capillaries. The oxygen-saturated blood reaches the organs and muscles via the capillaries, which branch out among all cells. As Bohr, Hasselbalch, and Krogh had shown, addition of CO_2 to blood lowers hemoglobin's affinity for oxygen, thus releasing oxygen to the cells where CO_2 is produced. While he was pretty sure that oxygen reaches the cells by diffusion from the capillaries, he did not know how this process could be regulated so as to adequately meet the demand of muscles during heavy work as well as at rest.

While studying the literature for his monograph on respiratory exchange, August read that the oxygen tension in the tissues, and particularly in muscles, was probably very low. He assumed that oxygen reached the tissue by diffusion from the capillaries at the same rate as it was used in tissue metabolism. But if its tension were low during rest, then what happened during heavy muscular work when the consumption of oxygen in the working muscles was increased around tenfold? The experiments he had been doing with Lindhard had shown that the increased oxygen consumption of the working muscles was accompanied by an enormous increase in blood flow, and he wondered how this could serve to increase the oxygen supply to the tissue. Anatomical studies had shown that

> the final arterioles in muscles are more or less at right angles to the muscle fibres; they branch into a comparatively large number of capil-

laries which run parallel to the fibres and finally—that is after about ½ mm—unite into small veins which are again at right angles to the fibres. . . . Every capillary could be conceived of as a tube with walls permeable to oxygen and surrounded by a cylinder of tissue through which the oxygen would diffuse toward the periphery, being reduced all the way by the metabolic processes. Now, if the supply was just right during rest, so that the oxygen pressure at the surface of the cylinder would be negligibly small, *no increase in the rate of flow through the same capillaries could make it sufficient during work,* when oxygen was used up, say, at tenfold the rate. If, on the other hand, the density of the capillary network was sufficient to provide by diffusion all the oxygen necessary during heavy work, the arrangement would be very wasteful during rest and would result in an oxygen pressure in the tissue practically identical with that of the venous blood.[1]

When Krogh made this observation it had already been two hundred years since the discovery of capillaries, but the interest in their structure and function had been minimal. Unknown to Krogh, this interest was about to awaken. It was "in the air." Ulrich Ebbecke in Germany, and Henry H. Dale and A. Newton Richards in England and America had initiated studies on capillary function at almost the same time as Krogh.

At the time, however, the generally accepted view was that capillaries were passive, that blood flowed continuously through all of them at rates determined by the state of contraction or dilation of the corresponding arterioles, and that the dilation of an arteriole would cause a rise of pressure in the corresponding capillaries. They would become passively expanded by the increased pressure, to contract again by their own elasticity when the pressure was reduced. This model clearly did not agree with the available facts because the distance for diffusion of oxygen would remain unchanged.[1,2] As Krogh sat pondering the problem in the university library, he was suddenly struck by the idea

> that the anatomical arrangement would work beautifully if it could be assumed that during rest, only a small fraction of the capillaries suitably distributed, are open to the passage of blood while all the rest are closed; and that increasing numbers are opened with increasing work. This mechanism would become ideal if local lack of oxygen forced the opening-up of the nearest capillary, while a certain higher concentration of the dissolved gas allowed the capillary to close, so that, in the resting muscle, or during moderate work, capillaries would open and close in a certain alternation.[1]

At home that same evening, August discussed his new idea with Marie, "who was always my nearest colleague"[1] and made a drawing for her to illustrate his point. Marie listened attentively and discussed his idea with great interest. Many years later in a talk at Harvard, August paid tribute to Marie as his sympathetic and critical colleague:

> The outcome was that it seemed worthwhile to make an experimental test. . . .

At this stage allow me a few words on the role of ideas. An idea or an hypothesis is a very insignificant, but very essential, part of an investigation. Most ideas are wrong and almost all are faulty: but even so experiments have to be planned so as to give an answer: right or wrong. Most ideas are quite vague. Nothing short of experimentation helps more to clarify them and bring them to the testing stage than discussion with a sympathetic and critical colleague."[1]

He must have gone to work on the experiments right away because late in December of 1915 he needed many frogs, which his friend Barcroft was able to ship from England in spite of the war.[3] While still occupied with many other studies, he went to work on the capillary problem. He designed four new instruments that permitted him to determine diffusion constants for oxygen through various tissues.[4] Next he had to know the total number of capillaries in muscles and other tissues from frog, cod, and a number of larger and smaller mammals. By injecting India ink or gelatin stained with Prussian blue through the aorta or large vessels, it was possible to stain the capillaries so that they could be counted on transverse sections. But he had difficulties in getting complete injections of all capillaries in muscles: "The best results have been obtained by injecting directly through a muscle artery. . . . I believe the material to be injected is best left a day or two after killing the animal before the injection is made."[5] The reason was that many capillaries were closed in the living animal but opened after death. The total number of capillaries was greatest in the muscles of the small mammal (the guinea pig) where he found as many as 3,000 capillaries per mm^2. In the horse there were only 1,400 capillaries per mm^2, and in the cold-blooded animals the numbers were much smaller.[5]

To calculate the oxygen pressure in the capillaries necessary to supply the tissue with sufficient oxygen, he went to a mathematician, Mr. K. Erlang, who worked out an equation for Krogh's model of a cylinder of tissue surrounding each capillary.[5] The calculations showed what he had suspected, namely that if all capillaries were open during rest, tissues everywhere in the body (and especially in the muscles) would have the same high oxygen pressure as in the capillaries. Obviously, this finding did not agree with the findings by other authors that the oxygen pressure in tissues is close to zero. Krogh wrote, "With constant conditions the facilities for transport [of oxygen] must either be ridiculously out of proportion to the requirements of the muscles during rest or ridiculously inadequate to meet their needs during heavy work."[1] Krogh and Lindhard had found that the oxygen tension of venous blood was only 12 mm Hg during work, compared to 35 mm Hg during rest. "It cannot, therefore, be doubted," wrote Krogh,

> that during work a much increased volume of oxygen diffuses from capillaries into the muscles, while the available pressure appears to be considerably diminished. . . . The increase in the rate of blood flow

through the capillaries and even a passive distention of them caused by the increased blood pressure would obviously be of no avail to explain the discrepancy, and I was led to the conclusion . . . the only possibility must be an increase in the number of available capillaries.[2]

Direct microscopic observations on living tissues confirmed what he suspected: "When the circulation of a muscle is not extremely feeble the open capillaries are generally seen to be arranged at fairly regular intervals (200–500 μm). By electrical stimulation or by gentle massage, an increased circulation can be brought about in any muscle where it was feeble beforehand with the invariable result that the number of visible capillaries is greatly increased, their average distance being diminished to 60–70 μm."[2]

A similar result for capillary distribution was obtained when he injected resting and working muscles with India ink and measured the density of capillaries on tissue sections: In resting muscles many capillaries were closed, in working muscles many were open. The distribution of open capillaries was such that the Erlang equation predicted that at rest the oxygen pressure was normally zero in considerable portions of the muscles and during work the pressure head was sufficient to supply the muscle with oxygen at the rate at which it was used.

Early in January 1919, August submitted the papers to Dr. Langley, editor of the *Journal of Physiology* in England, and on January 19 he wrote Barcroft:

> I am today sending two papers to you and in a few days one more will follow. They are intended for the Journal *[J. Physiol.]*. Langley has practically accepted them and why I send them to you is only because you might like to see the results and read part of them before they are printed. The two first are rather dull, though I hope useful, but I venture to believe that you will find the third one interesting. I at least found it very interesting when doing the work, but of course that may be a different matter. A short account of the work has been presented here in Denmark.[6]

The war had finally ended in November 1918 and the entire Krogh family (there were now four children) had been ill with the Spanish flu at Christmas. Only the baby born in November had avoided the flu. Marie had been quite ill, but did not take to her bed because she had to take care of the rest of the family. The end of the war occupied August's thoughts and he related to Barcroft his worries about what might happen to the German people and particularly the scientists:

> Here in Denmark we feel immensely relieved by the downfall of the Prussian militarism and officialdom, which oppressed, in the most grievous manner, our countrymen in Slesvig, interfered constantly with Danish affairs and was a consistent menace to our national existence. Now we look forward to joining hands after 55 years with our

brethren south of the frontier and we ought to be, and most of us certainly are, extremely grateful to the Powers to whom all this is due. In spite of all, we cannot help feeling sorry for the German people and anxious for the future of Germany. We know, and I am sure you will agree with me on this point, that the Germans have many excellent, nay wonderful qualities. We could not well do without them in science for instance. I cannot help looking with apprehension to the revengeful feelings worded by many in the Entente countries. I admit that justice would require sanctions, but I hope that they will be treated with so much leniency that it will be possible for them to join the League of Nations without bitterness of heart.

This was not idle talk for he continued in the letter:

However, since you are probably about as powerless in this matter as I am, it is of no use going further into it. The one direction in which I hope to be able to do something is the reestablishment of the scientific connection between the laboratories. When the time comes for that I know I can rely on your sympathy. I had a letter from dear old Zuntz a few days ago. He asked if I could get for him some N_2O for circulation rate experiments. I had to tell him that we had just as little of that here as in Germany. It will probably be impossible for you to get a cylinder sent to him from England.[6]

As a Quaker, Barcroft had at first not participated directly in the war efforts; but following the first use of poison gas by the Germans, he was, in 1915, called to national service in relation to the medical aspects of gas poisoning. In 1917 he had become chief physiologist and leader of a team at the Gas Warfare Center near Salisbury.

Returning home for a few days, his head full of what he had seen and worked on, Barcroft found Krogh's letter and manuscript. "They bring back such a forgotten world to me," Barcroft wrote, "as I have read no general physiology for a long time now and I feel very ignorant for I have forgotten most of it." He had picked up a book written by Arthur R. Cushny on the secretion of urine,[7] in which he found that he had once been regarded as an authority on that subject! But the book left him "quite cold" as he could not take the least interest in whether Ludwig's or Bowman's theory was correct.[8] Two weeks later, however, after he had received Krogh's third paper, he read all three papers and wrote Krogh, "You cannot imagine with what pleasure and enthusiasm I read them."[8] Barcroft also promised to help their friend Zuntz as best he could.

Back in Denmark, Krogh was also helping another of Barcroft's former collaborators, Professor Arnold Durig from Vienna, who in 1910 had participated with Barcroft and Zuntz in studies of respiration at high altitude on Pico de Teide in Tenerife. In December 1919, Durig wrote Krogh to get a spirometer. Now in the postwar period the suffering in Germany and Austria was great. As inflation worsened, the middle class, and with them the academicians, had little money and food.

August and Marie, feeling great empathy for Durig and his family, did their best to help. They gave him money for his instruments (300 Danish kroner then corresponded to 300,000 Austrian crowns!) and packages of food for his family. At the time, starving children from Vienna were sent to Copenhagen to stay with Danish families, and the Kroghs offered to take Durig's little girl, but it was unnecessary.[9]

After Krogh's three capillary papers were published in May 1919, the next problem to be investigated was the mechanism regulating the capillary circulation. During in vivo experiments on the tongues of deeply narcotized frogs, he studied the reaction of capillaries and small arteries to mechanical and chemical stimulation. In a paper published in May 1920, he wrote:

> Experiments are described which show that the arterial pressure is unable to dilate the capillaries to any appreciable extent or open them up when they are tonically contracted, while the venous pressure may be sufficient to fill them, when relaxed in response to weak mechanical or chemical stimulation locally applied. The state of filling of the capillary vessel does not depend, therefore, upon the arterial blood-pressure, but upon the degree of tonus and relaxation of the capillary wall.[10]

The apparently independent contractility of the capillaries and its regulation was to occupy Krogh and other investigators for many years to come.

For her part Marie Krogh had not been idle. She could not, as August did, devote most of her time to science. For her, August and the children came first. She ran her household well, making sure that August was always well taken care of, and she entertained family, friends, and visiting scientists generously. She bore two little girls during these busy years, Agnes Helga, born January 31, 1917, and me (Bodil Mimi) on November 3, 1918. Fortunately, domestic help was inexpensive in those days so Marie had two maids.

In 1914–15 Marie was clinical assistant under Professor Christian Gram at the Rigshospital. Through Gram's interest in diseases of the thyroid gland, Marie became involved in the study of the effect of the thyroid gland on metabolic rate. The study appealed to her as a physician and as a scientist. Using the techniques that she and August had employed during their Greenland expedition, she measured the metabolism in patients with hyperactive and hypoactive thyroid glands. In her first study on the subject Marie showed how measurements of metabolic rate could be used for diagnostic purposes in these diseases and how the effectiveness of the treatment could be followed by the changes in metabolic rate.[11]

In her private practice Marie used the same technique, and with time came to specialize in metabolic diseases. The procedure, however, involved the use of gas analyses, which were cumbersome and time consuming. Then in 1922, August, feeling sorry for Marie, constructed a new apparatus that could measure the metabolic rate accurately without gas analyses.[12] In a clinical study, Marie compared the old and the new methods and found the new method to be very accurate. Not only did Marie use this apparatus herself for as long as she lived, but, as she advocated, it became an important clinical tool for diagnosis of metabolic diseases.

Marie soon found that the metabolic measurements could also be used for biological standardization of preparations of the hormone thyroxin. She had already been involved in standardization of digitalis and strophanthin, following a request from the Løvens Chemical Company to collaborate in the production of a stable, well-standardized digitalis preparation. As a result, Marie published a series of papers on biological standardization of digitalis and other similar preparations between 1917 and 1929.

While Marie was using her physiological and medical training for the benefit of her growing family, she became convinced that homemakers needed a better education to properly care for their families' health and nutrition. Consequently, Marie gave lectures in physiology and nutrition for home economics teachers and worked toward having this education incorporated under the university. She was also appointed censor in physiology examinations at the Medical and Dental Schools in 1919.

Spring 1920 brought many worries for Marie. Erik frequently suffered from pneumonia and his parents feared for his life. Much later it was discovered that Erik had been infected with tuberculosis from the laboratory caretaker, Mr. Møller, and he repeatedly suffered from pleurisy. At the same time Marie's mother, Ane, was slowly dying from throat cancer while Marie's sister Kirsten, herself in poor health, cared for her. At the end of May, Ane died. While Marie was in mourning for her mother, a well-meaning lady, noticing Marie's black clothes, stopped her in the street and said, "Oh has he died the poor little fellow, but it was really the best!" The normally gentle Marie was outraged.

In July 1920, Marie was at Solrød Beach with the four children and two maids, while August was traveling to England, Paris, and Holland for physiological meetings. Feeling unwell, Marie had decided against accompanying him. Meanwhile, Marie found time to do proofreading for August and work on her own papers.

Then the happy, long-awaited event occurred: North Slesvig was reunited with Denmark. On July 9 the Danish King, Christian X, rode across the former border on a white horse while adults and children cheered and threw flowers. In Solrød the flag was raised all day, and Marie served extra cake with the afternoon coffee.[13]

August was in great spirits as he traveled through England. In Cambridge he thoroughly enjoyed staying with the Barcrofts in their comfortable house. "I have been received with the greatest kindness," he wrote Marie, "and have spent a delightful morning in the laboratory with Barcroft, Cohn (who visited us in Copenhagen), Hartridge, Parsons with his wife and a young man whose name I did not get."[14] On July 14, 1920, he thanked Marie for various papers she had sent him and pictures of their children. The photographs of the children delighted the Barcrofts and were also shown "at Haldane's where the interest was less pronounced." The meeting was held in London a few days later. To Marie, he wrote:

> The Physiological Society meetings were very successful. I had the opportunity to speak with Bayliss and Dale, with whom I shall later have a long discussion. I met [John J.] Abel from Baltimore, who spoke about getting me to America to give some lectures, and several others whom I knew slightly from before. My talk was received with great applause. There was no real discussion but Haldane and then Martin (Lister Institute) gave far too flattering talks about the significance of these investigations [capillary work]. Barcroft gave a report on oxygen tension in venous blood that he had revised on the basis of his calculations of oxygen diffusion and remarked that the results agreed well with yours. At one or two other occasions during the meeting they referred to results from the Copenhagen school, so that one would get the impression that we mean something.[14]

Following the meeting he went back to the Barcrofts and visited with several new friends in Cambridge. He even went to the service in "Kings College's wonderful old chapel, and the whole thing was so beautiful that it was worthwhile attending." The meeting in London was followed by another physiological meeting in Paris where August met so many people that he feared he would not be able to remember them. He was longing for Marie and wished she could have been with him. Arriving back in Ny Vestergade on July 22, he had a vague hope that Maric would be there waiting for him, but she was in Solrød and had not gotten his letter in time. "If you are longing for me as much as I am longing for you and if you can leave the youngsters then you will come to me. It would be wonderful to meet alone and spend the night together here."[15]

The rest of the summer vacation was spent in Solrød before the family went back to Copenhagen. But Marie was not well. She lost weight rapidly and was very tired. Never one to give in or admit to any weakness, Marie stubbornly continued her work but by the middle of September it worried August so much that he made her go to Fyn to stay with her brother Jørgen to rest. Marie had in fact developed diabetes, but at the time the diagnosis may not yet have been made. Instead efforts were made to make her gain weight. Erik, now twelve years old, was sent to a sanatorium at Refnæs for his tuberculosis. August was left in Ny Vestergade with his three daughters and the maids to take care of them. Since I was under two years old my little bed was placed next to his so that he could take care of me. "All is well here," he told Marie.

> The children are well behaved and both Miss Kønig and Miss Gram care for them in the nicest way. Bodil asks for you every morning when she comes over in my bed, but otherwise the little ones don't seem to miss you. The other day when I was eating alone for a little while I said in a singing voice, without thinking about it, "big live cod are good, cod are good" [a street vendor's song]. To this, Agnes, who was sitting on the floor, quietly remarked, "Father, we may not sing at the table." I had to pocket that![16]

Marie resented having to stay away from her family and work, so by early October she was home again resuming her busy schedule.

On October 28 the big event occurred. The Nobel committee in Stockholm awarded Krogh the Nobel Prize for physiology or medicine for the year 1920. The award was based on his first capillary papers, as well as the continuous stream of important papers coming from his laboratory. As soon as the news reached Copenhagen, a journalist located Krogh at the yearly university banquet and showed him the telegram. Taken aback, August exclaimed: "That cannot be true, why should I get it?"[17] But it was true, and as the news spread, numerous congratulatory letters arrived from far and near. Benedict wrote, "I cannot tell you what delight this gives me. I think I can consider myself one of the earliest to appreciate your extraordinary capacities, and never for one moment have I felt other than you were entitled to the first rank in biological science." Benedict, who had met August's mother on an earlier occasion, anticipated how Mimi would enjoy "the great pleasure that must have come to her from this recognition of her son."[18] Thanking Benedict, August wrote:

> The award of the Nobel Prize came as a perfect surprise to me and when it was first told me by a journalist I declined to believe it because in my opinion the work on the capillaries was so far only a promising beginning. I have learned later, that was just why. They wanted to give the prize for a definite piece of work before its value should be obvious to everybody. I believe the prize was as great a surprise to everyone here as it was to myself and you will readily understand that during the months of November and December I had a very glorious and very exacting [sic] time. Now at least I have approximately returned to my normal existence and I am pushing the work forward as hard as I can to do something to deserve the prize.[19]

Krogh had sent the collected papers from his institute to his many colleagues and friends shortly before the Nobel Prize was awarded. Durig wrote:

> Many heartfelt thanks for the imposing volume with the work by you and your students. I believe that I without exaggeration can say that

your institute today is at the top of all physiology, since no other single institute in Europe or America has contributed such a sum of original, fundamentally important studies and such wealth of new methods.[20]

Mimi Krogh had followed her son's success with fierce pride and interest. Once, after she and Viggo had been visiting in Solrød, August stood on the platform waving as the train pulled away. A fellow passenger turned to Mimi and said, "The young man is waving to you." Slightly offended, Mimi answered, "He is my son and he is a professor at the university." Now when August went to Stockholm to receive the Nobel Prize, Mimi accompanied her son and daughter-in-law. The presentation of the Nobel Prizes took place in the large hall of the Music Academy on December 10. Laudatory speeches were given to the three 1920 Nobel Prize winners, who were present, the Swiss physicist Charles-Edouard Guillaume, the Norwegian author Knut Hamsun, and August Krogh. Following each speech, the winners received their prizes from the king and music played. The grand ceremony was followed the same evening by a banquet, wrote *Stockholmstidningen*:

> The banquet for the Nobel Prize winners at the Grand Hotel Friday night was a shining festivity in the presence of all the capital can offer of its greatest in science and literature. At the table, which was richly and tastefully decorated with lily of the valley and red tulips, Prince Carl presided with Mrs. Guillaume on his right side. To his left the Prince had Mrs. Dr. Krogh, then the Nobel prize winner's mother and next to her Knut Hamsun had his place with Selma Lagerløf.[21]

August sat across from Prince Carl between Princess Ingeborg and Princess Märta. During the evening as the guests moved into the parlors, the royals entertained themselves especially with the Kroghs, the reporters noted. No doubt the lively Mimi, who had always taken a special interest in royalty, enjoyed herself. The next day, while walking on the icy street in Stockholm, Mimi slipped and broke her weak knee. She was brought to the hospital, where to her joy Princess Ingeborg, sister to the Danish and Norwegian kings, came to see her. The princess brought her flowers from the queen and herself, saying: "We are in this world to help and comfort one another." Mimi brought the flowers home and pressed them, and her daughter Frida framed them.

August himself did not share his mother's awe toward royalty and rather dreaded having to explain his work to people who did not understand it. Early in January 1921 he was in audience with the king of Denmark. As the king kindly asked him about his work, August, tired of trying to explain his work, replied, "I don't know anything about it."[22]

When August returned to Copenhagen, the work in the laboratory went into high gear. Among the many young people who had gravitated to his laboratory was the young zoologist Paul Brandt Rehberg, who was now scientific assistant in Krogh's laboratory.

Rehberg was the kind of person that August believed would make a first-rate scientist. Born in 1895, he came from a modest home, but his mother, an expert photographer and avid fighter for women's rights, saw to it that he had the right kind of opportunities for intellectual growth. Following a mathematical artium in 1913, he studied zoology at the university. Since he had to earn his living while studying, he taught twenty hours a week, and it took him seven years before he became cand. mag. in zoology.

Rehberg was interested in function and definitely not in systematics. During his studies he found that very few of his teachers had any understanding whatsoever of physics. "But that was what Krogh had," he thought, and Krogh taught function. Rehberg followed Krogh's lectures with rapture. "When Krogh found that a student in his class had a genuine interest in what he taught, his lectures became brilliant."[23]

In January 1920 Rehberg had finished his final examinations, but because he had to start military service in May he could not take a teaching position, so he thought he might enroll in a graduate course on scientific methods that Krogh gave for magister conference students. At Rehberg's final examination in zoophysiology, Krogh had been so pleased with his performance that he personally went to Rehberg and thanked him, "so little was he used to students truly interested in his subject." Now Rehberg took courage from Krogh's kindness and asked if he could take part in the course, while waiting for his military service.

After a couple of months, during which Rehberg had worked every day in the laboratory and shown his ability for independent research, Krogh asked Rehberg to stay. But in May, Rehberg's military service began. Assigned to the Medical Corps, he had to attend physiology lectures taught by an old physician. Finding the teaching utterly miserable and his military service a waste of time, Rehberg asked Krogh for help. Krogh answered that he ought to serve out his military duties at the Zoophysiological Laboratory because he was going to work with shock which was far more important for the military than what he was doing then. Rehberg's request was promptly denied and Rehberg was warned not to try such tactics again. But Krogh did not take no for an answer, he went directly to the war minister and told him in no uncertain terms what he felt was right. That helped. Rehberg, to the amazement of his fellow soldiers and secret resentment of his officers, was given orders to complete his military service in Krogh's laboratory. On September 1, 1920, Rehberg became Krogh's scientific assistant; by December he had finished his military duty.

Rehberg soon became involved in the capillary work. Krogh knew that Rehberg had previous training in photography (with his mother) and therefore asked him to work on the filming of the capillaries with him. They bought a primitive 32 mm movie camera for amateurs. Then Krogh changed it by putting a periscope into the camera, so that he could look at the image on the film directly with a mirror and a magnifying glass. This technique, never used before or since, made it possible for them to create absolutely sharp images. Even today the film is unique in its clarity. Electrically run movie cameras did not exist in 1921. But instead of rolling the film manually they used a flywheel to get a uniform speed and keep their hands free. But film was expensive and a brake had to be put on to stop the flywheel quickly. The two would film a short sequence and then Rehberg would rush into the darkroom to develop it. The camera is now in the Copenhagen film museum.[23]

Soon after the Nobel Prize ceremonies, invitations from all over the United States started coming. From Yale University, at the instigation of Yandell Henderson, came the invitation to present the Silliman Lectures. From Walter Boothby at the Mayo Clinic, who had corresponded with Krogh for several years, came not only an invitation to present a series of lectures, but Krogh was asked to join the staff. August was happy to lecture there but declined a permanent position. To Boothby he wrote, "I cannot think of leaving my own country, however, so long as the conditions for carrying on my scientific work here are reasonably decent, and I have some reason to expect that the authorities will pay a little more attention to my wishes now than they have done in the past." When Boothby tried once more, August explained: "I wish you to understand that I appreciate and value it very highly indeed, but very strong ties bind me to my native country and I feel I cannot leave it so long as I am not driven away by being seriously hampered in my work. I am, in fact, treated with all possible consideration, but like everybody else I must bear some of the consequences of the great financial difficulties of the State."[24]

From Rufus Cole at Harvard University came an invitation to give the Harvey Lecture and from John J. Abel in Baltimore an invitation to lecture at Johns Hopkins University.

In spite of being urged to come in 1921, August had to postpone his arrival until early in October 1922. In one letter he explained that he needed more time for his capillary work and because of a change in staff, but in later letters he explained that Marie could not accompany him until fall 1922. It might have been due to Erik's serious illnesses, but part of the reason could also have been Marie's poor health, which she did not wish to have discussed.

With the fame came some less pleasant publicity. The Kroghs were viciously attacked by anti-vivisectionists. One newspaper article bore the headline, "Great scientific achievement or torment of animals?" August had to give a public lecture on the subject to explain the relative merits of research. From Walter B. Cannon in the United States he received a sympathetic letter on the subject, with valuable advice on how to handle it. Another side effect of the publicity was that old acquaintances and former friends began asking for loans. August, always generous in the past, when he had little to spare, lent freely, but this sometimes resulted in his "friends" never writing again.

August's correspondence became so voluminous that he had to spend a good part of the summer vacation in Solrød sitting at his desk in his little house answering letters. He wrote long handwritten letters in Danish, English, German, and French.

In September 1921 August was in Edinburgh for scientific meetings and to receive an honorary doctoral degree. He greatly enjoyed the scientific discussions, but found the long excursions by car tiresome and quite unpleasant, even though the landscape was beautiful. "I shall strive to avoid it [such rides] in the future."[25]

During the academic year 1921–22 many aspects of capillary function were being studied by Krogh and his students. Several new people had come to take part in the work in August's laboratory and many more asked permission to come. But the laboratory was small, and August had to deny many of the requests. Among the people he accepted was the young Danish histologist Bjowulf Vimtrup, who came to work on the contractile elements in the capillary walls. Beatrice Carrier from Berkeley worked on reactions to drugs of human skin capillaries. George A. Harrop, a nephew of Rufus Cole from John J. Abel's laboratory in Baltimore, worked with Krogh and Rehberg on the effect of nerve fibers on capillary contraction. A feeling of excitement, happiness, and great friendship permeated the laboratory, and several of the participants later wrote that it was the happiest time of their lives. Dedicating his capillary book, August wrote, "To my wife and to my young comrades in the laboratory . . . this book is gratefully inscribed."[26]

As invitations continued to arrive, the trip to the United States became increasingly complicated. Following eight to ten days in New Haven for the Silliman Lectures, August and Marie were to visit Minnesota, Chicago, Cincinnati, New York, Boston, and Washington. In Washington they were to stay with Anna and Adam Bøving for rest and relaxation (Bøving had married a former student from Denmark in 1915 after he had moved to Washington). On July 31, 1922, he wrote Bøving:

> Many, many thanks for your excellent letter which contained much advice and orientation with respect to our America trip. I should have written long ago but I have toiled like a beast to finish the book on the capillaries, so it can be submitted to Yale University Press at the same time I give the lectures. During the past month I have been sitting in my little house here at the beach and written from morning to night with no other interruptions than going for meals in the larger summer house, where the family lives.[27]

The next day he was to return to Copenhagen to do more experiments before the trip. In Solrød it had been a cold, windy, and rainy summer, but it did not bother August as he sat buried in his work, gazing from time to time over the whitecaps on the gray sea. The Bøvings had invited Erik to come to Washington, but in the end August and Marie decided to leave him with Marie's brother Jørgen in Odense. They were to leave for England on September 10 and travel from Liverpool to Boston September 19–27. They hoped to start the return trip to Denmark the last days of November. "I don't think Mie can stand being without the children for a longer time and I suspect she will miss them terribly, long before that. I am, as behooves a man, more thick-skinned in this regard."[27]

August was looking forward with great anticipation to the adventure, but tragedy struck four days prior to their departure when August's youngest sister Frida drowned while bathing. Her body was never found. It was a cruel blow to her parents, with whom she had been living, and also to August and Marie. Frida had been a frequent and welcome visitor in Ny Vestergade, where she was a great friend of the children.

On September 10 the long trip began. Marie had arranged that the grandparents and her sister look in on her three little girls, who were being cared for by the maids. A big black teddy bear was purchased before they left, to be given to me on my fourth birthday. The Kroghs were interviewed and photographed on board the ship before they left. In the picture Marie looks drawn and tired.

12

The Insulin Story (1922–1925)

> Krogh's and Hagedorn's dynamic personalities, the fine combination of physiological and clinical insight and technical ingenuity they represented was determining for the quick build-up and development of "Nordisk Insulin Laboratorium."

It is not clear when Marie was first diagnosed with diabetes. She was so determined to keep her illness a secret that no letters or records mentioning her condition exist. I myself only learned about it in 1945, two years after her death.[1] Undoubtedly, as an excellent physician, Marie knew what was wrong early on. Her weight loss, thirst, and frequent urination told the story. Most likely she tested and found sugar in her urine. In those days, before insulin, the prognosis for diabetics was grim. The "adult-onset" diabetes, which Marie had, may develop gradually over many years, but Marie's case was severe and she could expect a continuous worsening resulting in cataracts, blindness, infections, gangrene, and eventually death.

Diabetes was long believed to result only from a failure to metabolize carbohydrates. Therefore, it was most often treated through dietary restrictions of carbohydrates to obtain sugar-free urine. To compensate for the weight loss and sugar loss in the urine, many European doctors increased the caloric intake of their patients and recommended a diet high in fat and protein but low in carbohydrates. In contrast, Frederick Madison Allen in America, following extensive research on mildly diabetic animals, had come to the conclusion that all food tended to overburden the metabolism of the diabetic. Consequently, he recommended severe restriction of food intake. In "Total Dietary Regulation in the Treatment of Diabetics," published in 1919, he recommended maintaining the already emaciated patients on a starvation diet of less than 1000 calories per day, sometimes as low as 350–600 calories per day. Allen treated a number of patients this way, and though they lived longer, most of them eventually died of starvation. Diabetes specialist Elliot Proctor Joslin of Boston advocated and used Allen's treatment.[2]

In Denmark a young physician, Hans Christian Hagedorn, specialized in diabetes while practicing medicine at a hospital in the small town of Brande. To follow the results of the treatment of his patients, he collaborated with the local pharmacist, Norman Jensen, and developed a method for determining sugar in small samples of blood from the earlobe. At a Copenhagen congress in summer 1918, Hagedorn and Jensen presented their new method, requiring only 0.1 ml of blood for sugar determination. Following the meeting, August sent Hagedorn his first paper on the capillaries. Hagedorn's thoughtful letter, in which he described his interest in capillary circulation in diabetics and the new ideas Krogh's paper had given him, must have impressed August, so a friendship began. In 1919 Hagedorn moved to Copenhagen to take up a position at the Rigshospital under the prominent internal medicine professor Knud Faber. Both August and Marie discussed their work with Hagedorn, and August helped Hagedorn with modifications and calibration of his instruments.[3] In 1919 Hagedorn published a paper in which he advocated the American Allen-Joslin treatment of diabetics.[4] Hagedorn's doctoral dissertation on blood sugar regulation followed in 1921.[5]

Since the Kroghs were fully aware of Hagedorn's expertise, there is no doubt that Hagedorn became Marie's doctor shortly after she discovered she had diabetes. Because of Krogh's interest in exchange of fluid between capillaries and tissue, by the time the Kroghs left for America, Hagedorn and Rehberg were working together in Krogh's laboratory to study edema.

The trip across the Atlantic was peaceful and uneventful. The Kroghs kept mostly to themselves among the six hundred passengers, but August, who loved children, occasionally visited the ship's playroom, "where I played a little with the children, and won the confidence of several of them."[6]

In Boston, they stayed with Dr. Walter R. Miles who worked with Benedict, and they were taken everywhere by car. August gave a lecture on insect physiology, because he was not permitted to speak about the capillaries before he had presented the Silliman Lectures at Yale. While in Boston they spent time in Benedict's laboratory and several other laboratories and were invited out for dinner every night.[7] They also met Joslin, who had been associated with Benedict at the Nutrition Laboratory of the Carnegie Institution in Washington, D.C., between 1908 and 1920. For several years they had been collaborating on measurements of respiratory exchange in diabetics. On October 4, the Kroghs had dinner in Joslin's home. Sitting next to Joslin, Marie told him about Hagedorn's blood sugar determination and later gave him Hagedorn's dissertation. In a letter to Hagedorn, Marie told him about the meeting and continued:

> In London Prof. Starling told us that they had succeeded in America in making an active preparation of the internal secretion from the pancreas, by first preventing the digestive enzymes in the gland from de-

stroying it. I asked Joslin more about it. He had the material for testing on his patients. As far as I understood him, it was still in the testing state. Joslin said that the present preparation was much better than in the beginning, because they had gradually been able to free it from protein contamination, whereby the danger of toxic effects from the injections was diminished. Joslin used it only in severe cases, where he had succeeded in lowering the blood sugar and increasing the tolerance to carbohydrates.[8]

Marie did not know the name of the man who had made the preparation, but had learned that August's friend the English physiologist Henry Hallett Dale was interested in it and had left for America because of it. (Dale had, in fact, gone to Toronto as representative of the British Research Council to get the insulin production started in England.) Since other doctors in Boston had received the preparation, "there is a possibility that you, too, might get some."

Two days later Marie wrote Hagedorn again, sending him a newspaper clipping about the pancreas preparation; but she added that according to Joslin, the effects seemed to be greatly exaggerated. After his week of lectures at Yale, where his film of capillary circulation excited great interest, August and Marie visited the Mayo Clinic in Rochester, Minnesota. Marie was getting excited about the possibilities of the pancreas preparation. She wrote Hagedorn from Chicago on October 28:

> Most of the places we visit, people are excited about the new pancreas preparation, Insulin, and do experiment with it. Dr. Boothby (Mayo Clinic) showed me figures from an experiment they had made with a factory-produced "Insulin" (that has another name), that is said not to be as good as the laboratory made. At a sanitorium in Battle Creek [Michigan], the chief of the laboratory had been sent to Toronto to learn the method so that they could make the preparation themselves (in collaboration with the laboratory in Toronto), and make experiments partly on animals and partly on diabetics. Dr. Lewis there told about a case of a very severe diabetic, whom they kept alive with intravenous injections three times daily. Since I think that you, from a theoretical as well as a practical point of view, will be interested in this preparation, I have persuaded my husband to write Dr. Macleod in Toronto and ask him if it is possible to get the production method so that it could be possible for you to make experiments with the preparation in Denmark.[8]

Marie, writing a strictly professional letter from one physician to another, makes no reference to her own condition! She suggests who might produce the pancreatic extract, which was now called "insulin," in Denmark and ways of administering the insulin to avoid painful intravenous injections. It is interesting to note that at this point there was no mention of Frederick G. Banting and Charles Best, who had done the experiments.

August continued his triumphant and hectic schedule of lectures and travel to Battle Creek, Michigan; Rochester, Minnesota; Minneapolis, Chicago, St. Louis, Cincinnati, Washington, Philadelphia, Baltimore, and Cleveland. In each city he gave one to three lectures. Marie told her mother-in-law, "People are very interested in A's investigations, are very kind and show us a lot of laboratories, buildings, landscapes, etc."[7] In spite of his schedule, August had found time to write a long letter to Macleod:

> During my visit to the United States—as a Silliman lecturer and as guest of the Mayo Foundation—I have been hearing everywhere about the experimental treatment of diabetes with insulin and I have been wondering if perhaps it might be consistent with the plan of yourself and your collaborators to have experiments carried out in Denmark also. A friend of mine, Dr. H. C. Hagedorn who is often working as a guest in my laboratory, is a very competent investigator and specialist in diabetes. He has done some very good work which has unfortunately so far only been published in Danish. He has worked out and thoroughly tested a new micromethod for blood sugar determination, which I think is the best in existence.[9]

August described in detail Hagedorn's investigations of the power of the organism to deal with sugar in diabetic and normal subjects. Hagedorn had also worked out a new respiration apparatus providing graphic records of the oxygen intake and the respiratory quotient, which August felt might be very useful in the study of sugar metabolism. (The respiratory quotient can distinguish between sugar metabolism and fat metabolism.) August mentioned that he had an organic chemist in his laboratory, that a plentiful supply of pancreas was available in Denmark, and that money was no problem.[9] A week later August received a courteous invitation from Macleod to visit Toronto, ending with, "I should like very much to go over our insulin work with you and to get the benefit of your advice and cooperation." It was arranged that Krogh should arrive in Toronto November 23 and stay as the houseguest of the Macleods.[10]

In Toronto, where the great discovery had taken place, the preceding year and a half had been eventful as progress was made, but turbulent as the relationship between the collaborators deteriorated. Michael Bliss gives a brilliant account of the events leading up to the clinical use of insulin.[2] I shall only present a few of the facts here in order to explain later developments in which Krogh was involved.

It all started with the idea of a young surgeon, Frederick G. Banting. It was known that animals became diabetic when the pancreas, which secretes digestive enzymes into the intestine, was removed. It was also known that it was not the lack of digestive enzymes that caused diabetes, but the lack of a mysterious internal secretion from certain cell groups in the pancreas, believed to be the islets of Langerhans. Several attempts to isolate the secretion had failed, seemingly due to the action of the powerful digestive enzymes produced by the pancreas. Banting thought that if he ligated the ducts of the pancreas he could eliminate the digestive enzyme secreting cells through atrophy. From the degenerated gland he could then try to isolate the internal secretion of the gland for treatment of diabetes.

Banting did not know and never acknowledged that a Rumanian, N. C. Poulesco, had just published his success in making a pancreatic extract with hypoglycemic effect. According to Bliss, Best misread the French article and therefore believed Poulesco had failed.

In April 1921, Banting asked J. J. R. Macleod, professor of physiology at the University of Toronto and an internationally known expert in carbohydrate metabolism, for facilities to experiment on dogs in ligation experiments. Macleod gave him space and gave him, as an assistant, Charles Best, a young biochemistry student. During Banting's first month Macleod advised and directed Banting and Best. He did not, as Banting later claimed, go away for the entire summer. Banting and Best made a great number of more or less successful experiments on dogs. By the end of the summer they were able to show that an extract, made from the degenerated gland, according to Macleod's instructions, could actually lower the blood sugar concentration in a dog made diabetic by pancreatic removal. Macleod, who had been in Scotland, learned of their success upon his return. He was interested, but felt that they needed better and more convincing data. Banting now suggested implanting degenerated gland tissue into diabetic dogs, but Macleod steered them away from this and told them to continue with extracts. Gradually during the fall, Banting and Best for lack of time started using increasingly less degenerated glands. Realizing that the internal pancreatic secretion is active in a fetus, while the digestive enzymes are not yet active, they started making extract from fetal pancreases (obtained at a slaughterhouse). Then, "on Dec. 8, they did a pancreatectomy on dog 35. Instead of throwing out its pancreas, they cut it up into slightly acid alcohol, macerated it, allowed it to stand for 48 hours. The solution was filtered, the alcohol was evaporated off in warm air current, and the dry residue redissolved in saline" (Quoted with permission from M. Bliss, 1982).[2]

The extract worked to lower the blood sugar concentration in a diabetic animal! No longer did Banting and Best need degenerated or fetal glands for extraction. In fact, degenerated glands had never been necessary. Paulesco used whole glands. It was at this point that Macleod permitted the highly qualified, well-trained biochemist James Bertram Collip to join the work. As pointed out by Bliss, Roberts's scathing criticism of Banting's idea and the two young investigators' haphazard studies was published in the *British Medical Journal* in December 1922. There was no reason to tie the ducts of the pancreas since the enzyme that would destroy insulin, trypsin, is present in an inactive form in the pancreas. It can become active after removal of the gland, but by using Macleod's suggestions of chilling the pancreas immediately and extracting the secretion with alcohol, the active secretion could be obtained.

Collip put his considerable skill to work trying to produce a purified extract. Sometime during the third week of January, Collip announced to Banting and Best, "Well, fellows I've got it." and to the great consternation of the two he refused to tell them how. The three men actually physically fought but fortunately Collip was not seriously hurt. As Bliss writes, a great deal of resentment had been building up between the players in the drama. One reason for this was that two weeks earlier, against the team's agreement, Banting had used his crude extract on a patient, and it had caused more harm than good. Banting had been seething with anger and resentment for a long time, as he felt that Macleod was taking the credit for his work. He bitterly resented it when Macleod spoke of the work using such terms as "ours" and "we." When the work was presented at a national meeting, Banting spoke so poorly that Macleod had to step in and answer all the questions for him.

Collip's extract was first given to a diabetic patient on January 23, 1922, with spectacular results. Then the clinical testing expanded to several other patients, while the experimental research in Collip's and Macleod's laboratories proceeded. Patients came out of diabetic coma. Emaciated diabetics were now able to metabolize carbohydrates and could gain weight. These results were unbelievable, a miracle. Arrangements were made for the Connaught Anti-Toxin Laboratories to cooperate in the production of the extract. The first successes were followed by a long, frustrating period during which the demands for the preparation increased while Collip and the Connaught Laboratories suddenly were unable to produce an effective extract. Finally, by mid-May, the group had recovered the ability to produce the extract, which they named "insulin." The major problem was that of acidity of the alcohol. At this time the Eli Lilly Company in the United States, who had long wanted to get involved in the manufacturing, finally convinced the Toronto group to give them a license. Lilly would supply the extract free of charge in the initial stages and later sell it at cost.

By the time the Kroghs came to the United States, a long series of failures and successes in insulin production had occurred in Canada as well as at Lilly. Krogh visited Macleod's laboratory November 23–25. He lectured on the capillaries and then the discussions about insulin got under way. In a ninety-page article, "Insulin, en Opdagelse og dens Betydning" (Insulin: A discovery and its significance) for the 1924 Festschrift for the University of Copenhagen,[11] Krogh wrote:

> I was received with the greatest kindness from all sides. I got an opportunity to see not only the insulin production and standardization, but in addition they reviewed for me the methods then used in treatment with insulin. I was invited to be present at meetings between clinicians, leaders of the insulin production and the insulin committee. At the time the difficulties in producing insulin from mammalian pancreas was very much on their minds since not only quantitatively but also qualitatively the insulin production left much to be desired. Prof.

Macleod felt that we in Denmark should try insulin production from fish pancreas, which in many regards was easier to work with and gave a cleaner product.[11]

Krogh was informed about the principles agreed upon by the Toronto Insulin Committee. (Bound by the Hippocratic oath, Macleod as well as Banting felt that insulin with its great benefits to humanity should be as widely distributed as possible and not be restricted by patents.) The possibility of losing the discovery, however, had seemed real, so a patent had been taken out in Banting, Collip, and Best's names, and then assigned to the Board of Governors of the University of Toronto (Bliss p. 133). The Insulin Committee said Krogh could take out a patent in Denmark and delegated insulin production control in Denmark to him. "This was not possible," said Krogh, because medicines could not be patented in Scandinavia. On the other hand, to ensure quality control of the product, Krogh maintained that absolutely he must have the exclusive rights in the three Scandinavian countries; he did not want to get involved in a race with other companies to market the extract. But Krogh told the committee that announcing his exclusive rights to the Scandinavian medical community and public would be a sufficient deterrent to possible competing enterprises. As we shall see, it was not enough.

The Kroghs returned to Denmark on December 12, 1922. The next day August met with Hagedorn and others to discuss the best way to proceed with production of insulin. The first step would be the intensive research that Hagedorn and Krogh would have to lead and mostly do themselves to become completely acquainted with insulin production and standardization of their product on animals. For this they needed money and decided they should approach a private company rather than the state. Negotiations with the state would drag out and valuable time could be lost. They turned to August Kongsted, owner of the pharmaceutical company Løven's Chemical Company, for whom Marie had made standardizations of digitalis in the past. Kongsted was willing to pay the expenses for the experiments and later, if they were successful, for starting insulin production.[12]

Now things were moving fast. A letter had arrived from Macleod giving details about insulin production.[13] Hagedorn and Krogh enlisted the pharmacist Norman Jensen. On December 21 the three produced the first insulin from shark and beef pancreas, and began experiments. During the Christmas holidays the work slowed down a little due to family obligations and lack of fresh glands. On January 2, 1923, August accepted an honorary membership in the Copenhagen Medical Society and gave his first talk on insulin. Following a review of the current knowledge of insulin's physiological effects, Krogh said, "I feel it is proper to put aside my own work, at least for a while, to promote this matter with the greatest strength possible." He spoke of his and Hagedorn's work and of Kongsted's involvement, adding:

> They [Løven] will pay the expenses for the preparatory experiments and commence the manufacturing as soon as possible. The price will here as in America be set as low as it possibly can. [It was essential to Krogh that no one should benefit economically from the insulin.] Naturally, I must warn you that it may take several months, possibly a whole year, before insulin becomes available to the clinicians. Great difficulties are associated with the production, and before it can be factory produced the necessary machinery and other materials must be procured. I ask you, however, to rest assured that we will spare no effort in as fast as possible producing a non-toxic and effective preparation in such amounts that the therapeutic use can begin.[12]

To evaluate the strength of their extracts, they had to use animals. Collip had injected his extracts into rabbits. When the blood sugar fell below a certain level, the animals went into convulsions, but the reaction could be reversed by the quick injection of a sugar solution. Thus, one insulin unit became the amount just sufficient to produce convulsions in a rabbit. In the limited Ny Vestergade facilities it was not easy to keep a large number of rabbits, and Krogh and Hagedorn decided to use mice. But something was wrong. The mice did not go into convulsions! They just curled up and became very quiet with backs bent and heads down. Then one day the mice were placed close to the stove that heated the laboratory, and lo and behold the mice went into convulsions! What had happened was that at the low room temperature customary in Denmark, the body temperature and metabolism of the mice fell as blood sugar decreased, and the mice went into something like hibernation. From then on the mice were kept warm in an incubator, and insulin injections caused convulsions just as in the rabbits.[11,14]

During January, as the intense work continued, the laboratory needed more manpower to replace Rehberg, who was to start work on his thesis research, and another assistant, Gad Andresen, who had left. Recalling this period at the hundredth anniversary of August Krogh's birthday, Professor Ditlev Müller recounted:

> It was by chance that I came to take part in the insulin work. Saturday, February 3, 1923 I gave my obligatory lecture for my magister conference. On the first row sat all the professors and Professor Krogh among them. . . . After my talk Krogh came up to me and said, "Come and see me on Monday, I have work for you." . . . I should inject white mice. A large glass thermostat was placed on a table and the mice sat in small glass cages on shelves. We should inject insulin and observe when they got convulsions. Then we gave them glucose right away. I don't think we lost a single mouse. Krogh came and talked with us. He was fabulous in dealing with numbers. . . . There was a specialist in diabetes, Sophus Bang from Kommune Hospitalet. He did not believe in insulin. One day he got one of the choreographer's [Ove Rasmussen,

Krogh's chemical assistant] very best preparations and gave it to a man in diabetic coma, because no harm could come of that. The man raised himself up in his bed, opened his eyes and looked at Sophus Bang! Never before had Bang seen anything like it! . . . Yes, it was two wonderful months. Never in my life have I experienced such intense, inspiring collaboration toward a common goal. Dear Professor Krogh, thank you![15]

Krogh soon found that there was not a sufficient supply of shark pancreas. Pigs in Denmark, however, were in plentiful supply, and were butchered throughout the year. An assistant posted next to the veterinarian who inspected each butchered pig could cut out the fresh pancreases and rush them in ice to the laboratory. But there were difficulties, because pig pancreas is rich in fat and contains a potent trypsin. Both difficulties were overcome by boiling the pancreas in alcohol before extracting the insulin. As Hagedorn and Krogh experimented with acid in the alcohol and with many other aspects of the production, they were able to get a considerably higher number of insulin units per kilogram of pancreas than with Collip's method.[11]

In March, as production increased, they moved it to the basement of Hagedorn's villa while the rest of the work stayed in Ny Vestergade. Because they used large amounts of pure alcohol, a government inspector occasionally checked the amounts. One day the inspector became quite concerned: a twenty-liter bottle was missing! "Then the professor must have drunk it!" said Hagedorn without looking up from his work. Krogh put a finger on the side of his nose and looking thoughtful said, "Has it been that much?" Soon they found the alcohol, thus satisfying the inspector.

These were hectic and also terrible days. Every day diabetics, especially young ones, died. Young diabetics lived an average of only one and a half to two years, while adults, like Marie, survived five to six years. People pleading for insulin telephoned Hagedorn and Krogh many times a day. But they had to harden themselves. Once a patient had been started on insulin they had to be sure there was enough to continue, even if the production should fail next week. They made many enemies as well as friends in those early days. Gradually during the spring of 1923, the insulin production increased. By June, Hagedorn and Krogh announced that they would be able to supply all that was needed to the hospitals as tablets of "Insulin Leo," that the patients could dissolve in sterile saline for injection.[14]

When Marie got her insulin, I do not know, but she was probably one of the first. Although there were still impurities in the insulin, causing local abscess when injected, it was an unbelievable blessing. Marie became very skillful in giving herself the correct doses, and we children never discovered that she was not completely well. In her purse she always carried a lump of sugar to take in case she should give herself too much and experience insulin shock. The diet Hagedorn recommended for a diabetic in those days was low in carbohydrates and sugar but high in fat and protein. We used to tease her that she ate the whipped cream off the pastries and discarded the rest, but we just thought that she liked it that way.

In October 1923, a pharmaceutical candidate, Thorvald Pedersen, who had recently completed his examinations, was hired to work with Hagedorn. He was the brother of the head machinist in Krogh's workshop at the Zoophysiological Laboratory, Harald Pedersen, a very able mechanic who had built many of Krogh's instruments for sale. He had also built a machine which shaved frozen pancreases. The shavings fell directly into ice-cold acid alcohol. In addition, the machinist's daughter was hired to help with the standardization in the laboratory.

But in spring 1924, Hagedorn had a fallout with Pedersen. (As Rehberg said, "Hagedorn could be very difficult well even Krogh could be difficult at times") The result was that Hagedorn fired Pedersen. Then the unthinkable happened. The machinist and his daughter left the Zoophysiological Laboratory to start producing insulin in their own cellar. The pharmacist had signed a declaration promising not to use what he learned in the laboratory for competitive purposes. The machinist and his daughter, however, had signed no such papers, and so learned from the pharmacist how to do it. The two Pedersen brothers, together with other family members, started producing insulin in 1925. From this beginning the now famous Novo Laboratories were founded.[14]

This was not the first time that someone from Krogh's laboratory profited from insulin. Krogh's former assistant Gad Andresen had started experimenting with insulin production after learning details in Krogh's laboratory. Andresen now owned a small company. A letter dated January 28, 1924, from Krogh to Andresen is still in the files. Other correspondence apparently was destroyed.

> Dear Andresen, I have with painful surprise learned that The Medical Company has taken steps to produce insulin. I believed that in my lecture I made it unambiguously clear that the right to do this had been given to me, but I see by rereading it that my pronouncement has not been as clear and categorical as was my intention. I believe that when you now learn the nature of the agreement that you will understand that The Medical Company cannot bring forth the insulin without breaking the rules of ethics normally adhered to in such matters and place me in a very awkward and unpleasant position with the public and the discoverer of insulin. . . .

Following an explanation of what went on in Toronto and his motives for bringing insulin to the Scandinavian countries, August ended with: "You will understand that when I have taken on this task, I should be able to expect that roadblocks are not placed in my way, and I think that I especially could expect it of you!"[16]

The matter did not end there. Not much was said in front of the children, but I recall discussions with reference to Andresen, whom I gathered was bad. The matter with the Pedersen brothers was also of some concern. Krogh wrote Macleod about it, and was told not to worry, they would never be able to produce as pure an insulin as Krogh and Hagedorn's.

The Pedersens and Gad Andresen were not the only ones producing insulin. In Norway insulin production had been tried and given up, and in Sweden a preparation named "Insulin Sal" was being sold. But according to Krogh it had many impurities. "It is not impossible," wrote Krogh, "that sharp competition will result, in that insulin production in the Scandinavian countries will come to an end due to the competition that will come from the factories in England and America with their large and secure home markets.[11] But insulin production did not come to an end.

In May 1923, Krogh and Hagedorn together with August Kongsted founded the first Nordisk Insulin Laboratory as part of Løven's Chemical Company. As a first step toward an export of insulin, they established an independent corporation for distribution of "Insulin Leo." In July 1924, the founders made Nordisk Insulin Laboratory an independent institution founded by royal charter, with Hagedorn as its director. As expressed by Jacob Poulsen, "Krogh's and Hagedorn's dynamic personalities, the fine combination of physiological and clinical insight and technical ingenuity they represented was determining for the quick build-up and development of Nordisk Insulin Laboratorium."[17] Thus insulin production flourished in Denmark, and in those years Krogh and Hagedorn's "Nordisk Insulin" produced insulin at a lower cost than anyone in the world.

On December 16, 1926, Nordisk Insulin Foundation was established with profits from the insulin production. The foundation's purpose was to support: (a) experimental scientific studies in physiology, and (b) clinical scientific studies in endocrinology and metabolism. The foundation was administered by a board of national and international scientists and directors of the insulin laboratory, with August Krogh as its first chairman (1926–31).[18] Then in 1932 Niels Stensen Hospital was established especially for the study and treatment of diabetes. The name of the hospital reflected the keen interest and admiration shared by Krogh, Hagedorn and Kongsted for the famous Danish biologist Niels Stensen (Nicolaus Steno).[19] The twenty-four-bed hospital was very advanced and luxurious for its time.

In 1923, Krogh recommended Banting and Macleod for the Nobel Prize "for the discovery of insulin and their exploration of its clinical and physiological characteristics." This was exactly the kind of discovery that Nobel had hoped to honor, Krogh felt—a discovery of great benefit to mankind. But he found it difficult to apportion credit for the work among Banting, Best, Macleod, and Collip, because the publications were the results of collaboration. The prize could not be given to four people. After much soul searching, he concluded that the prize should go to Macleod and Banting. Krogh reasoned that Best, as a young student assistant, had played a minor role in the discovery. Krogh wrote to the Nobel committee:

> According to the information I personally obtained in Toronto, and as it is contained in the publications, though not so distinctly, the situation is that credit for the idea unquestionably goes to Dr. Banting. He is a young and apparently very talented man. But he would surely never have been able to carry out the experiments on his own, which from the beginning and at all stages were directed by Professor Macleod. The other authors should be considered as Macleod and Banting's collaborators, but there is reason for special mentioning of the chemist J. B. Collip. He has made very important contributions in the method of producing insulin in a major practical way, beginning with the adult animal pancreas. But I do not think that is sufficient ground for the award of the prize.
>
> Macleod's special contribution in the experimental work has been only partly published at this time [January 31, 1923]. It is about locating insulin in the pancreas of several species of fish (and thereby proving the character of the hormone) and then exploring insulin's action on the total system and the respiratory quotient, and ongoing exploration of its action on carbohydrate metabolism—these all show clearly the action of the hormone, though as yet there is no explanation for its action.[2,20]

The Nobel committee also had difficulty in deciding. Two appraisers, John Sjöquist and J. C. Jacobaeus, were appointed to study the matter. Following a thorough investigation, both came to the same conclusion as Krogh: Banting had the idea and the initiative, but Macleod's guidance and knowledge were decisive for the final success. At the end, the Nobel committee voted for Banting and Macleod to share the 1923 prize for physiology or medicine.

Fred Banting, who for a long time had been telling other people what he thought and felt about Macleod, became livid when a friend called him by phone to congratulate him and told him that the prize had been awarded to him and Macleod. All he could answer was, "Go to hell." Then he saw the newspaper. Later he wrote:

> I rushed out and drove as fast as possible to the laboratory. I was going to tell Macleod what I thought of him. When I arrived at the building Fitzgerald was on the steps. He came to meet me and knowing I was furious he took me by the arm. I told him that I would not accept the prize; that I was going to cable Stockholm that not only would I not accept but they and that old foggy Krogh could go to hell. I defied Fitzgerald to name one idea in the whole research from beginning to end that had originated in Macleod's brain—or to name one experiment

that he had done with his own hands. Fitzgerald had no chance to talk.[2]

Eventually calming down, Banting did not take any of these drastic steps because he knew that the Nobel committee never changed or apologized for its decisions. Instead he gave half of his prize money to Best. When Macleod found out he donated half of his share to Collip. Neither Macleod nor Banting went to Stockholm to receive their prizes in 1923. To Macleod the Nobel Prize was a mixed blessing. In January 1924 he could no longer endure working with the insulin committee. He wrote Krogh January 15, 1924, "I have found it necessary to give up entirely all work in connection with this committee because it became by far too time consuming and was beginning to interfere seriously with my research work." He was still interested in the committee but did not attend any meetings.[21]

Because of Banting's anger and slander of Macleod, many believed that the Nobel committee had indeed made a mistake and that August Krogh was largely responsible for that mistake. Particularly damaging to Macleod was Banting's charge that Macleod had had no part in the experimental work; Banting and Best had worked alone in the laboratory all summer while Macleod was in Scotland. Banting forgot to mention, however, that Macleod helped and guided him in the laboratory for a whole month before Macleod left for the summer and after he returned. Banting also overlooked the fact (stressed by the Nobel committee) that at a crucial point during fall 1921, Macleod steered him and Best toward making extracts rather than using implanted panceatic tissue as a cure for diabetes. Had they followed their own idea, insulin would probably not have become available through their efforts.

Banting and Best became known to the public as the true discoverers of insulin. The hatred generated by Banting eventually drove Macleod away, and in 1928 he returned home to Scotland to become professor at the University of Aberdeen.

From the information available to Bliss, it becomes clear that the Nobel committee in 1923 did not make a mistake. Bliss writes, "Actually, given what happened in Toronto in 1921–22, and given the fact that the Nobel Prize could not have been awarded to insulin's four discoverers, it is hard to see how the Nobel Committee could have made a better recommendation than Banting and Macleod."

In Denmark the struggle that ensued with competing companies was also bitter, but in the long run it served medicine, science, and Denmark well. In 1989, with increasing competition from companies abroad, Novo and Nordisk Insulin merged under a new name, Novo Nordisk Pharmaceuticals, Inc. It has since become the largest producer of insulin and diabetes care systems in the world.

Mimi *(left)* **and** Viggo Krogh *(below)*, 1873.

Viggo Krogh with his firstborn son, August, 1877.

August and his siblings. From left: Johan, Edel, Misse, August, Emil, and Frida, 1886.

William Sørensen about 1885.

August as a student in Aarhus, 1892.

Professor Christian Bohr about 1894.

August working in Bohr's laboratory, 1900.

Marie (*left*) and August (*below*) at the time of their engagement, November 1904.

MK next to the respiration chamber in Greenland, July 1908.

The newborn Erik Krogh in the temperature-regulated box, 1908.

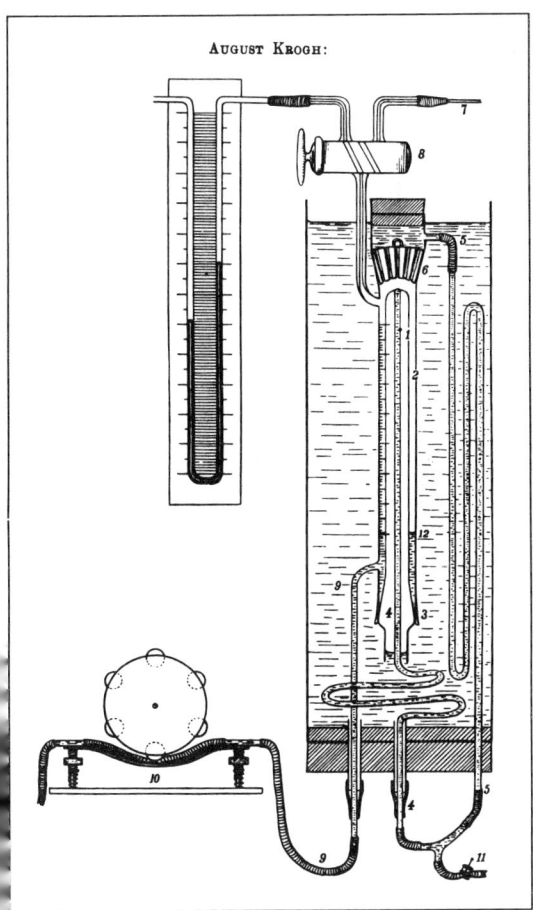

AK's modified Greenland tonometer.

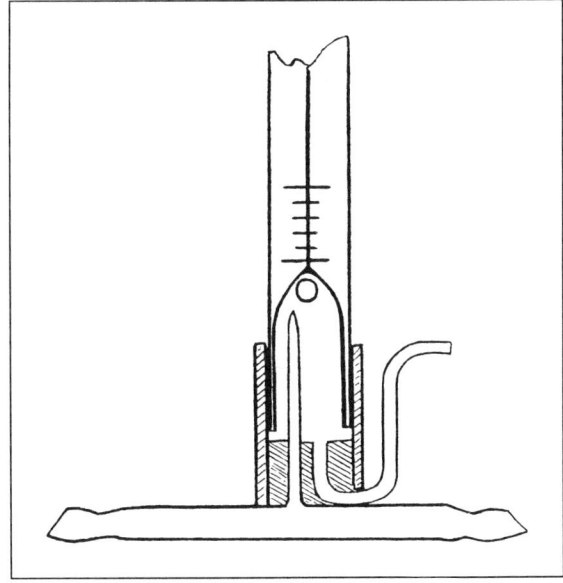

Microtonometer, to be inserted into a blood vessel of an animal.

AK writing at home, 1906.

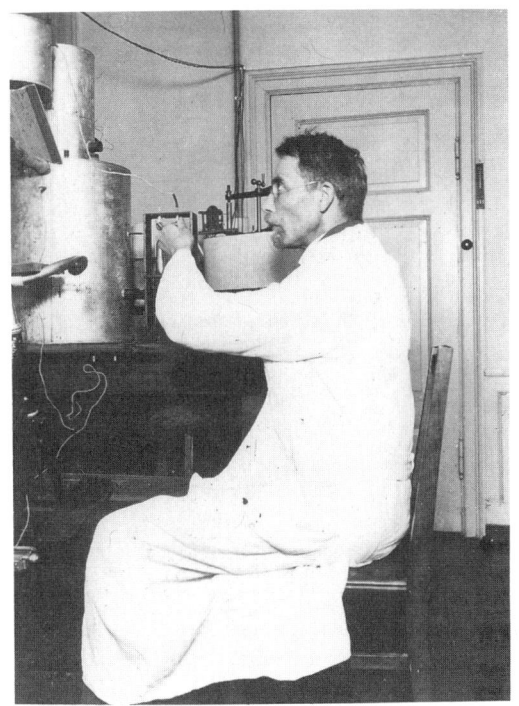 

(above, left) AK in his laboratory in Ny Vestergade about 1925. *(above, right)* AK and Johannes Lindhard on board.

MK defends her doctoral dissertation, 1914.

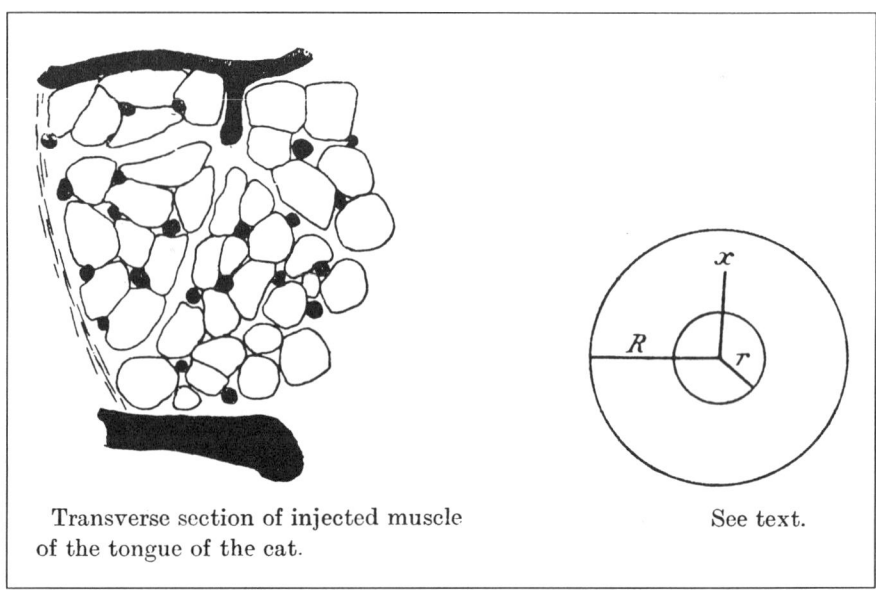

Illustration from AK's paper. *Left:* Transverse section of injected muscle of the tongue of a cat. *Right:* The diffusion distance for oxygen from a capillary with a radius r to the center of a muscle fiber.

AK the day after he got the Nobel Prize, October 1920.

(above, left) Christian Hagedorn about 1938. *(above, right)* Elliot P. Joslin (date unknown).

Francis Benedict in the United States, 1922.

MK at her desk in Ny Vestergade, 1924.

(above, left) Bodil and Agnes Krogh, "*de-to-smaa,*" about 1924. *(above, right)* Else Nicolaisen (Nic), later Mrs. Rahbek, about 1926.

The Krogh family at afternoon tea in the garden at the Rockefeller Institute, 1929. *From left:* Marie, Agnes, August, Bodil; *seated:* Ellen, Greta Kohl, Dagmar, and Erik.

The family in AK's sailboat in Lynæs Harbor, 1925. *From left:* MK, unidentified person, Agnes, Bodil, and AK.

The machine shop at the Rockefeller Institute, 1928.

The Physiological Institute, or the "Rockefeller Institute," as it was called, Juliane Mariesvej 26–34. The family lived in the villa to the left.

AK with his very accurate gas analysis apparatus, 1928.

MK in her laboratory at the new Rockefeller Institute, 1928.

AK and Cecil Drinker at Harvard University, 1922.

Eugene Landis in his laboratory at Harvard, 1929.

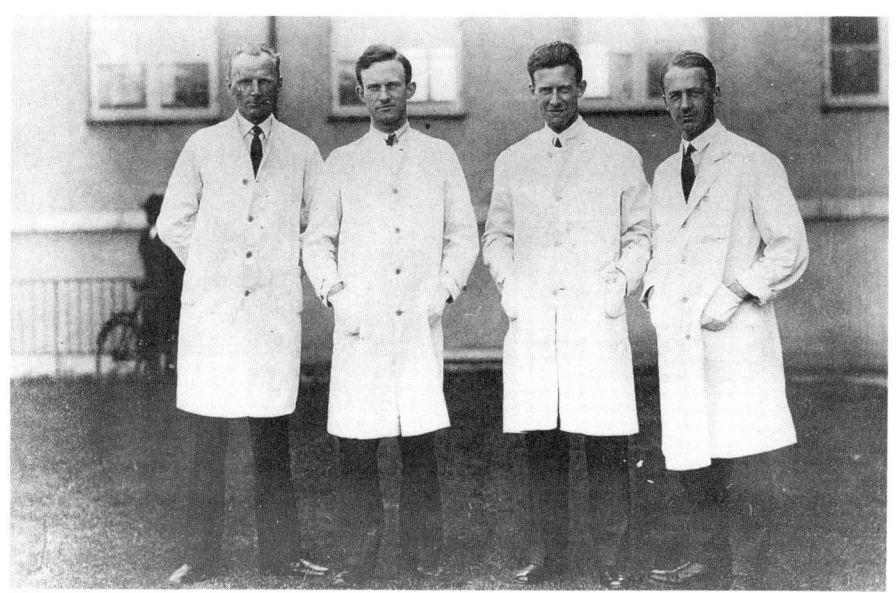

From left: Marius Nielsen, Ove Bøje, Holger Nielsen, and Hohwü.

(above, left) Erik Hohwü Christensen (Hohwü), 1933. *(above, right)* Paul Brandt Rehberg, 1935.

From left: Ellen, Bodil, Agnes, and Erik at the time of Marie's death, March 1943.

AK with Laurence Irving and C. L. Claff in Florida, 1946.

AK with Bodil and Knut in the Arizona desert, 1948.

Torkel Weis-Fogh with a locust, March 1949.

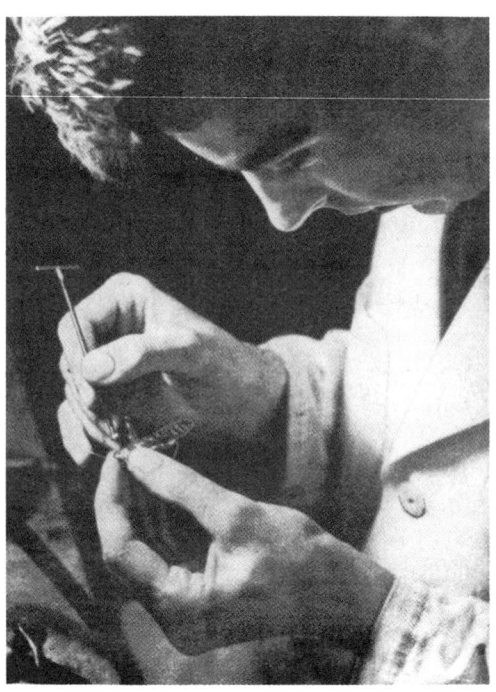

AK with the locust roundabout, March 1949.

13

The Happiest Years (1923–1938)

> Our gratitude shall be shown by work.

Returning from America, August turned his attention not only to insulin production and capillary physiology but also to getting a larger, better equipped laboratory. On January 10, 1923, he wrote a letter to Dr. Rufus Cole at the Hospital of the Rockefeller Institute for Medical Research in New York: "I take the liberty to approach you with a proposition which you will perhaps consider extremely preposterous. I am inclined to look upon it in that way myself but on the other hand it *might* be possible to take it seriously and I venture to believe that it would, if carried out, be of such value in furthering the study of experimental medicine that I feel justified in asking your opinion." He explained that the rooms in his present laboratory were few, small, and poorly lighted with no room for a library or even for a secretary, as they had to use every inch of space for experimental work. He regretted that there was never enough room for the American graduate students who wished to work with him. With improved laboratory facilities, he felt, it would be possible to increase, probably by 100 percent, "the amount of research work done in my laboratory without in any way lowering its standards. . . . I am now 48 years old. I am perfectly sound and expect to have about 20 years of useful experimental work before me. I believe that there is a fair chance that I shall repay in scientific work and in training of workers the outlay which it would require to put me in a position in which my capabilities for work could be utilized to the full."[1]

Cole referred Krogh to the president of the Rockefeller Foundation, Dr. George Vincent, who turned the matter over to the director of the Division of Medical Education, Dr. Richard M. Pearce. In a letter to Dr. Vincent April 17, Krogh emphasized the medical nature of many of his publications, but added: "I think it my duty to state expressly that my laboratory does not belong to the Medical School, but to the Science School and that I am not myself a medical man. I rely on the papers published from my laboratory to show that the objects of medical science have not been lost sight of in our work." Pearce was interested and visited Copenhagen during the summer. After his visit Pearce felt that "there was some question as to whether the division of medical education should handle it as a medical problem or the International Education Board as a general problem in biology."[2] He told Krogh that Dr. Wickliffe Rose, director of the latter board, expected to visit Copenhagen sometime in March 1924 and looked forward to meeting Krogh.

Krogh's request had actually struck a highly responsive note; the Rockefeller Foundation and the newly created International Education Board were involved in "A Scheme for the Promotion of Education on an International Scale." The inspired Rose had declared to the International Board, "Promotion of the development of science in a country is germinal, it affects the entire system of education and carries with it the remaking of civilization." Rose's guiding principle for the board was:

> Begin with physics, chemistry and biology. Locate the inspiring productive men in each of these fields; ascertain of each of these whether he would be willing to train students from other countries; if so, ascertain how many he could take at one time; provide the equipment needed, if any for operation on the scale desired. Provide by means of fellowships for international migration of select students to each of these centers of inspiration and training; students to be carefully selected, and to be trained with reference to definite service in their own counties after completion of their studies.[3]

In Rose's belief one of the most promising places was the University of Copenhagen. In addition to the truly great theoretical physicist, Niels Bohr, it included J. N. Brønsted in physical chemistry and August Krogh, both of whom enjoyed worldwide renown and attracted graduate students from many countries.

What resulted from Krogh's discussions with Rose, Pearce, and Simon Flexner, director of the Rockefeller Institute was a plan of far bigger scope than Krogh's original proposal. Rose was particularly interested in improving education in physics and chemistry, along with physiology, and plans for a comprehensive physiological center consisting of five separate institutes were drawn up. The rector of the University of Copenhagen, Dr. Torm, and Dr. Valdemar Henriques, Christian Bohr's successor as professor of medical physiology, joined the discussions. Krogh and Henriques drew up plans that were in turn supervised by two committees, one from the Faculty of Medicine and one from the Faculty of Science. With so many people involved the plans soon reached the press, where the prospect of a new Physiological Institute, due to a large gift from the Rockefeller Foundation, was announced in May 1924.

On June 28, 1924, Krogh, and Professors Henriques and H. M. Hansen submitted an informal plan to Dr. Pearce. The complex would house five institutes: (1) medical physiology, Chief Professor V. Henriques; (2) biochemistry, Chief Professor R. Ege; (3) zoophysiology, Chief Professor A. Krogh; (4) exercise physiology, Chief Professor J. Lindhard; and (5) biophysics, Chief Professor H. M. Hansen.

According to Danish university customs, the institute would house the residences for the professors, their assistants, and the caretakers, in addition to laboratories, lecture rooms, and so forth. This became a sticking point because, as Pearce wrote Rector Torm, "It is not the policy of the Foundation to take care of such items."[4] However, after Krogh's intervention the foundation gave in.

At a meeting of the Rockefeller Foundation on November 7, 1924, it was resolved that the foundation would pay $300 thousand for the building and equipment of a Physiological Institute in Copenhagen, while the rest would come from the International Education Board and private Danish sources (The Carlsberg and Rask-Ørsted Foundations). At the same time a grant was made to enlarge Niels Bohr's institute. Four years later a third grant was made for the construction of the Institute of Physical Chemistry.[3]

Now the work on the institutes began in earnest. To Krogh it meant that he could finally design a laboratory with all the special features he had envisioned. The laboratory had to be connected directly to his villa, so that he could continue his habit of going to his laboratory in his old dressing gown at seven in the morning to work undisturbed for two hours before anybody arrived. This created a serious architectural problem as the other professors felt that there should be free and unhampered circulation for the students around the complex. Following numerous memoranda and much discussion Krogh prevailed: the two villas, Henriques's and Krogh's, were attached to their laboratories through connecting hallways, and passages were made for the students to ride their bicycles under these hallways. In the Kroghs' house the connecting hall became a charming area where Marie kept her plants.

When all was settled concerning the various institutes, the total area for Krogh's was considerably smaller than that given to the other professors. Asked why his facility was smaller than the others he answered candidly, "I want limited space, as an excuse to say no to people I don't want." The quality of the work in his laboratory would decrease if there were too many students and visiting scientists at any one time. The laboratory area was increased from 300 square meters in the old Ny Vestergade building, to 850 square meters in the new institute. There was now space for ten guests in addition to the four permanent scientists: August and Marie Krogh and two scientific assistants.

While a large laboratory was not important to August, the design of the laboratory was all-important. With tireless enthusiasm he personally designed every room, making detailed drawings of all four walls. Benches and tables were made of parts that could be moved easily and placed in new ways according to experiments in progress. On or in the walls were all the piplines and basic services needed for a physiological laboratory. "These facilities were more convenient and efficient than any that I, at any rate, had seen before," wrote Landis.[5]

To avoid clutter in the rooms, all storage cabinets for glassware and other supplies were placed along the walls in the halls. A new design for dust-free rooms for instrument storage, which Krogh invented, was used, but it did not function well because inferior materials were used in the construction. Later, his concept was successfully used in the new university library.[6] To insure good lighting in his laboratories he measured the trees in Nørre Alle and calculated the shade they would cast at different times of year.[7]

In the cellar a large workshop was equipped with all the necessary machine tools for construction of his instruments for use in the laboratory and for sale to the national and international scientific community.

To make it possible to work on many kinds of animals, stables, terraria, and aquaria were built next to the laboratory. To guarantee a large, year-round supply of ice, an underground room was constructed in the front courtyard. It was Krogh's intention to have ice cut from the lakes and stored in sawdust, as his father had done at the brewery. Unfortunately, the project failed. The first year all the ice quickly melted, because pipes carrying steam from the heating plant at Rigshospitalet to the new institute were placed right next to the ice chamber!

Construction of the institute had taken longer than anticipated, but by January 1928 August moved into his new space and the family took possession of the beautiful new villa. The long hours spent in planning were over and August could again concentrate on the experimental work. At the entrance to the Zoophysiological Laboratory a marble plaque commemorated the Rockefeller Foundation gift. The inscription ended with the words, "Our gratitude shall be shown by work."

With a healthy Marie by his side, August was a happy, cheerful man with limitless energy and enthusiasm. In spite of his intense work schedule, he always knew how to organize his time and he loved children, all children. As far back as I can remember, my father was always willing to read to us, play with us, and talk with us. Whenever one of his children said something particularly clever or intelligent, August would ceremoniously extract one small coin (one øre) from his coin purse and reward the child with it. This was such a special honor that the coin was cherished as if it were a medal. Personally unassuming and not given to pomp and ceremony, he did not want his children to become conceited. Once Erik came home from school after a heated argument with another boy about whose father was more important. Erik asked his father, "Which is more prestigious, to be a professor or a chimney sweep?" To Erik's chagrin, his father promptly answered, "a chimney sweep."

It became a ritual that August would read aloud to his family after dinner on Saturday nights. Marie sat across from him mending clothes. (Belonging to the first generation of liberated women, Marie's sewing skills were rather rudimentary.) He read *Just So Stories, Puck of Pook's Hill, The Jungle Book,* and many other wonderful tales, translating into

Danish as he read. Often as he read, his emotions showed and tears ran down his cheeks.

August read widely and had an impressive library, but among all the authors Kipling was the one he valued the most. He felt deeply in the author's debt for the many hours of delight and pleasure he had received from Kipling's stories. After Kipling's death, August wrote an article in Danish titled "Rudyard Kipling: Some Words of Appreciation."[8] He had read what Pearl Buck had written about the enormous influence that the reading of Dickens had had on her life and understanding of people and it made August wish to express his own gratitude for Kipling: "But what must be easy for a writer, such as Pearl Buck, becomes very difficult for one who has never used his pen to express feelings, but only to present facts, and the only way out will be to translate the feelings into facts and try to make it clear to myself and eventually to others what it is in Kipling that has made such an impression upon me, widening my horizon, and moving me so deeply."

He felt a certain kinship to Kipling, his hard work, his vivid imagination, and his avoidance of public adoration and national honors. The great extent of Kipling's knowledge in so many different fields never ceased to delight him, as did Kipling's use of words and phrases from other languages and former times. August often traced such expressions to their source and always found them correct. The internal logic of Kipling's stories, which was not always obvious at the first reading, appealed to him and made him read and reread them. Kipling's genius for expression made him remember and frequently quote Kipling.

August found that the greatest and deepest in Kipling's writings was the understanding of human nature which they revealed. He was well aware that Kipling's understanding was limited to "healthy and distinctly virile" types whom Kipling shed light on through their words and actions. But in these types August often saw himself or others he knew.

It has been said of August Krogh that he saw people in terms of black and white, with no shades of gray between these poles, that his attitude toward people was frequently determined by a first impression or by some reaction to what a person had done. It is true that if he had reason to mistrust someone, he was through with that person, forever. As William Sørensen had done, he judged people by their character, applying the same motto: "Ultimately, everything depends on character." Krogh was not one for compromises. When he wished to further a course such as improving the working conditions for himself or those he believed in, he would often bring the situation to a head. "To those who benefited from it, it felt like a breath of fresh air—they did not mind . . .—but at times it met with strong opposition from other quarters."[9]

Those who became Krogh's friends remained so forever, and he spared no effort to help them. Among his and Marie's many close friends, none were closer than Adam and Anna Bøving. An extensive correspondence between the two families bears witness to the warm feelings they shared. They stayed with us in our summer home in Lynæs and in Copenhagen while visiting Denmark in 1925, 1929, and 1934. When Bøving's son, Bent, was severely scalded, August worried about him as if he were his own, and later he took great pleasure in Bent's academic achievements. On each of August's and Marie's five visits to the United States between 1922 and 1939, they arranged to visit with the Bøvings either in Washington or to have the Bøvings meet them in Woods Hole, Massachusetts. "We cannot think of being in the States and not seeing you," wrote August.[10]

When Adam Bøving in 1933 described to August how difficult and depressing his working conditions were, August got together with some of Bøving's friends in Denmark and the United States. Together they arranged for an invitation to Bøving to lecture at the University of Copenhagen and for a leave of absence from the Smithsonian Institution in 1934. Adam Bøving's touching letter to August and Marie after his return to the United States speaks for itself:

> When I think back on the two best months in my entire life and now write to thank both of you for what you have done for us, then I feel as a boy who wishes to let his parents feel how devoted he is to them.
>
> You understood what I am capable of and you helped me to come to Denmark so that I could see all my old friends again. But most of all I am grateful for the unspoken goodness toward me that I felt in your voices and the expressions in your eyes, in the little words and kind movements, that more than anything else reflect the mindset. When we were sitting in the living room and you read to us while Agnes patted your hair and Bodil stroked her mother's hair, or when you jested with Bent, or when I saw your's and Mrs. Krogh's eyes meet in understanding and satisfaction, then I was no longer a guest in your house but I belonged in the home.[11]

The day of the Bøvings' departure, my sister Agnes and I were granted leave from our school to see them off at the train station. Ellen and Erik had also shown up. As the train was pulling away and gathering speed we ran in our rubber boots as fast as we could with it. Bøving wrote: "Greet the flock of young people. What an elegant farewell they gave us. Hurrah for the lightning speed with which they ran following the moving train to the very end of the platform. It was a sight and a memory that can never fade.[11]

August instilled in his children the love of good books. If any of us were sick in bed, he would leave the laboratory briefly in the middle of the afternoon to come to our bedside to talk, read a story, or lend us a book.

At Christmas, he selected a good book for each of his children, while mother took care of all the other gifts. The lighting of the Christmas tree took place on Christmas Eve right after the traditional Christmas dinner of rice porridge followed by roast goose with red cabbage and brown potatoes. In Ny Vestergade we would sit in his study (the "green room") in total darkness while our father, behind the closed door leading to the living room, lighted the candles on the tree. He and our mother had decorated the tree earlier that day and none of us were permitted to see it before it was lighted. Finally, he would light a sparkler and open the door widely to the oohs and aahs of his admiring family.

On Sundays when the weather was good and during the summer vacation, he would take us on walks or outings in the woods or fields, teaching us about plants and insects. I remember he taught us to try to hold a dung beetle in a closed fist. The dung beetle always won, clawing and squeezing its way to freedom between our little fingers.

Long before the Kroghs could move into the new residence at the Rockefeller Institute,[12] they bought a bigger summer house to accommodate the large family, August's parents, and many other guests. This was made possible by the Nobel Prize. The house was in the fishing village Lynæs on Issefjord about fifty miles northwest of Copenhagen. Several factors led to this purchase: the area around Solrød had become crowded, the family needed more space, and August wanted to sail again. As a fourteen-year-old boy he had sailed with the Navy training vessel *Hauch,* on Issefjord and found it beautiful. Now his friend from the Greenland days, the polar explorer Knud Rasmussen, introduced August to an excellent boatbuilder, Christian Madsen, who lived near Lynæs Harbor. Rasmussen himself had a home north of Hundested. August and Marie first purchased a lot on Issefjord and arranged to spend the 1923 summer vacation with their children at a *pension* in Lynæs, while August's boat was built. In the meantime the Kroghs loaned the Solrød house to Marie's brother Jørgen and his family.

The *pension* was a beautiful villa, Lynæshus, on a hill overlooking the fjord and a grassy commons where the fishermen dried their nets. Facing the commons was a row of small houses belonging mostly to fishermen. Christian Madsen's boatyard was there. He mostly built the Lynæs fishing vessels, which by then were quite famous for their grace and efficiency. August had commissioned Madsen to build a sailboat and a dinghy of solid oak. It was an open spritsail-rigged boat with a half deck. Now while the family stayed in the *pension,* August visited the boatyard to talk to Madsen and follow the progress of his boat.

In the meantime, Marie learned that Lynæshus was for sale. She longed for a bigger and more elegant house for her own family and the visitors she would like to entertain. The house she had grown up in was a typical Danish farmhouse with tiny rooms, and she abhorred the darkness and dampness which had contributed to the tuberculosis in her family. She settled on Lynæshus, with its large airy rooms, vine-covered loggia, entry hall with marble floor, and impressive staircase reaching through three floors. There were plenty of bedrooms and a large kitchen and bathroom with imported Dutch tiles. Best of all, the master bedroom had its own balcony overlooking the commons and the sea. There was also a terraced garden, a pond planted with waterlilies, a stone grotto, many fruit trees, and lovely flowering shrubs and flowerbeds. The only blot on the beautiful view was an ugly house, which Marie claimed she would like to buy so that she could blow it up.

August took up sailing on the fjord with his family and friends. On one long expedition to the southern end of Issefjord, we became becalmed and all the children had to help row all the way back to Lynæs.

At the harbor our family rented a space on the westerly pier to build a small bridge leading to a bathhouse with stairs down to the water. There we would bathe and sun ourselves. Our father taught us to swim by holding on to an oar from the boat and we were soon strong swimmers. August himself would row out early in the morning to swim from the dinghy, a habit he kept up all his life.

The fields and woods around Lynæs were full of mushrooms and August taught his children to recognize the edible and the dangerous mushrooms. The fly mushrooms (amanitas) are particularly dangerous, but a few among them are edible and even good. One day August and Marie picked some of the edible kind, *Amanita rubescens,* and experimented with eating them, while we children watched and prayed that they would survive.

The following summer, 1925, Viggo developed pneumonia. It soon became serious and on July 27, he died. August picked a waterlily from the pond and placed it in Viggo's casket. Mimi became very lonely and aged rapidly after the loss of her lifelong companion. Daily, during the two years she lived after Viggo's death, August walked to Gunløgsgade to visit with her.

In March 1923 a young woman, later known to us all as "Nic" or affectionately as "little Nic," entered our lives. Nic, together with her husband and son, came to play an important role in August's life.

In 1922 and 1923, Erik's health had continued to be poor and he was far behind in his schoolwork. It was important that Erik, now fourteen, pass the middle school examination. Marie had hired an older woman to read with him to bring his skills up to level, but Erik disliked the woman, nicknamed her "Trissen," and said she had a mustache. So Marie advertised in the newspaper for a new teacher for her son. A young woman, Else Nicolaisen, daughter of a restaurant owner, read the announcement and applied for the position. She was only eighteen and had long corkscrew curls. To look older for the interview, she pinned up the curls in a tight knot and borrowed her mother's fur collar. Miss Nicolaisen had expected to meet a severe-looking scientist, but what she saw was a beautiful, feminine lady in a lovely dress. Marie, with her mild manners, soft voice, warm smile, and intelligent face made such a strong impression on the young applicant that she never forgot it. It was love and respect at first sight. While they talked, Erik, a tall, ungainly boy with straight, very blond hair, came in and threw himself into a chair to get a good look at his prospective teacher. He liked her; he liked her a lot. She was young and sweet. Marie liked her, too, and Miss Nicolaisen was hired. Marie never even asked her age.

Nic was a born teacher and under her able and loving tutelage, Erik's knowledge rapidly improved. In June he passed the middle school examination with flying colors. Nic continued to read with Erik for the next three years until he finished school (with the *preliminær examen*) to study forestry.

The fact that Nic came into the family had other far-reaching consequences for the Kroghs. Marie liked to have her children spend as much time as possible in the country. The air in Copenhagen, with every home using coal stoves, was unhealthy. We children used to call Copenhagen "the coal bin." The fumes and coal dust in the air may well have contributed to Erik's many bouts with pneumonia and pleurisy. When our parents had to go back to work in Copenhagen after the summer vacation, they had often left us in the Solrød summer house with a maid and cook to watch over us.

Agnes had started school in the fall of 1923. She was not happy in school and often complained of headaches. Having seen how well Erik took to Nic's teaching, Marie resolutely took Agnes out of school before the second grade to be taught by Nic. A year later when I was ready for school, Nic became the teacher for us both. Having a private teacher for *de-to-smaa* ("the two little ones," which we were always called) also meant we could remain in the summer house not only during the school vacation, but continuously from May through September. Then only the two older children were at home in Copenhagen, and Marie had more time for them and for her work. She did not care as much for the constant company of young children as August did. She was happier with us as we grew older.

In Lynæs, Nic and a housekeeper took care of our needs, while Marie with Ellen and sometimes August would come out to the country house on weekend visits during spring and fall. The prolonged stays in the country gave us freedom few children experience. We roamed around in the woods and along the shore, and we were permitted to take out the dinghy at any time we wished, without asking permission from anybody. We sometimes got into difficult situations with high waves and strong wind, but we learned from our mistakes and became strong and self-reliant. I have often wondered how my parents had the courage to trust our judgment, and I am sure that it was August who talked Marie into letting us have this freedom. It was also August who insisted that the children not be unnecessarily bundled up. We should be hardened by being lightly and comfortably dressed.

When we were old enough to go to balls at our friends' houses, August told Marie that she should trust us and not lie awake to hear us come in. This was not a license to do as we pleased, but a specific trust in our judgment, which we appreciated and honored.

I have always been grateful for my Mother's wisdom in letting us have a private teacher, and especially the gifted and loving Nic. It gave us genuine pleasure in learning and free time to pursue our own complicated and involved games and enterprises unfettered.

In my own memory, this time stands out as glorious and carefree as we grew up in an atmosphere of love, guidance, and understanding from both of our parents. These years were also some of the most fertile in the laboratory as new fields opened up and were explored.

In 1929, August Krogh was invited to deliver the opening address, "The Progress of Physiology," at the XIII International Congress of Physiological Sciences in Boston. He who was so used to writing and talking about scientific data was nervous about the prospect of giving a formal welcoming address and almost refused the invitation. Ultimately he gave in and traveled to New York with Marie and Ellen, then sixteen, on the famous "*Minnekahda* voyage" to the United States. Before his death in 1927, Ernest Starling had suggested that a ship be chartered to take the European physiologists participating in the congress across the Atlantic. A. V. Hill arranged for the charter of S.S. *Minnekahda,* a triple-screw steamer, sailing under the U.S. flag. It was booked for about four hundred physiologists and their families, who embarked in Tilbury in the Thames Estuary on August 9, 1929, for New York and Boston. With the war well behind them, the reunion of all the European scientists was exhilarating, and the experience on board appeared to many "like a voyage in Wonderland."[13]

As always, Marie enjoyed the party atmosphere far more than August did. Y. Zotterman, who wrote about the trip, commented: "I sat beside Marie Krogh, a charming and witty lady with an M.D. degree who took a very active part in her husband's respiratory experiments. Her Danish as well her English was much easier to follow than that of the famous August Krogh. They were accompanied by their lovely young blonde daughter Ellen." The reason Zotterman had trouble understanding August could well have been August's habit of mumbling. This was also the reason that he did not care for big meetings, but enjoyed himself much better in small groups. When he was invited to the one hundredth anniversary of the University of Chicago in 1933, he told Bøving: "I cannot say that I look forward with great enthusiasm to my stay in Chicago. I am afraid that it will be too overwhelming with respect to outside experiences and I don't believe that the atmosphere will be particularly favorable for scientific discussions or informal conversations."[14] But in smaller groups of scientists where he could exchange ideas, he enjoyed himself greatly.

August and Marie had made numerous friends among the scientists of all ages who came to work in the laboratory. As in the past, Marie's hospitality knew no limits. Foreign scientists and students of every nationality—Russians, Chinese, Japanese, English, German, Belgian,

The Happiest Years 149

French, Finnish, Norwegian, Swedish—were all welcome guests at our home at family gatherings as well as at more formal occasions. Two guest rooms for foreign visiting scientists, on the third floor of the laboratory building, were always occupied. Carl Schlieper, Eugene Landis, Madeleine Field, Abby Turner, Ancel B. Keys, Henri Koch, and numerous others used them. Marie saw to it that they would feel at home in Denmark and invited them for dinner with the family every Sunday night. The files from those years are full of letters from visitors expressing their gratitude and frequently saying that their time in Copenhagen was the happiest in their lives.

Marie's warmhearted kindness was not limited to the academic circles, but extended to all with whom she came in contact. A couple of little boys in Lynæs were poorly nourished so Marie arranged and paid for milk for them throughout the year, and when one of them needed eyeglasses she paid for those too. She arranged for her brother's son Erik Varn, whose mother had died in childbirth, to live with us during the years he studied law in Copenhagen. Marie also tried to make life easier for August's nephew, Johan, who was neglected and rejected by his father, Emil, because his mother, Sofie, had tricked Emil into having the child. When the child was born, Emil did not break up the marriage, but moved out and took a mistress.

Marie also treated her maids with kindness and consideration and helped their families with money, clothes, and other necessities and she continued to help her mother's maid, Trine, who had retired to Copenhagen.

Marie's patients apparently adored her, as her files are filled with letters from grateful patients asking for all kinds of personal advice and telling her how greatly she had helped them. Professor Starling once wrote August that he would like to be sick in Copenhagen, just to have Marie as his doctor. Even store owners took a special liking to Marie. Every day after lunch, prior to her consultation time, she had long, pleasant telephone conversations with the baker, the green grocer, the grocery store owner, and the butcher to find out what was freshest and best that day. Then she ordered what she needed and her orders were brought to the kitchen door by an errand boy on a bicycle.

To us children she was generous to the point of spoiling us. We would shop with our mother for the best fabrics, which a seamstress made into pretty new dresses and coats. Two new ball gowns every year was a must, because of the many balls we attended. Our mother treated us to hot chocolate and creampuffs when we shopped with her. Since August did not like the theater, she invited one or two of her daughters to accompany her to plays, ballet, or opera, whenever she went. When we wanted to give a party mother helped us make it as festive as possible. August usually disappeared into the laboratory when he heard dance music. He disliked music intensely, and when he wanted to go to bed he retired to the bedroom that had double doors to keep out the noise. But Marie stayed with the party. Often some of the young men would sit with her, preferring her company and intelligent conversation to dancing. Then we, in our young selfishness would say, "Mother, why do you keep the nicest young men from dancing?"

Marie sometimes helped us with our schoolwork and always put the commas in our essays. Every morning before we went to school, she personally made our sandwiches and saw to it that we got a proper breakfast. She even helped us find boys among the sons of her colleagues to ask to our balls. She rarely got angry with us. I recall being spanked only once when I was little and being ordered to stand in my mother's closet among all the coats and dresses a few times when I had been naughty. But mostly Marie was very forgiving. One time, she had invited us out for strawberries and cream in Jordbær Kælderen (a little restaurant) on Strøget. While waiting to go, Agnes and I, much against the rules, played ball in the living room. The inevitable happened; we broke one of Marie's favorite lamps. Crestfallen, we confessed, but were right away forgiven and, much to our surprise, taken out for strawberries anyway. When asked if she wasn't spoiling her children, Marie would answer, "the good they are getting now nobody can take away from them."

Every afternoon, Marie would leave her laboratory and come over to the villa to be with us as we returned from school. Then we had afternoon coffee or tea with her as we were served a fresh-baked, homemade bread. The bread was baked by the maid, according to Marie's own special recipe, which called for ten times the normal amount of yeast to make the bread especially high in vitamin B. Marie had experimented with this recipe and published the results together with Thyra Hansen from the School of Home Economics, where Marie taught. On our dining-room table there was always a bowl full of fresh fruit from which we could help ourselves freely. When Nic was still teaching us, Marie instructed her in how to get a vitamin-rich diet. One time Nic, worried about getting sufficient vitamin C, asked Marie to analyze a urine sample for her. Laughing Marie returned from her laboratory, saying, "Little Nic, you are getting so much that several people could live from it!"

Just before Marie's fiftieth birthday in December 1924, she was interviewed by Mrs. Loulou, the same reporter who had found August on the night his Nobel Prize was announced. Mrs. Loulou wrote: "It is very dangerous to be married to a famous person. That is an experience many women have had. They can be ever so intelligent or beautiful—the fame throws its shadow over them, and they are not themselves, they are their famous husband's wife." But the reporter added that Marie Krogh was nevertheless known and valued for her own sake. "Mrs. Krogh is a distinguished and amiable lady, the hair parting softly above a pair of intelligent, mild, brown eyes, her demeanor has its own quiet dignity, bordering on shyness. Her modesty is real and it is only by getting her to talk about her research, that we can make her speak about her own achievements."[15] I myself think that much of the reason for Marie's productivity and ability to remain her own person can be attributed not only to her own determination but also to the respect for her work and constant love that August gave her.

Marie had continued to do her research, teaching, and seeing patients in spite of her illness (before her diabetes was brought under control) and four active children. She taught physiology and nutrition to future teachers of home economics and gave lectures in various towns and on the radio. She was becoming quite famous in Denmark for advocating a healthier diet including vitamins, milk, fresh fruit, and vegetables for pregnant women, schoolchildren, and the general population. She pointed out that 33 percent of young Danish men were rejected for military service due to bad posture, curvature of the spine, varicose veins, and other defects caused by nutritional deficiencies, and she showed that schoolchildren were in similarly bad condition. In her laboratory, Marie carried out animal experiments on effects of vitamin deficiencies and continued work on biological standardization of drugs.

Marie was so universally loved by those who knew her that we found it highly amusing that the medical students were afraid of her and nicknamed her "Marie the Bloody." This was because Marie was a censor at the examinations in physiology for medical students. During the examinations, Marie, in deep concentration, would sit with a stern look upon her face, a look that made the students believe that she was severely critical of their performance.

Marie's laboratory in the new institute was next to August's, and could be reached from the villa by going through his. In the villa, Marie's mahogany desk stood in the living room in front of the antique cherry bookcase (from August's great-grandfather, brewer Andreas Krogh). Here she would write in the evening while we were doing our homework in our rooms upstairs, but she was ready to let us disturb her, whenever we wanted. The open door behind her let into August's study and he, too, would come to her when he needed to talk.

Around 1930, Marie entered into a fruitful collaborative study of the thyroid gland with the histologist Harald Okkles. This was a natural outgrowth of her clinical and experimental studies of the regulation of metabolic rate and her studies with standardization of medical preparations. Their collaboration resulted in a series of publications on the histology, physiology, and pathology of the thyroid. How she found time to do her work I do not know, but she did get behind as papers piled up.

Whenever she was giving lunch or dinner parties she took the unsightly piles of papers downstairs into her office and consultation rooms. There a series of many piles were left along the wall on a low shelf, to be sorted out later.

I don't think August ever helped Marie arrange the parties given for his colleagues, and sometimes he was even slightly aggravating when he failed to understand all that Marie was doing. There was the time when a foreign scientist of minor importance was invited for lunch. The table was full of delicious, expensive, beautifully arranged dishes. The man felt overwhelmed and deeply honored that this elaborate lunch had been put on for his sake and told Marie so, but August promptly deflated the poor man by saying, "Don't worry, these are only leftovers from our big dinner party last night."

In 1930 Marie was awarded Tagea Brandt's Rejselegat, a travel stipend in the amount of ten thousand kroner, an honor bestowed on outstanding Danish women, with no other obligations than to travel, and to travel comfortably. Marie wished to see the subtropics, and she and August decided to take a month-long trip to the Canary Islands in January–February 1931. Marie also wanted to give her two youngest daughters a new experience. At the time we had never been outside Denmark. August went with us, paying for his own trip. Agnes and I were then fourteen and twelve, respectively, and we were permitted to miss school for the length of the trip, because of all the new things we would see and learn. We traveled by train to Bremen. While we visited the wonderful zoological garden in Bremen, I was standing next to my mother, as she looked with keen interest at a huge walrus. Then she said, "he looks just like Professor ———." It seemed that the walrus didn't appreciate the comparison, because it made a tremendous splash that drenched my mother. I can still see her standing laughing in her bedraggled fur coat.

In Bremen we boarded a German ship bound for Madeira and the Canary Islands. We stayed on Tenerife in an idyllic little town, Guimar, where we were the only guests in a small German *pension*. Later we stayed in an English hotel on Grand Canary. While we were enjoying all the new sights, Marie keenly observed the nutritional condition of the native children. Their bone structure was good, with no signs of rickets and Marie concluded that the plentiful sunlight gave them sufficient vitamin D, but their stomachs were protruding badly due to protein deficiencies. From the Canary Islands we sailed on board a White Star Line luxury ship to London with stopovers in North Africa. While in London, our father showed us museums and the many sights that he had loved since he had first seen them thirty years earlier.

Early summer 1932 Erik (twenty-three) and Ellen (nineteen) both passed the *studenter examen*.[16] Ellen graduated from high school and Erik, who had studied forestry, had taken a special course to study for the exam. There he met a young woman named Dagmar Albrechtsen, to whom he soon became engaged. In the fall Erik and Ellen both started medical studies at the university.

In July 1932 Marie used the rest of the Tagea Brandt award money to travel to Italy with Ellen to attend the International Congress of Physiological Sciences. August had refused to go due to his dislike for and great mistrust of Mussolini's Fascist government. He was afraid of Mussolini, he said. Marie, always thinking of her children, shared her award

The Happiest Years

money to make life more interesting and educational for her three daughters.

As her children were growing up, Marie realized that Lynæshus would no longer serve the family's needs. On some of her many trips to America, Marie had seen the beautiful summer estate belonging to the Forbes family on the Elizabeth Islands near Cape Cod. There several generations could visit and have their own houses. Marie wanted her children to have the same opportunity so that they could continue to vacation in the same spot after they had families of their own. When a small, seven-acre farm in St. Karlsminde, a short distance from Lynæs, came up for sale, August and Marie bought it and put Lynæshus on the market. It is a beautiful piece of land with an old-fashioned thatched-roof farmhouse on it. Located on the shore of Kulhusrenden, an arm of Issefjord, it has a view over the water and the land around Issefjord. Steep clay cliffs lead to the shore, where August kept his rowboat and the family swam in the fjord. Thus, since 1938 it has been the family compound where the Krogh clan gathers for vacations.

14

Capillary Function and the Contractility Controversy (1923–1936)

> Rehberg has succeeded in my laboratory in demonstrating with absolute certainty the folding of the endothelium in strongly contracted capillaries.

While August was waiting for the new institute to be built, work continued in his small laboratory. The capillary book resulting from his Silliman Lectures had become an instant success. At an Alfred Benzon Symposium in 1969, Eugene M. Landis said, "Very few books yielded as prompt and as widespread stimulation of research as this monograph did when it was read by histologists, physiologists, pathologists, and clinicians."[1] In the foreword to the 1959 edition of Krogh's capillary book, Landis wrote:

> "It was written in a style, much more freely, much more *con amore* than his other books. He seems to be an artist painting a canvas of ideas in minutest detail wherever possible, but still willing with large brushstrokes, or even with exploratory pencil sketches to let the picture evolve fully rather than omit any challenging theoretical or practical implication. This is the reason for its provocative eliciting, from others, researches designed to amplify, test, or modify specific propositions."[2]

Although Krogh expressed numerous new ideas and observations, he did not have time to delve deeply into the literature at the time he wrote the first edition. It had to be ready when he arrived in America, but in the next edition (1929) this was remedied.[3] Actually, he had not researched the literature completely before he did the capillary experiments, following his own principle, which he later related to me: "Don't hamper your imagination by reading all the literature first. Do the experiments and then read the literature." Ulrich Ebbecke from Germany wrote him shortly after the publication of Krogh's first capillary papers. Krogh had missed Ebbecke's papers because of the war, but he became deeply impressed with Ebbecke's work, partly because Ebbecke, like himself, did not stop at collecting data, but thought about them and interpreted what he had seen. In the capillary book he wrote: "In 1917 Ebbecke published his paper on the local vasomotor reactions in skin and internal organs, the outcome of several years' observations and deep thinking. . . . I shall have to refer to it very often in the course of these lectures."[4] Ebbecke and his family soon became close friends of the Kroghs.

Several of Krogh's collaborators and most of the visiting scientists worked on problems connected with capillary function, while others worked on insulin and diabetes. Richard Ege[5] was studying respiratory mechanisms in insects as a continuation of Krogh's work with insect trachea, and another Dane, Th. B. Wernøe,[6] studied nervous control of capillaries in fishes. Rehberg worked with Krogh part of the time, but was mostly occupied with his own studies of kidney physiology. He was the only one in the laboratory who had his own room. Three Americans, Cecil Drinker, Edward D. Churchill, and A. Newton Richards shared one laboratory room in 1926–27. Drinker and Churchill developed a new injection method for capillaries and studied the effect of Pituitrin (an extract of the posterior lobe of the pituitary gland) on circulation and capillary permeabilities in the frog.[7]

Because Krogh was particularly interested in the exchange of fluid and substances between the capillaries and the tissue fluids, he, together with the Japanese scientist Fusakichi Nakazawa, developed a micro method for measuring colloid-osmotic pressure.[8]

Krogh's interest in capillary contraction led him to study the effect of pituitrin upon the capillaries. It is now known that the extract contains the vasoactive hormone *vasopressin*. In 1895, Oliver and Schäfer had reported that intravenous injection of this extract caused increased arterial pressure. Subsequent experimental results by these authors and by Howell led to the conclusion that the hormone acted on the peripheral circulation. Krogh and Rehberg now observed that the application of the extract caused contraction of the capillaries in the web of a frog's foot.[9]

The young Danish physician Bjowulf Vimtrup carried out anatomical work on the capillaries. Using histological techniques available in the 1920s, Vimtrup examined sections from frog tongues and tadpole tails suitably fixed and stained. He must have been a superb histologist because his descriptions (published in 1922 and 1923) of the cells surrounding the capillaries,[10] are almost identical to those given by authors in the 1990s, who have based their observations on modern scanning and electron microscopy. Vimtrup described richly branched cells closely associated with the capillaries. On the outside of capillaries, Vimtrup found certain nuclei slightly but distinctly different from ordinary endothelial nuclei. The form of these nuclei varied with the state of the contraction of the capillaries. When he stained the protoplasm with trioxyhematein in vitro or with methylene blue in vivo he could see how the branches encircled the capillary, like arms hugging the wall.

Vimtrup named them "Rouget cells," after the man who had first described them.[10] The cells are now called "pericytes," a name given by K. W. Zimmermann in 1923, who like Vimtrup was explicit about the muscular nature of the cells.[4,11] The most recent descriptions of pericytes are identical to Vimtrup's. Also the distribution and the gradual transition from muscle cells on the arterioles to Rouget cells, or pericytes, on the capillaries is the same in Vimtrup's paper of 1922 and Sims's papers of 1986 and 1991.[11]

On the arterioles Vimtrup found every stage of transition between normal, spindle-shaped muscle cells with an elongated nucleus and others with an oblique nucleus and the protoplasm split up into several ramifications. "These latter become more numerous on approaching the capillaries and there is no sharp distinction between them and the richly branched cells characteristic of the capillaries," wrote Vimtrup in 1922.[10] In 1991, Sims wrote, "When found on arteriole and venules proceeding toward capillaries, smooth muscle cells undergo gradual changes in shape that result in distinctive pericyte morphology."[11]

Vimtrup found that the Rouget cells contained fibrils in the protoplasmic branches which stained similarly to smooth muscle cells and concluded that the fibrils represent the contractile elements of the cells. In recent years this has been rediscovered with modern techniques. According to Sims, pericytes contain dense bands of filaments both near the nucleus and in the peripheral extensions of the cytoplasm (protoplasmic branches). The filament bundles contain actin, myosin, and tropomyosin, which are the molecules associated with cell contractility in both smooth and nonsmooth muscle cells.

Vimtrup also observed contraction of the Rouget cells. In his taperecorded memoirs, Rehberg told about the time in the 1920s when a steady stream of visitors came to Krogh's laboratory.[12] Rehberg often had to interrupt his experiments to demonstrate the capillaries. Then frequently Vimtrup would point to a place on the capillary and say, "There lies a Rouget cell outside the capillary wall." Rehberg recalled: "Nobody but Vimtrup was able to see it clearly, but when I electrically stimulated the place Vimtrup had pointed to, the cell contracted and the long threads of protoplasm were clearly seen to contract around the capillary. The observers would call out 'it gets legs, it gets legs' as the capillary was contracted by the Rouget cell."

When the Rouget cells contracted, the investigators observed a wrinkling of the capillary wall. Vimtrup and Bensley observed longitudinal folding of the endothelium, which could best be seen on venules. "This object can be recommended to any skilled microscopist who wishes to convince himself of the reality of the activities of Rouget cells," wrote Krogh in the capillary book, "Rehberg has succeeded in my laboratory in demonstrating with absolute certainty the folding of the endothelium in strongly contracted capillaries. When a capillary is watched under high power during the contraction, the formation of folds can be very distinctly seen. Occasionally the folds protrude into a red corpuscles which can be squeezed out into very strange forms."[4]

One of the many visitors to the laboratory was Queen Elizabeth of Belgium. She appeared unannounced, accompanied only by a lady-in-waiting. The daughter of a physician, the queen was an intelligent and well-educated lady who was especially interested in physiology. August interrupted his work to show her around, and explain his work. Then he took her to Rehberg who was doing an experiment and quickly mumbled something that Rehberg didn't understand. Rehberg, thinking she was a rich American lady with no understanding of physiology, was slightly irritated when he started to explain his work. But the lady asked questions—intelligent questions—and Rehberg began to enjoy the conversation. When he had finished, the lady-in-waiting stayed behind and whispered, "Do you know to whom you were talking? It is the Queen of Belgium." Rehberg was shocked.[12]

August then took the queen to Marie's laboratory. He knocked on Marie's door and when Marie opened it, he tried to introduce the guest. Busy and preoccupied, Marie did not hear what he mumbled. So she quickly closed the door on the queen saying that she had no time for visitors just then. Because an experiment must not be interrupted, August and the queen politely withdrew. Marie, on the other hand, was mortified and more than a little annoyed with August when she later learned in whose face she had closed the door.

The queen of Belgium was not offended by the casual way in which she had been received. After the new Rockefeller Institute was built, she announced another visit to the Zoophysiological Laboratory in the company of the Danish queen, Alexandrine. This time Marie was well prepared for the royal visitors. The villa was sparkling clean and Marie had bought two beautiful bouquets of flowers for Agnes and me to present to the two queens.

When they were first published in German, Vimtrup's findings were not generally accepted. In fact, Vimtrup had difficulty getting his papers published in English.[13] Neither were all of Krogh's findings and ideas accepted, which was particularly true of the independent contractility of the capillaries and the contractile, pericapillary cells, the Rouget cells, described by Vimtrup.[14] In all editions of his capillary book (the last in 1936), Krogh wrote with great conviction that he and other investigators had proven that the capillaries themselves show independent contractility and he cited numerous experimental findings supporting his view. One piece of evidence was that if he scratched along a small vein with a hair or a fine glass needle (in his experimental setup he used a frog tongue), "A small branch [capillary] opens up and is filled with blood, which becomes stagnant. By continuing the stimulus in front of the column of stagnant blood the relaxation is carried further, the blood flows slowly on in the direction from the vein, and at last connection is established with an arteriole, resulting, of course, in a sudden onset of current in the opposite direction, toward the vein."[4] This, of course, could only happen if the capillary had been contracted prior to the stimulation.

Were Krogh and Vimtrup right about the Rouget cells? The controversy had started in 1925, when "the Clarks, while studying the development of Rouget cells on the sprouting capillaries of very young tadpoles, came to the conclusion that certain cells which they assumed to be identical with Vimtrup's Rouget cells . . . were entirely devoid of contractility."[15] In Chicago, Robert R. Bensley worked with Vimtrup as well. He, too, observed the contraction of the Rouget cells. In December 1927, he wrote Krogh:

> In this field the only way to acquire confidence in experimental results is to do them oneself, and the chief difficulties that the theory has met in the literature has been due to discussions raised by observers who were not experimenters. The observations by the Clarks in this country are not so easily disposed of though I am convinced that they have not appreciated the fact that not all perivascular cells are Rouget cells. Their observations raise the question of independent contractility of the endothelium itself.[13]

In 1935 Zweifach concluded that the endothelium itself (the cells of capillary wall) acted as the contractile element and that none of the pericapillary cells played any part in the contraction of the capillaries.[16] Clark and Clark reached a similar conclusion in a 1935 review paper. It is probable that these papers induced Krogh to reinvestigate the problem. In 1936 two Americans, Madeleine Field and Henry K. Beecher, had joined him in the new laboratory. Field studied capillaries in several membranes in frogs and rats,[15] while Beecher studied capillaries in the ear of a rabbit.[17] Both found two types of capillary contraction, one caused by contraction of the Rouget cells, the other by the increase in size of the nuclei of the endothelial cells. The first type of contraction resulted in narrowing of the outer diameter of the capillary as its wall was creased by the contraction of an external force. The second type caused a narrowing of the capillary lumen through the enlargement of the nuclei bulging into the capillary.

Beecher, after giving a talk at a symposium in Memphis "On Mammalian Capillary Contractility" wrote Krogh, "Clark and I were each supposed to speak 20 minutes. I said what I had to say and sat down. Clark arose and spoke for 50 minutes almost entirely on capillary permeability . . . can it be that he is getting cold feet on his earlier stand on contractility?"[18]

But the scientific world was not convinced and the "Rouget cells" virtually disappeared from the scientific literature. They are now exclusively called pericytes and the question concerning their effect on capillary contractility is still being debated. Sims writes, "That they contract is no longer in dispute, however, the in vivo conditions that lead to contraction and the effects of pericyte contraction have not been thoroughly established."[11] Krogh and Rehberg continued to believe in the existence of the contractile Rouget cells, but this view was not shared by the scientific community in general in their time. Later capillary studies (particularly those of Chambers and Zweifach), using techniques not available in Krogh's time, indicated that single capillaries were controlled by precapillary sphincters (smooth muscle cells) and that blood can bypass the capillaries by moving through a thoroughfare or metarteriole.[19] For the next thirty years this view became the established dogma.[14]

Science, however, moves in its own mysterious way: sometimes forward, sometimes backwards, sometimes standing still. Once more it has moved forward as new and still better techniques have been developed. For example, studies using electron and scanning electron microscopy have revealed that pericytes are abundantly present on all capillaries and that in many cases pericytes, and not smooth muscle sphincters, control the arteriolar-capillary junction.[20] Over their entire length, all capillaries are encircled by numerous pericytes with long protoplasmic extensions ("legs" as Rehberg's spectators called them). At the same time the existence of the metarteriole is being questioned.[21]

Can the pericytes make the capillaries contract, as Krogh and Vimtrup said? They contain abundant contractile filaments and the creasing and contraction has been observed by some investigators recently. However, Vimtrup and Krogh's seventy-year-old proposal that pericytes contract the capillaries is still being debated!

Rehberg's study of kidney function was a direct outgrowth of the capillary studies. While Krogh was in America for the Silliman Lectures, Rehberg and Hagedorn were studying the permeability of kidney glomeruli and appearance of protein in urine in renal disease. Through these studies Rehberg became interested in measuring how much fluid was filtered by the glomerular capillaries, and he designed a method for measuring it. With this method, he gained important new insights into the function of the kidney tubules. At the time, Rehberg's method, using creatinine as the glomerular substance, was the most accurate measurement technique available.[22]

Among the visitors to Krogh's laboratory during this time were two outstanding kidney physiologists, E. K. Marshall, Jr., of Johns Hopkins University and A. Newton Richards of the University of Pennsylvania. Krogh knew Marshall from his visits to Abel's laboratory in Baltimore, and he had corresponded with Richards since 1918. Marshall had shown that the organic dye Phenol Red is actively secreted into the kidney tubules, but Rehberg did not believe in secretion. Richards, the pioneer in micropuncture studies of the kidney, sampled glomerular filtrate directly. He visited Krogh's laboratory for several months in 1927. Krogh's friendship with Richards was warm and long-lasting. Richards rejected Marshall's ideas and published a paper in which he tried to explain the obvious secretion of the dye into the kidney tubules as diffusion only.[23]

It is interesting that, although they accepted active transport out of kidney tubules, both Rehberg and Richards refused to believe that active secretion into the tubules could occur, even to the point of seriously misinterpreting their own findings. It was Marshall who proved beyond a doubt that organic dyes are actively transported into the kidney tubules of dogs and in aglomarular fish, but his proofs were not generally accepted until much later and failed to convince Rehberg for several more years.

In September 1930, when the new Zoophysiological Laboratory in the Rockefeller Institute was in full operation, Eugene Landis arrived in Copenhagen from the University of Pennsylvania. Two other students from United States arrived at about the same time, Ancel B. Keys, from the University of California at Berkeley, and Abby H. Turner, from Mt. Holyoke College in Massachusetts. Landis came warmly recommended by Richards, having already published several outstanding papers on capillary pressure. Landis wrote: "Each of us students had a separate room. Nevertheless, each of us also had the privilege of working literally elbow to elbow with Professor Krogh himself on at least one research problem, in addition to whatever we might be doing ourselves."[1]

Krogh took an active interest in all of the work in his laboratory, greeting each person as he or she arrived in the morning and talking with them during the day. Landis's initial conversation with Krogh took place within a few hours of his arrival. Landis writes:

> Professor Krogh began his conversation with a consideration of Starling's hypothesis. Ever since its publication in 1896 this had been highly attractive as a theory, but was still an induction based upon a few compelling, but indirect experiments. Even in 1930, quantitative data were limited to few studies on dogs and a few frogs. The first question Professor Krogh asked was whether in man capillary blood pressure could be high enough to explain filtration of fluid other than those that had been measured in the lower extremities during quiet standing on a tilt table. Under these conditions venous pressure in the legs, and hence local capillary blood pressure there, was exceptionally high and obviously capable of producing filtration. But what, he asked, occurred in other tissues and when venous pressure was normally low?[1]

Krogh suggested testing the Starling hypothesis in a number of ways and said; "would it not be interesting to measure capillary blood pressure and filtration rates in the trans-illuminated ear of a rabbit and in the frog mesentery." As Krogh continued to propose more and more ideas, Landis felt that this brief meeting had produced enough ideas to keep Turner and him busy for *a long time.*

As Turner and Landis got under way with the experiments, they found that none of the problems was easy. But as the Danish satirical poet Piet Hein had written, "Problems worthy of attack, show their worth by fighting back."

> And these problems did fight back, but Professor Krogh continued to suggest solutions for each complication. Almost every forenoon at about ten he would visit each of us in our respective laboratories. After a friendly handshake he would listen with obvious eagerness to our progress. He was pleased by successes, but I formed the impression that he enjoyed discussing difficulties just as much or perhaps even more. He would also transmit his own new thoughts on results, methods or research possibilities that had occurred to him overnight. Obviously, the laboratory, its people, and their research was always in his thoughts.[1]

Krogh's laboratory was "a cozy place," as Rehberg expressed it, with great camaraderie among all of the investigators, including Krogh. Every afternoon at three, coffee was served in the aquaria room, accompanied by lively scientific or political discussions. Sitting on the rack above the aquaria, Rehberg would often talk politics. Krogh, sitting on a laboratory bench, would discuss science or politics with equal interest. Anybody who had a birthday was obliged to give Danish pastry for the occasion. If one of us in the Krogh family had a birthday, the whole crew from the laboratory came over to the villa for hot chocolate with whipped cream and a huge birthday "kringle" (a large, pretzel-shaped Danish pastry). The socializing resulted in stimulating conversations, enhancing rather than hampering the productivity of the laboratory. Although Krogh contributed intellectually to all of the work carried out in his laboratory, he refrained from putting his name on papers resulting from studies in which he had not actively participated.

Sometimes when Landis was working late in the evening he could hear Krogh coming through the connecting hall from the villa, "to visit, chat a bit and often invite me to his study to share his evening coffee or chocolate. There conversation would meander from science to literature, languages, authors, personalities, humor and idioms of the day."[1]

Landis and Turner's research during one year in Copenhagen resulted in a series of important publications in 1932.[24] Landis's outstanding work on capillary pressure and exchange of fluid between capillaries and tissue won him international recognition and a professorship at Harvard University. The two were like members of the Krogh family and Landis learned to speak Danish quite fluently. I was only twelve years old then, and it flattered me that Landis liked to practice his Danish by speaking with me.

Many questions concerning capillary circulation and regulation still remained unanswered after Krogh in the mid-thirties turned his attention to problems in other fields. Krogh's suggestion that oxygen supply and demand in the tissue is a major factor in regulation of capillary circulation in working muscles gained general acceptance. To see the possibility of an autoregulated system with the oxygen pressure as an important factor was, to some, his major contribution to capillary physiology.[14]

As Krogh had told Barcroft in 1920, his work in capillary physiology, which had won him the Nobel Prize, was a promising beginning, but much remained to be done. In spite of the huge amount of work on microcirculation in the more than seventy years that have passed since then, it is still true that much work remains to be done.

In 1969, fifty years after the publication of Krogh's first capillary papers, an Alfred Benzon Symposium was held in Copenhagen on "Capillary Permeability: The Transfer of Molecules and Ions between Capillary Blood and Tissue." At the symposium, no fewer than six modified versions of Krogh's capillary-tissue cylinder model were presented.[25]

Even today, seventy years after Krogh's early publications on capillaries, his work is persistently quoted in the literature as the basis for capillary research. There is no doubt that the enormous interest in capillary function that occurred after 1922 was stimulated by his research and books. A new field had been opened wide.

15

New Fields of Investigation (1928–1943)

> Physiology does not go forward as an ordered line of battle on a continuous front, but must be carried on, . . . as a guerrilla warfare against the unknown conducted single-handedly or by quite small units.

Now that he finally had the perfect laboratory, it was as if Krogh's creative energy had been given free rein. In addition to the lines of study that continued to occupy him—circulatory physiology, insulin and diabetes research, comparative physiology of respiration, and exercise physiology—in the thirties Krogh embarked on several new fields: dissolved organic substances as food for aquatic animals, osmotic regulation, membrane physiology, and isotopes in biological research.

Krogh had told the Rockefeller Foundation that the new laboratory would make it possible to pursue several scientific problems at the same time and would double the amount of work done in his laboratory without in any way lowering the standard. What an understatement! The amount of pioneering work that came from the Zoophysiological Laboratory in the 1930s was astounding. Eugene Landis has expressed his admiration and appreciation of Krogh by quoting from Gilbert Highet's book, *Man's Unconquerable Mind:*[1]

> There are men who express the age and the milieu in which they were educated but who, by the intensity of their imagination, the sweep of their knowledge, and their astounding versatility, rise high above their era and their neighbors so that they inhabit both time and eternity at once. When we analyze their minds we can identify nearly all the component elements tracing this to family and that to school and the other to social climate, and yet the compound is far more than the sum of all these elements; richer, intenser, different in quality as diamond is different from carbon.

Wanting to accomplish a great deal while still strong and vigorous, Krogh found it necessary to economize his time. For many years he had steadfastly refused to serve as *decan* (head) of the Science School, even though the refusal caused more than a little animosity toward him from the other professors. Then in 1935, he applied for and got dispensation from lecturing at the university. In his place Rehberg, as newly appointed lecturer, took over.[2] Only occasionally did Krogh lecture to university students, but he continued to give yearly demonstrations and lectures in physiology to all students in Copenhagen gymnasium (high schools, which prepare students directly for the university and correspond more or less to the first two years of a U.S. college) and special lecture series to scientists.

In his teaching of university students, Krogh had made a clear distinction between future gymnasium teachers (cand. mag.) and researchers (magister conference). He taught the future teachers human physiology, primarily, which he felt was of more practical use. At the first lecture, Krogh would announce that the students need not go to his lectures; if they learned better by reading for themselves, he would not hold it against them. Unfortunately, as one of his student's put it, he was both the only lecturer with this policy and also the only one really worth listening to.

Undoubtedly influenced by Marie's great interest in nutrition, Krogh said in an address delivered to the American Academy of Arts and Sciences in 1939:

> I would like to have the fundamentals of nutrition introduced as a subject in all lower schools—at least in the cities. While it is no doubt true that the instinct of children could guide them to a right selection of natural foods, this does not hold at all in the highly artificial environment in which most children are brought up; and they should learn for their own sake and for that of future generations something about food values and the effect of stimulants in common use. I would also, on principle, include in the curriculum for all adolescents the elements of sex physiology, but how far this is practicable must depend on local conditions.[3]

In 1934 Krogh wrote a compendium, "Grundrids til forelæsninger over Menneskets Fysiologi" (Ground plan for lectures in human physiology).[4] The textbook he had written for students in the gymnasium also dealt exclusively with human physiology. It was published continuously, in ten editions, from 1908 to 1946, always updated to include new findings.[5] After several attempts to have it translated into English, the book was finally published in America, revised and edited by Katherine Drinker in 1932.[6]

For the magister conference students, a comprehensive course in zoophysiology was started in 1919, but mostly they were taught in Krogh's laboratory through an apprenticeship. There were rather few such students, because Krogh never encouraged anybody to become a scientist. To the contrary he discouraged it, because he felt that only a few had the calling and talent for a career in science.

Although Krogh stopped formal teaching outside his own laboratory, he continued to be an inspiration to many who came to see him for advice. Rehberg relates:

> For many years it was easy to come and talk with Krogh on scientific matters; nobody was refused an interview. In later years, however, Krogh found it necessary to economize with his time—so many things were left for him to do—and therefore he asked visitors to look for advice elsewhere. But if one was admitted, an interview took a very special course. First Krogh asked the visitor to talk about his problem. In the beginning he sat listening with his head somewhat bowed to the side and a scrutinizing glance in his eyes. Then he asked a single question, more questions, and somewhat later, maybe some hours later, he would start speaking, and if his interest had actually been awakened he was generous with his time. He then gave his advice, whether to continue or to stop, whether there was a practical way to go, and where it led.
>
> Not all who came understood that it was a good thing to follow his advice; maybe some actually did not want to learn, but would rather have had their own ideas confirmed, while others may have assumed that Krogh did not understand their problem as profoundly as they did themselves. Therefore they went away angry because he had not approved of their ideas. Many of them certainly regretted that they had not listened to him and relinquished a plan. Krogh's intuitive judgment of whether a goal could be reached in a given way was fabulous even in fields remote from his thoughts. This capability was also of enormous value in his own work. Beyond doubt there are few scientists who initiated so many diverse problems and yet were able to successfully complete so many.[7]

Most of those who looked for advice were scientists, physicians, or teachers. But one day Denmark's chief rabbi came for help. Animal protectionists had objected to the Jewish slaughtering ritual, *shechita*, which is carried out by cutting the neck in one stroke after the animal has been thrown down with its legs tied. Because the knife used by the rabbi was extremely sharp, and because the heart continued to pump, the animal lost consciousness instantly as blood drained from it depriving its brain of blood. The method used was probably more humane than that used on pigs in Denmark, but the authorities agreed with the activists, and a solution had to be found. How could the animal be anesthetized without making the meat unclean according to Mosaic and Talmudic law? August recalled from his youth that well diggers entering deep wells at falling barometric pressure became unconscious and died, apparently without feeling anything. He had solved the mystery: the air that seeped out of the ground into the well had become oxygen free. Now he suggested a method for using oxygen-free air (nitrogen) to anesthetize but not kill the animal just before its throat was cut. Later Krogh and Erik Hohwü Christensen experimented with the nitrogen anesthesia on themselves, registering no discomfort as they gradually lost consciousness. In a modified form, using nitrous oxide and nitrogen, the method worked on cattle, satisfying all concerned, without conflict with the Jewish ritual.[8]

In his 1929 address *"The Progress of Physiology"* at the XIII International Congress of Physiological Sciences in Boston,[9] Krogh found the opportunity to express many of his own strongly held convictions. He was not altogether pleased with the way science was conducted, often without the deep thinking that he himself employed in all of his work. He deplored what he had read in a recent book of instructions for medical writers, which stated that what was needed in scientific papers was facts and again facts and still more facts. "I venture to disagree emphatically with this statement. Facts are necessary of course, but unless fertilized by ideas, correlated with other facts, illuminated by thoughts, I consider them as material only for science. I am prepared to submit the thesis, revolting though it may seem, that too many experiments and observations are being made and too little thought is bestowed upon them."

Krogh was also emphatically against organizing science. In the same address, he voiced his protest against a proposal to "organize" physiology, even though in his younger days, he had thought this might be useful:

> I imagined a central laboratory, to which all new methods could be submitted for testing and from which only the most reliable and quickest methods would emanate. I see clearly now that all such schemes are dreams. They can never be realized and should never be realized if it could be done. The individual freedom is our chief asset, the mainspring of the really new ideas, the guarantee of progress. Physiology does not go forward as an ordered line of battle on a continuous front, but must be carried on, . . . as a guerrilla warfare against the unknown conducted single-handedly or by quite small units.[9]

These statements won applause in the United States, where E. C. Rosenow from the Mayo Foundation wrote expressing how heartily he agreed, adding, "Your own great accomplishments and your wonderful spirit as I learned to know it during the series of Mayo Foundation lectures, you gave here several years ago, I shall ever regard as expressions of the individual freedom which you, as every true scientist, must cherish as a priceless heritage."[10] (Too bad that in this day and age these sentiments seem to be partly forgotten!)

Krogh suggested the creation of laboratories of comparative physiology in the science schools and a close cooperation between them and the zoology departments. He added: "In my opinion a general physiology which can describe the essential characteristics of matter in the living state is an ideal to which we may hope that our successors may attain after many generations, and I want to emphasize that the route by which we can strive toward the ideal is by a study of the vital functions in all their aspects throughout the myriads of organisms." And he stated what Hans Krebs later called the Krogh principle:

> For a large number of problems there will be some animal of choice or a few such animals on which it can be most conveniently studied. Many years ago when my teacher, Christian Bohr, was interested in the respiratory mechanism of the lung and devised the method of studying the exchange through each lung separately, he found that a certain kind of tortoise possessed a trachea dividing into the main bronchi high up in the neck, and we used to say as a laboratory joke that this animal had been created expressly for the purpose of respiratory physiology. I have no doubt that there is quite a number of animals which are similarly "created" for special physiological purposes, but I am afraid that most of them are unknown to the men for whom they were "created" and we must apply to the zoologists to find them and lay our hands on them.[9]

But his love of comparative physiology was best expressed when he said: "I want to say a word for the study of comparative physiology also for its own sake. You will find in lower animals mechanisms and adaptations of exquisite beauty and the most surprising character. . . ."

While the capillary work continued, Krogh, returning to his original interest in lower animals, took up his private "guerrilla warfare." He began an investigation of dissolved organic substances as food for aquatic organisms which in turn led him into studies of ion transport, osmoregulation and use of isotopes in biology. It started through a chance observation by a young scientist, Ragnar Spärck, who worked in Krogh's laboratory during the twenties. Spärck was interested in growing oysters commercially in Danish waters. In 1926, while studying the effect of temperature and food sources on the growth of larvae and adult oysters, Spärck noticed that starved oysters became so weak that they could no longer close their shells. However, if he added a small amount of sugar to the water the oysters regained their strength. It seemed that the oysters might be able to take up sugar directly from the water.[11]

The problem interested Krogh. August Pütter, in 1907-9 had pointed out that there were simply not enough of the necessary plankton organisms in ocean water to serve as nutrition for the seawater protozoans, while, on the other hand, dissolved organic substances were found in very large quantities and could serve as food for the aquatic animals. Pütter's work was much criticized and Krogh felt that it was time to reinvestigate the problem with better and more accurate methods than those available to Pütter. Working alone and undisturbed during the early morning hours, Krogh devised and tested an elaborate apparatus for determining the total quantity of combustible organic material in samples of fresh water from various lakes.[12] He chose not to use seawater because it was too difficult to isolate the organic material in the presence of the huge amounts of salt in seawater. As Barker Jørgensen later showed, this was the reason he found no uptake, because only in seawater is there a small uptake of dissolved amino acids (which can be shown with radioactively labeled amino acids).

Krogh presented the first paper on this work, "Dissolved Substances as Food for Aquatic Animals," at the International Congress of Physiological Sciences in 1929.[13] Now followed a series of publications on dissolved organic matter in various lakes, the amounts given off by algae, the chemical composition of phytoplankton, and the role of these compounds as food for aquatic animals.[14] In 1931, Krogh wrote a review for *Biological Reviews* on the subject.[15] Although dissolved organic substances are present in large amounts in freshwater lakes, 10 mg per liter or more (about 3.3 mg of protein and 5.3 mg of carbohydrate), he found no convincing evidence that any freshwater animal takes them up in any significant amount. But he could not entirely dismiss the possibility, since other authors had made it probable that certain protozoans can do so. For the first time Krogh mentioned active transport as a distinct possibility:

> There are two essentially different ways in which dissolved substances can become absorbed into living beings. One is by diffusion, that is, by movement of dissolved molecules from a medium where their concentration is higher, into another where the concentration is lower. The other is by an active process involving energy by which a substance is transported from a medium where its concentration is low, into another in which the concentration is higher.[15]

At the time, it was generally accepted that processes of the second kind, the active transport, take place in kidney tubules, and there was reason to believe that they could also take place in the intestines of animals, generally. Rehberg himself called the reabsorption of chloride in kidney tubules "active transport."

Having finished his research with freshwater organisms, Krogh, together with Ancel B. Keys, during the next two years laboriously worked out methods (using wet combustion) for determining the amounts of dissolved organic substances present in seawater.[16] Krogh and Spärck designed "a new bottom sampler for investigation of the micro fauna of the sea bottom," and measured the weight and numbers of invertebrate species they collected at different depths in Danish waters (calculated from the amounts of organic nitrogen and carbon).

In 1929, following the International Congress of Physiological Sciences in Boston, the Kroghs had gone to Woods Hole, where Krogh had an opportunity to participate in a trial cruise on board the new marine research vessel *Atlantis,* built in Denmark by Burmeister. "I made tentative agreements for collecting of bottom samples from the depth of the Atlantic ocean," Krogh wrote Bøving, in December 1932. "It is possible that when the time comes I must go out and get them myself whether it be with the Danish *Dana* or the American *Atlantis* from Woods Hole."[17]

His laboratory had acquired a five-ton research vessel in 1931, which Krogh used for sampling in the Kattegat during the summer months. Then in 1933 he and Marie went to Woods Hole again. August brought with him all his instruments for a summer's work in Woods Hole, but first he went to Chicago to receive an honorary degree and to present two papers on the conditions for life in the ocean, particularly at great depth. "I'm not wildly enthusiastic about the trip to Chicago," wrote Krogh. He was afraid that the meeting would be too overwhelming and not conducive to exchange of ideas, but he greatly looked forward to the time at Woods Hole and a trip on board *Atlantis* to Bermuda.[17]

At the Woods Hole Oceanographic Institution August analyzed samples of sea water collected on board the *Atlantis*. The samples were taken from the surface down to 5,400 meters (3.4 miles). What he found was a uniform distribution of organic material per liter of seawater at all depths and anywhere in the ocean. The amounts were about 1.5 mg protein or amino acids and 3.9 mg carbohydrates. This does not seem like much, but Krogh calculated that it represents 300 to 1,000 times the amount present in all marine organisms per liter of seawater at any time. The dissolved organic matter appeared to be lost from living marine organisms and to remain largely inaccessible to practically all living forms, including bacteria.[18]

Later Krogh's findings were confirmed, and by carbon 14 determinations it was shown that the organic material in the sea has a turnover rate of several thousand years. "The main results and conclusion of Krogh's investigation were so convincing that research in the field almost stopped for about 30 years. Only when radioactively labelled molecules, especially amino acids, became available was the problem again taken up for further research," wrote C. Barker Jørgensen, who later continued work in this field using radioactively labeled amino acids.[2]

Having investigated whether dissolved organic molecules can be taken up by aquatic animals, it was natural for Krogh to turn to inorganic molecules. Thus his other major interest in these years was osmoregulation in aquatic animals. The question he was exploring was "How do animals living in fresh or sea water maintain the concentrations of salts and other soluble molecules in their body fluids at concentrations that differ markedly from the surrounding water?"[19] For many years, Krogh had been wondering off and on about this problem. Then one summer day in 1930 he had a casual conversation with a fisherman at Lynæs harbor, which made him decide to study the problem. In Issefjord there is a lively and profitable eel fishery. Eels live for most of their lives in fresh water, but they breed in seawater, in the Sargasso Sea. During late summer and early fall they swim down the rivers and start their journey toward the sea. Thus, in late summer they come out of the rivers into the salt water of Issefjord, where the fishermen are prepared to catch them with numerous pound nets set up between stakes.

The interesting fact the fisherman told Krogh was that certain changes in the appearance of eels occur when they are transferred from sea water to fresh water. In March of the same year Ancel B. Keys had asked if he could come and study in Krogh's laboratory. Keys was just finishing his Ph.D. research at La Jolla and was sending the papers he had written to Krogh. He had been working with marine animals, his interests being "largely in respiratory and blood phenomena."[20] Keys had an excellent record and Krogh had immediately wired his acceptance to him. Now, while standing on the pier in Lynæs listening to the fisherman, Krogh began thinking about experiments that Keys might do in his laboratory.

Keys arrived in September 1930 and, after discussions with Krogh, began work on methods for determining chloride and water movements across eel gills in fresh water and sea water. The work called for a highly accurate chloride method. In those years before radioactive sodium became available it was practical only to determine chloride ions, a fact that explains the great emphasis on chloride transport. It was during this work that Krogh and Keys developed the precision syringe pipette, accurate to 0.01%.[21] Not only was it many times faster than ordinary pipettes but it was also far more accurate than any pipettes in use at the time. Syringe pipettes became standard equipment in Krogh's and many other investigators' laboratories. They were manufactured in the workshop and sold all over the world.[22]

Keys worked out a special technique for perfusion of a heart-gill preparation, in which the heart and gills were perfused by one balanced solution while the mouth and branchial cavities were bathed by another aerated circulating solution. Measuring the volume and concentrations of both solutions before and after the experiment, the transfer of salt and water across the gills could be measured. Keys developed an extremely sensitive and accurate method for chloride determination (based on the Volhard titration) in which he used the syringe pipette for measuring the volumes of samples and reagents with the greatest precision. His results showed conclusively, for the first time, that chloride ions are actively secreted (transported) across the gill epithelium from blood to seawater. But no chloride secretion took place when the gills were bathed by fresh water.[23] In 1933 Carl Schlieper, who had been working on osmoregulation for some years, came to Krogh's laboratory, where he reexamined Key's work and found that the chloride secretion is independent of water movements across the gills.[24]

But Keys's and Schlieper's work did not solve the problem that interested Krogh the most: can freshwater animals take up chloride from very dilute solutions? Keys's experiments with eels in fresh water remained inconclusive, while results from plants indicated that such mechanisms did exist. A quotation from a short note in *Nature* (May 1937) introduces Krogh's ideas:

> In recent papers (1933–37), Lundegårdh has demonstrated, in roots of plants, a mechanism for absorbing and concentrating salts out of very dilute solutions. The mechanism utilizes energy derived from the oxidation of sugar and acts by transport of anions (in Lundegårdh experiments $NO_3{;}^-$ and Cl^-) from the outside medium through the active cells to the inside. It is a specially important point that the energy used up is proportional to the anion exchange, while cations cause no increase in respiration. In carbonate solutions no active transport can take place and the exchanges of cations are slight only.[25]
>
> I submit that a mechanism closely resembling Lundegårdh is of widespread occurrence and of great biological significance in the animal kingdom.[26]

At the time Krogh published the note in *Nature*, he and his young colleagues had for some time been studying chloride uptake in frogs, crabs, and insects.[27] In 1934 a young investigator from Belgium, Henri Koch, published data indicating that certain cells in insect anal papillae and crab gills may absorb chloride from fresh water.[28] Krogh invited Koch to come to his laboratory in 1936, where Koch was able to show conclusively that the anal papillae of insect larvae actively absorb chloride ions.[29]

The same year another highly talented visitor, V. B. Wigglesworth, came to Krogh's laboratory to study insect physiology. Wigglesworth, a young English physician, shared Krogh's great love for insects. He was employed by the London School of Hygiene and Tropical Medicine. With the increasing use of insecticides it was felt that more knowledge of insect physiology was needed. Before Wigglesworth came to Krogh's laboratory he had worked with tracheae respiration in insects, but the day after his arrival, Krogh told him to attend a lecture he was going to present in Danish on chloride absorption by insects. Because Wigglesworth did not understand Danish, Krogh explained ahead of time what he was going to say. This made it possible for Wigglesworth to ask a question following the lecture. Krogh had explained that because of the small size of mosquito larvae, the experiments had to be done on a large number of them at the same time. "But wouldn't it be better to do it on a single larva?" asked Wigglesworth. "Yes, of course," said Krogh, "but that is not possible with our methods." "Yes, but shouldn't I try?" said Wigglesworth.[30] Krogh agreed and three weeks later Wigglesworth had developed an ultramicromethod for chloride,[31] and he proceeded to make observations involving single larvae.

Krogh and his collaborators were finding that animals and plants possess mechanisms that enable them to take up chloride actively from extremely dilute solutions.[33] They also found that the mechanism was regulated in animals, as it only took place if the animal had been salt depleted.

In 1939 Cambridge University Press published Krogh's monograph *Osmotic Regulation in Aquatic Animals*.[19] In the preface to the book Krogh explained what had prompted him to write it:

> I lectured on the general subject in the spring of 1935 and was asked to publish these lectures, but too many points seemed obscure and we have since been busy in the laboratory trying to elucidate some of these. Although new material keeps pouring in I venture to believe that stocktaking and a general review is opportune at the present moment. My aim has been to present the essential features of the problem and to direct attention to points about which information is highly desirable.

The book is written in the same style as the capillary book, quoting published and unpublished work that suggested new ideas and thoughts. As he intended, the book inspired an upsurge in the field of osmoregulation, most of which came after World War II. Because of the war, Krogh was never able to write a second edition, but the book was reprinted unabridged and unaltered in 1965 as a Dover publication.

In the thirties Krogh was also working on another monograph, *The Comparative Physiology of Respiratory Mechanisms*, published two years after the osmoregulation monograph by the University of Pennsylvania Press.[33] The book was based on a series of lectures delivered at Swarthmore College in the spring of 1939. Krogh completed the manuscript in 1939, but difficulties in communication across the Atlantic delayed its publication. Both the osmoregulation monograph and the respiration monograph deal with the physiological mechanisms used by animals to adapt to widely varying environments and needs of the animals. Both monographs amply illustrate what Krogh had called "mechanisms and adaptations of exquisite beauty and the most surprising character."

16

Exercise Physiology (1918–1944)

The Three Musketeers.

In 1918 little was known about the supply of energy to working muscles and nothing was known about the role of adenosine triphosphate (ATP) in muscle contraction. Neither was it known that the partial breakdown of sugars (glycolysis) can release energy when oxygen is lacking (via the formation of ATP). While studying oxygen uptake during exercise, Krogh and Lindhard came to wonder about the source of energy for muscular work. At the time, there were two schools of thought. In Germany, Nathan Zuntz and his students had found that muscles can utilize and convert into mechanical work a constant fraction of the energy liberated by combustion from any available substance—provided the substance can be oxidized in the body.[1] In contrast, the Cambridge school, represented by Walter M. Fletcher, Frederick G. Hopkins, Archibald V. Hill, and others, suggested that muscular contraction depended on the splitting of a definite molecule (unknown but closely allied to carbohydrate), resulting in the formation of lactic acid.[2] If the Cambridge school were correct, it seemed inconceivable to Krogh that substances such as fat could be utilized by the muscles without a chemical transformation involving the loss of energy.

The discrepancy between the two schools of thought "caused a growing uneasiness in our minds," wrote Krogh and Lindhard, "which has at last compelled us to take up the problem and see whether Zuntz's conclusions will stand the test of a renewed experimental investigation."[3] Consequently, the two embarked on a major study to determine if the mechanical energy that can be derived from the metabolism of fat is the same or lower than for carbohydrate.

Which food substances are oxidized during muscular work can be estimated from the ratio of the amounts of oxygen used and CO_2 formed by the metabolic processes in the body. This ratio, called the respiratory quotient (R.Q.), is 1.0 for carbohydrate and 0.71 for fat. When the diet contains a minimal amount of protein, the relative amounts of fat and carbohydrate catabolized in the body can be calculated from the R.Q.

Thus, if R.Q. is close to 1, carbohydrate has been metabolized; but when it is close to 0.7, fat has been metabolized.

For the study, Krogh completed the new gas-analysis apparatus that he had worked on for several years. Accurate to 0.001%, it could measure R.Q. with great accuracy (0.005%).[4] During 1918 and 1919 they measured metabolism and the respiratory quotient during rest and work, using themselves and others in the laboratory as subjects. For weeks they had to be on strict diets with very little protein consisting of either mostly fat or mostly carbohydrate. The work was measured on a bicycle ergometer and the subject was placed in a small, airtight respiratory chamber where incoming and outgoing air could be measured and analyzed. Their seventy-page paper was submitted in August 1919. One of the major conclusions was that work is more efficiently performed on a carbohydrate diet than on a fat diet; on the average, 11% of the energy used is wasted when fat is the source of energy for muscular work:

> Four series of experiments (about 220 determinations) on six different subjects, living during the experiments on a diet poor in protein, have been made to study the relative value of fat and carbohydrate as a source of muscular energy. All the series agree in showing that work is more economically performed on carbohydrate than on fat. When the work was sufficiently severe the subjects performed it with greater difficulty on fat than on carbohydrate and became much more tired.[3]

The result did not resolve the dilemma. According to the literature quoted by Zuntz, 30% of the energy of fat should become lost if fat were converted into sugar. This and other calculations did not agree with Krogh and Lindhard's finding. They suggested that during work the proportion of fat to carbohydrate that is utilized (catabolized) depends on the available supply. In other words they agreed with Zuntz that the available energy sources were interchangeable. This conclusion turned out to be correct. We now know that metabolic breakdown of fatty acids as well as carbohydrate (particularly glycogen) are utilized by working muscles to form ATP, which fuels the muscle machine.

Krogh and Lindhard refrained from trying to explain the 11% waste of energy when fat fueled muscular work. Subsequent experimenters confirmed the 11% waste of energy, but even fifty years later no satisfactory explanation had yet been found. (The discrepancy cannot be explained by the yield of ATP from the combustion of fat because the yield is only 3% lower for fat than for carbohydrate. In 1974 Erling Asmussen discussed the problem and suggested as a possible explanation that white and red muscle fibers may be fueled by fat and carbohydrate, respectively, and that the energy efficiency may be lower for the white fibers than for the red.)[5] For years to come, the Krogh-Lindhard study and the questions it raised became the model for numerous other studies by their students.

With Krogh's new, accurate gas analyzer, it was possible to measure the small increase in CO_2 and decrease in oxygen percentage in the streets of Copenhagen. From these values, Krogh was even able to estimate the R.Q. of Copenhagen! He figured that the R.Q. for the burning of wood and peat in Copenhagen would be about 0.95 and this is approximately what he found. To monitor the changes in the earth's atmosphere, he suggested that a thorough study should be made, including samples taken from great heights by airplanes and kites.[6]

In 1915, Göran Liljestrand, a young Swedish medical doctor, joined Krogh and Lindhard in the old laboratory, where they taught him the method for determining blood flow through the heart (cardiac output), and the use of Krogh's bicycle ergometer and other equipment used in the experiments. Early in 1917 Liljestrand wrote Krogh heartily thanking him for the stay in the laboratory, adding, "I could never have come to a place where I could learn more." After another visit in 1918, he wrote Krogh, "I always get the feeling that I have come to a place where intense work is the order of the day."[7]

Liljestrand published several papers on respiration and cardiac output from Krogh's laboratory. As always, when Krogh became impressed with the ability of a young scientist, he wished to help him and, in the process, further the cause of a branch of physiology in which he was interested. Thus in 1917, when Hasselbalch was leaving the Finsen Institute, and Liljestrand had just finished his doctoral dissertation, Krogh recommended him as the new director of the Finsen Institute. To Krogh there was no reason not to choose the best candidate for the position, regardless of his nationality, but Professors Johannes Bock and Thorkild Rovsing of the medical faculty viewed the situation differently. Carl Sonne was appointed director of the institute. In spite of the outcome, the recommendation was beneficial to Liljestrand, whose position in Stockholm was greatly improved. He was highly thought of and later became professor of pharmacology at the Karolinska Institutionen in the Swedish capital.[8]

Liljestrand and Krogh became close friends. In 1919 after Liljestrand had worked at Kristineberg on metabolic rate during swimming, Krogh and Lindhard invited him to participate in their study of the utilization of fat and carbohydrate during exercise. When Krogh was awarded the Nobel Prize, Liljestrand, now at the Karolinska Institution, was among the first to congratulate him. Liljestrand continued to collaborate with Lindhard for some time. Liljestrand and Krogh maintained a lively and affectionate correspondence which continued until Krogh's death. The letters dealt mainly with their joint interest in *Skandinavische Archiv für Physiologie,* the official journal of the Scandinavian Physiological Society. For economic reasons it was printed in Leipzig, Germany. In 1934, Krogh arranged to have the Insulin Foundation support the journal and discussed the possibility of publishing it in one of the Scandinavian countries under the name *Acta Physiologica Scandinavica*. This did not happen until 1940 after the war broke out. The editors chosen from each of the Scandinavian countries were, Y. Reenpää, Finland; A. Krogh, Denmark; E. Langfeldt, Norway; and G. Liljestrand, Sweden.

The close collaboration between Krogh and Lindhard was interrupted when Krogh became too busy in 1920 after the Nobel Prize. However, when Krogh drew up the plans for the new Rockefeller Institute, he included a "Laboratory for Theoretical Gymnastics,"[9] with Lindhard as director. It occupied the second floor, directly above the Zoophysiological Laboratory, in the west wing of the Rockefeller Institute and consisted of a number of laboratories and offices.

The atmosphere in Lindhard's laboratory was very different from Krogh's. Although Lindhard spoke and wrote several foreign languages, he had an unconquerable fear of speaking to foreigners. According to his collaborator, Erling Asmussen,[10] Lindhard refused, almost categorically, to receive foreign visitors. The research in his laboratory was based entirely on Lindhard's ideas, with his students and assistants doing the experimental work. On the basis of his own ideas and logic, Lindhard attacked other physiologists in his field without mercy. In a manner unsurpassed in the contemporary literature, he attacked from a position of arrogance and superior knowledge, while "lecturing" his opponents about their mistakes.[10] As Krogh kindly put it, "he was an inflexible and relentless logician."[11] It is not surprising that the gentle Benedict was shocked when first exposed to Lindhard's vitriolic style. Nevertheless, Lindhard's laboratory was thriving; its strengths were the care and accuracy with which the assistants carried out the experiments and the theoretical papers and chapters for handbooks written by Lindhard and his assistant Emanuel Hansen.[10]

Surprisingly, Lindhard and Krogh, both by nature strong and uncompromising, continued to be friends. They had their problems, but according to Erik Hohwü Christensen,[12] who knew them both well, it was Marie Krogh, with her capacity to accept good as well as bad in people's characters, who steered August away from serious confrontations with Lindhard and others.

In 1928 Hohwü Christensen (born 1904), came to work in Lindhard's laboratory; and in 1931, in Krogh's. This resulted in renewed contact and collaboration between the two laboratories. It also led to a long, important series of investigations on the physiology of heavy work in Krogh's laboratory.

Hohwü, as everyone called him, came to Copenhagen in 1924 from South Jutland. Having grown up in a small farming community south of what was until 1920 the border between Germany and Denmark, he shared Krogh's strong patriotic feelings against the German annexation of Slesvig in 1864. Because Hohwü had gone to a German school, he spoke and wrote German fluently, with the result that almost all of his publications were in German. He came to Copenhagen to study natural sciences, chemistry, philosophy, and geography. He majored in the theory of gymnastics, and an important part of his education was in Lindhard's laboratory. As Rehberg before him, he became enraptured by Krogh's lectures. According to Hohwü, it was Krogh's fundamental, basic biological curiosity, quantitative approach, and ability to look at complex problems and, with unbelievable intuition, break them up into several smaller and simpler problems that captured and held his interest. He went to all of Krogh's lectures, not because he had to but because of his deep interest.[10,12]

In 1928 Hohwü started work on his thesis in the Laboratory for Theoretical Gymnastics, and Lindhard asked him to test Krogh and Lindhard's N_2O method for measuring cardiac output.[13] It was during this work that Hohwü became interested in the physiology of high-intensity, prolonged physical work. Krogh and Lindhard had worked at moderate intensities, but Hohwü used well-trained young men, namely himself, Marius Nielsen, Ove Bøje, and Holger E. Nielsen. All were fellow students and had become friends at "Studentergården," the fraternity where Hohwü lived as a student. Marius Nielsen came from a farm on Fyn and in 1924 came to Copenhagen to study for a teaching degree as cand. mag. in natural history and geography. Ove Bøje and Holger E. Nielsen were medical students.

Hohwü compared the N_2O method for measuring cardiac output with Grollman's acetylene method, which was easier to use for high-intensity exercise, and he tested both methods for accuracy. He standardized the experimental conditions, such as diet, mealtimes, time, and previous training, while he followed a strict protocol, making measurements before, during, and after heavy muscular work. This made his results far more reliable than those in the past and raised new and interesting questions. His three experimental subjects became so interested in the project that they willingly exposed themselves to the rigor and sometimes extreme discomfort of the experiments.[10] The work started at 7 A.M., and the heavy exercise lasted from two to four hours. Because the laboratory was located right under biochemistry professor H. M. Hansen's bedroom, the noise from the laboratory woke up Mrs. Hansen every morning. When this had been going on for some time, H. M. Hansen went to Lindhard and asked him to discontinue the experiments. Without hesitation Lindhard answered that if Hansen didn't like the noise he could move. The purpose of the institute was for experimental work and not for residences for the professors! That ended the argument.[11]

Hohwü defended his doctoral dissertation in 1931. His two official opponents, Krogh and Lindhard, both congratulated him on his fine work. Krogh then invited Hohwü to become assistant in the Zoophysiological Laboratory where Rehberg now was promoted to *amanuensis* (a rank corresponding to assistant professor).

In 1931, the Health Organization under the League of Nations held an international meeting in Copenhagen on the effects on the body of physical activity, especially sports and games involving maximal muscular work. A rapidly growing worldwide interest in sports was already apparent before World War I and many countries supported sports with public funds. Little was known about what actually happened in the body of the athlete during such performances. A number of experts were invited to the meeting, among them Krogh and Lindhard. Meeting participants agreed that metabolic rate, respiration, cardiac output, blood concentrations, kidney function, temperature regulation, body temperature, and fatigue should be studied during maximum athletic performances.[10,12]

Shortly after the meeting, Krogh and Lindhard suggested that a major part of the agreed-upon program could be carried out at their two laboratories, where Hohwü and his friends were actively engaged in exactly such investigations. The proposal was accepted and money was granted for a two-year investigation. Hohwü's well-trained experimental subjects, Marius Nielsen, Ove Bøje, and Ove Hansen (another cand. mag., who had replaced Holger E. Nielsen), agreed to continue with the experiments. In the meantime they had finished their formal education, and they now became active investigators themselves while continuing to function as experimental subjects for each other. Krogh and Lindhard divided the problems to be investigated among them, and at the completion of the work, each of them wrote his doctoral dissertation on an aspect of the work.

As the study progressed Krogh and Lindhard were kept informed about progress at frequent meetings. Krogh took great delight in the experiments and the findings. Often when he had listened to a progress report he would exclaim, "What fun it is!"[14] Krogh took particular delight in solving technical problems that arose. Following the study for the League of Nations, research on exercise physiology continued and gradually moved from Lindhard's to Krogh's laboratory.

Besides Hohwü's group, other groups in the laboratory took part in the League of Nations project. F. Grande Covian from Spain worked with Rehberg and Krogh on kidney function during exercise.[15] Carsten Trolle worked on insensible perspiration during work and rest. For this work it became desirable to be able to weigh the amount of water lost from the body by evaporation (insensible perspiration). This meant weighing a 70 kg man within an accuracy of ±1 g. It seemed almost impossible, but Krogh designed a balance that could do the job as the man resting on a stretcher was suspended under the scale.[16] The balance was suspended on ball bearings and the proportion of the lever arms was 1 to 5. A steel plate dipping in oil damped the oscillations, cutting the number of oscillations down to three, and oscillation time to 7½ sec. Later, when Nielsen needed to weigh his subjects during active work on the bicycle ergometer, Krogh said, "Why not weigh the man and the bicycle ergometer together?" Doubting that it could work, Nielsen tried it anyway. A man and the bicycle ergometer were hoisted up and weighed while he was vigorously pedaling. The balance oscillated from the movements, but it was still possible to weigh the person with an accuracy of ±3–4 g.[14]

The investigations involved an ongoing study of fat and carbohydrate as fuel for muscular work. It is very important that the breathing of the experimental subject is as natural as possible and not influenced by the technique used to collect the respiratory gasses. Breathing appliances like mouthpieces, nosepieces, or masks have a tendency to disturb normal breathing and produce spurious changes in the R.Q. Earlier Krogh and Lindhard had used a respiratory chamber for their experiments at rest and moderate work. However, when experiments were carried out during heavy muscular work, it became necessary to monitor the stores of CO_2 in the body by taking frequent samples of arterial blood. This could not be done when the experimental subject was in a chamber. Krogh then modified the Benedict helmet for use during vigorous work. The suspended, water cooled helmet could be fitted over the person's head with minimal restriction to the respiration and movements of the head.[17]

When Hohwü and Ove Hansen reinvestigated the problem at high-intensity work, they could confirm what Krogh and Lindhard had found. The muscles work better and more efficiently when carbohydrate is available. However, during very heavy and prolonged work (intensity: 1,120 kg/min. or 183 watts for 160 minutes) the percentage of carbohydrate used gradually decreases from around 70 to 30–35, while the percentage of fat burned increases proportionally.[18]

What limits the duration of the performance is, in some situations, the blood-sugar concentration, which can no longer be maintained when the carbohydrate reserves in muscles and liver are used up. Ove Bøje showed that the organism begins to conserve carbohydrate as soon as the blood-sugar concentration begins to fall. On a high-fat diet, the men were unable to continue work for a long period of time, because carbohydrate reserves became depleted early.[19]

All the findings indicated that muscular work is best performed on carbohydrates and for prolonged optimal performances, the body's stores of carbohydrate (glycogen) should be maximally filled. These stores fill rather slowly over a period of two days. It is interesting to note that as early as 1934 Hohwü, Krogh, and Lindhard were able to recommend: "In athletic sports requiring long continued severe work, the same person ought not to take part in several contests in immediate succession, but periods of two days' rest ought to be interposed. This holds, of course, also for games like football, where the rule is often disregarded to the certain detriment of both players and play."[20]

The results of the kidney studies by Grande Covian and Rehberg showed that urine production is reduced during high-intensity work mainly due to greater tubular reabsorption of water. However, when the work is prolonged the glomerular filtration rate may become reduced to 35% of its resting value, which further reduces urine production.[15]

In his careful study of temperature regulation, Nielsen, following up on one of Hohwü's findings, found that body temperature rose considerably during the first thirty to forty minutes of work, but once body temperature had reached a plateau it would remain constant for hours while the work continued at the same intensity. The height of the plateau varied with the work intensity and was within a wide range independent of the external conditions for heat dissipation. He reached the interesting conclusion that the set-point for the body's thermostat varies with work intensity.[21]

When the work for the League of Nations was finished in 1934, Krogh found money to support Nielsen and invited him to continue at the Zoophysiological Laboratory. His major interest became the regulation of respiration during work. Krogh and Lindhard had suggested that the abrupt rise in ventilation, like the increase in heart rate at the onset of work, is brought about by "a sudden increase in excitability of the respiratory center induced by irradiation of impulses from the motor cortex."[22] In the course of his work, Nielsen had obtained results indicating that the excitability of the respiratory center (to CO_2) was not increased during prolonged work. He went to Krogh showing his results, saying, "If this is so then I cannot understand how the increased respiration during muscular work is maintained." Krogh answered, "No I don't understand it either," and then he added, "You must go and find out." According to Nielsen, Krogh said this with such intensity and urgency and in such a stimulating manner that it became decisive for his (Nielsen's) future work.[14] Nielsen continued to contribute significantly to this field for many years. There was no simple answer to the question that he had raised, and there is still a great deal of controversy concerning the mechanism underlying the regulation of ventilation during exercise.[23]

The long series of papers resulting from the support from the League of Nations, as well as the work that followed, were published in German during the mid- to late thirties, some of them just before the war broke out. The unfortunate result was that to a large extent they went unnoticed by the English-speaking world. Only after Hohwü's later publications in English did the importance of these studies become fully appreciated.

While the theoretical work was in full swing, purely practical investigations were also undertaken at the Rockefeller Institute. In the early thirties Krogh designed a respirator based on Cecil Drinker's principles. It was used for victims of polio.[24] The large machine, which enclosed the whole body, was built in the laboratory workshop. The pumping mechanism (Krogh's invention) was powered by water from a faucet so that no electricity was required to run the machine. Frequently, during a severe polio epidemic in Denmark, the hospital sent an ambulance to Krogh's laboratory to pick up the respirator, which saved many lives. Then in 1934 Krogh designed a tilting table to be used for artificial respiration of drowning victims. It worked on the principle that the inner organs pressed on the diaphragm and forced air out of the lungs when the head was down. However, it also made the person quite seasick![25]

Colonel Holger Nielsen developed a better method for artificial respiration while he was director of the Institute for Gymnastics in Nørre Alle, across from the Rockefeller Institute.[2] His method differed from earlier, purely manual methods in that not only was air pushed out of the person's lungs by pressing on the rib case from behind but air was sucked into the lungs when the head and shoulders were lifted. The method was tested in Lindhard's laboratory while, according to Erling Asmussen on whom it was tested, Krogh and Lindhard were reading the spirometer to measure the amount of air coming into the victim's lungs. The method proved superior to others, and Krogh took such a delight in it that Holger Nielsen thanked him by presenting him with a silver model of artificial respiration being given to a victim.

Holger Nielsen became world famous for the method, which for many years was the method of choice for artificial respiration. The Danish Red Cross introduced it as their standard method, and later it was universally adapted and used by the U.S. Army in Korea. After 1958, it was replaced by the mouth-to-mouth procedure.[10]

In the late thirties Krogh was asked to become chairman of a committee to recommend physiological and practical solutions for home heating. Krogh worked hard on this committee and took great interest in solving many problems. There was talk of heating by radiation (rather by than convection) from radiating panels in the ceiling. This meant heating the people, not the room. It became desirable "to record the temperature and humidity relations inside the clothes of men." Krogh then designed and built a microclimate recorder, which is made from a wrist watch. The hour-hand axle projects into a chamber where it carries a disc on which the recording instruments are mounted. The temperature recorder is a bimetal spiral, and the humidity recorder is a single human hair. Both were provided with fine writing points to write on a sooted disc covering the chamber. The variations in temperature and humidity could then be traced over a twelve-hour period and the curves read under a microscope.[26]

Another practical investigation involved the testing of air force pilots. A large (twenty-seven cubic meters capacity) low-pressure steel chamber had become the property of the Zoophysiological Laboratory. It was no longer needed by the Finsen Institute, where it had been built for Hasselbalch and Lindhard. Situated in a special building next to the Zoophysiological Laboratory, it was used for various physiological experiments, and Hohwü and Krogh tested the ability of prospective pilots to maintain consciousness at high altitudes (where low oxygen pressures would be encountered). In those days fighter planes were not pressurized. The effect of oxygen deficiency is not noticed by the pilot, who believes that he is perfectly well and is in full control of his senses even when he is barely conscious.

The young men were told to write the alphabet while the atmospheric pressure was gradually lowered. When the test person began to write poorly and repeated the letter he had just written, the investigators interrupted the experiment. Often the young man would protest saying that he felt great. Only when he was confronted with what he had written did he understand what had happened.

Individual differences in tolerance to low oxygen pressure in the inspired air were pronounced. Hohwü and Krogh could determine by their measurements that the differences were due to how deeply the persons were normally breathing and not to differences in rate of diffusion through the lung epithelium. In every person oxygen tension in the alveoli and in the central nervous system were identical (about 30 mmHg) at the time they became confused while the men with greater tolerance could tolerate lower oxygen tension in the inhaled air because of their better lung ventilation.[27]

On one occasion the use of the low pressure chamber had near fatal consequences. Hohwü's group wanted to investigate the respiratory effect of breathing a high percentage of CO_2. The chamber had been in use for a long time but the air had always been constantly renewed during the experiments. This time the scientists decided to recirculate most of the air, which made it easier to maintain a constant CO_2 pressure. Hohwü and Nielsen planned to spend three to four days in the chamber with a 4.5% CO_2 content. At 9:40 P.M. they were locked into the chamber. They were both newlyweds and their nervous wives insisted on staying the night to watch their husbands through the chamber's observation window. Early on the only sign was the increased respiration caused by the effect of CO_2 on the respiratory center of the brain. The two men went to bed but a few hours later their wives noticed that their sleep was disturbed; they were coughing and seemed to be in considerable distress. The wives now insisted that they come out. By that time they were so ill that they were promptly hospitalized and diagnosed with severe lung edema. Experimental animals, guinea pigs, mice, and rats subsequently placed in the chamber all died within twelve hours. Their lungs were then as solid as liver from edema!

A careful analysis by a number of specialists (including Marie Krogh and the two victims) showed that the symptoms were caused by mercury poisoning. Gas analyses had been performed in the chamber and mercury, which nobody worried about, was spilled and gradually became finely distributed over the floor by scrubbing. The combination of the recirculation of the chamber air, which greatly increased the mercury vapor in the air, and the hyperventilation, resulting from the high CO_2, was a deadly combination.[11,28]

It seems that Krogh should have been worried about mercury poisoning earlier. After all, in his experiments on nitrogen excretion in 1905 he had diagnosed that it was mercury vapors in his apparatus that killed his experimental animals. He himself, without realizing it, had also suffered from mercury poisoning in his youth. But it was not until this incident that everyone in his laboratory realized the danger of mercury. For the first time, precautions were taken. All the laboratories were full of mercury droplets that had found their way into the cracks of the floor coverings. Ib Holm-Jensen, one of Krogh's students, published a simple but effective quantitative method for testing the mercury content of the air by keeping an aquarium with daphnia in the room. The sensitive daphnia died at relatively low concentrations of mercury. Holm-Jensen also developed a white paint for the wall, which turned black when exposed to mercury vapors.[10]

Hohwü and Nielsen apparently did not suffer any long-term effects from their ordeal, but another member of the team was not so lucky. Ove Hansen, an important member of the group, is presumed to have been a victim of mercury poisoning. He was regularly using Krogh's ultra-accurate gas analysis apparatus[4] in his work on the use of fat and carbohydrate. Mercury was spilled all around it and Hansen worked with it daily in the poorly ventilated cellar room that was his laboratory. According to his colleagues, Hansen's personality suddenly underwent a peculiar change. Though he had been a mild and fun-loving man, Hansen became aggressive, high-strung, and totally unreasonable. He became unable to write his papers and had to leave the work for a prolonged period. Hansen finally completed his doctoral dissertation in 1942, but never fully regained his health.[10,11,14]

In the midthirties another young scientist, Erling Asmussen, joined Hohwü and Nielsen at the Zoophysiological Laboratory. Asmussen had been working in Lindhard's laboratory, isolating frog muscle fibers since 1931. Then in 1932, Fritz Buchtahl came to Lindhard's laboratory from Germany, because of the beginning hostilities against Jews. An excellent electrophysiologist, Buchtahl gradually took over the field of muscle physiology in Lindhard's laboratory, while Asmussen shifted to physiology of intact human beings. This drew him closer to the work that Hohwü and Nielsen were engaged in.[9] Soon a highly productive collaboration on the regulation of circulation and respiration during rest and muscular activity was under way.[29] For several years, Hohwü, Nielsen, and Asmussen would meet every morning in a laboratory in the basement of the Zoophysiological Laboratory, where the assistant had prepared for the experiments. Krogh visited daily the trio, which he called "the Three Musketeers," and often brought visitors to learn about the work.[10] In the evening Krogh frequently would visit whoever was still at work and, as Nielsen has told, at leisure he would then discuss problems and suggest technical improvements.[14]

Krogh helped arrange that each of the Three Musketeers, Hohwü,

Nielsen, and Asmussen, could go abroad to broaden their training. He was well acquainted with the Harvard Fatigue Laboratory, a leading institute in exercise physiology. The head of the institute was L. J. Henderson, who was succeeded by Bruce Dill. Hohwü went in 1935 and participated in the famous Andes expedition with Bruce Dill and F. G. Hall.[10,11,30]

Nielsen went to the John B. Pierce Foundation Laboratory in New Haven in 1938 and later to the Fatigue Laboratory in Boston. Then he went to the Mississippi Delta to study the effect of high temperature and humidity on the sharecroppers. Asmussen joined him in Mississippi in 1939 and later went to the Fatigue Laboratory and on a high-altitude expedition to Mt. Evans in Colorado.[10]

Hohwü was in the United States when Lindhard in 1935 announced his impending retirement. To Krogh, Hohwü was the logical successor to the professorship, but Lindhard had other plans. He felt that his long-term assistant and collaborator Emanuel Hansen should not be bypassed by the younger and more qualified Hohwü. Because Krogh had suggested that Hohwü apply, the situation caused Lindhard a great deal of anxiety. He wrote Hohwü: "I will not accept that he [Krogh] makes himself master of my little laboratory. It is not his work and he must not make it a branch of Zoophysiological Laboratory." He added that if Krogh would try to force the issue, "then the only solution is that you do not apply."[31] But Krogh did not try to force the issue and Lindhard's fears were calmed. Lindhard's attitude created a very difficult situation for Hohwü, for whom there was no available professorship in Denmark.

Eventually, however, each of the Three Musketeers became leaders in theoretical gymnastics. Hohwü was appointed professor in physiology at the College of Physical Education in Stockholm in 1941, but it was not until 1944 that he was able to move into a good laboratory. Many times Krogh visited his department and for several years worked to get Hohwü back to Denmark. Hohwü continued and initiated research with roots in the Krogh-Lindhard tradition: effects of high altitude, temperature regulation during exercise, effects of dehydration, effect of extreme fat and protein-carbohydrate diets on physical performance. In the sixties, by doing biopsy during work, it became possible to measure the muscle stores of glycogen directly. Now published in English his earlier papers became well known.[32]

Erling Asmussen succeeded Emanuel Hansen as professor in theoretical gymnastics in Copenhagen in 1961 and Marius Nielsen became professor at the same institute in 1964. In 1970 the Department of Theoretical Gymnastics moved to its new location in the just completed August Krogh Institute. There Nielsen and Asmussen continued their collaboration for several years.

17

The Introduction of Isotopes (1935–1944)

> It is my task today to present some thoughts about a new and, as I believe, extremely powerful tool in biological and biochemical research: A small number of isotopes which can be readily distinguished and quantitatively determined by relatively simple physical means.

In 1935 Niels Bohr and Georg von Hevesy invited Krogh to collaborate in biological experiments with "heavy" water, i.e. water in which some of the hydrogen ions are replaced with the isotope deuterium (D) bearing twice the atomic weight of hydrogen.[1]

At about the same time, Hans Ussing, a young man who was working on his doctoral dissertation in zoology, came to see Krogh. Working with Arctic plankton, he had found it difficult to identify the larval stages of the organisms, because they all looked alike. It occurred to him that if he could make antibodies to the various forms he could use them on the larvae. So he came to Krogh to ask advice on how to carry out this project. Impressed with the ingenious idea, Krogh listened carefully to Ussing and suggested that he contact the Serum Institute concerning procedure. Then when they were about to part, Krogh took a small glass vial out of his pocket and said, "Let me show you something amusing." As Krogh held up the vial, Ussing could see that it contained what appeared to be pure water. Krogh explained that it was heavy water just obtained from its discoverer, H. C. Urey in the United States. Two days later Krogh called Ussing and said he had funding for him and would he like to come work on the biological effects of heavy water.[2] Krogh may have felt that Ussing's obvious talent and imagination could be put to better use on a more interesting problem than classifying plankton.

Animals living in fresh water are exposed to a steady (osmotic) influx of water through their outer surface, while most animals living in salt water lose water by diffusion in the other direction. Krogh was naturally interested in measuring the rate of water diffusion through various animal membranes, a rather tedious procedure when carried out by measuring volume of water moving across the membrane. However, if water could be "labeled" with heavy water, diffusion through a membrane could be measured quite easily. But first Krogh and Ussing had to know if heavy water (D_2O) is toxic to living organisms. Embryos are far more sensitive to toxicity than mature organisms, so Krogh suggested that Ussing test D_2O on the development of frog eggs.[2] The toxicity of D_2O was found to be only slight; increasing concentrations increasingly delayed embryonic development.[3]

In the meantime, Krogh, his assistant Fenger-Eriksen, and Ussing developed a method for determination of D_2O concentration in water. Krogh's daughter Agnes also worked with Ussing on this project. A precisely measured drop of the mixture was introduced into a density gradient where the rate of fall was measured with great accuracy.[4] As with all Krogh's methods, this one was incredibly accurate; the concentration could be determined within 0.001%, due to the utmost attention to detail. Rehberg and Ussing have both told me that nobody working in Krogh's laboratory was permitted to use precalibrated weights or ready-made standard solutions. Weights had to be calibrated in the laboratory and standard solutions made by the investigators. Once, Ussing was in a hurry and, hoping that Krogh wouldn't notice, called the commercial supplier for a $\frac{1}{10}$ normal HCl solution. Krogh did notice, and to Ussing's amusement, Krogh, in a hurry himself, came very quietly and borrowed some of Ussing's HCl solution![5]

Krogh, in collaboration with Hevesy and E. Hofer, compared the permeabilities of frog skin to D_2O and water. In this study Krogh used whole frogs and (for the first time) isolated pieces of frog skin. Contrary to their expectations, they found that water flow resulting from an osmotic gradient across a membrane was five times faster than diffusional flow resulting from a difference in concentration of D_2O on the two sides of the membrane. This discrepancy could not be explained at the time, and they had to conclude that D_2O could not be used for measuring water permeability because osmotic water flow is different from diffusional water flow for unknown reasons.[6] Many years later (1953), Ussing and Koefoed-Johnsen found that the reason osmotic water flow is much greater than the diffusional movement of water molecules is that water, driven by an osmotic gradient, moves as bulk flow through channels in the membrane.[7]

Even though heavy water could not be used for quantitative measurements of diffusion rates, it could be used for determining whether membranes were permeable to water or not. Results obtained on frog and trout eggs revealed that frog eggs are permeable to water for a period of time while trout eggs become practically impermeable shortly after fertilization.[8]

Ussing now turned his attention to synthesis of protein, from amino acids labeled with deuterium. (In proteins and amino acids some hydrogen ions exchange rapidly, while others will be built into fixed linkages.)[9] Krogh recommended that Ussing work at the Carlsberg Laboratory with S. P. L. Sørensen and K. Linderstrøm-Lang, who knew more about protein synthesis.

Krogh's association with Hevesy and Bohr became of the utmost importance for future research involving the use of isotopes in biological sciences. Hevesy also introduced Krogh to radioactive phosphorus and later to other isotopes. It did not take Krogh long to see the enormous potentials afforded by isotopes as powerful new research tools. In 1937 and 1938, Krogh wrote two reviews on the subject, "The Use of Isotopes as Indicators in Biological Research"[10] and "The Use of Deuterium in Biological Work."[10] In his introduction to the first paper Krogh wrote:

> While it is undoubtedly true that the chief tool and weapon is thought and ideas and that a large amount of experimental work in biology is more or less wasted for lack of thought, it is not less true that progress depends to a very large extent upon methods and that new methods may open up new and fruitful fields. It is my task today to present some thoughts about a new and, as I believe, extremely powerful tool in biological and biochemical research: A small number of isotopes which can be readily distinguished and quantitatively determined by relatively simple physical means.[10]

The man who first introduced isotopes as tracers in biology was Hevesy. Born in Hungary in 1885, he was educated as a chemist. He married a Danish woman and lived in Copenhagen from 1922 to 1926, while working at Niels Bohr's Institute for Theoretical Physics. From 1926 to 1934 he worked in Freiburg, but returned to Copenhagen in 1934 after Adolf Hitler came to power in Germany. Hevesy remained in Copenhagen even after the start of the German occupation in 1940, but fled to Sweden in 1943 when the persecution of Jews began in Denmark. Hevesy's two most outstanding achievements were his discovery, in 1922, of the missing element 72 in the periodic table, which he named "hafnium" after the Latin name for Copenhagen, Hafnia, and the introduction of radioactive indicators. Hevesy conceived the idea of radioactive indicators in 1912 while working with Ernest Rutherford in Manchester, England. Rutherford asked him to separate a radioactive material, radium D, from lead. However hard Hevesy tried, he could not separate the two, and he became convinced that they were chemically identical. In his Nobel Lecture in 1943, he said, "In order to make the best of this depressing situation I decided to use RaD [radioactive lead] as an indicator of lead." In his classic experiments on lead turnover in plants, published in 1921, he used radioactive lead as a tracer. While still in Manchester, Hevesy also used radioactive lead as an indicator at the boarding house where he lived. He suspected that the hash that was often served was mixed with the leftovers from their plates and served again. So he introduced a little radioactive lead on his own plate. Sure enough, a week later traces of radioactivity could still be detected in the hash the landlady served.[11]

In 1935 at Bohr's institute, Hevesy and his associates prepared a radioactive phosphorus isotope from sulfur and used it in a number of experiments on plants and animals. By the time Krogh became associated with Hevesy and Bohr, they had produced a number of isotopes, most of them with too short a half-life to be of any practical use. This had come about after the discovery of induced radioactivity by the Joliot-Curies. Enrico Fermi had told Bohr in a letter that he had produced radioactive isotopes in many different elements, and Hevesy and Bohr enthusiastically started producing isotopes.[11,12]

In spite of his great achievements, Hevesy was quite inept in the laboratory. In Copenhagen his coworkers used to joke, "It is lucky that Hevesy is a genius, because he is not good enough to be an ordinary chemist." But Hevesy, the true genius, was fired up by his mission to introduce the use of isotopes into biological research and went around talking to biologists about it. The problem was that Hevesy had no understanding of biology and most biologists were not interested. Krogh became the only one among the biologists who could foresee the immense future benefits of isotopes to biological research. As Ussing told me, "There is no doubt that your father filled the role as Hevesy's teacher. But to impart understanding of biology to Hevesy took time. In fact, it took an inordinate amount of time before Hevesy reached a reasonable level of understanding."[5]

In the meantime, as Ussing worked with Krogh, he found that the other biologists, including Rehberg, were highly critical and pessimistic concerning this new and strange method. During the laboratory coffee hour, Rehberg, as was his habit when any experiment was discussed, would bring up all the reasons why a method, or experiment couldn't work, while the always optimistic Krogh would counter the arguments with fresh ideas. In 1936, when Krogh was in America, Ussing felt extremely lonely because there was nobody he could talk with about his experiments. Even the brilliant and famous S. P. L. Sørensen[13] at the Carlsberg Laboratory told Ussing that it was a waste of time to work with isotopes, but one other scientist at the Carlsberg Laboratory who did understand the value of isotopes from the beginning was Kai Linderstrøm-Lang. Rehberg's pessimism concerning isotopes did not last. As questions and answers became more clearly formulated, Rehberg became an enthusiastic supporter of work with isotopes and of Ussing himself.[5]

In the years preceding the war, heavy water was supplied by a plant in Riukan, Norway. Bohr's institute made radioactive phosphorus. Bohr and Hevesy first used the radiation sources available at the Finsen Institute, but the amounts that could be produced there were very limited. It happened that Ernest Lawrence in Berkeley had recently built the first cyclotron in the world, and Bohr wondered if one could be built at his institute. Bohr desired the cyclotron for his physics experiments, but there was no possibility for obtaining the large amount of money necessary from Danish sources. The Rockefeller Foundation, however, had just decided that the recent advances in physics should benefit biological research. When Krogh explained that biology would *need* isotopes, Bohr, Hevesy, and Krogh jointly prepared an application, which Bohr signed. The application was granted and Bohr's cyclotron became the first in Europe, a fact that gave Denmark a lead in the production of isotopes.[12,14]

Krogh felt "exceptionally fortunate in having become associated with Hevesy and through him with Bohr," and wrote, "The study of radioactive isotopes is to be pushed forward in Copenhagen and a powerful plant is being erected for their generation."[11]

Niels Bohr, one of this century's greatest minds and the indisputable leader among the world's greatest physicists in quantum mechanics, was born in Copenhagen in 1885, eleven years after Krogh. He was the son of Krogh's mentor, Christian Bohr and Bohr's lovely and highly intelligent wife Ellen (Adler). Krogh had known Niels Bohr as a young boy in the years when he was a frequent guest in Christian Bohr's home. Niels Bohr's rise to fame had been fast. He spent the years of World War I with Rutherford in Manchester, where he broke with classical physics and developed his famous theories in quantum mechanics. In spite of Bohr's growing fame, his first application for a (new) professorship in theoretical physics in Copenhagen was denied for lack of funds. In 1916, the Danish government, afraid of losing him to another country, granted him an institute and a professorship in theoretical physics. In 1922, Bohr was awarded the Nobel Prize for physics.[12]

The collaboration between Bohr, Hevesy, and Krogh lasted until the fall of 1943. Then the persecution of the Jews forced Hevesy and Bohr (whose mother was Jewish) to flee Denmark to Sweden. Shortly after his arrival there, Bohr was spirited to Scotland and then to the United States to work on the Manhattan Project. Hevesy remained in Sweden, where he was awarded the Nobel Prize for chemistry in 1943. As a Nobel laureate he took advantage of his option to become a Swedish citizen. Hilde Levi was another Jewish physicist who, after she fled Germany in 1934, had been working at Bohr's institute and at Krogh's laboratory. Levi also went to Sweden, but returned to Denmark after the war.

During the thirties and early forties Hevesy could frequently be seen arriving on his bicycle in the courtyard of the Rockefeller Institute in Copenhagen, often carrying radioactive material.[11] In those days very little was known about the dangers of exposure to radioactivity. Radioactive phosphorus (^{32}P) was administered to humans without qualms. Once, a cat injected with radioactive phosphorus got loose and Hevesy combed the neighborhood for it, not because it represented any danger to anybody, but because of the investment in time and money the cat represented. Hevesy, however, did take one precaution when he traveled by streetcar carrying a rather large amount of radioactivity in a lead container: he left the container with the driver of the streetcar, to avoid the continuous exposure himself![5]

In 1937 Professor J. Holst from the School of Dentistry was drawn into the project to study the exchange of phosphorus in rat and human teeth.[15] And in 1941, when I was a dental student, my professor, P. O. Pedersen, asked me to join him in a study of exchange of ^{32}P in human teeth.[16] Granted, the radioactivity was low and the half-life of ^{32}P only fourteen days, but I still shudder when I recall that, without permission, we administered the radioactive isotope in a piece of chocolate to an unsuspecting child who had to have a fresh tooth extracted.

The radioactivity was determined with Geiger-Müller counters, constructed according to the principles worked out by Hilde Levi at Bohr's institute. At Krogh's institute, one counter was set up on a table in the middle of his personal laboratory, with the space under the table crowded with a host of batteries that powered the Geiger counter.

With the low radioactivity, counting was a tedious process in which samples had to be counted alternately with background for six to eight hours at a time. Because I was married and lived elsewhere, my father sometimes helped me by changing my samples in the Geiger counter. One morning in the laboratory he pointed to the protocol to show me that he had changed my samples at 2 A.M.! I was deeply touched.

The research with heavy water came to an abrupt stop when the heavy water plant in Norway was blown up by the Norwegian resistance movement to prevent the Nazis from using it, but work with radioisotopes in biology continued in several laboratories. It became clear that the accepted view that cell membranes are impermeable to cations was erroneous, a finding that triggered renewed interest in how the concentrations inside cells are regulated. This led Krogh into studies of ion exchange between cells and extracellular fluid, in the heart muscle as well in plant cells. He continued this work after the war broke out until he had to flee to Sweden in summer 1944. The work he had started led to the Croonian Lectures, which he completed in Sweden and sent to the Royal Society in London in February 1945, while the war was still raging.

Before Krogh had to flee Denmark, his plan had been to initiate and supervise a program to study active and passive exchanges of inorganic ions through the surface membranes of living cells, using radioactive isotopes. Ussing writes:

> The idea [Krogh's] was that the constant exchange of inorganic ions between cells and their surroundings must mean an active transport of certain (maybe all?) species in one direction and leakage in the opposite direction. If a certain ion species exhibits a sufficiently large con-

centration drop across the cell membrane, one must assume that the flow of ions is almost exclusively active in one direction and passive in the other. In such cases the ion exchange as measured with an isotope under steady-state conditions should simultaneously yield the rate of active transport and the leak permeability. . . . This argument does not always hold, but conceptually it was a very important step forward. The work of Hevesy and other pioneers in the use of isotopes had revealed that many ionic species, thought to be non-penetrating, exhibited a more or less lively "exchange" across cell membranes, but the mechanisms underlying the exchanges had not been rigorously analyzed. Now Krogh postulated that the process could be resolved into two well-defined processes: an active transport that consumed metabolic energy, and a passive leak that was a simple physical process.[14]

Krogh had planned to locate the project at the Zoophysiological Laboratory and staff it with a few young physiologists under his guidance. He must have planned this after he was forced by the war to delay his retirement until he was seventy years old. However, the many changes and hardships brought on by the war delayed the project, and he was not able to return to Denmark until he had reached the mandatory retirement age. Upon his return, he asked Hans Ussing to supervise the project until it was well under way:

In the first place it was essential that so important a project not go astray in its initial phase. Second, as Krogh pointed out, the fact that our University had a cyclotron at the Bohr Institute and that Niels Bohr actively supported biological applications of isotopes gave us a unique chance to do pioneer work with respect to transport of inorganic ions. Carbon-14 had just become available for biochemical applications and everybody in the isotope field would soon rush to apply carbon-labeled substances in metabolic studies. In the meantime we might have the inorganic ions to ourselves for a while.[14]

Ussing accepted the task, planning to get back to his own studies with amino acids and protein synthesis in a year or two. But the supposedly temporary project never ended. Ussing's first teammates became Hilde Levi and Barker Jørgensen. The work continued successfully, and Ussing would from time to time confer with Krogh at his private laboratory in Gentofte. Ussing found that both sodium ions (Na^+) and chloride ions (Cl^-) moved across the frog skin, but that Na^+ moved faster than Cl^-. His data did not permit him to determine if both Na^+ and Cl^- were actively transported or if Cl^- moved only because of the electrical potential generated by the Na^+ transport.

The XVIII International Congress of Physiological Sciences was scheduled to be held in Copenhagen in 1950, and Krogh, who had been asked to be congress president, invited Ussing to give one of the three introductory talks devoted to membrane transport problems. Alan L. Hodgkin and Edward J. Conway were the other two speakers. Ussing felt that he needed something striking to justify that he, a relative newcomer, occupied this prominent place on the program. With only a few months left before the congress, Ussing consulted his list of future projects and settled on a short-circuiting experiment. During his stay in Berkeley, California, Ussing had conceived the idea that if he could bring the electrical potential across the frog skin to zero then only the actively transported ions could contribute to the current passing through the skin and he could determine if both Cl^- and Na^+ were actively transported.

Needing an efficient coworker, Ussing contacted K. Zerahn who had worked with Hevesy. Thanks to their combined skills—Ussing's glass-blowing (learned from Krogh) and Zerahn's knowledge of electrical circuits—they made their apparatus, the now famous Ussing chamber. Within two weeks they had enough data, proving that only Na^+ transport is responsible for the current across the frog skin and that Cl^- is passively transported, and Ussing had obtained the "striking" new results that he could present in his lecture at the congress. Ussing's ingenious work led to an unprecedented explosion in the study of membrane transport, bringing numerous foreign visitors to study in Copenhagen.

As Hevesy and Krogh expected, the use of isotopes came to be, and still is, one of the most important research tools in modern biological sciences.

18
Dark Clouds (1938–1944)

> Mother probably knows how serious it is, but it is an implicit understanding between us that we don't talk about it. Mother does not want to be pitied and we pretend that she will soon be well.

In 1938 August was thinking about retiring. The eighteen years since he had won the Nobel Prize had been productive, hectic, and exciting, but August was beginning to tire from the pace and the many commitments and responsibilities. He wanted more time to think and do uninterrupted research; what he needed was a small laboratory where he could work for the rest of his life. By retiring in 1939 at age sixty-five rather than seventy, he felt that he could get his new work under way before he grew too old.

But even a small laboratory costs money and requires supporting facilities such as a workshop in which to build instruments. The best solution would have been to build a small private laboratory and become associated with a larger, better-equipped institute such as Nordisk Insulin Laboratory, where Hans Christian Hagedorn, August's partner and friend for thirty years, was director. The laboratory could be paid for partly with his own money and loans from his two brothers, and partly by grants from the Insulin Foundation.[1] This was a reasonable solution because, after all, it was due to August's initiative that the Insulin Laboratory existed.

But to August's immense disappointment his retirement plan met with unexpected resistance from two sides. Marie cringed at the idea of moving away from the comfortable villa, the laboratory, and surrounding area where she had been so happy. The other and more formidable obstacle was Hagedorn, who did not want Krogh to become associated with his laboratory. Krogh first discussed his plan with Hagedorn in the summer of 1938. Hagedorn was more than willing to recommend financial support for Krogh's laboratory, but he emphasized that it was not a good idea for Krogh to become associated with Nordisk Insulin Laboratory.

Krogh became uneasy, but could not believe that his old friend meant to turn him down. In early August 1938, he went looking for a suitable house lot in Gentofte near the Insulin Laboratory. Finding two lots near Gentofte Lake that bordered on the bog belonging to the Insulin Laboratory, he wrote Hagedorn, "I would like to know, if I decide on one of them, if I can have access to the bog [belonging to the Insulin Laboratory] through a private gate and if I can establish a connection to the house phone in the Insulin Laboratory."[2] Hagedorn wrote back that he was willing to support the grant application to the Insulin Foundation. But the lines he added hurt and angered Krogh, "Once more I wish to emphasize the qualms I have concerning the way in which you wish to be affiliated with Nordisk Insulin laboratory. I was hoping that after thinking it over you would accept my point of view. My own qualms have not diminished by further reflection."[3]

Hagedorn suggested calling a directors meeting. Krogh was chairman of the board of directors for Nordisk Insulin Laboratory. Several letters and a discussion, where Marie was present, followed, but Hagedorn stood firm, that Krogh could in no way become affiliated with Nordisk Insulin Laboratory.

Why was Hagedorn so much against Krogh's plan? August and Marie guessed that Hagedorn's resistance was prompted by jealousy, and that Hagedorn did not want to be overshadowed in his own laboratory by Krogh. This suspicion was corroborated by the Swede, Professor Torsten Thunberg, when he came to Denmark for the directors meeting. Marie was then in Trondheim, where I was hospitalized, seriously ill following a month-long illness in the Norwegian mountains. August wrote her: "I had a discussion with Thunberg today. He fully confirmed what we suspected that H. at any price wishes to avoid my influence and 'wanted to keep all lines, even the telephone lines, in his own hand.' I repeated that I had solemnly promised to stay out of everything, but this is apparently far from enough. . . . Thunberg assured me that they were willing to go far to satisfy me and hoped that I would find a way."[4] August repeated to Thunberg that without a big laboratory behind him with workshop and other facilities, he was afraid of starting anything. He shocked Thunberg by confiding that he was planning to resign as chairman of the board of directors. Hagedorn had already told Thunberg that he (Hagedorn) was upset about the whole situation and threatened to withdraw from everything. "This way of thinking has to a high degree strengthened my resolve to terminate all connections with the Insulin Laboratory," wrote August. Basically such a happy man, August was deeply discouraged. His letter to Marie continued:

> I cannot deny that these difficulties in combination with your absence trouble me greatly. The talk to Squibbs weighs heavily on me and will not take form. I have tried to look at the lectures for the spring [lectures at Swarthmore College on respiratory mechanisms], but they too present great difficulties because the material is too big to concentrate into five lectures. I don't see any way out. I wish you were home again,

but on the other hand you must not run any risks with Bodil. Greet her and say that she must keep her spirit and courage up. All will probably be well. Your own August.[4]

The last two sentences were probably directed to himself as much as to me. Years later it was learned from people close to Hagedorn that he had several times been angry and annoyed with Krogh when they worked together on the board of Nordisk Insulin Laboratory. More than once it happened that, before a meeting, Hagedorn would ask for Krogh's support in a certain course of action. Krogh would gladly agree, but later, having completely forgotten his promise (he had a notoriously poor memory when it did not concern science directly), would suggest something else at the meeting.[5] There was probably considerable truth in both Krogh's and Hagedorn's versions. Hagedorn, an immensely authoritarian man, could not tolerate anyone interfering with his personal authority over the Insulin Laboratory. August also may have been more than normally irritable during 1938. He was plagued by an enlarged prostate. His colleagues found him uncharacteristically irritable and difficult to get along with during that period. Over a period of several years he was treated three times with X-rays, but was not operated on until August 1940.[6]

In spite of the setback, August continued with his plans for the private laboratory. The lot was purchased and architectural plans were drawn. The villa was placed on a sloping lot where the lowest floor (part cellar) housed laboratory rooms for himself and Marie, workshop, office space, and so on, while the comfortable living area was on the two upper floors. The balcony leading from the dining room had a view over the bog and Gentofte Lake. Upstairs there were five bedrooms for himself and Marie and their visiting children with families.

During 1938 the news from Germany was becoming increasingly threatening and war seemed inevitable. In March the Anschluss between the Reich and Austria took place. Then on September 22, Hitler demanded the annexation of the Sudetenland, the German-speaking part of Czechoslovakia. On September 29–30, Chamberlain and Daladier went to Munich to confer with Hitler. The result was appeasement; Germany took over the Sudetenland, leaving Czechoslovakia with borders that could no longer be defended.[7] No one in Denmark believed the headlines in our newspapers, which read "PEACE" in very large letters.

During the spring of 1939, August and Marie went to the United States on a three-month trip. At Swarthmore College in Pennsylvania, August delivered the series of lectures on the comparative physiology of respiratory mechanisms, which later resulted in his monograph. Afterwards he lectured in several other American cities. In the meantime the situation in Europe had worsened when, on March 11, Hitler took over a large part of Czechoslovakia, and on March 23 occupied Memel in

Lithuania. Back in Denmark the family was nervous, but August and Marie returned safely. Then following a peaceful summer vacation in St. Karlsminde, the bad news arrived that German troops had invaded Poland on September 1. Two days later, France and Britain issued separate ultimatums demanding German troop withdrawal from Poland and when the ultimatums were not met, France and Britain were at war with Germany.

While in the United States, August had arranged with Laurence Irving at Swarthmore College for Dr. Per F. Scholander to go to United States to work with Irving because of their common interest in diving mammals. Krogh was impressed with the brilliant young Norwegian, who had been studying diving seals while working under the most primitive conditions in a cellar at the University of Oslo. Whenever Krogh saw real talent, he spared no effort. He recommended Scholander for a Rockefeller Fellowship, which was granted. In September 1939, however, Scholander received a letter from the foundation announcing that all fellowships had been cancelled due to the war. Alarmed, Scholander asked Krogh, "What do I do now?" Krogh did not want Scholander's talent to be wasted in Norway for the duration of the war. "Board the first ship to America and pretend the letter has not reached you," said Krogh. "Once in America you will be taken care of." Scholander worried, but told himself, "If papa Krogh wants me to go, I will." This he did and, as Krogh had promised, he got the fellowship.[8]

In Denmark it was hoped that the Scandinavian countries could remain neutral as during the First World War. Even so, the uncertainty created by the war made it undesirable for Krogh to retire. He postponed retirement, but continued the building of his new home and laboratory in Gentofte.

Toward the end of the decade, all of us in "Krogh's fun-loving young family," as Landis had called us, had become more serious-minded. We had grown up. By the beginning of the war we were all married.

For my brother Erik life had been rather difficult due to his poor health. He had divorced his first wife and was given to long periods of depression and sometimes to manic phases. (In fact Erik suffered from manic depression, a genetic disease that afflicted two of August's siblings.) When he was depressed, Erik became quite disorganized and found it difficult to do any work at all. In spite of these handicaps, Erik was brilliant and a charming, lovable brother with a great sense of humor and in June 1939 he finished his last examination for his medical degree and married Karen Hjort, a lovely young medical student with flaming red hair.

Ellen wanted to study medicine. But after two years of premedical and medical studies, she found that it was too much work and reasoned that if she wanted to be married it would be easier to be a dentist. So she switched to the School of Dentistry and graduated in 1936. Following her marriage to a young Swedish doctor, Einar Ljunghusen, she practiced dentistry in Sweden.

In the summer of 1935, when she was seventeen, my sister Agnes was taken by August on a trip on the laboratory boat to the Swedish Marine Biological Station in Kristineberg. In Kristineberg a young Swedish zoology student, Christer Wernstedt, saw her on the boat and fell in love. At the end of the summer, he came to Copenhagen and formally asked August and Marie for Agnes's hand in marriage. Following a year of studying home economics in Stockholm, Agnes studied at the University of Copenhagen, working in her father's laboratory with Hans Ussing on the experiments with heavy water at the Zoophysiological Laboratory. Agnes and Christer were married at Eastertime in 1938, when they were both working at the Zoophysiological Laboratory and Christer was studying at the University of Copenhagen.

My father took me to Norway in 1936 to visit the oyster ponds, where my father and Dr. Spärck were studying the growth of young oysters. My young friends teased me that my father wanted me to find a Norwegian, but it didn't happen on that trip. After I graduated from the gymnasium in 1937, I studied for the premedical examination, which I completed in 1938. From the age of three, it had been my intention to study medicine just like my mother, but Ellen changed my mind when she told me that it would be better to become a dentist if I wanted to marry. Definitely wanting to marry, I followed Ellen's example. When in the fall of 1937, I told my father that I had decided on dentistry, he said, "To find out if you have the necessary dexterity to become a dentist, I will teach you glassblowing in the laboratory during Christmas vacation." So he taught me glassblowing, which I took to easily, so my father declared that I had passed the test. My glassblowing skill became invaluable to me later when I switched to physiological research.

In fall 1937 a handsome young Norwegian zoology student, Knut Schmidt-Nielsen, came to work in my father's laboratory and at Christmastime he proposed to me. To no avail, my mother had tried to prevent the union by placing us far from each other at dinner parties. When we asked her why, she said, "I don't want Bodil to move to Norway, that is too far away." When the war broke out in September 1939, I was the only child left at home. Knut and I were still studying, I at the School of Dentistry and Knut in the Zoophysiological Laboratory. One day my father said to me, "Your mother and I have talked about it, and we think you might want to get married. If you do, you can live in the villa with us until you have finished your studies and can afford an apartment of your own." Gratefully, we accepted the offer, and on September 24, 1939, we were married.

That same year, August and Marie's first grandchildren started to arrive. Agnes had a son, Lars, and Ellen a daughter, Bodil, in 1939. During the next two years two more grandchildren arrived; Erik and Karen had a daughter, Inger Marie, and I a daughter, Astrid, in 1941.

When a lady friend of my mother's remarked on all the babies arriving, Marie unsentimentally remarked, "Yes, they marry and multiply like a cage full of white mice." The lady was shocked at Marie's cynicism, but Marie was not cynical, she had a good sense of humor. Both she and August took enormous pleasure in their grandchildren.

In the meantime the situation in Europe became increasingly ominous. With the cooperation of Russia, Hitler's blitzkrieg had defeated Poland; by October 7, 1939, all resistance there ceased. When Molotov and Ribbentrop signed the Soviet-German Nonaggression Pact in August 1939, it was secretly agreed that Russia could annex Poland up to the line of the Vistula River and annex the Baltic states of Latvia, Lithuania, and Estonia. Russia immediately demanded basing rights for its troops in the Baltic states and then confronted Finland with demands for naval basing rights. When the Finns refused, the Russians attacked Finland with four armies on November 30, 1939.[7]

The "Winter War" became a great inspiration to all Scandinavians, as the small Finnish army successfully fought against the Russians. In white uniforms, which made them almost invisible in the snow, the Finnish soldiers, combining their prowess on skis with their knowledge of their native forests, were able to cut off and encircle the disoriented enemy. The Danes reveled in the stories of their heroic feats as the Finns, far outnumbered by Russians, fought with skill and cunning.

The Danes took up collections to aid the Finns, prompting August to donate his large, solid gold Nobel Prize medal to aid their cause. Before he gave it away, I got permission to take it to the School of Dentistry, where I made a silver casting of it which was later gold plated. Unhappily, the Russians eventually overwhelmed the Finns with a million troops to their 175,000 soldiers. On March 12, 1940, a peace treaty was signed which conceded the demands made by the Russians.[7]

As long as Denmark was free, August could freely correspond with his many friends in England and America; work continued in the laboratory, but without foreign visitors other than Scandinavians. Knut, who had been in the laboratory, was now trying to complete his studies in Oslo. During the Easter vacation at the end of March 1940, I went to Norway to go skiing with him. Agnes and Christer were living in their own little apartment and Christer was studying for his degree in zoology and working in the Zoophysiological Laboratory.

Then on April 9, 1940, at four o'clock in the morning an overwhelming roar was heard over Copenhagen as hundreds of German warplanes flew in over the city. In the villa, I got up. The phone started ringing downstairs. It was Christer calling to report what we most feared: the Germans had taken over our country. Christer, awakened by the noise, had gone down from their apartment into the dark street, where he found numerous flyers telling the Danes that their country was now under German occupation. Ellen, who had been home with her parents following a protracted illness, came out at the top of the stairs hearing me crying, "Oh no, no!"

We were stunned. From the radio we learned that only minimal fighting had taken place as the German army rolled in over our southern border, and troops landed on our shores. Denmark, defenseless against the overwhelming military force, had capitulated when the Germans threatened to bomb Copenhagen. As I went to the School of Dentistry that morning, I saw the hated and feared German soldiers on every street corner. In the villa, Marie and the maid got busy putting up blinds over the windows, as ordered by the occupation force. It took time as black cloth had to be bought and fitted. In the beginning, only August's study was sufficiently darkened and that is where the family gathered in the evenings that followed. For the first time in my life, I saw my father disheartened. What he said one evening was, "It is no longer a joy to wake up in morning!" I couldn't help reflecting on the fact that up to then it had always been a joy to wake up in the morning. What a happy man he had been!

It became clear that the Swedish members of the family had to leave Denmark. Christer had to return to help defend his country. He suffered from chronic kidney disease and could not join the army, but even so he had to return to Sweden promptly to join the home guard. Before the end of April, Agnes, Christer, and their little son left for Stockholm. Ellen's husband, Einar, wanted his family home in Sweden, and so they left for northern Sweden, where Einar was practicing.

Now in the darkened villa, gloom descended on my parents and me. We did not know where my husband was, because all communication with Norway had been cut off. Fierce fighting had broken out in and around Oslo, where Knut had been studying. As German troop ships were sunk on their way to Norway, we cheered, but for me the situation was almost unbearable until, late in May, a letter arrived through the Red Cross that Knut was safe and was coming to Denmark. By that time fighting in northern Norway had ceased and the Allied troops had been evacuated from Norway.

The invasion which took us by surprise had been in the planning state since December 1939 and in February 1940 Hitler had agreed to the plan. The purpose was to deny Norwegian territorial waters to the British, and the decision was made to invade and occupy not only Norway but to use Denmark as a land bridge to Norway.[7]

By the end of the summer it looked as if Sweden, which was armed to the utmost with modern weapons and a huge army (one million men under weapon in a small country of only 7.5 million!) would be spared a German invasion. Every German plane that had violated Swedish air space since the beginning of the war had been shot down with great precision. Hitler realized that taking Sweden would be too expensive. However, he obtained what he wanted through the concessions Sweden made concerning transport of troops through Sweden and shipment of iron ore for the German war machine from Kiruna in northern Sweden.

That Sweden remained neutral during the war was a blessing to many in the Scandinavian countries, because it provided a safe haven for the many refugees from Denmark and Norway. Even so, the concessions made by the Swedish government were severely criticized by many Norwegians and Danes.

In the summer and early fall of 1940, as the blitzkrieg raged on and Holland, Belgium, and finally France fell, the situation seemed increasingly hopeless. Trying to visualize what our future would be, should Germany win and Denmark never be free again, was such a grim prospect that we could hardly bear it. Of the heroic evacuation from Dunkirk and the fierce Battle of Britain we heard little. Not until Germany, during summer 1941, turned against Russia did we dare to hope that Hitler would eventually lose the war. Our hopes were further raised when the United States was drawn into the war in December 1941. Much as we despised the Nazis, there was only minimal resistance to the occupation forces during the early years of the war. Hitler thinking of the Danes as pure Aryans treated Denmark with kid gloves.

No one in the family knows when Marie first felt a lump in her breast. It could have been around 1941. Never wanting to complain or even talk about her own health, she did not confide in August. The only treatment she accepted was some X-irradiation. We never learned why she did not accept a more radical treatment. Knut and I had been living in our own small apartment since fall 1940 and Marie and August were alone in the large villa, where they missed their family. Marie's thoughts centered on how to help her children and grandchildren. Travel between Sweden and Denmark became an ordeal. To obtain visas for her children to come home to Denmark, or for herself and August to travel to Sweden, application after application had to be submitted, letters had to be written, and excuses had to be invented. Sometimes the visas were granted, but often they were denied, and they were always delayed.[9]

Marie also worried about her children's health. As some food supplies dwindled in Denmark, we supplemented our diet with cod liver oil, boiled yeast, and dried rose hips to add vitamins A, B, and C. The Germans took advantage of Denmark's dairy products, pork, and eggs, and shipped large quantities to Germany. Even so, we never actually starved; we were usually able to buy some meats by standing in line, when they became available. Fuel, however, was scarce, resulting in cold houses and no hot water in the pipes.

Cut off from its regular suppliers, Sweden had more trouble feeding its population. When Agnes came home on a vacation, Marie detected that she was malnourished. Lack of protein had made her edematous. Her family's dinners had in fact consisted of fried potatoes served with boiled potatoes. From then until a few weeks before she died, Marie sent numerous packages of meat, cheese, and eggs to Agnes and Ellen in Sweden. To her dismay Agnes found that a ham, which had been traveling for only three days, was spoiled and made her family ill. Now Marie had to contact her supplier to make sure that the food was not spoiled.[10]

During summer 1940, Marie succeeded in getting Ellen and her little Bodil home for a much needed rest. The next summer, Agnes and her son Lars came, but in spite of all Marie's efforts Ellen's visa was denied. Marie missed her bitterly. Finally at Christmas she succeeded in getting Ellen and little Bodil home. Ellen was pregnant again and Marie went to Sweden to be with her after her little boy, Bjørn, was born. It was not the happy occasion she had expected. Ellen's husband Einar was drinking and threatened both Ellen and Marie.[9]

Knowing she did not have long to live and deeply distressed about Ellen's problems, Marie was even more eager to have Ellen home for the summer vacation in 1942. All was planned and Ellen could come to St. Karlsminde with her two children during her summer vacation. It looked promising by the end of June, but the permission did not come. Week after week it dragged on. Finally, by the end of July when most of Ellen's summer vacation was over, the visa was granted. Ellen got her vacation prolonged, and at last Marie had the pleasure of having all of her children and grandchildren with her in St. Karlsminde. By then the cancer had spread to her bones, and although she was having severe pains, she continued, as if nothing ailed her, to partake in the family life as her children and grandchildren enjoyed the summer in St. Karlsminde.

In November, Marie finally admitted that something was wrong and called it arthritis. She struggled along without complaining, giving the traditional birthday party for August, but early in December she took to her bed with a bad cold. From her bed she telephoned in her orders for Christmas gifts and food packages for her daughters in Sweden. Marie had furthermore found a good seamstress who made clothes for the grandchildren out of discarded coats, suits, and dresses.

Following the traditional Christmas celebration, Marie became bedridden because of increasing pain. August then moved her bed downstairs into his study so that she would be near the activities in the house. He himself spent the nights on the divan to be close at hand if she needed help, which she rarely did. A nurse came every morning, and the rest of the time, August and the maid looked in on her as often as they could.[11]

She started a series of X-ray treatments that made her ill and weak, but she assured her children that she was getting better. By early March she had had thirty-five X-ray treatments, but the pain did not subside and she was getting weaker. I'm not quite sure when she told August what she had known for a long time—that she had cancer. My father told me sometime in January, saying that I should not talk about it because my mother did not want to be pitied. I had been coming daily with my little Astrid, to work in the laboratory and to sit by her bed and talk with her. She wanted to talk about the experiments I was doing and gave me good advice, while Astrid sat on her bed or walked around in the study looking at the books. Once when we were talking about the biography of Madame Curie I was reading, my mother said with pride, "The only person who has ever been awarded two Noble Prizes, is a woman, Madame Curie!"

At the time, I was practicing dentistry three days a week in a dental clinic for schoolchildren. I needed the money and I felt that I had to practice to earn my *jus practicandi,* the right to practice independently. I disliked the practice and was unhappy with the time away from the laboratory, but I fully expected to put up with it. Then one day when I came to see my mother, my father said, "Your mother and I would like to help you by giving you 2,000 kroner so that you can give up the job and spend more time in the laboratory." In the middle of their own worries, they took time to think of my small problems. I was never one for crying, but this time tears came to my eyes.

My father also asked me to collaborate with him on an experiment on the exchange of ions between cells and extracellular fluid. It had been his plan that he, my mother, and I should do it together, but now he had to ask my mother's assistant Anna-Louise Lindberg to work with us.

Early in March, August wrote Agnes and Ellen that they should seek permission to come to Denmark because their mother was failing rapidly. He added, "Mother probably knows how serious it is but it is an implicit understanding between us that we don't talk about it. Mother does not want to be pitied and we pretend that she will soon be well. You will have to do the same when you write."[11] On March 18 he wrote, "Mother's condition is worse and she has for some time suffered severe pains. Usually she sleeps nights and she is very brave."[12] Around that time she said to me, "I am sorry to leave you. I wish I could stay longer with all of you."

All her children came and we sat around her during the day and night when she lay dying. It was August who kept our courage up. Then, as her life ebbed, he gathered us around his chair and told us about how they had met and became engaged, and for the first time he told us about the little boy Marie had borne who died at birth. We slept in the villa that night, a forlorn little flock. But the next morning as I came downstairs, my father took my hand, saying, "Come, let us go over and work in the laboratory." Even then, when life had dealt him its severest blow, work was his salvation.

Numerous letters of condolence came during the coming months, all bearing witness to how beloved and admired Marie was, and many wondered how August could live without his wife, who had meant so much to him. But August hid his sorrow. From his letters to colleagues, friends, and family from the time after her death, it sounds as if nothing of importance had happened to him. I understood him because I too behaved as if nothing had happened. When someone asked me how I was, I smiled and said, "Fine." It was when an acquaintance in surprise asked me, "But didn't you just lose your mother?" that I suddenly understood that I had to seem unconcerned because my feelings were far too deep to discuss. When Hohwü Christensen in a letter to August specifically mentioned how deeply saddened he, personally, was because of Marie's death, August answered that he admired his wife even more from the way she had borne the knowledge of her illness alone, sparing him the agony by not mentioning it to him.[13]

August had carefully considered how he would live after Marie died, and he now asked if my husband and I would move back to the villa and live with him so that I could run his household. He dearly loved our little year-and-a-half-old Astrid; she would help cheer him up. August was pleased with the way I ran his house and wrote Ellen in April that I was a good and capable housewife. He became increasingly fond of Astrid, telling Ellen, "I have much pleasure of Astrid who is very intelligent and sweet. I find it neither very difficult nor bothersome to be tyrannized by her. As soon as she sees me it is 'Come,' and then she takes a finger and pulls me along to show me or tell me something and I must repay as best I can."[14] To the surprise of visitors and to Astrid's delight, August would do somersaults for her and even taught her to play wheelbarrow with him where he walked on his hands while she followed behind laughingly, holding both of his feet.

August continued to be busy. He was head of a committee studying the most advantageous way of heating homes from a physiological point of view. Less than three weeks after Marie's death he had to represent the committee with speeches and a lecture. "I have the impression that it was all very successful," he wrote Ellen. But it was particularly his experiments which occupied him. In the middle of March, when he told Hohwü about Marie's illness, he added, "In spite of all the difficulties I continue to work diligently in the laboratory and I believe that I am on the trail of very important phenomena concerning the salt uptake and its regulation in living cells."[15] It was one of these experiments that he had planned as a family project. "The exchange of potassium and calcium between the frog heart muscle and the bathing fluid." Besides his own methods, it involved using Marie's preparation for the perfused frog heart and the calcium method I was using in my own experiments.

During the early part of the occupation we Danes had mostly shown our contempt and hatred for the occupation forces by ridicule. The Danes have a strong sense of humor, which made the situation bearable. From the beginning of the occupation, small groups of resistance fighters had spontaneously sprung up all over Denmark. Gradually, as the Allies were beginning to win the war, the resistance movement grew, and by 1943 there were six or seven major acts of sabotage every day.[16]

As we learned about the rounding up of Jews in other countries and the dismal conditions in the concentration camps (although we had not the slightest idea of the magnitude of the Nazi crimes), the anger and hatred toward the Nazis mounted steadily. Adding to the anger was the fact that the Germans recalled from Russia the Schalburg Corps to fight against the growing sabotage. The Schalburg Corps consisted of Danish traitors, mainly criminals released from our prisons when they volunteered to fight for Hitler.

Up until the fall of 1943, the Germans had left the eight thousand Danish Jews alone. Werner Best and before him Cecil von Renthe-Fink, the Nazi chief administrators in Denmark, knew that the Danes would react with violent anger should the Nazis try to round up the Jews because in Denmark, one of the world's oldest true democracies, the population harbored no trace of anti-Semitism. The Danish Jews were fellow Danes and an act against them would be considered an act against the Danish citizenry in general. The Danish opposition to anti-Semitism goes back to 1690 when a police chief was relieved of his duties for suggesting that Denmark establish a ghetto in Copenhagen. The Danish Parliament then passed a resolution condemning the very idea of a ghetto as an inhuman way of life. Later in 1814 a bill was passed in the Danish Parliament making all racial discrimination punishable by law.[16]

A series of events now led to the attempts at rounding up all Danish Jews. In August 1943 Hitler called Best to Berlin telling him that the idea of Danish Jews walking around free was "loathsome." Next the Germans issued an ultimatum to the Danish government on August 28, which was flatly rejected. On August 29 Hitler replaced Werner Best with General von Hannecken, who declared a state of emergency in all of Denmark. The cabinet resigned and the king declared himself a prisoner of war. The Danish Navy scuttled itself. To save face, Best, who had been set aside in favor of Hannecken, was now willing to cooperate with Hitler in the arrest and deportation of the Danish Jews and telegraphed him accordingly. Eventually, the raid was set for the night between September 30 and October 1.

A warning reached the Jews, however, before it was too late. The warning came from Georg F. Duckwitz, who was Best's head of shipping operations. Duckwitz had lived in Denmark since 1928 and had many friends among the heads of the Danish Social Democrat Party. The night before the raid he secretly warned Hans Hedtoft, head of the party, thus setting in motion a chain of warnings. Niels Bohr, whose mother was a Jew, was secretly taken to Sweden on September 30, where he personally contacted the Swedish king, requesting that Sweden accept the eight thousand Danish Jews for the duration of the war.

The night of the raid all but a couple of hundred Jews were in hiding in numerous Danish homes, hospitals, cloisters, hotels, and other places. Escapes to Sweden by boats, primarily fishing boats, and empty railroad cars were spontaneously organized and subsidized by freedom fighters and ordinary people from all walks of life.[16]

The Rockefeller Institute became one of the focal points when the professor in biochemistry, Richard Ege, became involved. Dr. Paul Astrup, Ege's associate, who was already active in the underground, first told Ege about the impending raid. Ege set out on bicycle to warn all his Jewish acquaintances. When some of them did not know where to hide, Ege simply told them to come to his apartment at the Rockefeller Institute. From then on, Ege and his wife were both actively involved also in collecting funds to help those who could not afford the transportation cost. Krogh's associate P. Brandt Rehberg and Kai Linderstrøm-Lang, head of the Carlsberg Laboratory, were likewise involved in hiding Jews and arranging for their transportation to Sweden.

In December, Bohr's institute was taken over by the Germans on the pretext that it had worked for the Allies. Promptly, everyone connected with the institute went underground. A woman and her eight-year-old son stayed in the basement of Krogh's villa for a short time.[17] Two of Hevesy's collaborators were able to move a substantial part of their work to the Zoophysiology Laboratory. When it was rumored that the cyclotron would be dismantled and shipped to Germany, the resistance movement made preparations to blow up Bohr's institute by placing bombs in its sewage system. The danger was averted through much activity behind the scenes by Professor Ole Chievitch and others. The institute was finally freed following a visit by the famous German physicist Werner Heisenberg, a former colleague and collaborator of Bohr, accompanied by a high-ranking Nazi physicist. The duo declared that there was nothing of interest at the institute, and it was released.[18]

August continued to be busy in the laboratory. As usual we celebrated his birthday in November with a roast goose dinner. The family members who came had to stay overnight because of the 8 P.M. curfew ordered by the Germans. By the end of 1943, the underground movement had greatly increased in Denmark. Our freedom fighters were becoming bolder and more effective in blowing up railroads and factories that served the Germans. Nobody knew who the freedom fighters were. It could be the one working next to you during the day, it could be a brother, husband, or friend. It was best not to know, because then you could reveal no secrets should you be caught and tortured. Thus, I did not know that my husband was making parts for rifles in the workshop in the Zoophysiological Institute. In the academic year 1943–44, I was again teaching at the School of Dentistry, when one day one of our very best instructors was caught and executed for his underground activities. For each successful act of sabotage the Germans retaliated by blowing up beloved buildings and killing some of our best-known people.

Shots and explosions rang out during the hours of darkness, and we only learned later from the illegal underground papers some of what had actually happened. Sometimes it was our people killing a Dane caught in collaboration with the Germans; sometimes one of our people was shot. Air raids were becoming frequent as the British Royal Air Force bombed strategic sites in Denmark. In the villa we had a room in the cellar dedicated as a bomb shelter, but mostly we avoided going down there even when the eerie sound of the alarm was heard. As Danish railroads were blown up, food shipments to Germany were greatly hampered, and suddenly there would be large amounts of eggs or other commodities available on the black market.

None of these events could be told in the letters going back and forth between Denmark and Sweden. All letters were censored and a line was painted across each letter to test for invisible ink. After Hevesy, Bohr, Buchtahl, and others had fled to Sweden and Bohr's institute was occupied by the Gestapo, all August could write his daughter in Sweden was, "It is going quite well, even though our work is greatly hampered by the events."[17]

In spite of increasing unrest, life was relatively normal during the spring of 1944. My son Bent was born in March. We were all busy with our research. It pleased August that two of his children, Erik and I, were doing research, publishing papers, lecturing, and teaching. Rehberg was now deeply involved in the underground movement and was still around. He helped arrange for a steady flow of shipments of food packages to the Danish prisoners in Theresienstadt. In the meantime, Ege had had to go into hiding after the Gestapo early one morning came banging on his door. He had escaped by leaving his apartment through a back door.

In June 1944, in reprisal for the sabotage of the railroads, the Danish Riffelsyndikat, and Globus arms factory, the Gestapo began murdering Danish patriots and other well-known Danish citizens. The beloved patriot author Kai Munch was found shot in a ditch early in June. On June 5 and 6 the invasion of Normandy was underway. In the villa all was calm when on the twelfth of June a mysterious telephone call changed it all. Knut answered. A man with a heavy German accent asked for Professor Krogh and identified himself as Professor Arnold. When we checked on it, we found that the actual Professor Arnold did not have a German accent and had not called. The same afternoon a well-dressed man rang the doorbell. When I opened the door he asked for Professor Krogh, but his accent made me suspicious, and I assured him that Krogh was not at home. Rehberg and the Danish police advised Krogh to promptly go underground. They discovered that August Krogh was next in line on the list of prominent Danes the Gestapo was planning to murder. Had my father opened the door himself, he most likely would have been shot. Krogh was scheduled to be an opponent at a doctoral dissertation on June 13, but instead he bicycled out of Copenhagen to stay for short periods of time with various friends and relatives north of Copenhagen.

In the meantime, the violence in Copenhagen increased, as the Germans let loose the Schalburg Corps to shoot innocent Danish citizens. The disturbance spread throughout Copenhagen, barricades were built, and a general strike ensued. June 30, as the strike took effect, Knut and I bicycled out of Copenhagen. We went on to St. Karlsminde with our two young children, the baby in a sidecar and Astrid in a seat on the handlebars.

August came to St. Karlsminde for a brief visit on July 5. The same day a telegram from Agnes arrived from Sweden sent through the Red Cross. She told him that her husband's kidney ailment had become very serious and she begged her father to come to Stockholm right away. August had been planning to spend the summer in a small laboratory on Zealand, but now he went back to Copenhagen. When he wrote Ellen after his arrival in Stockholm he explained:

> It was not very dangerous since I had changed my looks considerably, full beard, long tie [he used to always wear a bow tie] no glasses. With good help and a lot of energy I succeeded in getting all taken care of such as Danish, German and Swedish visa as well as money. As early as Saturday I could travel [to Sweden] via Helsingør [Elsinor]. There I was almost stopped because my name was not yet on the list of those who could leave. I got through, but had to leave all my scientific notes for a paper I was planning to write. I hope I will get them back because they promised to send them to Copenhagen.[19]

It appears that the German authorities who gave him his visa were not working directly with the Gestapo and that they were glad to get Krogh safely out of Denmark.

As the Allies were winning the war, violence continued to escalate in Denmark. The Danish police force was rounded up and sent to concentration camps. A similar attempt was made to round up the university students, but it was effectively prevented by letting the word out that the students should stay away from lectures and other university functions. By the fall of 1944 the resistance leaders asked the Royal Air Force to bomb Aarhus University to destroy the large, dangerous Gestapo files on the Danish freedom fighters.[20] The plan was to bomb the student quarters that had been taken over by the Gestapo, but the bombardiers' aim was not precise and the main building where my brother Erik was working in his laboratory was also hit. Erik was slightly injured and his scientific notes were destroyed.

March 1, 1945, Erik was arrested in his home where he was hiding a freedom fighter, who had been busy blowing up railroads. Both were taken prisoner. But Erik's wife Karen was able to deceive the two Gestapo men who came to arrest them. One went upstairs to the bedrooms while the other was looking through a pile of papers on Erik's desk. While he was in the middle of the pile the other called him upstairs. Quickly, Karen took out the illegal papers in the pile and put them with those the officer had already looked at. Thus, when the officer returned to the task he found no illegal papers! As soon as they had left with their prisoners, Karen took off on her bicycle to warn those that had been implicated by papers found in her guest's coat pocket.[21]

In early 1945 Rehberg was taken prisoner by the Gestapo and was interrogated and tortured. He was imprisoned in the Shell House in Copenhagen which served as Gestapo headquarters. On the top floor of the building thirty-two of the most important leaders of the resistance movement were jailed. In spite of this the resistance leaders asked the Royal Air Force to bomb the building. The British were reluctant to grant the request because of the prisoners, but the Danish resistance people insisted that the material held in the Gestapo files was so damaging to them that the bombing had to take place. On March 20, nineteen Mosquito bombers and twenty-eight P-51 Mustang fighters took off from Norfolk. The planes came in low over the North Sea to avoid German radar. Then most of the bombers skipped their bombs low into the base of the Shell House. The upper floor shook violently but about half of the prisoners were able to escape alive. Rehberg and the others had to jump over the dead Gestapo men as they reached the lower floors. Rehberg managed to run through the streets to the communal hospital and was later spirited to Sweden.

As a result of the loss of their files on resistance people, the Gestapo had no records on my brother Erik and he was released after only a month in prison. Although the bombing of the Shell House was a success, it was also the cause of a horrible tragedy. One of the Mosquito bombers clipped a wing on a railroad tower and crashed into the French Jean d'Arc School. The school burst into flames. The heavy clouds of smoke from the fire caused the last wave of bombers to mistake the school for the target and they released their bombs over the school where over two hundred children died.[20]

19

Exile in Sweden (1944–1945)

> I am mainly occupied in writing a paper on the exchange of ions between living cells and their surroundings.

August's enforced stay in Sweden was to last ten months. It was a difficult period, and a few times he came close to despair as he visualized his life without Marie after the war. But mostly he adapted to the circumstances with his usual vigor. He helped and comforted his two daughters, wrote his famous paper on active transport by cell membranes (the Croonian Lecture), finished a paper for Marie and a study on bud development in trees, lectured in Stockholm and Lund, and attended the celebrations in Stockholm when Hevesy was awarded the Nobel Prize.

Arriving in Stockholm on July 9, 1944, August soon learned the background for Agnes's cry of distress. Due to an infection, chronic kidney disease, and resulting inflammation of the retina, Christer had been seriously ill for seven weeks and had lost most of his vision. To restore the blood supply to his kidneys, Dr. Hilding Berglund (Sweden's foremost specialist in kidney diseases) proposed an operation on each kidney with recuperation in between. Agnes was pregnant and suffered from a stomach ulcer. Had Marie still been alive, she would have been the one to take over, but now August came to his daughter's aid.[1] Supplying moral as well as practical support, August stayed with Agnes in Stockholm until Christer came home from the first operation and then went with them on recreation to a summer cottage in Skärgården (Stockholm's archipelago). When his sight improved sufficiently to permit Christer to read with one eye by using a magnifying glass, August helped him by writing an abstract of his thesis research for *Nature*. Always considering work the best healer, he encouraged Christer to write his doctoral dissertation as soon as he was able.

Another important task that August accomplished during this time was to write a paper for Marie. Before she died, Marie had asked him to publish her study on the effect of thyroid extract on guinea pigs. He finished the first draft of the paper but, needing a few more data, did not submit the final version to the journal until he returned to Denmark.[2] In vain, August tried to work on the material he had brought with him on ion exchange in cells, but gave it up because of lack of space and library resources.

When Christer had recovered from the second operation and his disease was in remission, August considered his mission ended and wished to go home. He was even willing to stay in hiding as long as he could be in his own country. But in Denmark the situation was becoming increasingly dangerous as the Germans became more desperate and the Danish saboteurs became bolder. Urged to stay, August reluctantly gave in and settled in Eslöv with Ellen and her family.

Eslöv is only twenty minutes by train from Lund, where August was given a room at Lund University's Physiological Institute. This is where he worked until the war ended. He even received a salary. In a letter to Cecil Drinker in Boston, Krogh wrote, "I am mainly occupied in writing a paper on the exchange of ions between living cells and their surroundings, discussing the literature and new experiments to show that a power of active transport of certain ions is a general property of living cells."[3]

In Lund, he found numerous friends, among them Fritz Buchtahl, a fellow refugee from Denmark, who also came from the Rockefeller Institute. But August longed for home and also for his American friends: "Even though the Swedes are extremely kind to the 15,000 Danish refugees who are now here, and I myself am among very good friends, we are deeply grateful for any greetings from our friends overseas, and we all look forward to the day when we can get back home."[3]

In his letter to Drinker he told about his research plans. Telling Drinker that he had now submitted his resignation from his professorship, he added that Rehberg would be appointed as his successor.

> I feel quite fit and hope that it may be possible for me to move into the house in Gentofte and go on working. I am especially fascinated by problems concerning the flight of insects and birds and hope to make determinations of the cost of flying at varying rates; but much depends on conditions in Denmark, when I am allowed to return, and there are also personal difficulties in the way. Perhaps I shall have to take a small house in Århus, where my son Erik is assistant at the Institute of Anatomy and where they will be glad to give me room and facilities.

Proudly he added, "Erik has been doing some very nice work in physiological anatomy of the motor cells in the spinal cord and their reaction to oxygen lack."[3]

The personal difficulty that August alluded to was his great worry about living alone in his Gentofte villa and laboratory close to the Insulin Laboratory. He knew that Knut and I with our children could only stay with him for a limited time before our next career move. We were both working on our doctoral thesis research and were expecting to move to

Norway following a study trip to America. August missed Marie badly. He did not speak of it during this time, but wrote of it to the Bøvings; several years later, he admitted to Nic that loosing Marie had been extremely hard on him. He needed company and someone to take over the job of running his household. Before he left Denmark, August had asked Anna-Louise Lindberg, Marie's faithful assistant for many years, to marry him.

Miss Lindberg was an unusually intelligent, energetic, and resourceful lady in her early forties. She took a warm and genuine interest in the entire Krogh family and the laboratory. She had never married and now lived alone. Over the years she had formed a close personal friendship with Rehberg, which many saw as a romantic attachment. Following Marie's death, August worked with her. They coauthored a couple of ion exchange papers and together completed Marie's thyroid hormone study.

August had written Miss Lindberg asking her for a decision because his own decision concerning the house in Gentofte depended on hers: I cannot imagine living and working alone in that big house without anyone that I am close to, in other words, I cannot do it unless you come with me. Will you?[4] She could still work at Zoophysiological Laboratory. All she had to do was live there with him, and he could afford a small car, if she would drive herself. It would please him to stay in contact with his old laboratory through her. Before he left for Sweden, he had asked her to give him an answer, which she had not done, and now he was afraid that she had misunderstood him. Miss Lindberg was compelled to write:

> It saddens me deeply that there could have been a misunderstanding last summer. The agreement was that if the answer to the letter was no then I need not answer but could pretend that it was not written. Therefore, I waited two weeks before making my yearly trip to St. Karlsminde to visit the entire family and to talk with the professor about the experimental results and curves, and I tried to pretend that your ever so beautiful letter had never been written.[5]

Lindberg went on to say that she could not live in Gentofte, she preferred her own easy household, private apartment, and the freedom that she had finally acquired five years earlier when her mother died. Then she added: "I will just add that the professor must move to Gentofte, it will be so sad otherwise, for the professor, the children and their families. From the early planning stages they have been looking forward to having a place for vacations and for work in your home. Now their father must not let them down and deprive himself of some good years in Gentofte."[5]

I, too, wrote my father stressing how much we needed him and that he must not let all his plans depend on Miss Lindberg. It was the first and only time that he wrote me a letter of reproach, saying that I had no understanding at all of what a serious blow he had received, but that could not be expected either. In retrospect, I know that I had not understood; nor did I have the slightest inkling that he had proposed to Miss Lindberg. Our letters, however, had an effect. Following the initial disappointment, August saw that, in reality, he had no choice, as he put it; he had to continue with the house-laboratory in Gentofte. As it turned out this was the best possible arrangement. He did great work in his Gentofte laboratory, and he was never alone in the big house. The place became a haven for his children and grandchildren, as well as for many good friends. Then fate brought him Nic and her family when he needed them the most, and a short time later a truly outstanding scientific assistant, Torkel Weis-Fogh.

Before August left Denmark he had done a series of experiments on plant cells and vertebrate tissues to study movements of ions between cells and their surroundings. He had published some of these studies. Some were still unfinished by the time he was forced to leave, but he brought the data with him. His notes were confiscated at the border but were later mailed to him. In Lund, with access to a good university library and the newest literature, he worked on a major treatise.

The opening statement of his the paper reads, "The main object of this paper is to discuss the large differences in concentration of individual ions between the interior of living cells and the fluid surrounding them, to bring out the point that such differences are normally, and perhaps always brought about and also maintained by some special activity on the part of the cell, while diffusion processes are all the time tending to reduce them."[6] What Krogh meant by "special activity on the part of the cell," was active ion transport requiring expenditure of metabolic energy.

His views differed from those of Hugh Davson and James Frederick Danielli, who in 1943 had published their book *The Permeability of Natural Membranes*. Assuming that all exchanges of ions and other solutes take place by diffusion, these authors discussed at length what they called "equilibrium conditions of cells." Placing the emphasis on diffusion through natural membranes, they barely consider the possibility of active transport processes. In contrast, in the paper he was writing, Krogh made it clear that "where large differences in concentration of single ions are maintained between organisms and the surrounding water or between cells and the surrounding extracellular fluid, one has to do *not* with a true equilibrium, but with a *steady state* maintained against a passive diffusion."[6]

Krogh's own interest in active transport of ions had been particularly inspired by the work by H. Lundegårdh (1933–37) on active uptake of ions by plant roots. This had led him to study uptake of chloride from very dilute solutions by gills and skin in animals (such as crustaceans, fishes and frogs). Through such active transports of ions, freshwater and some brackish-water animals maintain a higher osmotic concentration and different ion concentrations in their body fluids than the surrounding water. The studies that followed resulted in his book on osmoregulation in aquatic animals.[7] Not only do whole animals maintain different concentrations from that of their surroundings, but within each organism the fluid within the cells (the protoplasm or intracellular fluid) has an ionic composition different from that of the body fluid surrounding them (extracellular fluid and blood), with much higher K^+ concentration and much lower Na^+ concentrations in the cells than in the blood.

The question raised by several investigators was, How do animal cells maintain these concentration differences? There was no consensus among investigators as to this point. Archibald V. Hill (1931) categorically claimed that muscle cells are normally impermeable to Na, K, and Cl ions, while Wallace O. Fenn (1936) acknowledged that the membrane was permeable to K^+. It was a widely held, almost dogmatic belief that cell membranes, such as the membrane of red cells, were impermeable to positively charged ions (cations) while still permeable to negatively charged ions (anions). The maintenance of the cation concentration differences were explained by the postulated impermeability.

This dogma could no longer hold up when Hevesy and his collaborators (1939, 1941), by means of isotopes, showed that a regular, albeit slow exchange of cations as well as anions takes place through the cell membranes in muscle, red cells, liver, brain, and yeast cells, thus proving that the membranes are not impermeable to cations.[12] How then could the ion concentrations be so different inside and outside the cells? As early as 1941, R. B. Dean concluded, "The muscle can actively move both Na^+ and K^+ against a concentration gradient and therefore there must be some sort of a pump possibly located in the fiber membrane." While still in occupied Denmark, Krogh had not had access to the new literature and was probably unaware of Dean's paper. It may not have been available in Lund, because it is not in Krogh's list of references.

Krogh reasoned that, as a consequence of the free permeability for water of cell membranes,[9] it followed that the cells must be in osmotic equilibrium with the extracellular fluid and a large fraction of the ions inside the cells must be free and not bound. Therefore, K^+ ions would be lost by diffusion across the cell membrane while Na^+ would diffuse into the cells. These passive movements of ions would have to be counteracted by active transports of Na^+ and K^+ ions in the opposite directions of the passive diffusion processes.

Having developed a very accurate microanalytical method for K determination, Krogh proceeded to investigate K^+ movements into cells. In three separate studies on animal cells, "The Exchange of Ions between Cells and Extracellular Fluid I, II, and III," which he carried out and published in 1943 and 1944, Krogh showed that cells that had been depleted of K^+ and then returned to a K-containing solution could take up K^+ actively and probably also extrude Na^+, actively.[10] Krogh was inspired by a paper by Lundegårdh from 1940. Lundegårdh had had the great foresight to visualize what we now know as the transporter molecules, inserted in the cell membrane at right angles to the surface. Lundegårdh considered "the boundary layer of plant cells as a mosaic containing both indifferent micellae [long lipoid molecules] and others, spaced at certain intervals, which have at both ends very definite affinities."[11] Krogh became deeply interested in this model of ion transport molecules to which the ions would become attached and then released at the other side of the membrane. From his results on K uptake by cells, performed on isolated chorion membranes, Krogh was able to estimate the distance between membrane transport molecules to be approximately 150 Å.[12]

In a fourth study on ion exchange between cells and extracellular fluid, Krogh collaborated with Ib Holm-Jensen and the Finnish scientist Veijo Wartiovaara. The study was designed to determine the diffusion rate for K^+ and Na^+ through the cell membranes of plants.[13] If, in a steady state, diffusion losses of K^+ were exactly balanced by active uptake of the ion, then the rate of active transport should equal the diffusion rate. In these experiments Krogh and his two collaborators used the radioactive isotopes ^{42}K and ^{24}Na, supplied by the cyclotron in Bohr's institute.

Because of the war and the German occupation of Denmark, all of these studies were carried out under rather trying conditions and the experiments were terminated when Krogh had to flee Denmark. In one of his papers he wrote, "These experiments ought to be repeated and extended, but as it appears unlikely that we shall get an opportunity to do so we feel justified in publishing them in this fragmentary state." Even more difficulties were encountered when Krogh and his colleagues were using radioactive potassium (^{42}K). The study was undertaken on Krogh and Collander's initiative as a continuation of Collander's work. Veijo Wartiovaara, arrived in Copenhagen in September 1942 bringing with him a supply of a special aquatic weed, *Tolypellopsis stelligera,* which has very large cells. But then the cyclotron in Bohr's laboratory failed. It was working again in the fall of 1943 and the experiments got under way, but Wartiovaara had already returned to Finland where the Germans were fighting the Russians. Then the Germans seized Bohr's institute and the resistance movement threatened to blow it up. Finally, following Heisenberg's visit to Copenhagen which resulted in the release of the cyclotron, isotopes were again produced late in February, but by that time the *Tolypellopsis* had been in the laboratory for five months and were no longer in perfect condition. Krogh and Holm-Jensen supplemented the material with the freshwater plant *Nitella,* and the experiments could continue until Krogh had to flee the country.[13]

Krogh's treatise "The Active and Passive Exchange of Inorganic Ions through the Surfaces of Living Cells and through Living Membranes Generally" is characteristic of his way of thinking and writing. He deals at length with the literature as well as with his own finished and unfinished studies. Just as in the capillary book, he reports the results of individual experiments, supplying his own interpretation rather than relying on the interpretations given by the authors. His discussion covers all types of living cells from the animal as well as the plant kingdom. His final conclusion, "The power of active transport of ions is a common occurrence both in vegetable and in the animal kingdom and is possibly a general characteristic of the protoplasmic surface membrane," is as true today as it was when he wrote it.

He had followed his plan of finishing the paper by the time he officially retired from his professorship. On that date, February 2, 1945, he wrote his friend Sir Henry Dale, director of the Royal Institute, while sending him the paper through the British Council in Stockholm. "I want to ask your advice, or rather to leave it to you what to do with it. You are certainly too busy to read it, but if you will look through the summary I think you will understand my problem. The paper contains too much of original material and personal viewpoints to go as a review. I fear it is too long and contains too much discussion of other people's experiments to be published in *J. Physiol.*"[14] He went on to say that he would like to have it published in the *Proceedings of the Royal Society.*

Dale accepted the paper for the *Proceedings*, and the Society invited Krogh to give the Croonian Lecture in the fall of 1945. In May he also received a letter from the registrar of the Royal College of Physicians in London, asking him if he would accept the Baly Medal.

The Croonian Lecture had a great impact on future research. It was not the first time that such ideas had been expressed, but it was the first time that so much evidence for the concept was presented. Krogh's considerable international prestige lent credence to the new concept, which henceforth became widely accepted.

Having submitted his large manuscript in which he discussed the active uptake of ions by plant roots, the question of how the ions and other material are supplied to the buds was a natural extension. Consequently, in collaboration with the Swedish plant physiologist Hans Burström, Krogh began a study on the development of buds in trees.[15] "At an early stage in spring, different for different trees and shrubs, the buds formed during the preceding summer and autumn begin to develop," he wrote in the introduction to the paper. "A great deal more than water appears to be necessary for the growth process in the buds." Burström and Krogh collected material from the University of Lund's botanical garden and Krogh collected samples around Eslöv. It became a large study. Buds at several stages of development were analyzed for sugars, ions, and nitrogen, and so was bleeding sap from trunks and branches. Analyses for sugars and nitrogen compounds were made in Lund, while the analyses of minerals by spectral analysis were made at Lundegårdh's Institute for Plant Physiology at Ultuna-Uppsala. Burström and Krogh found a great increase in sugar and minerals in the buds during development, but it could not be resolved how this material could be supplied from the sap, which had a much lower concentration.[15]

While working in Lund, August had lunch with Fritz Buchtahl and his lovely wife, Ellen, each day. They knew each other rather well from the Rockefeller Institute in Copenhagen, but these lunches became the beginning of warm friendship that meant a great deal to August during his years in Gentofte.

As the war was drawing to an end the news from Denmark became more encouraging. In Copenhagen, the Gestapo headquarters was bombed by the Royal Air Force and Rehberg escaped. He arrived in Lund and could tell Krogh about his torture and his miraculous escape from the collapsing and burning building. News of his son Erik's release from prison in Aarhus also reached August. Krogh's private laboratory and home in Gentofte were gradually being completed. I followed my father's instructions about moving and what to do with the family's belongings. He told us that he planned to live in the basement next to his office and laboratory rather than upstairs in the comfortable bedroom he had planned before Marie died. We moved the first of May.

Then in the evening of the fourth of May came the glorious, unbelievable news that Admiral Dönitz had capitulated in northern Europe. At long last Denmark was free and safe. Until then, we were never sure that our country would not be devastated by the retreating Germans before we were liberated. In Finland the Germans had applied a scorched-earth policy, and we knew this could happen to us. The night we learned that we were free I went into my little daughter's room, woke her up and said, "Astrid, the war is over, we are free!" Astrid replied, "Then grandfather will come home!"

Through a strange coincidence something happened that was to save August's life early in June. At the time Denmark was liberated, my one-year-old son, Bent, had been ill for a couple of months with a severe ear infection. Since there was very little heat at the Rockefeller Institute and none in the Gentofte house, the doctors insisted that Bent stay in the hospital. He was not getting any better and it was heartbreaking to see how listless and depressed the little fellow was in the hospital. I wrote my father, asking him to please bring penicillin with him to cure Bent. Promptly, August contacted Liljestrand, who let him have a sample, which should be sufficient to cure Bent.

Having just completed his study with Burström, now for a full week August applied all of his energy to the task of obtaining permission to go home. With fifteen thousand Danish refugees in Sweden, it looked as if it might take several weeks. Then on May 18 he received a telegram from Stockholm with permission to travel. The next day he arrived in Copenhagen totally unexpected. No taxis were available; he had to find us at work before we could go home to his new residence and laboratory on Søbredden in Gentofte.

20

The Private Laboratory in Gentofte (1945–1947)

> My wind-tunnel will suddenly become an apparatus of practical importance and the whole project is so big and important that I cannot possibly refuse my cooperation or even postpone it. In reality it concerns creating the foundation for a world-wide control of migrating grasshoppers.

Following joyous welcomes from family and friends, August busily arranged his study and applied for funds to equip his new laboratory. His work was briefly interrupted when he developed pneumonia after a trip to Møen with the Buchtahls. He had brought with him the penicillin that I had asked for, but in the meantime my little son was cured of his ear infection by sulfa drugs. So August himself got the penicillin, which worked its usual miracle. In two days he was cured.

In the years after his return to Denmark, August worked toward two main goals: to continue his own research, and to help promising young scientists and thereby science in general. While he pursued these goals with relentless energy, he also took time for his archeological interest.

Immediately after his return, with no laboratory assistant and little money, August had to exert a major effort to get his private laboratory in working order for his new experiments. He was determined to spend the winter in the United States if he could not work productively in postwar Denmark. A. N. Richards had informed August that the Rockefeller Foundation would authorize Harvard University to invite him for a prolonged period and pay the expenses at a very generous rate. When August found that the conditions in Denmark were not as bad as he had feared, he accepted the invitation for a three-month stay beginning in early March. For two reasons he could not go for a longer visit:

> One is my private laboratory which I must get going and at least start the experiments which I have been planning for the last six years. They are to deal with the propulsion of fishes in water and insects in the air and to measure, if possible, the relationship between velocity of progress and energy expenditure. I hope to make some quite prelimi-

nary insect experiments just after the summer holidays and to do something with the fishes in the winter months."

The second reason was his chairmanship of the committee to study home heating problems. "We are going to try and clear up the problem of the distribution of heat loss from the human body between convection and radiation and I feel that my active participation is necessary."[1]

Following the hiatus of the war, honors were bestowed upon Krogh from many sides. In September 1945, accompanied by much festivity, August was made honorary citizen of his birthplace, Grenaa, where a commemorative plaque was placed on the wall of the house where he was born. A letter from the daughter of his former teacher Carl Nilsson meant more to him than did the festivities. August had expressed to the press how much Nilsson had meant to him, and this prompted his daughter to thank him. August thanked her in a long letter.

In October, he traveled to London to receive the Baly Medal and present the Croonian Lecture. At a solemn ceremony at the Royal College of Physicians on October 18, Sir Alexander Fleming and August Krogh each received the medal. Neither of the two would have been there, had not Fleming discovered penicillin and Krogh not been cured by it. At the stately dinner the same evening, the prime minister, the archbishop of Canterbury, and the minister for foreign affairs were among the speakers. Then on October 25 Krogh presented the Croonian Lecture to the Royal Society.[2]

The London visit was particularly pleasant when August visited with his longtime friends Sir Edward and Lady Mellanby. Both of the Mellanbys wrote August regularly, but May Mellanby, a scientist in her own right, wrote him more often. This time May warmed August's heart by speaking about Marie. He admitted how brave Marie had been during her illness and how terribly he missed her.[3]

Several other close friends brightened August's life during the Gentofte years. Besides the Buchtahls, these were Claus Munch Plum, Erik Tetens Nielsen, Torkel Weis-Fogh. They and their families became frequent guests in August's home.

The warm friendship with Claus Munch Plum, his wife and children started the year before August had to leave Denmark.[4] Plum was a young man who had studied medicine, but failed the first part of the medical examinations three times. He was seriously dyslexic, but was a talented experimenter and had done work on the ripening of red blood cells while working in the laboratory of the medical firm Medicinalco Ltd. The work was excellent and Plum had written a doctoral thesis. But how could he get a doctoral degree without first having an academic degree? He came to Krogh to ask advice. Impressed by the work and sympathetic to Plum's dilemma, Krogh suggested that the university could give dispensation in this case. Looking over the manuscript, Krogh did not appreciate the historical review in the first chapter. He said, "Throw that away, it is the medical people who want you to show that you have read so many papers, but in my opinion you should stick to the problem and cite only the necessary literature." Following Krogh's advice the first chapter was thrown out, and the second rewritten. A dissertation has to be accepted by two independent official opponents; Krogh would be one and he thought it best that the other was from the medical faculty, precisely because Plum had failed the medical examinations three times. Einar Lundsgaard, a physiology professor (also at the Rockefeller Institute), was asked.[5] Lundsgaard found the paper acceptable, except that it lacked a chapter on earlier studies. Even though Plum told him that Krogh didn't want it, Lundsgaard insisted. When Plum told Krogh, he said, "Wait here a moment, I will go over and talk with Lundsgaard." A while later he came back saying that now Lundsgaard had changed his mind.[4]

While Krogh spared no effort helping promising young scientists like Plum, there were others to whom he was less than generous. Once when Plum was talking with Krogh, the secretary came to announce that Dr. so-and-so wanted to see him. Krogh said, "I have already told him that I am not available today." A while later when Krogh and Plum came out of the office they saw the man sitting in the laboratory hallway. The man got up, saying, "Mr. Professor—" Interrupting him, Krogh said, "I told you that I cannot be seen today, can't you see that?"[4]

Another close friend was Erik Tetens Nielsen. In the early twenties, he was studying zoology and knew Krogh through his lectures.[5] Krogh first noticed him when Tetens was giving a talk at the Natural History Society. Independently, while studying at the university, Tetens had made extensive studies of solitary digging wasps. He was very clever at making simple, ingenious instruments for his work. During his talk he handed out a special funnel through which he could pour melted metal that would make a complete cast of the wasp's tunnel, regardless of its angle to the surface. Krogh studied the funnel throughout the lecture and invited Tetens home for lunch the next day.

Tetens married a young woman, Astrid, who with her widowed father owned a lovely old farmhouse surrounded by willow trees in Tisville. Astrid named it "Pilehuset" (the willow house). Tetens came upon the house as he wandered around studying wasps in 1925. He fell in love with the girl and the house and became a frequent visitor, prompting Astrid's father to make a small laboratory for him in one end of the house. In 1928, when the laboratory had just been finished, Krogh asked to see it. "It is not much of a laboratory," said Tetens apologetically. "Ah, but I have seen those that were smaller, where it was still possible to do good work," answered Krogh. In the following years, Krogh bicycled from Lynæshus to Pilehuset several times each summer. Sometimes I came along. The house and family were charming and interesting, and Tetens always had insect experiments and apparatus to show us.

When Tetens had finished a series of papers on solitary wasps and their nests, he submitted them for a doctoral degree. Unfortunately for Tetens, the faculty decided on two zoology professors as the official opponents, and not Krogh. Having had problems with one of the two professors, Tetens withdrew the dissertation. In a year he wrote another thesis on the metabolism of the wasps, so that Krogh would have to be an official opponent.[5] The professor Tetens had trouble with was the famous zoologist Carl Wesenberg-Lund. According to Tetens he was "an inspiration among teachers at the University of Copenhagen and a field naturalist by the grace of God." But he was capricious in his relations with people and could without apparent provocation suddenly take an intense dislike to anyone, among them Tetens.

While praising Tetens's work at the defense ceremony, Krogh compared Tetens to the little kingbird who lets the eagle (Wesenberg-Lund) lift it to great heights and then flies even higher than the eagle itself. Wesenberg-Lund was not amused!

From 1929 to 1936, Tetens had a position at the Insulin Laboratory. Then Krogh helped him get a stipend from the Carlsberg Foundation. Tetens and his father-in-law built on to Pilehuset to make a larger laboratory. This is where Krogh was working while he was hiding from the Gestapo in June and early July 1944. As shall be told later, Tetens was to play an important role in getting Krogh's insect work off to a "flying start."

Arriving in Boston early in March 1946, Krogh began what was to become a major safari in the United States during which he renewed many friendships and worked hard on behalf of his young friends back home and in the States. But he also took time to see new, interesting places and indulge in his more recent interest in Norse archaeological sites on the North American continent.

Coming to Harvard University was like a homecoming to Krogh, as no less than five of the current professors at the School of Medicine had trained with him in Copenhagen. These were James Howard Means, Jackson Professor of Clinical Medicine since 1923; Cecil K. Drinker, professor of physiology since 1923 and dean of the School of Public Health Science since 1935; Edward D. Churchill, John Homans Professor of Surgery since 1931; Henry K. Beecher, Henry Isaia Door Professor of Research in Anesthesia since 1941; and Eugene Landis, George Higginson Professor of Physiology, who had become Walter B. Cannon's successor in 1943.[6] As Drinker wrote Krogh, they had each played a role in Landis's appointment. "I congratulate myself on having the most to do with bringing him here and you may congratulate yourself on your assertion to me that he would be by far the best appointment. It has turned out splendidly and I think he is very happy!"[1]

During the three months in the United States, August's schedule was almost unbelievable for a seventy-one-year-old man. But he never seemed to tire and enjoyed himself immensely as he visited with his numerous former students and friends and gave lectures in the East and Midwest. His only luggage was a small suitcase with a wickerwork cover, no bigger than the small carry-on suitcases of today.[7] It contained all he needed for his three-month stay. Shirts and underwear he washed in his room. How he found space for his papers and slides and probably another suit, I cannot imagine.

At first, August stayed and worked at Harvard University in Cambridge, but then gave a number of lectures and visited friends, traveling from one city to the next in rapid succession: Washington; Edgewood and Lansdowne, Pennsylvania; Philadelphia; Atlantic City; Swarthmore; New York; Wilton, Connecticut; New Haven, and back to Boston. While in Swarthmore, Laurence Irving and Pete Scholander persuaded Krogh to visit Florida. So on March 28 he flew to Jacksonville, Irving and Scholander boarding the same plane in Philadelphia. They went on to Marineland, where Irving and Scholander had studied diving in porpoises and manatees just before the war. Now with great pleasure they showed Krogh what was then the world's largest oceanarium. Krogh loved it and was filmed feeding the trained porpoises. Next in Jensen Beach, they visited a friend of Irving's, C. L. Claff, a wealthy industrialist and protozoologist. Krogh was taken out on long fishing trips and drives and was also introduced to Mr. Bloomingdale who owned a large estate on Jensen Beach.[2,8]

Krogh flew back north to visit Abby Turner at Mt. Holyoke and then went back to Harvard until April 26, when he flew to Washington for a conference in field physiology arranged by Irving. Following a visit with the Bøvings and yet another lecture, he was off for Chicago to visit Melvin Knisely. Afterwards he went on to Rochester, Minnesota, and Minneapolis and back to Washington to stay with the Bøvings for a short vacation. Of all the places he visited he felt most at home and happiest with the Bøvings. He also took a great interest in their son Bent, whom he helped in his scientific career. On May 22 he sadly bid the Bøvings good-bye, assuring them that he would soon come back to the United States.

Now followed a special mission unrelated to physiology, but a mission he had looked forward to with great pleasure. He was to visit the site where the Kensington Stone had been found and other places supposedly visited by Norsemen in 1362. The Kensington Stone had come to light in western Minnesota in 1898, when a farmer named Ohlman tried to remove the roots of a large aspen. The roots were entangled around a large, flat stone weighing 90 kilograms (198 pounds). On the flat side of the stone were runic inscriptions that were deciphered to read that a group of eight Swedes and twenty-two Norsemen had camped there. After some of them returned from a fishing trip, they found ten men red with blood (scalped) and dead. The year on the stone was 1362. Battleaxes and other artifacts supposedly of Norse origin were also found on the site.

Krogh's interest in the Kensington Stone stemmed from reading Hjalmar Holand's 1940 book detailing his findings and opinions on the Kensington Stone and other artifacts. The book so impressed Krogh that he published an article in a Danish newspaper about the find and the many arguments in favor of Holand's theory.[9] According to Holand, the Norsemen who had carved the runes in the Kensington Stone were connected with a well-documented expedition led by Paal Knutsson sent out by the king of Sweden and Norway, Magnus II Eriksson in 1354. The expedition's purpose was to find and bring back to Christianity the remnants of Vesterbygden, the Norse colony in West Greenland. They had returned in 1364, but there are no records of their travels. According to Holand, the expedition went on to Vinland from Greenland in search of the people and eventually reached the Fergus Falls in Minnesota via Hudson Bay and the Nelson River.

Following a few days with the Kniselys in Chicago, Krogh went by train and bus to Ephraim, Wisconsin, far out on a long, narrow peninsula on the western shore of Lake Michigan, where he met with Holand, a naturalized Norwegian who managed a large cherry farm there.[10] Krogh found Holand to be a well-educated man with many interests besides history. In Holand's car the two now drove for two days to Fergus Falls, Minnesota, where the Kensington Stone had been discovered and toured localities where Holand had found what he believed to be mooring stones from the Norse expedition. What Krogh saw and learned from Holand completely convinced him, and he made up his mind to further the course by writing a review of Holand's newest book upon his return to Denmark.

There were several other causes that Krogh wanted to further before he could return home. He went to Minneapolis to see what kind of work Wallace Armstrong was doing in dental research because I was interested in working with Armstrong. August, however, did not find the work very interesting. From there he went back to Chicago because he wanted to talk with Knisely again about the work on sludged blood. He was deeply impressed with Knisely's work and was planning to propose him for the Nobel Prize. From Chicago he flew to New York the same day to talk with Magnus Gregersen about Bent Bøving and about a van Gogh painting that Erik's wife Karen had asked him to sell. August also talked with the Rockefeller Foundation about a stipend for Fritz Buchtahl. Upon learning about the successful treatment of kidney ailments with the Kempner rice diet, August sent rice home for Christer in addition to other foods not obtainable in postwar Denmark.

Back in Boston a sailing trip with Cecil Drinker did not materialize, because Drinker was in poor health. However, Krogh discussed Knisely's work with Drinker, who did not exactly share Krogh's enthusiasm.[10]

August had still more to do about his interest in Norse archeological sites in America. This time he discussed the Newport Tower of Newport, Rhode Island, with J. Howard Means, a professor at Harvard who had studied with him in Copenhagen in 1913. Means's late brother, Philip, an archaeologist, had published a book about the tower, showing that it could have existed before the pilgrims arrived. Holand had published a book in which he proposed that the structure was of Scandinavian origin and built by Norsemen as a round church, a type of church known in the Scandinavian countries from the Middle Ages.[11] According to Holand it was built by Paal Knutsson. Means was not too impressed by Holand's ideas, but was sufficiently interested in a possible excavation to determine the tower's origin.

Still not tired from all his travels, August flew to London on his way back to Denmark for a visit with the Mellanbys and other friends. The Mellanby visit also involved helping us. Knut had asked him to look into the possibility that we could work somewhere in the British colonies, and the Mellanbys were exploring this idea.[12]

Back in Denmark after the stimulating trip, Krogh had much to attend to. While in the United States, he had bought and shipped to Denmark instruments for the insect experiments. From Sweden he had ordered a wind tunnel in which the insects could fly. It took time before it all arrived. In the meantime, he had electricity and running water installed in the house in St. Karlsminde. Needing a small laboratory on summer holiday in St. Karlsminde, he rearranged his little thatched-roof house into a bedroom, study, and laboratory. It had previously served as his and Marie's bedroom and study, and had been moved from Solrød to St. Karlsminde when they bought the property. In his new wind tunnel he tested the available insects. The tethered insect was suspended in the tunnel and the air speed adjusted to its speed. The trouble was that most of the insects would not continue to fly. After many disappointments he finally found a fly *(Lucilia)*. "It flew with constant speed for more than half an hour and reasonably constant for a whole hour, so it is certain that the experiments can be made. I have a couple more [insects] that seem promising and will probably find more."[13]

During the first part of July, Agnes and Christer were with him while Knut and I were in Norway with our children and Knut's parents. Knut had defended his doctoral dissertation in mid-June, and I was to defend mine early in the fall. At midsummer Christer's condition worsened; he and Agnes went to Stockholm where Christer was hospitalized. "I don't expect that we will see him again," wrote August. Christer died the first of August in Stockholm and Agnes returned to Denmark early in September.

Irving and Scholander were touring the Scandinavian countries in a jeep that summer. On my father's suggestion they came to see Knut and me on the Norwegian mountain farm where we were vacationing. With them we hiked and camped in the mountains, botanizing along the way. It was then that Irving invited us to come to Swarthmore and work with them. All I knew at the time was that Irving was looking for two research associates to bring back to the United States to work with him and Scholander at Swarthmore. My father, I strongly suspect, had suggested us to Irving. He did not tell us this, and I think that in most cases where he helped young scientists, he did not tell them.

In late summer, after our return to St. Karlsminde, Irving and Scholander came there to visit my father and us and we worked out the details for our year at Swarthmore. October 16, I defended my dissertation and was celebrated with a very festive dinner at my father's house. My daughter Astrid, then five years old, participated in the dinner, sitting at a small table with her cousin Lars. On November 5 we left Denmark for Sarpsborg, Norway, where we boarded an old Liberty ship bound for Norfolk, Virginia, to bring coal back to Norway. It was very sad for our children and us to take leave of my father, and apparently it was equally sad for him, for in his letters to his close friends he wrote, "I shall greatly miss them."

August's interest in Norsemen had deepened while he was in America and although his main interest was insect flight, he formed a small club of men who were as interested as he was in solving the Newport Tower and the Kensington Stone mysteries, naming the club "the Conspirators." One member was Vilhelm Marstrand, a civil engineer at the Academy for Technical Sciences in Copenhagen. Marstrand understood runic inscriptions and was interested in measurements from the Middle Ages.[14] He corresponded with Holand and with Captain Raidar Fladmark, who studied Mayan writings on his long sea voyages. Fladmark believed that Norsemen had reached the Yucatán Peninsula. Another member was Professor William Thalbitzer, who had studied the Eskimos in Greenland and the Norse colony established by Erik the Red. A third was Johannes Brønsted, head of the National Museum, who had written about prehistoric times in Denmark. Members of the club met fairly often, and letters from Holand, Means, and Fladmark circulated among them.

Not all of Krogh's friends agreed with him about Holand's objectivity. Reviews of Means's and Holand's books that Krogh submitted to the Göteborg shipping gazette *Sjöfart ock Handelstidning* were rejected, and civil engineer Paul Bergsøe was not impressed with Holand's books. When invited to lecture in Oslo, Krogh suggested talking about Holand's theories as well as Knisely's work, but he was not asked to talk about Holand, nor was there any interest in giving Holand an honorary doctoral degree as suggested by Krogh. In fact, none of the Scandinavian archeologists believed in Holand's theories. When Howard Means read Holand's book *Westward from Vinland* and a new book entitled *America: 1355–1364*, he was rather skeptical about the second. "The first half is devoted to the Newport Tower, and I think is nothing more than a rehash of my brother's book, but I think he has been less scientific in drawing conclusions than my brother."[15]

In spite of his skepticism, Means was interested and discussed the origin of the tower with Kenneth Conant, who showed considerable interest, but believed that the tower was built by the early English. Much encouraged, Krogh suggested that Danish and American archaeologists collaborate in excavations around the Newport Tower. During the following months plans proceeded. Henry Luce, who was then president of the Newport Historical Society, approved, and Conant suggested that Krogh make a quick trip in late autumn 1947 to make preliminary plans with Luce and his directors. Krogh, however, suggested Dr. Nørlund, head of the Danish National Museum, be consulted about who should participate. Nørlund was prepared to raise money for the project for Danish participation. However, all their plans came to naught when the Newport Preservation Society succeeded in getting definite and exclusive permission from the city authorities of Newport to make excavations and raised the necessary funds from a resident in Newport, Robert R. Young, chairman of the Chesapeake and Ohio Railroad. "Apparently the Historical Society moved too slowly and lost out to the Preservation Society," wrote Means.[15]

The Preservation Society finished the excavation in September 1948, finding no conclusive evidence for a Norse origin of the tower. Nørlund and Krogh tried and failed in efforts to send a Danish archaeologist to the dig, but at the same time the Scandinavian American Foundation invited Professor Brøndsted to go to the United States and review the evidence. Having spent a week with Holand and visited the Newport Tower, Brøndsted came back not convinced one way or another with respect to the tower, but quite convinced about the Kensington Stone.[16]

By the time Krogh died, no conclusions had been reached. The Norse origin of the Newport Tower was eventually refuted. The Kensington Stone was exhibited at the Smithsonian from February 1948 to February 1949. Skepticism, however, continued and the stone was deemed a hoax perpetrated by Farmer Ohlman after the stone had been found. Ohlman's son remembered that the stone was used as doorstep, but he did not recall seeing any runic inscriptions until several years after the stone was found.[17]

During fall 1946 and winter 1947 August's home life caused him considerable trouble. After we had left for the United States, my sister Agnes did not stay long with her father. She suffered from a stomach ulcer and left in late November to seek treatment in Stockholm. Left alone with two maids and Agnes's two little boys, August kept busy with his many projects, traveling to give lectures in Stockholm, Göteborg, Lund, and Aarhus. But at home he felt lonely. For company, he invited friends and family for lunch, but often had to eat alone. He read to the little Christer, but the older boy, Lars, preferred to be by himself. The thought of having to spend Christmas alone worried him. Ellen, however, saved him by coming over for the holidays with her children.

In January he wrote to me that Agnes was coming home although her health was not improved, and he was disturbed that she did not stay to complete the treatment. "Otherwise it is all right here, except that the food I get is so boring that I don't have much appetite and I have become rather skinny."[18] Alarmed by this, I sent a list of his favorite dishes for the cook to use and August himself wrote a similar list. Apparently, his meals improved.

The winter was extremely cold, and by the end of February the shortage of solid fuel in Copenhagen was severe. Even though there was no apparent shortage of oil, August's oil rationing was cut and he had to fight to get what he needed. He wrote the official in charge of the rationing that a ration that permitted him to exist but not to work was of no interest to him. If his work was so unimportant that they would not allot him what he had asked for, he would shut down his household and go to the United States, where his presence was wanted. In Swarthmore I told Irving, who promptly wired August an invitation to his laboratory. By then, however, August's letter had already had the desired effect and his oil allotment was increased.[16]

What happened next eventually solved his household problems. In a letter to me February 22, 1947, he mentioned, "The Rahbek family [Nic, her husband, and fourteen-year-old son] temporarily live here because they have no fuel at all, and Nic is in charge of the household, because Agnes has suddenly left for Stockholm to visit her friend. She is expected home in a week."[19] Earlier in February, Agnes had contacted Nic. Upon learning how the Rahbeks were suffering in their freezing-cold apartment, she had invited them to come and stay in August's warm house. As the bitter cold continued and Agnes's stay in Stockholm dragged out, the Rahbeks stayed. August enjoyed their company and was happy with the way Nic took charge of his household. Agnes finally returned from Stockholm with her friend Olaf (Olle) Lindberg, whom she had met when she was a student at Stockholm University, and now intended to marry. Learning that Agnes later wanted to spend several months in Stockholm, August began making plans with the Rahbeks to stay in his house during Agnes's absences. Eventually it became clear that the best arrangement for all concerned was for the Rahbeks to move to Søbredden permanently, and Nic would be in charge of the household. Having settled their affairs, the Rahbeks moved in with August on July 1, 1947. The cold winter and the acute fuel shortage had combined to solve August's problem and create an ideal, harmonious living arrangement for him and the Rahbeks as well.

The study of insect flight had not been proceeding quickly. Krogh had hired a mechanic, Helge Nielsen, to help him with his instruments, and together they were working on a better wind tunnel design, but in addition he needed an assistant. Not only was it difficult to find the right person, but he also needed money for the salary. Tetens came to his rescue. Tetens had several very good friends and colleagues in England. One of these was D. L. Gunn, Lancelot Hogben's scientific assistant in Birmingham. Gunn now worked for Dr. B. P. Uvarov, director and founder of the Anti-Locust Research Center in England. Gunn and Tetens had often talked about how marvelous it would be to get the two great men, Krogh and Uvarov, together. Already in January 1947 he started talking to Krogh about working with grasshoppers. Later he recommended a young zoology student, Torkel Weis-Fogh, for Krogh's assistant.[5]

During August's many difficulties with fuel and household arrangements, Irving, Knut, and I again urged him to come to Swarthmore. August wrote, "I was sorely tempted, and until lunch considered it probable that I would come . . . but now the situation has totally changed and there is no doubt that I must stay here and at the most take a shorter trip to the USA."[20] What had happened was that Dr. Gunn, who was visiting Tetens, arrived with a proposal from the Anti-Locust Research Center that Krogh lead a series of investigations of climatic effects on migrating grasshoppers. "My wind-tunnel will suddenly become an apparatus of practical importance and the whole project is so big and important that I cannot possibly refuse my cooperation or even postpone it. In reality it concerns creating the foundation for a worldwide control of migrating grasshoppers." Adding that his difficulties would have to be solved in ways other than by fleeing them, he told us about the final arrangement with Nic and her family.[20]

Finally, the insect work began to progress in earnest.

21

Last Scientific Work (1945–1949)

> The Academy of Sciences must come out of its shadow of prestige and in full public view apply its insight and ability in the service of society.

Krogh's interest in insect flight can be traced back to the time when he realized and subsequently proved that oxygen is not secreted but diffuses passively through the lung epithelium and the tissues. While this realization led him to study vertebrate capillaries and the delivery of oxygen to working muscles, it also made him wonder about insect respiratory systems. Thus, while working with capillaries and measuring diffusion coefficients in different tissues, he simultaneously investigated the respiratory system of a large insect (*Cossus*) larva by injecting the tracheal system with India ink and measuring the dimensions of the tracheae.

Krogh calculated that the *Cossus* tracheal system could adequately supply the working muscles, without respiratory movements, even during muscular exertions. The reason is that diffusion rates in air are 100,000 to 1 million times greater than in tissues. In other, more active insects, where respiration-ventilation was a necessity, he found collapsible tracheae as well as the pure diffusion tracheae. This finding might explain how sufficient oxygen could be supplied to the working flight muscles in insects during high intensity metabolic rate, but he lacked quantitative data on these rates.[1]

The stimulus to study the metabolism of flying insects and swimming fishes had come in 1938, when Marius Nielsen found that muscular work in humans is closely correlated with a rise in body temperature (chapter 16). Ten years earlier K. Dotterweich had published his observation that moths, before they would fly, would beat their wings rapidly, sometimes for six minutes, until their body temperature reached 32–34°C. Dotterweich concluded that the higher temperature was necessary for the nerves conducting the stimulus to the flight muscles.

So Krogh, with a young zoology student, Erik Zeuthen, began a study of insect flight in 1939 (published 1941).[2] They concluded that warming up was required more for the muscles than for the nerves. It was necessary, they found, only in the "bad" fliers, such as bees and moths, which needed a maximum effort of their flight muscles to fly.

The discussion in the paper ends with the statement: "The line of investigation initiated in this paper will be followed up in two distinct directions. One of us (E. Z.), who began these experiments is mainly interested in the problems of heat regulation. . . . The senior author has been interested for years in problems concerning economy of locomotion and proposes to study the metabolism of insects during flight at various known velocities and to discover, if possible, the influence of temperature upon the maximal rate of flight."[2]

After preliminary experiments in the spring of 1940 at the Zoophysiological Laboratory, Krogh realized that the investigation was so complicated that it might take years and the outcome was uncertain. It was a luxury he could not afford while directing his laboratory. Thus, he put the project on hold, while turning his attention to ion exchange in cells.

During the summer of 1947, when Weis-Fogh began working with him, Krogh had succeeded in making some insects fly in front of a wind tunnel, but he could not measure metabolic rate during flight, and the setup was not suited for studying the effect of climatic conditions on swarms of locusts (*Schistocerca gregarius*). Other investigators had found that a suspended locust will move its wings when exposed to an air current. Now Weis-Fogh discovered that the wing movement is a reflex from an "aerodynamic sense organ," consisting of hair patches on top of the locust's head. When the insect was suspended and an air current blew on its head the locust started to fly.[3]

This discovery made it possible to study a single grasshopper in a respiration chamber using the principle Krogh and Lindhard used when they studied human metabolism and respiratory quotient (R.Q.) during muscular work on a bicycle ergometer. Then they had enclosed the subject in a respiration chamber whose circulating air they sampled for gas analyses. Krogh and Weis-Fogh now suspended the tethered locust in a small respiration chamber consisting of a container in which the air could be circulated by a pump and delivered as a jet directed toward the upper part of the insect's head. When they needed a pump to circulate the air, Krogh brought out the old one he had built for his frog research in 1903.[4] With the air jet properly adjusted, the locust could be made to fly continuously for one and a half hours while air-analysis samples were taken at intervals through a special tube from the container.[5]

Late in 1948 Krogh and Weis-Fogh adapted the roundabout proposed by T. S. Kennedy et al. in 1948. To study effects of climatic variations on the flight performance of a "swarm" of locusts at their own chosen speed, they constructed a roundabout where the animals were suspended from a ring two meters in diameter. "The ring was suspended by means of thin spokes originating from the hub which rested on ball-bearings. The lowest part of the hub was provided with a 16-bladed mill, which was driven by means of four jets of air." Through measurements and adjustments of the air jets, the mill provided exactly the amount of power needed to eliminate the drag of the roundabout with its attachments. So the locusts were propelling only their own bodies through the air and could fly unimpeded until exhausted.[6]

The animals and their wing movements were observed with red strobe-light. (Flashes of white light disturbed the flight, while red light had no effect.) The performance was comparable to that in nature. A swarm of 16–32 locusts on the roundabout regularly flew 4–5 hrs., even up to 9 hrs., at a constant speed of 3 m/sec (6.75 m.p.h.). Weis-Fogh and Krogh studied conditions affecting flight performance, such as temperature and humidity, and the relationship between flying speed and metabolic rate.[6,7] Another young man, Martin Jensen, collaborated in a study of the energetics of flapping flight, to investigate how a flying animal musters enough muscle power to fly.

R.Q. measurements showed that the fuel used by the flying locust was fat and not carbohydrate. The insect uses an amount of fat corresponding to six to eight percent of its body weight during five hours of flight, a large percentage of its total fat deposit.

Weis-Fogh answered the question of how the tracheae are ventilated and oxygen reaches the working flight muscles. He showed that air sacs connected to the large tracheae supplying the muscles are ventilated by the wing movements. The wings are cobbled to a shield on the insect's back. When the wing goes up the shield goes down pressing air out of the sacs, and when the wing goes down, the reverse happens. In this way the tracheae supplying the flight muscles with oxygen are automatically ventilated.[7]

August took great pleasure in all the studies and developed a warm friendship with Weis-Fogh. It is evident that he became increasingly impressed with Weis-Fogh's ability. After several times making references to how competent his new assistant was, he wrote me on October 30, 1947, "Magister Weis-Fogh is phenomenally capable and very nice."[8] The year before August died, Sir Edward Mellanby, when visiting the laboratory, asked Weis-Fogh if he did not feel lonely in the laboratory so far away from his peers. "Overcome by surprise by such a question," wrote Weis-Fogh, "I was barely able to answer: It had never occurred to me that an age difference of nearly 50 years should be an obstacle to an intimate collaboration. To the very end, Professor Krogh was so young and alive, with such an ability to fill my life that an outsider had to make me realize that it was not a matter of course."[9]

While the insect work was progressing, August continued his busy schedule in many other areas. On July 20, 1947, he cut short his St. Karlsminde vacation to attend the International Congress of Physiology in Oxford. He bicycled fifty miles to Copenhagen, then flew to London the next day, bringing with him cheese and bacon for the Mellanbys. (There was still rationing and shortages of certain foods in England as well as in Denmark.) At the conclusion of the meeting five physiologists (Krogh, Albert Szent-Györgyi, Herbert S. Gasser, Bernardo A. Houssay, and Charles H. Best) received the honorary doctorates from Oxford University. At the same meeting Krogh was elected president of the 1950 International Congress of Physiological Sciences, to be held in Copenhagen. Typically, he was not seeking this kind of honor, "I was sorry about it," he wrote me, "but could not prevent it."[8]

August's health first began to falter at New Year's 1948, when he became ill from a flu that kept him bedridden and unable to work for three weeks.[8] After recovering, he resumed working in his laboratory and planned a visit with me and my family in the United States.

Because we could not come home, we urged my father to come to the U.S. for a visit. His finances were strained from having many family members at home and because the Insulin Foundation could not give him the amount of money originally agreed upon. He was sure, however, he could support his trip by giving lectures. What tempted him to come, he wrote, was "1. to visit you and the children, 2. to visit Knisely to talk about his plans, 3. to visit Dr. Moore in Ann Arbor."[8] So Knut helped arrange a lecture tour. August left Denmark on April 16 and came to Swarthmore to visit with us and Irving for nine days. From there he went to Washington, Ann Arbor, and Chicago, before joining us at Santa Rita Station in Arizona, where we had traveled by car and were working on water metabolism of kangaroo rats.

At Santa Rita, he helped us in the laboratory and taught me how to calibrate the microclimate recorders. We were measuring temperature and humidity in the burrows of the kangaroo rats and using his recorders, which he had shipped to us. By trapping a kangaroo rat in a live trap during the night and tying the recorder to its tail, we could make the animal itself bring the recorder down in its burrow, without disturbing the burrow. Then twelve hours later we would dig out the burrow and reclaim the recorder, and a complete record of temperature and humidity during the past twelve hours could be read under a microscope from the curves on the sooted glass plate.

Later Irving and Scholander joined us, and we traveled by car to the Grand Canyon and then to California and Stanford University. Irving had arranged for Knut and me to move our work to Stanford after the summer. August was to give lectures at Stanford. He disliked long car trips, but this one seemed particularly hard on him. At breakfast one morning, after the noise from the highway had kept him awake, August wore a suffering expression, was in a bad mood, and found the price too high. Irving broke the ice with a warm smile saying, "Yes, but the noise was free!"

The visit to the Grand Canyon was a great success. My father walked up to the rim just ahead of me. There is no warning in the landscape, before you stand on the rim looking out over the mighty, magnificent canyon. Overwhelmed, August's only comment was, "It is a lie!"

The time at Stanford went quickly, August made new friends and his lectures were well received. We parted at San Francisco airport, he to fly back East, we to go back to the desert before returning to Palo Alto and a new home. I knew then that his health was not good. He had a persistent cough and looked tired. Parting was painful.

In September 1948, a long-anticipated visit to Denmark by Sir Edward and Lady Mellanby occurred. They spent a week vacationing at Hornbæk House before an official dinner in Copenhagen with Nils Bohr and Robert Oppenheimer. During the rest of their time in Denmark, both of them gave lectures in Copenhagen. August had arranged that he and Lady Mellanby give lectures together at the School of Dentistry. During their stay the Mellanbys used August's house as their headquarters, to which they returned no less than four times. The arrangement was of great mutual satisfaction.

August's health was not improving. In October 1948 he consulted Professor Hechscher about problems he had breathing, especially at night. Hechscher told him that it was emphysema, caused by his bad posture. To alleviate the problem he had to lean forward from his hips and straighten his back. It wasn't easy, but August thought he could get into the habit. In fact he was quite optimistic about it. In December he said he felt better and enjoyed having Karl von Frisch and his wife as his houseguests.[8]

August had several disappointments during the fall. For the second year, Knisely did not receive the Nobel Prize. The chances for our return to Denmark and Norway seemed very slim. After lecturing in Oslo for a couple of months, Knut felt increasingly pessimistic about his future in Norway. In addition, August's friend Tetens might also be lost to the United States. He was now in America on Irving's invitation. Vigorous efforts by Krogh and Danish zoologists to save Tetens's private laboratory, Pilehuset, and to establish a position for him at the Zoological Museum in Copenhagen were stranded when the secretary of the treasury rejected the university proposal. He stated that Tetens was now too old for such a position. This meant that Tetens had to remain in the United States indefinitely, and Pilehuset was put up for sale. The event was much lamented in the newspapers. When interviewed by the press about it, Krogh expressed anger over the rejection, saying, "What notion does the government department have about these things?"[10]

Then on January 14, 1949, August dropped a bombshell on the Danish Royal Academy of Sciences. As the meeting was about to begin, Weis-Fogh arrived and handed a letter to the secretary. The opening words read: "By this letter I take the liberty to announce that from the time of its receipt, I resign from the Academy of Sciences. This step, which is simultaneously announced to the public, has been carefully considered for more than a year." Never in the two hundred-year history of the venerable old academy had any member resigned. Krogh went on to reiterate what he had proposed two years earlier: that the academy substantially increase its membership, partly by electing younger members and making members over seventy years old inactive. He suggested that in a few years the academy would be called upon to take up such problems as mobilizing the country's research (independent of academic teaching) and improving the conditions for scientists in Denmark, and for such actions younger and more-active members were needed.

Krogh's first proposal had been studied by a committee during most of 1947 and was finally rejected in December of that year, when a minor increase in membership was unanimously agreed upon. The idea that the academy should actively work toward improving conditions for scientific research was put aside, and emphasis was placed on the special honor it was, and should continue to be, to be chosen a member. Krogh's response was to boycott the academy for all of 1948. His letter continued:

> I do not disagree that it should be an honor, but I think that the honor should be associated with a responsibility to work collectively for the conditions for science and the scientists in the Danish society, for the understanding of the importance of scientific research and for the use by the academy of the research.
>
> My deliberations have led to the realization that I possess neither the ability nor the strength to work within the academy for these principles and that all I *can* do is to direct public attention to these matters, through a demonstrative, motivated resignation.

In the second part of his open letter Krogh addressed the public more than the academy, pointing out that in the entire civilized world a situation now existed where governments understood or had begun to understand the importance of science for the national welfare and that investment in research can be highly profitable. This was true not only for research in technical and medical fields, but equally true for basic research.

While in Denmark the public and the government were beginning to understand this, they had little understanding of what is involved in research and its demands. The poor conditions offered scientists bore witness to this. The best scientists were leaving, while to the academy it seemed unheard of that they should do something about it.

> It is this attitude that must be changed. The Academy of Sciences must come out of its shadow of prestige and in full public view apply its insight and ability in the service of society by: (1) speaking up on

all questions that deeply concern the position of research and its tasks; (2) striving to become accepted as the official adviser to the government in questions concerning scientific research; (3) working for the establishment of an advisory panel for natural sciences, consisting of active scientists with the purpose of administering the funds made available by the government.[11]

On January 16 he wrote me, "All the large papers have published the letter and given it their full support, but it looks like the academy will stick its head in the bush." On February 2 he again wrote to me:

The affair concerning the academy evolves in the normal fashion. Following the meeting on the 28th, the secretary, following the president's instructions, had put together a long and somewhat reproachful letter. But several younger members opposed strongly, while the older felt that they shouldn't answer at all. The compromise was a very short acknowledgment of the receipt of the letter of which they took cognizance with deep regret. In a few months some of the younger (Buchtahl) will begin an action to, at least to some degree, activate the academy. The press and some younger scientists are more elated with my "courageous" action than I can see any reason for.[12]

Krogh gave an interview to the press, explaining in more detail the hard work involved in research. "It is not rare that it takes years to find out how a thing should be done and then only months or weeks to do it. Let me mention an example from my own experience. The work with the capillaries was started in the beginning of 1915 and demanded seven years of such intensive work that it was difficult for me to carry out my not extensive teaching obligations and I had to withdraw from all administrative tasks." He came back to the problem that had occupied him for years: "The greatest danger is that the best of our young scientists will be deprived our country, because the circumstances offered them are too poor and because other countries, particularly the USA and Canada, have a clearer understanding of the value of scientists to society." Finally, he told how he himself, thanks to Marie, had been able to remain in Denmark and, in spite of a poor salary, devote his time to research: "I can also, from my own experience, declare that it is a necessary condition for intensive scientific work that one does not daily have to worry about where the bread is coming from and take on all kinds of irrelevant jobs to obtain it. Personally, I have never taken on anything irrelevant, but it was only because of my wife's efforts that I was able to avoid it during the critical years."[13] When asked by the reporter if he was a personal friend of Niels Bohr, president of the Academy of Sciences, Krogh answered: "Yes, but that has nothing to do with it. I did not say anything to him in advance, nor to anyone else." He was told by other members of the academy that Bohr was not amused.

An illustrated article of the work with locusts appeared in *Billedbladet* on March 1. After that August considered his own involvement in the matter over. But the public interest did not end, and for years (even recently) the newspapers were still writing about it. In the years that followed Krogh's death, Danish government support for science declined, but the press kept the issue alive. In September 1975, *Politiken,* a leading Copenhagen paper, published an editorial titled "Awkward Silence: Academy of Sciences—Wake Up!" where Krogh's 1949 action is recounted. The article concludes: "The learned academy did not speak up. While sister societies in other countries have been engaged in the upheaval between science and society, to preserve its prestige the Academy of Sciences reduced its interaction with government to mere formalities. From fear of changing its character and lowering its scientific level not only does the Academy of Sciences risk dying, but science may die as well."[14]

In spring 1949, August's health was failing. His letters became less frequent and I started to worry a lot. In mid May he went back to Dr. Hechscher. This time, the doctor ordered a number of X-rays. By the end of May, however, August had not received a diagnosis. He told me it was only a pain in the chest muscles, which he had treated with heat.[15]

In early June, August was planning a trip to Jutland with the Buchtahls, but the plan was scrapped when August entered the Niels Stensen Hospital for more examinations. He wrote me that he was sure it was nothing serious. He was up and about, but admitted that his hand was shaking when he wrote. He planned a vacation in St. Karlsminde with the Rahbeks, but was too tired to have anybody else there. While in St. Karlsminde he became severely ill and was taken by ambulance to Kommune Hospitalet in Copenhagen. This time he was told that he suffered from a liver infection, which was treated with penicillin and, when that did not work, neomycin. By the end of July he returned to his home.

During his last hospital stay he must have realized that he had cancer. But apparently the doctors never told him. In those days, it was quite common for physicians not to tell their patients when they had a fatal disease. While we were in Arizona, my father had told me about Barcroft's death. He was diagnosed with serious heart disease, and might have lived longer if he was very cautious. However, in consultation with Mrs. Barcroft, his physician decided to let Barcroft enjoy what was left of his life and not to tell him anything. Barcroft died in March 1947 while running to catch a streetcar.

But August did know. Nic and Gustav came to see him in the hospital and, finding him asleep, they left a loving note. Finding the note, August wrote back that he had wanted them to wake him up; "I will have plenty of time to sleep later."[16]

One evening after he was home in Gentofte, he rose from his bed, dressed, and came upstairs to the living room, carrying a small green book, "Many Inventions" by Rudyard Kipling. He said, "Now we need a fairy tale." He read aloud "The Children of Zodiac": "Thousands of years ago, when men were greater than they are to-day, the children of Zodiac lived in the world . . ." The story tells about how they, even though they were immortal, became more and more afraid as they heard the stories of mortal men and women and how their loved ones were killed. Leo and the girl fall in love and decide never to leave each other, even though they become more afraid for the sake of the other. Through their love, they begin to understand mankind and they themselves become mortal. The girl dies first, then Leo several years later. Leo understands that whatever happens, "man must never be afraid."[17]

Each time I heard from my father I became more alarmed; although he told me not to come home, I wrote him that I had to disobey. At the end of July I flew to Denmark with my three children. August was up and dressed when I arrived, but that was the only time I saw him dressed after I came home, and he was a shadow of himself.

Later, when he was back in bed, I found him reading "100 Poems" by the Swedish author Hjalmar Guldberg. He showed me the poem he was reading, "Efterlyses" (Advertisement of loss).[18] The author is advertising for his lost childhood faith, promising a reward for the finder. August also read the Bible but failed to find his childhood faith. In a note he wrote shortly before his death, he specified that he did not wish to have clerical assistance at his funeral.

When I arrived, a small group of people were there, my brother Erik, Nic, Gustav, and Ib and Weis-Fogh. I was told that my father had a liver infection and Erik and I kept up the pretense that he was going to get better. Soon we established a routine, Erik and I would give my father his injections for pain and we helped him with his meals. But Erik's first words to me were, "You must help me finish my dissertation, that is all-important." It was of immense importance to August that Erik get his Dr. med. degree. In Denmark the scientific doctoral degree is needed for advancement in the academic world. In spite of much prodding and help from August, Erik had been unable to finish the writing. So we went to work. Erik arranged that our children, his and mine, be sent out to St. Karlsminde with two maids. Now we could concentrate completely upon our tasks, taking care of my father and finishing the dissertation. Every minute we did not spend with my father, we were writing Erik's dissertation. It became teamwork, organizing the material, putting it together, and revising the manuscript. Weis-Fogh helped us from time to time.

In the month and a half that I was there before my father died, nothing else in the world seemed to matter. There was no room for other people. As my father became weaker, the little group around him grew closer, sharing the intense sorrow of our loss.

The first week of September, Erik and I finished his dissertation. It was handed over to the official opponent, Dr. Busch, who read it immediately and came over to tell August that Erik's dissertation was accepted. I was by his side when he heard the good news. The relief showed in his face. It may have been shortly after that when as I was helping him, he looked up at me, and said, "It is good to have good children." He went downhill fast after that and his physician told us he only had a few days left. To August he said, "Now you are really getting better," and August agreed with him. I did not understand, but the physician explained that dying people are often euphoric. He died at home September 13 surrounded by his family. The enormity of the event would change our lives—a bright and shining light had gone out.

Epilogue

Before his death August made several applications to the Insulin Foundation for continued support for his laboratory. He estimated that the laboratory would have to operate until 1952 to make it possible for Weis-Fogh to complete the locust research. Not knowing that Krogh was dying, Hagedorn hesitated because of the losses suffered by the Insulin Laboratory during the war. By the end of March 1949, however, Hagedorn could assure Krogh that the Insulin Foundation had enough money and that support for Krogh's laboratory could continue. August was greatly relieved. The research was continued and brought to completion by Weis-Fogh and Martin Jensen.

When the International Physiological Congress was held in Copenhagen in 1950, many of his friends and colleagues came to visit the laboratory in Gentofte.

It is impossible to say in how many ways August Krogh's work is still alive. Even today, I continue to receive current newspaper clippings from Denmark, discussing Krogh and his scientific contributions. In Copenhagen the August Krogh Institute was completed in 1970. There several of his former students continued work initiated by him. An August Krogh Lecture is given at each International Congress of Physiological Sciences. In 1994 the first August Krogh Distinguished Lecture of the American Physiological Society's Comparative Physiology Section was given. (I was invited to give it.) Attesting to the continued interest that his work has generated, I have been asked to speak about my father's work at national and international meetings five separate times over the past seven years. Even so, I was surprised to learn how current his work is considered to be. In April 1993 Dr. Brian Duling (president-elect of the American Physiological Society) told me that he has listed August Krogh's name on his door as one of the active investigators in his laboratory!

According to an old Danish saying, "No good thoughts can die until even better thoughts have germinated from their seeds." This is what August Krogh would have wanted and it appears to be happening.

Notes and References

Reference material includes a large collection of Krogh family letters as well as August and Marie Krogh's letters from friends and colleagues. AK's letters to his mother and father were saved by them and are included in the collection. AK had the habit of saving the handwritten drafts of many of his letters. Most of this material is now in the Danish Royal Library in Copenhagen. Letters from AK to Adam Bøving and Hohwü Christensen have been given to me, and my sister Ellen Krogh has lent me her letters from her parents.

Direct quotations included in the text are from material written in English, Danish, and other languages. Those written in languages other than English have been translated into English by me. Such references are marked by an asterisk. References to AK's own publications refer to the list of AK's publications starting on page 261.

Introduction
1. From contemporary newspaper articles and from a talk given by P. Brandt Rehberg, Symposium in honor of August Krogh's one-hundredth birthday, 1974, sponsored by the August Krogh Institute in Copenhagen. It is available on tape in the institute.
2. From Eugene Landis in commemorative words on August Krogh presented to the American Physiological Society in 1950.

Chapter 1. Ancestry
1. Alex Krogh: *En Nordslesvisk bondeslægts historie. Slægten Krogh 1653–1933.* J. Thomsen, Viborg, 1933.
2. Palle Lauring: *A short history of Denmark.* Høst & Son, Copenhagen, 1973.
3. Mimi Krogh's memoirs. Mimi Krogh, AK's mother wrote her memoirs (in Danish) in the years after she and Viggo moved to Copenhagen. Written in longhand by Mimi, they were never printed but were copied in longhand by Viggo and her granddaughter, Helga Christiani.
4. Letters between Mimi Dreckman and Viggo Krogh.
5. Carl Svendstrup: *Grenaa bys historie* (A history of the town of Grenaa). Grenaa Byraad. De forenede Bogtrykkerier, Aarhus, 1945.

Chapter 2. Childhood in Grenaa (1874–1890)
1. Mimi Krogh's memoirs and a speech given by Viggo Krogh at their golden wedding anniversary, Oct. 16, 1923.
2. *Mimi Krogh to AK, Nov. 15, 1905.
3. *Johan Krogh's memoirs, written in Chile, 1948.

4. *Viggo's memoirs.
   5. *Mimi to AK, July 4, 1881.
   6. *AK to Mimi, July 8, 1881.
   7. *From a few pages of handwritten memoirs written by AK shortly before his death.
   8. *Mimi to a friend, no date.
   9. *AK to Marie Jørgensen (MJ), Aug. 18, 1904.
   10. *AK Publ. #88.
   11. *Sofus Franck: William Sørensen. *Danmark* 5: 269–273, 1945.
   12. *W. S. to Viggo, Oct. 23, 1867.
   13. *AK to Mimi, March 1, 1889.
   14. *AK to Mimi, July 7, 1889.

Chapter 3. School Years in Aarhus (1891–1893)
   1. *AK to Mimi, May 10, 1891.
   2. *AK to Mimi, June 7, 1891.
   3. *AK to Mimi, Sept., 1891.
   4. *AK to Mimi, Oct. 11, 1891.
   5. *AK to Mimi, Nov. 1791.
   6. *AK to Mimi, May 3, 1892.
   7. *AK to Mimi, Sept. 3, 1982.
   8. *AK to Mimi, Sept. 1892.
   9. *AK to Mimi, Oct. 7, 1892.
   10. *AK's essay, sent to Mimi Dec. 19, 1892.
   11. *AK to Mimi, May 16, 1893.
   12. Artium is the Danish word for the degree qualifying the candidate for acceptance at the university. Three separate lines of study can be pursued in the higher school (the gymnasium, which corresponds more or less to the first two years of a U.S. college.): mathematics-science, classical languages, or modern languages.

Chapter 4. Becoming a Zoologist (1893–1895)
   1. *AK to Mimi, Sept. 7, 1893.
   2. *AK to Mimi, Dec. 1, 1893.
   3. *Viggo Sørensen: En Videnkabsmands Hjem (A scientist's home). In *Danske Hjem ved Aarhundredeskiftet,* Ny Samling. (Danish homes at the turn of the century). Hirschsprungs Forlag, Copenhagen, 1949. In this article Sørensen's son, Viggo, gives a lively description of his parents' home.
   4. *AK to Mimi, Nov. 23, 1893.
   5. *AK to Mimi, April 4, 1894, Author's emphasis.
   6. *AK to Mimi, May 18, 1894.
   7. *AK to Mimi, June 1, 1894.
   8. *AK to Viggo, summer 1894. The examination, candidatus magisterii or cand. mag. as it is commonly called, permits the candidate to teach in the higher school, the gymnasium. The magister conference, which is somewhat more than a master's degree in the U.S., prepares the candidate for scientific research.
   9. *AK to Mimi, Sept. 9, 1894.
   10. *AK to Mimi, Feb. 21, 1895.

11. *AK to Mimi, March 11, 1895.
12. *AK to Mimi, May 22, 1895.
13. *AK to Mimi, June 7, 1895.
14. *Misse to AK, spring 1949.

Chapter 5. Becoming a Physiologist (1895–1899)

1. *AK to Mimi Krogh, September 16, 1895.
2. *AK to Mimi Krogh, October 18, 1895.
3. AK to Mimi Krogh. Letter written in English, December 3, 1895.
4. *AK to Mimi Krogh, September 26, 1896.
5. Robert Tigerstedt: Christian Bohr. Ein Nachruf. (*Skand. Archiv. f. Physiol.*, 25, 1911, and from *Politiken*, Feb. 4, 1911).
6. *Christian Bohr: Definition und Methode zur Bestimmung der Invasions- und Evasionskoeffizienten bei der Auflösung von Gasen in Flüssigkeiten. Werte der genannten Konstanten sowie der Absorptionskoeffizienten der Kohlensaüre bei Auflösung in Wasser und Chlornatriumlösungen. (*Ann. d. Physiol. und Chem. N. F.*, 68, 1899b).
7. *Christian Bohr: Experimentelle Untersuchungen über die Saurstofaufnahme des Blutes. Copenhagen, 1885. Der Saurstoffgehalt der Oxyhämoglobinskristalle. (*Skand. Archiv. f. Physiol.*, 3, 1891). Über die Verbindung des Hämoglobins mit Saurstoff. (*Skand. Archiv. f. Physiol.*, 3, 1891).
8. *AK to Mimi, Jan. 4, 1897.
9. *AK to Mimi, Oct. 4, 1897.
10. *AK to Mimi, Oct. 14, 1897.
11. *AK to Mimi, May 10, 1897.
12. AK to Mimi, June 7, 1897.
13. *AK to Mimi, Nov. 25, 1896.
14. *AK to Mimi, Nov. 19, 1897.
15. *AK to Mimi, Dec. 7, 1897.
16. *AK to Mimi, Feb. 9, 1898.
17. *AK to Mimi, May 17, 1898.
18. *AK to Mimi, June 2, 1898.
19. *AK to Mimi, April 24, 1898. A year later AK gave a similar talk to the Biological Society in Copenhagen. AK Publ. #1.
20. *AK to Mimi, April 26, 1899.
21. *AK to C. Bohr, April 24, 1899.
22. Told by AK to friends and family. T. Weis-Fogh, Symposium in honor of August Krogh's one-hundredth birthday, 1974, sponsored by the August Krogh Institute in Copenhagen. It is available on tape in the institute.
23. *AK to Mimi, Jan. 10, 1899.
24. *AK to Mimi, Nov. 29, 1898.
25. *AK to Viggo Krogh, Feb. 1899.
26. *AK to Mimi, March 8, 1899.
27. *AK to Mimi, April 4, 1899.
28. August Krogh's handwritten thesis for the magister conference: En Fremstilling af Lungernes og Luftsækkenes Bygning og Funktion hos Fuglene (An account of the structure and function of the lungs and air sacs of birds). Unpublished.
29. *AK to Mimi, June 7, 1899.

30. *AK to Mimi, June 16, 1899.
31. *AK to Mimi, Oct. 7, 1899.

Chapter 6. The Beginning of Zoophysiology (1899–1904)

1. *AK to Mimi, Oct. 17, 1899.
2. *AK to Mimi, Oct. 31, 1899.
3. John T. Edsall: The controversy over oxygen secretion. Talk presented at History satellite symposium at the International Congress of Physiological Sciences, Vancouver, 1987; J. S. Millege: The great oxygen secretion controversy. (Lancet, 2, 1408–1411, 1985).
4. Christian Bohr: Ueber die Lungenathmung. (Skand. Archiv Physiol., 2, 1890).
5. AK Publ. #2.
6. AK Publ. #51.
7. *AK to Mimi, Aug. 28, 1900.
8. After working in Bohr's Laboratory, Hasselbalch became director of the Finsen Institute in Copenhagen. He later worked with Henderson and is famous for the Henderson-Hasselbalch equation. In 1916, when he inherited the family estates, he gave up science for agriculture.
9. AK Publ. #5.
10. *AK to Mimi, Sept. 27, 1900.
11. *AK to Mimi, Oct. 10, 1900.
12. AK Publ. #1.
13. *AK to Mimi, Nov. 28, 1900.
14. *AK to Mimi, Dec. 18, 1900.
15. E. Hohwü Christensen, M. Krogh, & M. Nielsen: Acute mercury poisoning in a respiratory chamber. (Nature, 139, 1937). E. Hohwü Christensen, M. Krogh, & M. Nielsen. Beobachtungen und Versuche über Quecksilbervergiftung im Laboratorium. (Skand. Arch. f. Physiol., 76, 1937).
16. *AK to Mimi, March 10, 1901.
17. *AK to Mimi, April 4, 1901.
18. *AK to Mimi, June 6, 1901.
19. *AK to Mimi, July 14, 1901.
20. *AK to Mimi, July 21, 1901.
21. *AK to Mimi, Jan. 15, 1902.
22. *AK to Mimi, June 8, 1902.
23. AK Publ. #11, 12.
24. *AK to Mimi, Feb. 1903.
25. AK Publ. #15, 16, 17.
26. Emil Krogh to AK, June 1902.
27. *AK to Mimi, Oct. 28, 1902.
28. *AK to Mimi, Dec. 29, 1902.
29. *AK to Mimi, June 3, 1903.
30. AK Publ. #7, 13.
31. *AK to Mimi, Feb. 1903.
32. *AK to Mimi, June 17, 1903.
33. AK Publ. #26.
34. A Danish doctoral degree does not require any further course work and is awarded upon completion of a thesis based on independent scientific re-

search. The thesis must be accepted by two professors, the official opponents. It is later defended by the candidate in front of a large audience.
35. *AK to Mimi, Nov. 1903.
36. AK Publ. #14.
37. *AK to Mimi, Dec. 17, 1903.
38. *AK to Mimi, Jan. 3, 1904.

Chapter 7. August and Marie (1904)
1. *AK to Viggo and Mimi, Nov. 11, 1904.
2. *AK to Marie Jørgensen (MJ), July 7, 1904.
3. *AK to MJ, June 9, 1904.
4. *MJ to AK, June 9, 1904.
5. A copyhold farm was leased to the farmer but the lease could be inherited by the son after the death of the farmer. Part of the rent, the manorial due, was worked off by the farmer on the land belonging to the manor of the estate. The landowner, however, still had the right to transfer a farmer from a prosperous to a neglected farm so that he might redevelop it. A hundred years earlier, ascription had ended under King Christian VI and the peasants were no longer "bound to the soil."
6. William Norvin: Wedellsborg, Husby sogn, Vendsherred, Odense Amt. Pages 373–394. In: *Danske slotte og Herregårde*, vol. 9 Nordvestfyn. Ed. Aage Roussell, Hassings Forlag, Copenhagen 1965.
7. The family tree was written by my cousin Helga Hansen (daughter of Kirsten and Lorens Hansen).
8. Personal communication from my cousin Emma Gjerløv (daughter of Kirsten and Lorens Hansen).
9. *Clara Black, Estrid Hein, Lis Jacobsen, & Marie Krogh: *Kvindelige Akademikere, 1875–1925*. Gyldendalske Boghandel, Nordisk Forlag, Copenhagen, 1925. Pages 117–153.
10. *AK to MJ, June 17, 1904.
11. *AK to MJ, June 20, 1904.
12. *MJ to AK, June 28, 1904.
13. *AK to Mimi, July 6, 1904.
14. *AK to MJ, July 5, 1904.
15. *MJ to AK, July 6, 1904.
16. *AK to MJ, July 7, 1904.
17. *MJ to AK, July 9, 1904.
18. *AK to MJ, July 17, 1904.
19. *MJ to AK, July 17, 1904.
20. *AK to MJ, July 26, 1904.
21. *Correspondence between MJ to AK, summer 1904.
22. *AK to MJ, Aug. 21, 1904.
23. *Ane Jørgensen to MJ, Sept. 20, 1904.
24. *Ane Jørgensen to MJ, Sept. 21, 1904.
25. *MJ to AK, Oct. 1904.
26. *MJ to AK, Oct. 1904.
27. *AK to Viggo and Mimi, Nov. 6, 1904.
28. *Mimi to AK, Nov. 7, 1904.
29. *MJ to Mimi, Jan. 12, 1905.
30. *Mimi to MJ, Jan. 18, 1905.

Chapter 8. Marriage and the Seegen Prize (1904–1906)
1. AK Publ. #22, 23.
2. *AK to MJ, Jan. 17, 1905.
3. *AK to MJ, Jan. 22, 1905.
4. *Frida Krogh to Mimi, March 15, 1905.
5. *Marie Krogh (MK) to Mimi, March 28, 1905.
6. *MK to Mimi, April 9, 1905.
7. *Mimi to MK, April 10, 1905.
8. *AK to Mimi, May 10, 1905.
9. *MK to Mimi, May 22, 1905.
10. *MK to Mimi, Aug. 28, 1905.
11. *AK to Mimi, Sept. 27, 1905.
12. *MK to Mimi, Oct. 29, 1905.
13. *AK to Mimi, Dec. 12, 1905.
14. *MK to Mimi, Jan. 16, 1906.
15. *MK to Mimi, Jan. 31, 1906.
16. *MK to Mimi, June 7, 1906.
17. *Viggo to AK, May 31, 1906.

Chapter 9. The Oxygen Secretion Controversy (1906–1910)
1. AK Publ. #166.
2. AK Publ. #35.
3. AK Publ. #11.
4. AK Publ. #44.
5. C. Bohr: Ueber die Lungenathmung. (*Skand. Arch. Physiol.*, 2, 1890).
6. AK to Robert Tigerstedt, 1909.
7. *MK to Mimi, Oct. 6, 1906.
8. The first results were published in AK Publ. #29.
9. *AK to Mimi, Feb. 8, 1907.
10. AK Publ. #46.
11. AK Publ. #13.
12. AK Publ. #46.
13. *AK to Mimi, April 17, 1907.
14. *AK to Mimi, April 22, 1907.
15. AK Publ. #36.
16. AK Publ. #45.
17. *MK to Mimi, March 20, 1907.
18. *AK to Mimi, Aug. 2, 1907.
19. Kenneth J. Franklin: *Joseph Barcroft, 1872–1947*. Blackwell Scientific Publications, Oxford, 1953. Page 381.
20. *MK to Mimi, Oct. 3, 1907.
21. *MK to Mimi, Dec. 28, 1907.
22. AK Publ. #31.
23. AK Publ. #25, 26, 27, 28, 29.
24. AK Publ. #58.
25. Correspondence between AK and Francis Benedict, January–April, 1908.
26. *MK to Mimi, June 6, 1908.

27. *MK to Mimi, July 29, 1908.
28. Told by AK.
29. Knud Rasmussen: preface to one of the books published by the Greenland Society. *Kajakmænd, Fortælllinger af Grønlandske Sælhundefangere* (Kayakmen, stories by Greenland seal hunters). Milo'ske Bogtrykkeri, Odense, 1896
30. AK to Benedict, Oct. 1, 1908.
31. *Mimi to MK, Oct. 15, 1908.
32. AK to Benedict, Jan. 1912.
33. *University of Copenhagen: Yearbook 1910.
34. *AK to Ane Jørgensen, Oct. 31, 1908.
35. Told by AK and MK.
36. *Frida Krogh to Mimi, Dec. 1908.
37. AK to Benedict, Dec. 1908.
38. AK to Benedict, July 1909.
39. *Marie Krogh, in Clara Black, Estrid Hein, Lis Jacobsen, & Marie Krogh: *Kvindelige Akademikere, 1875–1925*. Gyldendalske Boghandel, Nordisk Forlag, Copenhagen, 1925. Pages 117–153.
40. AK to Haldane, March 1909. As expressed by Krogh (in AK Publ. #50): "The Haldane and Smith method starts from a series of determinations of the relative amounts of CO and O_2 taken up by hemoglobin from a definite mixture (i.e. at definite tensions) of these two gasses. A trustworthy curve being obtained for the percentage-saturation of hemoglobin with varying percentages of the gas in air, it becomes possible to calculate the oxygen-tension in the blood of an animal, breathing air with a known percentage of CO, from the CO-tension of the air breathed and determinations of the percentage-saturation of the blood with CO." The discrepancy with Haldane and Smith was that they found a mean oxygen saturation of rabbit blood of 27.4%. "when my experiment was calculated on the basis of my own determinations in vitro on rabbit's blood, an arterial O_2-tension of 14–15% resulted, in perfect agreement with the tonometric determinations given in my proceeding paper." AK Publ. #50.
41. Haldane to AK, April 15, 1909.
42. AK Publ. #47.
43. J. S. Millege: The great oxygen secretion controversy. *Lancet*, 2, 1408–1411, 1985.
44. AK Publ. #49. The diffusion constants for O_2 and CO_2 could be calculated from the absorption coefficients of O_2, CO_2, and CO when the diffusion constant for CO was known.
45. *Robert Tigerstedt, Finnish physiologist, to AK, Dec. 1909.
46. C. Bohr. (*Zentralbl. Physiol.*, 23, 1909).
47. *AK to C. Bohr, Aug. 1909.
48. *C. Bohr to AK, Aug. 11, 1909.
49. C. Bohr: Ueber die specifische Tätigheit der Lungen bei respiratorishen Gasaufnahme und ihr Verhalten zu derdurch die Alveolarwand stattfinden Gasdiffusion. (*Skand. Arch. für Physiol.*, 22, 221–280, 1909).
50. AK Publ. #50.
51. Haldane to Krogh, Feb. 19, 1910.
52. AK Publ. #39. Discussion following Krogh's talk; AK to MK, July 29, 1910.
53. *AK to Professor George Dreyer, 1910.

Chapter 10. The Zoophysiological Laboratory and the Beginning of Exercise Physiology (1910–1916)

1. AK to Roald Amundsen, Jan. 1, 1909, and Roald Amundsen to AK, Feb. 11, 1909. The ship *Fram* was built for Fridtjof Nansen for his North Pole expedition in 1884 to freeze into the polar ice cap and drift with the ice across the North Pole. The enormously strong keel, designed to withstand the pressure of the ice, was sloped so that it would not be crushed, but rather the ship would be lifted up by the ice.

2. Roland Huntford: *The last place on earth*. Atheneum, New York, 1985, 565 pages.

3. Correspondence between AK and B. Helland Hansen. April, 1909–July. 1910.

4. *MK to AK, Jan. 27, 1910.

5. Correspondence between AK and MK, Jan.–Feb. 1910.

6. *Bilag til Ændringsforslag til 3. Behandling af Finanslovforslag for 1910–11* (Amendment to 3. treatment of the proposed finance law for 1910–11). Pages 952–953.

7. AK to Benedict, May 1910.

8. AK Publ. #249.

9. AK Publ. #51.

10. A. Krogh: Reminiscence of work on capillaries. A lecture to the students in the Harvard Medical School, 1946. (*Isis. Official Quarterly J. of the History of Science Society, 41,* 1950).

11. *A. Krogh: Johannes Lindhard. 25 April 1870–11 October 1947. Speech to the Danish Royal Academy of Sciences, Jan. 23, 1948. Unpublished.

12. AK Publ. #60.

13. AK Publ. #56, 57, 69, 75, 76.

14. AK Publ. #53, 63. Bornstein's principle amounts to this: To produce a definite tension difference between the blood and the alveolar air with regard to a certain neutral gas (e.g. nitrogen) and to measure the quantity of gas liberated or absorbed during a certain time. On the assumption that the blood leaving the lungs is in tension equilibrium with the alveolar air, the quantity of blood that must have passed during the time can be calculated from these data.

15. AK Publ. #54.

16. AK Publ. #55.

17. AK Publ. #59.

18. AK Publ. #67.

19. AK Publ. #68.

20. AK Publ. #80.

21. AK to Benedict, July 1915.

22. Benedict to AK, Aug. 13, 1915.

23. AK Publ. #166.

24. Benedict to AK, Dec. 15, 1915.

25. AK Publ. #79.

26. AK to Benedict, Jan. 1, 1916.

27. *AK to faculty dean.

28. *MK, in Clara Black, Estrid Hein, Lis Jacobsen, & Marie Krogh: *Kvindelige Akademikere, 1875–1925*. Gyldendalske Boghandel, Nordisk Forlag, Copenhagen, 1925. Pages 117–153.

Notes and References 249

29. AK Publ. #58.
30. Marie Krogh: The diffusion of gasses through the lungs of man. (*J. Physiol.*, 49, 1915). The paper was first published in Danish in 1914, when Marie defended her dissertation.
31. Douglas, Haldane, Henderson, and Schneider. The physiological effects of low atmospheric pressures as observed on Pike's Peak, Colorado: preliminary communication. *Phil. Trans. Roy. Soc. B*, 1913.
32. Julius Comroe: *Retro spectro scope, insights into medical discoveries.* Von Gehr Press, Menlo Park, California.
33. Kenneth J. Franklin: *Joseph Barcroft, 1872–1947.* Blackwell Scientific Publications, Oxford, 1953.
34. J. Scott Haldane: *Respiration.* Yale Univ. Press, [1923?].
35. Newspaper articles, 1914.
36. Marc Faro: *The great war, 1914–1918.* Routledge & Kegan Paul, London, 1973; John Terraine: *White heat, The new warfare, 1914–18.* Sidgewick & Jackson, London, 1982.
37. *MK to AK, Aug. 2 or 3, 1914.
38. *Correspondence between MK and AK, early August 1914.
39. Douglas to AK, March 3, 1915.
40. AK to Starling, Oct. 1914.
41. Starling to AK, no date.
42. Applications from AK to the University of Copenhagen, 1911–20. AK to Academic Council, Jan. 12, 1920.
43. *Torkild Rowsing, for Academic Council of University of Copenhagen, to AK, Jan. 15, 1920.
44. *AK's application to Cabinet for Church and Education, April 1, 1915.
45. *University of Copenhagen: Yearbook 1915–1920.

Chapter 11. Capillaries and the Nobel Prize (1916–1922)

1. AK Publ. #297.
2. AK Publ. #95.
3. Correspondence between J. Barcroft and AK, 1915.
4. AK Publ. #93.
5. AK Publ. #94. The Erlang equation: $T_o - T_x = P/d[1/2\ R^2 \ln\{x/r - (x^2 - r^2)/4\}]$; $T_o - T_x = P/d[1.15\ R^2 \log\{R/r - (R^2 - r^2)/4\}]$.
6. AK to J. Barcroft, Jan. 1920.
7. A. R. Cushny: *The secretion of urine.* Longmans Green, London, 1917.
8. Barcroft to AK, Jan. 1920.
9. Correspondence between A. Durig and AK. Dec. 1919–July 1920.
10. AK Publ. #107.
11. L. S. Fredericia: *Marie Krogh. Dec. 25, 1874–March 25, 1943.* Akademiet for de tekniske videnskaber, Copenhagen, 1943; Marie Krogh: Patalogiske forandringer i hvilestofskiftet (Pathological changes in resting metabolic rate). (*Ugeskrift for Læger*, 537–577, 1920).
12. AK Publ. #127 and 128.
13. *MK to AK, July 1920.
14. *AK to MK, July 1920.
15. *AK to MK, July 22, 1920.

16. *AK to MK, Sept. 1920.
17. P. B. Rehberg, Symposium in honor of August Krogh's one-hundredth birthday, 1974.
18. Benedict to AK, Dec. 3, 1920.
19. AK to Benedict, Jan. 11, 1921.
20. *Durig to AK, Oct. 30, 1920.
21. *Stockholmstidning*, December 11, 1920.
22. *Told by AK and MK.
23. P. B. Rehberg's tape-recorded memoirs, 1975, in the Danish Royal Library, Copenhagen.
24. AK to Boothby, Jan. 1921.
25. *AK to MK, Sept. 12, 1921.
26. AK Publ. #121.
27. *Correspondence between AK and Adam Bøving, 1922.

Chapter 12. The Insulin Story (1922–1925)

1. While sorting out my mother's belongings in preparation for the move to Gentofte after her death, I came across a large number of insulin bottles in my mother's closet. When the war ended and my father returned from Sweden, I asked him if my mother had had diabetes and learned the truth. Had I not asked, he would never have told anybody because of his promise to Marie.
2. Michael Bliss: *The discovery of insulin*. The University of Chicago Press, 1982.
3. Correspondence between H. C. Hagedorn and AK.
4. H. C. Hagedorn: Nogle Bemærkninger om Diabetesbehandling i almindelig Praksis (Some remarks concerning diabetes treatment in a common praksis). (*Ugeskrift for Læger, nr. 10,* 1–7, 1919).
5. H. C. Hagedorn: Undersøgelser vedrørende Blodsukkerregulationen hos Mennesket (Investigations concerning the regulation of blood sugar in humans). *Disputats,* Copenhagen, 1921.
6. *AK to Mimi, Sept. 1922.
7. MK to Mimi, 1922.
8. *MK to Hagedorn, Oct. 1922.
9. AK to Macleod, Oct. 23, 1922.
10. Macleod to AK, Oct. 23, 1922.
11. AK Publ. #139.
12. AK Publ. #133.
13. Macleod to AK, Jan. 1924.
14. P. B. Rehberg, Symposium in honor of August Krogh's one hundredth birthday, 1974.
15. Detlev Müller, Ibid. Müller is the discoverer of the enzyme glucoseoxydase. The enzyme is used throughout the world to diagnose diabetes.
16. AK to Gad Andresen, Jan. 28, 1924.
17. Jacob Poulsen: August Krogh's hundredårsdag den 15 November 1974 (August Krogh's hundredth birthday, November 15, 1974). (*Medicinsk Forum,* 27:177–184, 1974).
18. Jacob Poulsen: *Hans Christian Hagedorn (1888–1971)*. Dansk medicinhistorisk årbog, 1978.
19. The hospital was named after the Danish biologist Niels Stensen (Nico-

laus Steno), 1638–1686. Krogh published a translation of some of his work and a short biography. AK Publ. #5, 238.
20. Draft to the Nobel committee in Krogh's files.
21. Macleod to AK, Jan. 1924.

Chapter 13. The Happiest Years (1923–1938)

1. AK to R. Cole, Jan. 10, 1923.
2. AK to Vincent of the Rockefeller Foundation, April 17, 1923.
3. Raymond B. Fosdick: *The Story of the Rockefeller Foundation*. Transaction Publishers, Oxford, 1989.
4. Pearce to Torm, Oct. 8, 1924.
5. Eugene M. Landis: Professor August Krogh: An appreciation. In *Capillary Permeability, the transfer of molecules and ions between capillary blood and tissue*. Alfred Benzon Symposium II, 1969. Munksgård, Copenhagen, 1970.
6. C. Barker Jørgensen: Dyrefysiologi og Gymnastikteori. In *Københavns Universitet 1479–1979*. Copenhagen, 1979. Pages 447–488.
7. P. Brandt Rehberg: August Krogh. November 15, 1874–September 13, 1949. (*Yale J. Biol. Med.*, 24, 1951).
8. AK Publ. #242.
9. Axel M. Hemmingsen: August Krogh. (*Naturhistorisk Tidende*, 14, 8–16, 1950).
10. AK to A. Bøving, Aug. 22, 1929.
11. A. Bøving to AK, 1934.
12. The institute was officially named the Physiological Institute, but unofficially it was referred to as the Rockefeller Institute.
13. Yngve Zotterman: The *Minnekahda* Voyage. In Wallace Fenn, editor: *A short history of the International Congresses of Physiological Sciences 1889–1968*. Published by the American Physiological Society. Washington, D.C., 1968, 100 pages.
14. AK to Bøving, Dec. 7, 1932.
15. Interview with Marie Krogh for *Dame Tidene*, Dec. 1924.
16. The *Studenter examen* is the same as the *artium*. It qualifies the student to study at a Danish university.

Chapter 14. Capillary Function and the Contractility Controversy (1923–1936)

1. Eugene M. Landis: Professor August Krogh: An appreciation. In *Capillary Permeability, the transfer of molecules and ions between capillary blood and tissue*. Alfred Benzon Symposium II, 1969. Munksgård, Copenhagen, 1970.
2. E. Landis: Preface to the reprinted edition of A. Krogh's *The Anatomy and Physiology of Capillaries*. Hafner, New York, 1959.
3. P. Brandt Rehberg: August Krogh, November 15, 1874–September 13, 1949. (*Yale J. Biol. Med.*, 24, 1951).
4. AK Publ. #121.
5. Richard Ege later became professor of biochemistry and had his laboratory at the Rockefeller Institute in Copenhagen.
6. Th. B. Wernøe's doctoral dissertation from the Zoophysiological Laboratory was published as *Viscero-Cutane Reflexe*. Springer Verlag, 1925; and Über den Verlauf und die Verteilung präganlionärer sympatischen Bahnen bei Fischen, in Physiological papers dedicated to Prof. A. Krogh, 1926.

7. C. K. Drinker & E. D. Churchill: A graphite suspension for intravital injection of capillaries. (*Proc. Royal Soc. B., 101,* 1927). C. K. Drinker, The permeability and diameter of the capillaries in the web of the brown frog (*R. temporia*) when perfused with solutions containing pituitary extract and horse serum. (*J. Physiol., 63,* 1927).

8. AK Publ. #155.

9. AK Publ. #149; Leonard Share: Vasopressin and regulation of water homeostasis. In *Endocrinology. People and ideas.* Ed. S. M. McCann. American Physiological Society, Bethesda, Maryland, 1988. Pages 1–21.

10. Bj. Vimtrup: Beiträge zur Anatomie der Capillaren. I Über contractile elementen in der gefässwand der Blutcapillaren. (*Zeitschr. f. Anat. u. Entwicklungsgeschichte, 65,* 1922); Beiträge zur Anatomie der Capillaren. II Weitere Untersuchungen über contractile elementen in der gefässwand der Blutcapillaren. (*Zeitschr. f. Anat. u. Entwicklungsgeschichte, 68,* 1923).

11. David E. Sims: The pericyte—a review. (*Tissue and Cell, 18,* 153–174, 1986); Recent advances in pericyte biology—Implications for health and disease. (*Can. J. Cardiol., 7,* 431–443, 1991).

12. Rehberg's tape-recorded memoirs, 1975, in the Royal Library of Denmark.

13. Bensley to AK. Dec. 22, 1927.

14. Christian Crone: Træk af Kapillærfysiologiens Udvikling. Festschrift udgivet af Københavns Universitet i anledning af Universitetets Årsfest 1974. Bianco Lunos Bogtrykkeri A/S, Copenhagen, 1974.

15. Madeleine Field: The reactions of blood capillaries in the frog and rat to mechanical and electrical stimulation. (*Skand. Arch. f. Physiol., 72,* 1935).

16. B. W. Zweifach: A micromanipulative study of blood capillaries. (*Anat. Rec., 59,* 83–108, 1934).

17. Henry K. Beecher: The active control of all parts of the capillary wall by the sympathetic nervous system. (*Skand. Archiv. f. Physiol., 73,* 1936).

18. Beecher to AK, June 26, 1937.

19. Robert Chambers & B. W. Zweifach: Topography and function of the mesenteric capillary circulation. (*Am. J. Anat., 75,* 173–205, 1947).

20. J. A. G. Rhodin, personal communication; J. A. G. Rhodin & H. Fujita: Capillary growth in the mesentery of normal young rats. Intravital and electron microscope analysis. (*J. Submicrosc. Pathology, 21,* 1–34, 1989).

21. J. Stingl: Zur Ultrastruktur des terminalen Gefässbettes der Skeletmuskulatur. (*Acta Anat., 80,* 255–272, 1971).

22. P. B. Rehberg: Studies on kidney function. I. The rate of filtration and reabsorption in the human kidney; Studies on kidney function. II. The excretion of urea and chlorine analyzed according to a modified filtration reabsorption theory. (*The Biochem. Journ., 20,* 447–482, 1926).

23. A. N. Richards & J. B. Barnwell: Experiments concerning the question of secretion of phenolsulphonephthalein by the renal tubules. (*Proc. Royal Soc. B., 102,* 1927).

24. E. M. Landis: Capillary pressure and hyperemia in muscle and skin of the frog. (*Am. J. Physiol., 98,* 1931); Abby H. Turner: The validity of determination of colloid osmotic pressure of serum. (*J. Biol. Chem., 96,* 1932); A. Krogh, A. H. Turner & E. M. Landis: A celluloid capsule for measuring venous pressure. (*J. Clin. Invest., 11,* 1932); A. Krogh, E. M. Landis & A. H. Turner: The movement of fluid through the human capillary wall in relation to venous

pressure and to the colloid osmotic pressure of the blood. (*J. Clin. Invest., 11*, 1933).

25. *Capillary Permeability, the transfer of molecules and ions between capillary blood and tissue.* Alfred Benzon Symposium II, 1969. Munksgård, Copenhagen, 1970.

Chapter 15. New Fields of Investigation (1928–1943)

1. Eugene M. Landis: Professor August Krogh: An appreciation. In *Capillary Permeability, the transfer of molecules and ions between capillary blood and tissue.* Alfred Benzon Symposium II, 1969. Munksgard, Copenhagen, 1970.
2. C. Barker Jørgensen: Dyrefysiologi og Gymnastikteori. In *Københavns Universitet 1479–1979.* Copenhagen, 1979. Pages 447–488.
3. AK Publ. #258.
4. AK Publ. #200.
5. AK Publ. #31, 32, 33.
6. AK Publ. #191. The English edition was translated by Kathrine Drinker, wife of Cecil Drinker.
7. P. Brandt Rehberg: August Krogh, November 15, 1874–September 13, 1949. (*Yale J. Biol. Med., 24*, 1951).
8. AK Publ. #259.
9. AK Publ. #166.
10. Rosenow to AK, Oct. 15, 1929.
11. R. Spärck: Studies on the Biology of Oysters (*Ostrea edulis*) II–III. (*Report of the Danish Biological Station, 33*, 1927).
12. AK Publ. #173.
13. AK Publ. #167.
14. AK Publ. #172, 173, 175, 180, 183, 184.
15. AK Publ. #181.
16. AK Publ. #194, 198.
17. AK letter to Bøving, Dec. 7, 1932.
18. AK Publ. #199.
19. AK Publ. #255.
20. A. B. Keys to AK. March 3, 1930.
21. AK Publ. #185
22. AK Publ. #208.
23. Ancel B. Keys: The determination of chlorides with the highest accuracy. (*J. Chem. Soc.*, Sept. 1931); The heart gill preparation of the eel and its perfusion for the study of a natural membrane in situ. (*Z. verg. Physiol., 15*, 1931); Chloride and water secretion and absorption by the gills of the eel. (*Z. verg. Physiol., 15*, 1931); A. B. Keys & E. N. Willmer: Chloride secreting cells in the gills of fishes with special reference to the common eel. (*J. Physiol., 76*, 1932).
24. Carl Schlieper: Ueber die osmoregulatorische Function der Aalkiemen. (*Z. verg. Physiol., 18*, 1933); Die Brackishwassertiere und ihre lebens bedingungen vom physiologischen Standpunkt ausbetrachtet. (*Verh. Int. Ver. theor. angew. Liminologie, 6*, 1933); Ueber die Permeabilität der Aalkiemen. I. Die Wasserdurchlässigkeit und der angebliche Wassertransport der Aalkiemen in hypertonischem Aussenmedium (*Z. verg. Physiol., 19*, 1933).
25. The term *active ion transport* is a more rigorous term now than in Krogh's time, when it only meant that the ion was transported uphill. At that

time it was not yet possible to distinguish between primary and secondary active chloride transport. It has since been shown that Cl^- ions are most often transported by either passively following the Na^+ ion or coupled to Na^+ transport through an electrically neutral Na^+ carrier. However, the argument used by Lundegård does indicate that Cl^- transport may be independent of Na^+ movements. In recent years, evidence—from plants, insects, and other invertebrates—is mounting for the existence of a primary active Cl^- pump. George A. Gerenzer et al. Is there a chloride pump? (*Am. J. Physiol.*, 254, 1988).

26. AK Publ. #237.
27. AK Publ. #240, 241, 244, 251, 253, 254, 257.
28. Henri Koch: Essai d'interpretation de la soi-disant "reduction vitale" de sels d'argent par certain organes d'Artopodes. (*Ann. Soc. Sci. Méd. Nat. Brux. Sér. B.*, 54, 1934). In this paper Koch showed the curious affinity for salts exhibited by special cells in a number of arthropods. The cells will absorb silver from very dilute solutions of silver nitrate. The metal becomes precipitated as an insoluble silver salt. Koch suggested that they absorb salt, while Wigglesworth believed the anal papillae absorbed water.
29. AK Publ. #221; H. Koch: The absorption of chloride ions by the anal papillae of diptera larvae. (*J. exp. Biol.*, 15, 1938).
30. Torkel Weis-Fogh, Symposium in honor of August Krogh's one-hundredth birthday, 1974. Not published.
31. V. B. Wigglesworth: A simple method of volumetric analysis for small quantities of fluid: estimation of chloride in 0.3 μl of tissue fluid. (*Biochem. J.*, 31, 1719–1722, 1938). The regulation of osmotic pressure and chloride concentration in the hemolymph of mosquito larva. (*J. exp. Biol.*, 15, 235–247, 1938).
32. AK Publ. #240. "Frog which have been deprived of a certain amount of salt will take up Cl^- ions from solutions down to 10^{-5} molar or less, either with Na^+, (K^+) or in exchange against HCO_3^-. While in plant roots the process is apparently going on indiscriminately all the time, in the frog's skin it is definitely regulated. It take place only when the salt content of the body has been depleted. When potassium chloride only is available it soon stops."
33. AK Publ. #265.

Chapter 16. Exercise Physiology (1918–1944)

1. N. Zuntz: (*Oppenheimer's Handb. Biochemie*, 41, 281, 1911).
2. W. M. Fletcher & Hopkins: (*Proc. Roy. Soc. B.*, 89, 444, 1917).
3. AK Publ. #101.

Title & MSPP:
4. AK Publ. #99.
5. Erling Assmusen, symposium in honor of August Krogh's one-hundredth birthday, 1974.
6. AK Publ. #97.
7. Liljestrand to AK, Jan. 6, 1918.
8. Correspondence between AK and Liljestrand.
9. In Danish, the laboratory was called "Gymnastik Teoretisk Laboratorium." The English translation of the name varied, but in later publications the name Laboratory for Theoretical Gymnastics was used consistently.
10. Erling Asmussen: Gymnastikstudiet og det gymnastikteoretiske laboratorium ved Københavns universitet. Tilbageblik på trekvart århundredes hænde-

lser (The study of gymnastics and the laboratory for theoretical gymnastics at the university of Copenhagen. A look back on the events of three quarters of a century). Unpublished typescript, 1984, available only through the Laboratory for Theoretical Gymnastics at the August Krogh Institute. Page 278.

11. August Krogh: Johannes Lindhard, 25. April 1870–11. Oct. 1947. Speech to the Danish Royal Academy of Sciences, Jan. 23, 1948. Unpublished.

12. Interview with Professor Erik Hohwü Christensen, 1988.

13. AK Publ. #53.

14. Interview with Professor Marius Nielsen, 1988.

15. F. Grande Covian & P. B. Rehberg: Über die Nierenfunktion wärend schwerer Muskelarbeit. (*Skand. Arch. f. Physiol.*, 75, 1936); AK Publ. #218.

16. AK Publ. #231.

17. AK Publ. #217.

18. E. Hohwü Christensen & Ove Hansen: I. Zür methodik de Repiratorichen Quotient-Bestimmung in Ruhe und bei Arbeit. II. Untersuchungen über Verbrennungsvorgänge bei langdaurnder, schwerer Muskelarbeit. III. Arbeitsfähigheit und Ernärung. IV Hypoglykämie, Arbeitsfähigheit und Ermüdung. IV. Respiratorischer Quotient un 02-Aufnahme. (*Skand. Arch. f. Physiol.*, 81, 1939).

19. Ove Bøje: Der Blutzucker wärend und nach körperlicher Arbeit. (*Skand. Arch. f. Physiol. Suppl. Nr. 10*, 74, 1936).

20. E. Hohwü Christensen, A. Krogh & J. Lindhard: Investigations on heavy muscular work. (*Quarterly Bulletin of the Health Organization of the League of Nations*, 3, 1933).

21. Marius Nielsen: Die Regulation der Körpertemperatur bei Muskelarbeit. (*Skand. Arch. f. Physiol.*, 79, 1938).

22. AK Publ. #57.

23. Per-Olof Åstrand & Kaare Rohdahl: *Textbook of workphysiology. Physiological basis of Exercise*. McGraw-Hill, 1986. The book's dedication reads, "To Professor Erik Hohwü Christensen who first introduced us to the field of work physiology."

24. AK Publ. #186.

25. AK Publ. #202.

26. AK Publ. #260. Microclimate recorder and several other publications on physiological problems concerning home heating, AK Publ. #268, 272, 278, 289, 291.

27. AK Publ. #228, 230.

28. E. Hohwü Christensen, M. Krogh, & M. Nielsen: Beobachtungen und Versuche über Quicksilververrgiftung im Laboratorium. (*Skand. Arch. f. Physiol.*, 76, 1937); and by the same authors: Acute mercury poisoning in a respiration chamber. (*Nature*, 139, 1937).

29. Erling Asmussen, E. Hohwü Christensen & Marius Nielsen: Über die Beinflussung der Pulsfrequenz durch Änderung des arteriellen Blutdruckes. (*Skand. Arch. f. Physiol.*, 79, 1938). I. Pulsfrequenz und Köperstellung. II. Die effectivität der Blutdruckregulation in verscheidenen Köperstellung. III. Ueber die Kreislaufsufficienz in stehenden Stellung bei normalem arteriellen Druck und herabgesetztem Minutvolumen. IV. Die Bedeutung der Köberstellung für Pulsfrequenz bei Arbeit. (*Skand. Arch. f. Physiol.*, 81, 1939).

30. E. Hohwü Christensen: Saurstoffaufnahme und respiratorishe Functionen in grossen Höhen. (*Skand. Arch. f. Physiol.*, 76, 1937); E. Hohwü Chris-

tensen & W. H. Forbes: Der Kreislauf in grossen Höhen. (*Skand. Arch. f. Physiol.*, 76, 1937).
   31. J. Lindhard to Hohwü, 1934.
   32. Åstrand and Hohwü, personal communication.

Chapter 17. The Introduction of Isotopes (1935–1944)
   1. AK Publ. #247.
   2. Hans H. Ussing. Symposium in honor of August Krogh's one-hundredth birthday, 1974.
   3. Hans H. Ussing: The influence of heavy water on the development of amphibian eggs. (*Skand. Arch. f. Physiol.*, 72, 1935).
   4. AK Publ. #222. D_2O was determined in a density gradient with an accuracy of between 1.00001 and 1.000001.
   5. Author's interview with Hans Ussing, 1988.
   6. AK Publ. #220.
   7. Valborg Koefoed-Johnsen & Hans H. Ussing: The contributions of diffusion and flow to the passage of D_2O through living membranes. Effects of neurohypophyseal hormone on isolated Anuran skin. (*Acta Physiol. Scand.*, 28, 60–76, 1953).
   8. AK Publ. #235 and 252.
   9. AK Publ. #246.
   10. AK Publ. #239 and 247.
   11. Hilde Levi, Georg von Hevesy Memorial Lecture: Georg Hevesy and his concept of radioactive indicators—in retrospect. (*European J. Nuclear Medicine*, 1, 1976).
   12. Niels Blædel: *Harmoni og enhed. En Biografi af Niels Bohr* (*Harmony and unity. A biography of Niels Bohr*). Published by Carlsberg Fondet and Rhodos, Copenhagen, 1985.
   13. S. P. L Sørensen is the famous Danish chemist who introduced the pH concept.
   14. Hans H. Ussing: Life with tracers. (*Ann. Rev. Physiol.*, 42, 1980).
   15. AK Publ. #236.
   16. P. O. Pedersen & Bodil Schmidt-Nielsen: Untersuchungen über Stoffwechsel in den Zazhnhartgeweben menschlicher Zähne unter Anwendung radioaktiven Phosphors als Indikator. (*Schweizerischen Monatschrift für Zahnheilkunde, 51*, 1941).

Chapter 18. Dark Clouds (1938–1944)
   1. August Krogh's will, handwritten among his papers.
   2. *AK to Hagedorn, Aug. 1938.
   3. *Hagedorn to AK, Aug. 8, 1938.
   4. AK to MK, Sept. 1938.
   5. Told to Ellen Krogh by Professor Jacob Poulsen.
   6. MK to Ellen, Aug. 24, 1940.
   7. John Keegan: *The Second World War*. Viking Penguin Group, New York, 1989.
   8. Told by P. F. Scholander. As expected by Krogh, Scholander became one of the world's foremost comparative physiologists. He stayed in America, having obtained his American citizenship after he had joined the U.S. Army.

9. Correspondence between MK and Ellen, 1940–43.
10. Correspondence between MK and Agnes, 1940–43.
11. AK to Ellen, March 3, 1943.
12. AK to Ellen, March 17, 1943.
13. Correspondence between AK and E. Hohwü Christensen.
14. AK to Ellen, May 9, 1943.
15. AK to Ellen, April 19, 1943. The paper he planned to write became the Croonian Lecture to the Royal Society in 1945. AK Publ. #285.
16. Harold Flender: *Rescue in Denmark*. Simon and Schuster, New York, 1963.
17. AK to Ellen, Dec. 26, 1943.
18. Niels Blædel: *Harmonie og enhed, Niels Bohr en Biografi (Harmony and unity, Niels Bohr a biography)*. Carlsberg Fondet and Rhodos, Copenhagen, 1985.
19. AK to Ellen, July 11, 1944.
20. John Toland: *The last days*. Random House, New York, 1965.
21. Told by Karen Krogh.

Chapter 19. Exile in Sweden (1944–1945)

1. From various letters to Ellen, myself, and several friends.
2. Marie Krogh & Anna-Louise Lindberg: The effect of active thyroid substance on metabolism and other functions in guinea pigs. (*Acta Physiol. Scand.*, 10, 1945).
3. AK to Cecil Drinker, Nov. 1944.
4. AK to Lindberg, Nov. 25, 1944.
5. Lindberg to AK, Dec. 5, 1944.
6. AK Publ. #285.
7. AK Publ. #255.
8. A series of papers published by Hevesy and collaborators in *Kongelige Danske Vidensk. Selsk. Biol. Medd.*, 1939, 1940, and 1941 and in *Acta Physiol. Scand.*, 1941 and 1942.
9. Using heavy water, Krogh and Ussing had investigated the water permeability of many cell membranes and found most to be highly water permeable. See chapter 18.
10. AK Publ. #273, 276, 277.
11. H. Lundegårdh publ.
12. AK Publ. #273. In this paper Krogh foresaw that the number of transport molecules inserted in the membrane would vary according to need for transport. Because Krogh could not obtain cell cultures, the experiments were made on chorion membranes from chick embryos.
13. AK Publ. #275.
14. AK to H. H. Dale, Feb. 2, 1945. The paper (AK Publ. #285) was two hundred pages long when published in 1946.
15. AK Publ. #284.

Chapter 20. The Private Laboratory in Gentofte (1945–1947)

1. AK to Cecil Drinker, July 11, 1945.
2. AK to Adam Bøving, Oct. 1945.
3. Lady May Mellanby to AK, Oct. 24, 1945.

4. Author's interview with Claus Munch Plum and his wife Dr. Ruth Plum and a detailed letter from Claus Plum, 1989.
5. Taped interview with Erik Tetens Nielsen, 1988, and a short paper written for his friends, "On Scientific Roots."
6. Donald S. Gair: August Krogh 1874–1949. (*Harvard Medical Alumni Bulletin*, 1950).
7. This little suitcase is now in the Museum for Medical History in Copenhagen.
8. AK travel account to his family, 1946.
9. AK Publ. #266.
10. Correspondence between J. Howard Means and AK.
11. Hjalmar Rued Holand's first book on the Kensington Stone was written in 1907. At the time all authorities in Sweden and Norway had dismissed the find as a hoax. The farmer, Ohlman, who had found the stone gave it to Holand. Holand subsequently wrote *Westward from Vinland; an account of Norse discoveries and explorations*. Duell–Sloan and Pearce, New York, 1940; and Hjalmar Rued Holand: *America: 1355–1364*. Duell–Sloan and Pearce, New York, 1946.
12. From correspondence between AK and Lady Mellanby.
13. AK to Bøving, July 27, 1946.
14. From an extensive correspondence between Marstrand and AK with copies of letters from Fladmark, Holand, and Thalbitzer.
15. Howard Means to AK. Oct. 6, 1948.
16. AK to Bodil, 1946–49.
17. Erik Wahlgren: *The Kensington Stone, a mystery solved*. The University of Wisconsin Press, Madison, 1958.
18. AK to Bodil, Jan. 5, 1947.
19. AK to Bodil, Feb. 2, 1947.
20. AK to Knut, May 5, 1947.

Chapter 21. Last Scientific Work (1945–1949)
1. AK Publ. #85 and 110.
2. AK Publ. #267.
3. T. Weis-Fogh: (*Nature, 164,* 873, 1949); T. Weis-Fogh: (**the Int. Congress Entom. Proc.*, page 584, 1950).
4. AK Publ. #7.
5. AK Publ. #298.
6. AK Publ. #299.
7. This information comes from three sources, (1) the author's discussions with Weis-Fogh, (2) a talk given by Weis-Fogh at the symposium in honor of August Krogh's one-hundredth birthday, and (3) Torkel Weis-Fogh: The flight of locusts. (*Scientific American*, page 116, March 1956).
8. AK to Bodil, 1947 through 1949.
9. T. Weis-Fogh: (*Naturens Verden, 34,* 19, 1950).
10. *Politiken*, 1949.
11. Open letter from AK to the Danish Royal Academy of Sciences, hand-delivered at the meeting of Jan. 14, 1949.
12. AK to Bodil, Feb. 2, 1949.
13. Further comments by AK to the press concerning his resignation from the Academy. The handwritten comments are found in the AK archives.

14. *Politiken*, Sept. 1974.
15. During his illness, I learned that he was suffering from lung cancer, which had metastasized to the liver.
16. Author's interview with the Rahbeks in 1987.
17. The book is from AK's collection of Kipling's writings. In the story of the children of Zodiac, AK has marked several paragraphs referring to Leo's love for the girl.
18. Hjalmar Guldberg: *100 Dikter* (100 poems). Norstedts, Stockholm, 1940. Efterlyses. Undertecknads barnatro / har försvunnit från sit bo / utan mössa, rock och sko.
Här, i hopp att det blir känt,/ vart han sig i världen vänt, / gives hans signalement.
Rösten som en fågeldrill, / ögon blå med blank pupill, / blicken hör ej jorden till.
Den som innan ägarn dör / den förvunne återför, / lovas hederlig dusör.

*The signer's childhood faith / has disappeared from its home / without cap, coat or shoes.
Here in the hope that it is known / where in the world he has gone / his description is given.
The voice is like a bird shrill / the eyes blue with clear pupil / the expression does not belong to this earth.
Anyone who finds him / before the owner dies / is promised a reasonable award.

August Krogh's Publications

Revised by Axel M. Hemmingsen

From *H. C. Hagedorn:* August Krogh. November 15, 1874–September 13, 1949. (*Meddelelser fra Akademiet for de TekniskeVidenskaber.* A. V. T. No. 1: 33–50, 1949).

1901   1) Om Turgescensens Betydning for Plantelegemets Fasthed og Spalteaabningernes Mekanik. (*Biol. Selsk. Forh.* i Vinterhalvaaret 1900/01. Kbh. 1901).

2) Om hydrostatiske Forhold i Dyreriget. (*Biol. Selsk. Forh.* i Vinterhalvaaret 1900/01. Kbh. 1901).

3) *Vejledning til Brug ved de fysiologisk-kemiske Øvelser paa Universitetets fysiologiske Lab.* Trykt som Manuscript. Kbh. 1901; 2. omarb. Udg. 1905.

1902   4) Om Stofskiftet i Havet saaledes som det giver sig Udslag gennem Luftarternes Mængde i Havvandet. (*Biol. Selsk. Forh.* i Vinterhalvaaret 1901/02. Kbh. 1902).

5) A. KROGH & V. MAAR: Oversættelse med Indledning og Noter af NICOLAUS STENO: *Foreløbig Meddelelse til en Afhandling om faste Legemer, der findes naturlig indlejrede i andre faste Legemer.* Kbhvn. 1902.

6) Hr. M. JANTZEN's Saftstigningsteori. En Kritik. (*Vid. Medd. Nat. For.*, 54, 1902).

1903   7) *Frøernes Hud- og Lungerespiration.* Disp. København. 1903. (Ogsaa Vid. Medd. Nat. For., 55, 1903).

8) On shells floating on the surface of the sea. (*Proc. Malacol. Soc. Lond.* 5, 1903).

1904   9) Om Hudrespirationen. (*Biol. Selsk. Forh.* i Vinterhalvaaret 1903/04, Kbh. 1904).

10) A. KROGH & E. KROGH: Moderne Loddeapparater. (*Dansk Søfartstid.*, 11, 1904).

11) On the tension of carbonic acid in natural waters and especially in the sea. (*Medd. om Grønland*, 26, 1904).

12) The abnormal CO_2-percentage in the air in Greenland and the general relations between atmospheric and oceanic carbonic acid. (*Medd. om Grønland*, 26, 1904).

13) On the cutaneous and pulmonary respiration of the frog. (*Skand. Arch. Physiol.*, 15, 1904). Translation of Nr. 7.
14) Some experiments on the cutaneous respiration of vertebrate animals. (*Skand. Arch. Physiol.*, 16, 1904).
15) Apparate und Methoden zur Bestimmung der Aufnahme von Gasen im Blute bei verschiedenen Spannungen der Gase. (*Skand. Arch. Physiol.*, 16, 1904).
16) CHR. BOHR, K. HASSELBALCH & A. KROGH: Ueber einen in biologischer Beziehung wichtigen Einfluss, den die Kohlensäurespannung des Blutes auf dessen Sauerstoffbindung übt. (*Skand. Arch. Physiol.*, 16, 1904).
17) CHR. BOHR, K. HASSELBALCH & A. KROGH: Ueber den Einfluss der Kohlensäurespannung auf die Sauerstoffaufnahme im Blute. (*Zentralbl. Physiol.*, 17, 1904).

1905 18) Landøkonomisk Forsøgslaboratorium. En Kritik af Virksomheden. (Anmeldelse i *Berl. Tidende,*). May 19, 1905.
19) Eine einfache Methode, um den herabsetzenden Einfluss der Kohlensäure auf die Sauerstoffaufnahme des Blutes zu demonstrieren. (*Zentralbl. Physiol.*, 18, 1905).

1906 20) Demonstration eines Vorlesungsapparates zu Farbenmischungen. (*Biol. Selsk. Forh.* 1905–06 in *Skand. Arch. Physiol.*, 18, 1906, p. 320).
21) *Forelæsninger over Fysiologi*. A mimeographed Manuscript. Kbh. 1906.
22) Experimentelle Untersuchungen über die Ausatmung freien Stickstoffes aus dem Körper. Mit dem Seegen-Preis gekrönte Abhandlung. (*Sitzber. Kais. Akad. Wiss. Wien. Math. nat. Klasse*, 115, 1906).
23) Experimental researches on the expiration of free nitrogen from the body. (*Skand. Arch. Physiol.*, 18, 1906). Same as Nr. 22.

1907 24) Ulykken ombord i Dampskibet »Ruth«. (*Berl. Tidende*, 1. 6. 1907).
25) Ueber die Prinzipien der exakten Respirationsversuche. (*Biochem. Zeitschr.*, 7, 1907–08).
26) Om Kvælning ved Iltmangel. (*Hospitalstid.*, 50, 1907).
27) Insektlarver som ingeniører. (*Nordisk tidskrift för vetenskap, konst och industri*, 1907).
28) Ueber die Bildung freien Stickstoffes bei der Darmgährung. (*Zeitschr. physiol. Chem.*, 50, 1907).
29) Ueber vasomotorische Nerven zu den Lungen. Vorläufige Mitteilung. (*Zentralbl. Physiol.*, 20, 1907).

1908 30) *Alm. Naturhistorie og Fysiologi*. II. Del af P. HEEGAARD, M. VAHL & A. KROGH: *Naturkundskab for Gymnasiets sproglige Linier*. 1. Udg. 1908; 2. Udg. 1910.
31) *Kortfattet Lærebog i Menneskets Fysiologi* (for Gymnasiets mat.-naturv. Linie). 1. Udg. 1908; 2. Udg. 1912.
32) *Lærebog i Menneskets Fysiologi for Gymnasiet*. 3.—8. Editions of the former two. *1917—1938.* See also Nr. 191.

33) A. KROGH & P. BRANDT REHBERG: *Lærebog i Menneskets Fysiologi.* 9. og 10. Udg. af de tre foregaaende. 1942 og 1946.

34) POUL HARDER, A. C. JOHANSEN, AUG. KROGH, N. V. USSING med flere: Diskussion om V. HINTZE's Foredrag: Den nordeuropæiske Fastlandstid. (Summary in *Medd. Dansk geol. Foren.*, 3, 1908).

35) Some new methods for the tonometric determination of gastensions in fluids. (*Skand. Arch. Physiol.*, 20, 1908).

36) On micro-analysis of gases. (*Skand. Arch. Physiol.*, 20, 1908).

1909 37) A. KROGH & M. KROGH: Versuche über die Diffusion von Kohlenoxyd durch die Lungen des Menschen. (*Zentralbl. Physiol.*, 23, 1909).

1910 38) Tonometric determination of dissolved gases. (*Brit. Med. Journ.*, 2, 1910).

39) The forces governing the gas exchange in the lungs. (*Brit. Med. Journ.*, 2, 1910).

40) Om Kulsyre som Regulator i Organismen og Aarsagerne til kirurgisk Shock. En Oversigt over nogle nyere Undersøgelser. (*Hospitalstid.*, 53, 1910).

41) Nogle Bemærkninger om Overtryksrespiration. (*Hospitalstid.* 53, 1910).

42) Om Overtryksrespiration og Kulsyreudvaskning. Et Gensvar til Hr. Assistent Mollgaard. (*Hospitalstid.*, 53, 1910).

43) Om Akapni ved Kirurgiske Operationer. (*Hospitalstid.*, 53, 1910).

44) A. KROGH & M. KROGH: On the tension of gases in the arterial blood. The mechanism of gas-exchange. I. (*Skand. Arch. Physiol.*, 23, 1910).

45) On the oxygen-metabolism of the blood. The mechanism of gas exchange. II. (*Skand. Arch. Physiol.*, 23, 1910).

46) On the mechanism of the gas-exchange in the lungs of the tortoise. The mechanism of gas-exchange. III. (*Skand. Arch. Physiol.*, 23, 1910).

47) On the combination of hæmoglobin with mixtures of oxygen and carbonic oxide. The mechanism of gas-exchange. IV. (*Skand. Arch. Physiol.*, 23, 1910).

48) Some experiments on the invasion of oxygen and carbonic oxide into water. The mechanism of gas-exchange. V. (*Skand. Arch. Physiol.*, 23, 1910).

49) A. KROGH & M. KROGH: On the rate of diffusion of carbonic oxide into the lungs of man. The mechanism of gas-exchange. VI. (*Skand. Arch. Physiol.*, 23, 1910).

50) On the mechanism of the gas-exchange in the lungs. The mechanism of gas-exchange. VII. (*Skand. Arch. Physiol.*, 23, 1910).

1911 51) On the hydrostatic mechanism of the *Corethra* larva with an account of methods of microscopical gas analysis. (*Skand. Arch. Physiol.*, 25, 1911).

1912 52) Kredsløbets Regulering gennem Hjertets Forsyning med venøst Blod. (*Hospitalstid.*, 55, 1912).

53) A. KROGH & J. LINDHARD: Measurements of the blood flow through the lungs of man. (*Skand. Arch. Physiol.*, 27, 1912).

54) On the influence of the venous supply upon the output of the heart. (*Skand. Arch. Physiol.*, 27, 1912).

55) The regulation of the supply of blood to the right heart. (*Skand. Arch. Physiol.*, 27, 1912).

1913

56) A. KROGH & J. LINDHARD: The volume of the "dead space" in breathing. (*Journ. Physiol.*, 47, 1913).

57) A. KROGH & J. LINDHARD: The regulation of respiration and circulation during the initial stages of muscular work. (*Journ. Physiol.*, 47, 1913).

58) A. KROGH & M. KROGH: A study of the diet and metabolism of eskimos undertaken in 1908 on an expedition to Greenland. (*Medd. om Grønland*, 51, 1913).

59) On the composition of the air in the tracheal system of some insects. (*Skand. Arch. Physiol.*, 29, 1913). See Nr. 110.

60) A bicycle ergometer and respiration apparatus for the experimental study of muscular work. (*Skand. Arch. Physiol.*, 30, 1913).

61) Eine einfache automatische Druckluftinstallation und einige Anwendungen der Druckluft. *Zeitschr. biol. Techn.*, 3, 1913).

62) Thermostate und Thermoregulation. (*Zeitschr. biol. Techn.*, 3, 1913).

1914

63) A. KROGH & J. LINDHARD: Ueber die von den Respirationsbewegungen bedingten Schwankungen des Gaswechsels und Blutstroms in den Lungen des Menschen. (*Biochem. Zeitschr.*, 59, 1914).

64) Ein Mikrorespirationsapparat und einige damit ausgeführte Versuche über die Temperatur-Stoffwechselkurve von Insektpuppen. (*Biochem. Zeitschr.*, 62; Berichtigung 66, 1914).

65) A. C. JOHANSEN & A. KROGH: The influence of temperature and certain other factors upon the rate of development of the eggs of fishes. (*Cons. internat. pour l'explor. de la mer. Publ. de circonstance* Nr. 68, 1914).

66) Ethyl urethane as a narcotic for aquatic animals. (*Internat. Rev. Hydrobiol.*, 7, 1914).

67) R. EGE & A. KROGH: On the relation between the temperature and the respiratory exchange in fishes. (*Internat. Rev. Hydrobiol.*, 7, 1914).

68) The quantitative relation between temperature and standard metabolism in animals. (*Internat. Zeitschr. physik-chem. Biol.*, 1, 1914).

69) A. KROGH & J. LINDHARD: On the average composition of the alveolar air and its variations during the respiratory cycle. (*Journ. Physiol.*, 47, 1914).

70) On the influence of the temperature on the rate of embryonic development. (*Zeitschr. allg. Physiol.*, 16, 1914).

71) On the rate of development and CO_2-production of chrysalides of

Tenebrio molitor at different temperatures. (*Zeitschr. allg. Physiol., 16,* 1914).

1915   72) Die Mikroluftanalyse und ihre Anwendungen. (*Abderhaldens Handb. der biochem. Arbeitsmethoden, 8,* 1915).

73) Ueber Mikrospirometrie. (*Abderhaldens Handb. der biochem. Arbeitsmethoden, 8,* 1915).

74) Funktionsuntersuchungen an den Lungen des Menschen mittelst gas-analytischer Methoden. *Abderhaldens Handb. der biochem. Arbeitsmethoden, 8,* 1915).

75) A. KROGH & J. LINDHARD: Om Blanding af Luft i Menneskets Lunger. Forsøg og Kritik. (*Hospitalstid., 58,* p. 1025, 1915; Discussion p. 1045, 1070, 1091, 1112, 1122 og 1166).

76) A. KROGH & J. LINDHARD: Om Expirationstrykket m. m. (*Hospitalstid., 58,* p. 1091, 1915).

77) A note on the colour of blood and its oxygen content. (*Proc. Physiol. Soc.—Journ. Physiol., 49,* 1915).

78) An automatic device for regulating the work per revolution of the bicycle ergometer. (*Proc. Physiol. Soc.—Journ. Physiol., 49,* 1915).

1916   79) Videnskabsmanden William Sørensen. Nogle Mindeord. (*Berl. Tidende,* 4. 7. 1916).

80) *The respiratory exchange of animals and man.* (Monographs on Biochemistry). London, 1916.

1917   81) A. KROGH & J. LINDHARD: The volume of the dead space in breathing and the mixing of gases in the lungs of man. (*Journ. Physiol., 51,* 1917).

82) A. KROGH & J. LINDHARD: A comparison between voluntary and electrically induced muscular work in man. (*Journ. Physiol., 51,* 1917).

83) Respirationsundersøgelser paa malkende Kvæg. (*Tidsskr. f. Landø*

84) *Forgiftning som Følge af Gassens forandrede Sammensætning.* (*Ugeskr. f. Læger, 79,* 1917).

85) Meddelelse om Traché-Respirationens Mekanisme. (*Vid. Medd. Nat. For., 68,* 1917).

86) Injection preparation of the tracheal system of insects. (*Vid. Medd. Nat. For., 68,* 1917).

1918   87) Vævenes Forsyning med Ilt og Kapillærkredsløbets Regulering. (*K. D. Vid. Selsk. Biol. Medd.,* I, 6, 1918).

88) Tale ved Afsløringen af Mindestenen paa dr. phil. William Sørensens Grav. (*Naturens Verden,* 2, 1918).

89) Meddelelse om 1) Pincetsax 2) Lampeholder. (*Vid. Medd. Nat. Foren., 69,* 1918, p. XVI).

1919   90) Energy exchange in man. (*Proc. Physiol. Soc.—Journ. Physiol., 52,* 1919).

91) The spectrocomparator. An apparatus designed for the determina-

tion of the percentage saturation of blood with oxygen or carbon monoxide. (*Journ. Physiol.*, 52, 1919).

92) A. KROGH & J. LEITCH: The respiratory function of the blood in fishes. (*Journ. Physiol.*, 52, 1919).

93) The rate of diffusion of gases through animal tissues with some remarks on the coefficient of invasion. (*Journ. Physiol.*, 52, 1919).

94) The number and distribution of capillaries in muscles with calculations of the oxygen pressure head necessary for supplying the tissue. (*Journ. Physiol.*, 52, 1919).

95) The supply of oxygen to the tissues and the regulation of the capillary circulation. (*Journ. Physiol.*, 52, 1919).

96) The contractility and innervation of capillaries. A preliminary notice. (*Proc. Physiol. Soc.-Journ. Physiol.*, 53, 1919).

97) The composition of the atmosphere. An account of preliminary investigations and a programme. (*K. D. Vid. Selsk. Math.-fys. Med.*, I, 12, 1919).

98) *Vejledning ved Kursus i zoologisk Mikrokemi og Zoofysiologi.* Mimeographed at Univ. Zoofysiol. Lab. 1919. Revised 1927.

1920
99) A gas analysis apparatus accurate to 0.001% mainly designed for respiratory exchange work. (*Biochem. Journ.*, 14, 1920).

100) The calibration, accuracy and use of gas meters. (*Biochem. Journ.*, 14, 1920).

101) A. KROGH & J. LINDHARD, with the collaboration of G. LILJESTRAND and K. GAD-ANDRESEN: The relative value of fat and carbohydrate as sources of muscular energy. With appendices on the correlation between standard metabolism and the respiratory quotient during rest and work. (*Biochem. Journ.*, 14, 1920).

102) A. KROGH & H. O. SCHMIT-JENSEN: The fermentation of cellulose in the paunch of the ox and its significance in metabolism experiments. (*Biochem. Journ.*, 14, 1920).

103) A. KROGH & G. LILJESTRAND: Eine Mikrometode zur Bestimmung der Kohlensäure des Blutes. (*Biochem. Zeitschr.*, 104, 1920).

104) Sur le mécanisme de la respiration trachéenne. (*Compt. rend. Soc. Biol.*, 83, 1920).

105) Contractilité et innervation de capillaires. (*Compt. rend. Soc. Biol.*, 83, 1920).

106) Dyrebeskyttelse og Fysiologi. (*Dyrevennen*, 41, 1920).

107) Studies on the capillariomotor mechanism. I. The reaction to stimuli and the innervation of the blood vessels in the tongue of the frog. (*Journ. Physiol.*, 53, 1920).

108) A. KROGH & J. LINDHARD: The changes in respiration at the transition from work to rest. (*Journ. Physiol.*, 53, 1920).

109) Om Biernes Farvesans, Formsans og Lugtesans. (*Naturens Verden*, 4, 1920).

110) Studien über Tracheenrespiration. II. Ueber Gasdiffusion in den Tracheen. (*Pflügers Arch.*, 179, 1920). I same as Nr. 59.

111) Studien über Tracheenrespiration. III. Die Kombination von mechanischer Ventilation mit Gasdiffusion nach Versuchen an *Dytiscus*larven. (*Pflügers Arch., 179,* 1920).

1921
112) A. KROGH & H. O. SCHMIT-JENSEN: Sur la fermentation cellulosique dans la panse des ruminants et son importance pour l'étude des échanges respiratoires. (*Compt. rend. Soc. Biol., 84,* 1921).

113) A. KROGH & G. A. HARROP: Quelques remarques sur les stases et les oedèmes. (*Compt. rend. Soc. Biol., 84,* 1921). Same as Nr 115.

114) Reactions vasomotrices locales dans la peau de la grenouille. (*Compt. rend. Soc. Biol., 84,* 1921).

115) A. KROGH & G. A. HARROP: Some observations on stasis and oedema. (*Proc. Physiol. Soc.—Journ. Physiol., 54,* 1921). Same as Nr. 113.

116) A. KROGH & G. A. HARROP: On the substance responsible for capillary tonus. (*Proc. Physiol. Soc.—Journ. Physiol., 54,* 1921).

117) Studies on the physiology of capillaries. II. The reaction to local stimuli on the blood-vessels in the skin and the web of the frog. (*Journ. Physiol., 55,* 1921).

118) Fortsatte Studier over Kapillærernes Fysiologi. (*K. D. Vid. Selsk. Biol. Medd., III, 3,* 1921).

119) Shock og Blodtab. Et Referat af den engelske Shockkomités Undersøgelser. (*Ugeskr. f. Læger, 83,* p. 333, 1921; Discussion: *Kbh. med. Selsk. Forh.,* 1920—21. Kbh. 1921).

120) Gummisaltvand. (*Ugeskr. f. Læger, 83,* p. 1407, 1921).

1922
121) *The anatomy and physiology of capillaries.* Yale Univ. Press, New Haven, 1922 and 1924. Revised and enlarged edition 1929, 1930, and 1936. See also Nr. 138.

122) Sur un appareil respiratoire enregistreur, servant a déterminer l'absorption d'oxygène et les échanges caloriques chez l'homme. (*Compt. rend. Soc. Biol., 87,* 1922).

123) A. KROGH & P. B. REHBERG: Sur l'influence de l'hypophyse sur la tonicité des capillaires. (*Compt. rend. Soc. Biol., 87,* 1922).

124) A. KROGH, G. A. HARROP & P. BRANDT REHBERG: Studies on the physiology of capillaries. III. The innervation of the blood-vessels in the hind leg of the frog. (*Journ. Physiol., 56,* 1922).

125) Bidrag til Kapillærernes Fysiologi. Nobelforedrag afholdt d. 11. Dec. 1920 i Stockholm. (*Les prix Nobel en 1919—1920,* Stockholm, 1922).

126) Blodkapillærernes Bygning og Funktion. (*Svenska Läkartidn., 19,* 1922).

127) Et Respirationsapparat til klinisk Bestemmelse af Menneskets Energiomsætning. (*Ugeskr. f. Læger, 84,* p. 525, 1922). Same as Nr. 128.

128) Ein Respirationsapparat zur klinischen Bestimmung des Energieumsatzes des Menschen. (*Wiener klin. Wochenschrift, 35,* 1922). Same as Nr. 127.

1923 129) Determination of standard (basal) metabolism of patients by a recording apparatus. (*Boston Med. and Surg. Journ., 189*, 1923).

130) Die Wirkungen von Insulin im Organismus. (*Deutsche Med. Wochenschr., 49*, 1923).

131) The exchange of substances through the capillary wall. (*Proc. Inst. Med. Chicago, 4*, 1923).

132) De nordiske landes forsyning med insulin. En redogörelse. (*Svenska Läkartidn., 20*, p. 516 og 587, 1923). Same as Nr. 134.

133) Pankreashormonet Insulin og dets Anvendelse i Diabetesterapien. (*Ugeskr. f. Læger, 85*, p. 21, 1923; Diskussion i *Kbh. med. Selsk. Forh.*, 1922–23. Kbh. 1923, p. 26).

134) De nordiske Landes Forsyning med Insulin. En Redegørelse. (*Ugeskr. f. Læger, 85*, p. 392 og 443, 1923). Same as Nr. 132.

135) Det medicinske Fakultet og Medicinen. (*Ugeskr. f. Læger, 85*, p. 662, 1923).

136) H. C. Hagedorn & A. Krogh: Insulinstandardisering. (*Ugeskr. f. Læger, 85*, p. 913, 1923).

1924 137) A. Krogh & P. Brandt Rehberg: Kinematographic methods in the study of capillary circulation. (*Amer. Journ. Physiol., 68*, 1924).

138) *Anatomie und Physiologie der Capillaren*. Berlin. Springer. 1. Aufl 1924 (Translation by U. Ebbecke of Nr. 121, 1922); 2. Aufl. 1929 (Translation by W. Feldberg of Nr. 121, 1929).

139) Insulin, en Opdagelse og dens Betydning. (*Festskr. Kbh. Univ.*, Nov. 1924).

140) De nordiske Landes Forsyning med Insulin. (*Svenska Läkartidn., 21*, and *Ugeskr. f. Læger, 86*, p. 224, 1924). The two articles are not quite identical.

1925 141) A. Krogh & P. Brandt Rehberg: The influence of insulin on metabolic processes. (*Festschr. f. Prof. Pavlov*. Leningrad, 1925).

142) Die Wirkungen von Insulin im Organismus. Lecture at Congress. (*Nord. Bibl. Terapi, 4*, 1925, p. 7; Discussion. p. 24).

143) *Recording respiration apparatus*. Tables for computing standard metabolism from respiration experiments. Tables of normal metabolic rates. After Du Bois, Bierring and Benedict-Harris. 1925 and 1942.

144) Kinematographic methods in research and teaching. (*Skand. Arch. Physiol., 46*, 1925).

145) Nogle Bemærkninger om Insulin. (*Svenska Läkartidn., 22*, 1925).

146) Den anden internationale Konference om biologisk Standardisering af Lægemidler. (*Ugeskr. f. Læger, 87*, p. 987, 1925).

1926 147) Die Mikrogasanalyse und ihre Anwendungen. (*Abderhaldens Handb. der biol. Arbeitsmethoden*, Abt. IV, Teil 10, 1926).

148) A. Krogh & P. Brandt Rehberg: Titrimetric determination of CO_2 in 50 or 100 cc atmospheric air. (*Auszug d. Vortr. geh. auf d. XII.*

Internat. Physiologen-Kongress in Stockholm, 3—6. VIII, 1926: 93).

149) The pituitary (posterior lobe) principle in circulating blood. (*Journ. Pharm. Exp. Therapeutics, 29,* 1926).

150) A. KROGH and A. M. HEMMINGSEN: The assay of insulin by the convulsive-dose method on white mice. (*Publications of the League of Nations III. Health* 1926, III, 7, p. 40).

151) Insulinforsyningen til ubemidlede. (*Ugeskr. f. Læger, 88,* p. 1013, 1926).

1927
152) Ledelsen af Statens Gymnastikinstitut. (*Berl. Tidende,* 6. 5. 1927).

153) Kapillærnerverne og deres reflektoriske Virksomhed. (*Bibl. f. Læger, 119,* 1927). Samme Indhold som Nr. 158.

154) Stofskiftet gennem Kapillærvæggene. Ødemteorien. (*Bibl. f. Læger, 119,* 1927). Samme Indhold som Nr. 159.

155) A. KROGH & FUSAKICHI NAKAZAWA: Beiträge zur Messung des kolloid-osmotischen Druckes in biologischen Flüssigkeiten. (*Biochem. Zeitschr., 188,* 1927).

156) On the accuracy to be obtained by repetition of simple measurements. (*Journ. Biol. Chem., 74,* 1927).

157) A. KROGH & P. BRANDT REHBERG: The active relaxation of capillaries and venules in "reflex flare". (*Proc. Physiol. Soc.—Journ. Physiol., 64,* 1927).

158) Die Capillarnerven und ihre reflektorische Tätigkeit. (*Klin. Wochenschr., 6,* 1927). Indhold som Nr. 153.

159) Der Stoffaustausch durch die Capillarwände. (*Klin. Wochenschr. 6,* 1927). Indhold som Nr. 154.

160) Statens Gymnastikinstitut og Universitetets Gymnastikstudium. (*Nationaltidende,* 5. 8. 1927).

1928
161) A. KROGH & A. M. HEMMINGSEN: The destructive action of heat on insulin solutions. (*Biochem. Journ., 22,* 1928).

162) Insulinets Fysiologi. (*Dansk med. Selsk. Forh.,* 1928).

163) Experiments concerning the biology of *Pyrausta nubilalis* Hb. (*Intern. Corn Borer Investig. Scientific Reports.,* 1928).

164) A. KROGH & A. M. HEMMINGSEN: The assay of insulin on rabbits and mice. (*K. D. Vid. Selsk. Biol. Medd.,* VII, 6, 1928).

165) WILLIAM HARVEY.Fysiologiens Grundlægger. (*Politiken,* 5. 6. 1928).

1929
166) The Progress of Physiology. (*Amer. Journ. Physiol., 90,* og *Science, 70,* 1929). Se Nr. 171.

167) The utilization of dissolved organic substances by aquatic animals. (*Amer. J. Physiol., 90,* 1929).

168) Determination of CO_2 in fluids by microtitration. (*Amer. J. Physiol., 90,* 1929).

169) A. KROGH & P. BRANDT REHBERG: CO_2-BESTIMMUNG IN DER ATMOSPHÄRISCHEN LUFT DURCH MIKROTITRATION. (*Biochem. Zeitschr., 205,* 1929).

170) Om Insulin. (*Farmaceutisk Tidende*, 39, 1929).

171) Fysiologiens Fremskridt. (*Nordisk Med. Tidsskr.*, 1, 1929). Translation of Nr. 166.

1930 172) A. KROGH & E. LANGE with the collaboration of WILLIE SMITH: On the organic matter given off by algae. (*Biochem. Journ.*, 24, 1930).

173) Eine Mikromethode für die organische Verbrennungsanalyse, besonders von gelösten Substanzen. (*Biochem. Zeitschr.*, 221, 1930).

174) A. KROGH & E. LANGE: Ueber die Anwendung von Celluloid, besonders Celluloidröhren im Laboratorium. (*Biochem. Zeitschr.*, 221, 1930).

175) A. KROGH & P. BRANDT REHBERG: CO_2-Bestimmung in Flüssigkeiten und Geweben durch Mikrotitration. (*Biochem. Zeitschr.*, 225, 1930).

176) Dyr og Menneske. I. II. III. (*Flensborg Avis* 7., 9., and 10. Sept. 1930). See Nr. 189.

177) Om Hjernens Kredsløbsforhold. (*Hospitalstid.*, 73, 1930).

178) Institute of Physiology, University of Copenhagen. (*Methods & Problems of Med. Educ.* 18th Series. The Rockefeller Found. New York, 1930).

179) Pavlov's Undersøgelser over Storhjærnens Fysiologi. (*Naturens Verden*, 14, 1930).

180) Ueber die Bedeutung von gelösten organischen Substanzen bei der Ernährung von Wassertieren. (*Zeitschr. vergl. Physiol.*, 12, 1930).

1931 181) Dissolved substances as food of aquatic organisms. (*Biol. Reviews*, 6, 1931 & *Cons. internat. pour l'explor. de la mer. Rapports et Procès-Verbaux*, 75, 1931).

182) *Forplantningen*. En Fremstilling til Brug ved Undervisningen i Gymnasiet. Kbh. 1931. Included in Nr. 32 seventh edition onward.

183) A. KROGH & K. BERG: Ueber die chemische Zusammensetzung des Phytoplanktons aus dem Frederiksborg-Schlosssee und ihre Bedeutung für die Maxima der Cladoceren. (*Int. Rev. Hydrobiol.* 25, 1931).

184) A. KROGH & E. LANGE: Quantitative Untersuchungen über Plankton, Kolloide und gelöste organischen und anorganischen Substanzen in dem Furesee. (*Int. Rev. Hydrobiol.* 26, 1931).

185) A. KROGH & ANCEL B. KEYS: A syringe-pipette for precise analytical usage. (*Journ. Chem. Soc.*, 1931, p. 2436).

1932 186) En Respirator efter Philip Drinker's Princip. (*Hospitalstid.*, 75, 1932).

187) A. KROGH, E. M. LANDIS & A. H. TURNER: The movement of fluid through the human capillary wall in relation to venous pressure and to the colloid osmotic pressure of the blood. (*Journ. Clin. Invest.*, 11, 1932).

188) A. KROGH, A. H. TURNER & E. M. LANDIS: A celluloid capsule for measuring venous pressures. (*Journ. Clin. Invest.*, 11, 1932).

189) Dyr og Menneske. (*Naturens Verden, 16,* 1932). Nr. 176 edited and enlarged.
190) Dansk Naturvidenskab og Universitetsbiblioteket. U. B.'s 450 Aars Jubilæum. (*Politiken,* 9. 12. 1932).
191) A *text-book of human physiology.* Revised and edited by Katherine R. Drinker. Philadelphia, 1932. Revised translation of Nr. 32.

1933 192) Om indretning af støvfri rum. (*Bygmesteren,* 1933).
193) Conditions of life in the depths of the ocean. (*The Collecting Net,* 8, 1933).
194) Kvælningsrisiko. (*Flensborg Avis,* March 28 and 29 1933, also *Tidsskrift for Ingeniørofficerer,* 4, 1933; *Flensborg Avis* April 2 1933).
195) Indledning til V. Meisen's oversættelse af Nicolaus Steno. Dissektion af et Hajhoved. (*Stenoniana,* Bind I, Kbh. 1933).
196) Om standardisering af hæmometre. (*Ugeskr. f. Læger, 95,* p. 173, 1933).

1934 197) A method for the determination of ammonia in water and air. (*Biol. Bull., 67,* 1934).
198) A. Krogh & A. Keys: Methods for the determination of dissolved organic carbon and nitrogen in sea water. (*Biol. Bull., 67,* 1934).
199) Conditions of life in the ocean. Conditions of life at great depths in the ocean. (*Ecological Monogr.,* 4, 1934).
200) *Grundrids til Forelæsninger over Menneskets Fysiologi.* Mimeographed at Univ. Zoofysiol. Lab. 1934.
201) Om målesprøjter og deres anvendelse navnlig til nøjagtig iltbestemmelse i vand efter Winkler. (*Kemisk Maanedsblad,* 15, 1934).
202) En vippebaare til kunstigt aandedræt. (*Militærlægen,* 40, 1934).
203) Physiology of the blue whale. (*Nature, London, 133,* 1934).
204) G. C. C. Damant & A. Krogh: Physiology of deep diving in the whale. (*Nature, London 133,* 1934).
205) Nogle nyere undersøgelser over hvalernes biologi. (almost the same in *Naturens Verden,* 18, and *Naturen,* 58, 1934).
206) E. Hohwü Christensen, A. Krogh & J. Lindhard: Investigations on heavy muscular work. (*Quart. Bull. of the Health Org. of the League of Nations,* 3, 1934).
207) A reflex showing sympathetic innervation of cold spots. Kongresberetning. (*Skand. Arch. Physiol.,* 71, 1934).
208) Syringe pipettes and some of their uses. Kongresberetning. (*Skand. Arch. Physiol.,* 71, 1934).
209) Sympathetic innervation of the cold spots, brought about in a reflex from the pharynx to the skin in man. (*Skand. Arch. Physiol.,* 71, 1934).
210) Opstilling, anvendelse og pasning af selvregistrerende stofskifteapparat. (Ugeskr. f. Læger, 96, p. 737, 1934).

1935 211) E. Hohwü Christensen, A. Krogh og J. Lindhard: Undersøgelser over haardt muskelarbejde. (*Bibl. f. Læger, 127,* 1935).

212) Syringe pipets. (*Industr. and Engin. Chem.*, 7, 1935).
213) Precise determination of oxygen in water by syringe pipets. (*Industr. and Engin. Chem.*, 7, 1935).
214) ANCEL KEYS, E. H. CHRISTENSEN & A. KROGH: The organic metabolism of sea-water with special reference to the ultimate food cycle in the sea. (*Journ. Mar. Biol. Ass. Unit. Kingd.*, 20, 1935).
215) Den produktionsøkonomiske vexelvirkning mellem nogle plante- og dyresamfund. Lecture presented at det nordiske Studentermøde Juni 1935. (*Naturens Verden*, 19, 1935).
216) The use of isotopes in biological research. (*Orvosi Hétilap, Budapest*, 1935).
217) OVE HANSEN & A. KROGH: An arrangement for determining gas exchange and respiratory quotient during severe work. (*Skand. Arch. Physiol.*, 71, 1935).
218) FR. GRANDE COVIAN and A. KROGH: The changes in osmotic pressure and total concentration of the blood in man during and after muscular work. (*Skand. Arch. Physiol.*, 71, 1935).
219) TH. V. BRAND & A. KROGH: Das Verhalten der Kohlehydrate bei Ratten in einer auf erschöpfende Arbeit folgende Ruheperiode. (*Skand. Arch. Physiol.*, 72, 1935).
220) G. V. HEVESY, E. HOFER & A. KROGH: The permeability of the skin of frogs to water as determined by D_2O and H_2O. (*Skand. Arch. Physiol.*, 72, 1935).

1936 221) H. KOCH & A. KROGH: La fonction des papilles anales des larves de diptères. (*Ann. Soc. Scien. Bruxelles Sér. B. Sciences phisiques et naturelles*, 56, 1936).
222) K. FENGER-ERIKSEN, A. KROGH & H. H. USSING: A micro-method for accurate determination of D_2O in water. (*Biochem. Journ.*, 30, 1936).
223) Stoftransport ved diffusion og sekretion i organismen. (*Hospitalstid.*, 79, 1936).
224) A. KROGH and R. SPÄRCK: On a new bottom-sampler for investigation of the micro fauna of the sea bottom with remarks on the quantity and significance of the benthonic micro fauna. (*K. D. Vid. Selsk. Biol. Medd.*, XIII, 4, 1936).
225) H. K. BEECHER & A. KROGH: Microscopic observation of the absorption of insulin and protamine-insulinate. (*Nature, London*, 137, 1936).
226) Nicolaus Steno, Danmarks største biolog. (*Politiken* 25. 5. 1936).
227) H. K. BEECHER, M. E. FIELD & A. KROGH: A method of measuring venous pressure in the human leg during walking. (*Skand. Arch. Physiol.*, 73, 1936).
228) E. HOHWÜ CHRISTENSEN & A. KROGH: Fliegeruntersuchungen. 1 Mitt. Methodik der Prüfungen von Höhenfliegern. (*Skand. Arch. Physiol.*, 73, 1936).
229) H. K. BEECHER, M. E. FIELD & A. KROGH: The effect of walking

on the venous pressure at the ankle. (*Skand. Arch. Physiol.*, 73, 1936).

230) E. HOHWÜ CHRISTENSEN & A. KROGH: Fliegeruntersuchungen. 2. Mitt. Die Wirkung niedriger O_2Spannung auf Höhenflieger. (*Skand. Arch. Physiol.*, 73, 1936).

231) A. KROGH & C. TROLLE: A balance for the determination of insensible perspiration in man and its use. (*Skand. Arch. Physiol.*, 73, 1936). Indhold som Nr. 234.

232) E. HOHWÜ CHRISTENSEN, A. KROGH & J. LINDHARD: An introduction to the studies of severe muscular exercise published in the present supplementary volume and other papers in the Skand. Arch. (*Skand. Arch. Physiol.* Suppl. Nr. 10 til 74, 1936).

233) A. KROGH & H. H. USSING: The exchange of hydrogen between the free water and the organic substances in the living organism. (*Skand. Arch. Physiol.*, 75, 1936).

234) A. KROGH & CARSTEN TROLLE: En vægt til bestemmelse af perspiratio insensibilis hos mennesket og dens anvendelse. (*Ugeskr. f. Læger*, 98, p. 113, 1936). Same as Nr. 231.

1937 235) A. KROGH & H. H. USSING: A note on the permeability of trout eggs to D_2O and H_2O. (*Journ. Exp. Biol.*, 14, 1937).

236) G. HEVESY, J. J. HOLST & A. KROGH : Investigations on the exchange of phosphorus in teeth using radioactive phosphorus as indicator. (*K. D. Vid. Selsk. Biol. Medd.*, XIII, 13, 1937).

237) Active absorption of anions in the animal kingdom. (*Nature, London*, 139, 1937).

238) Biologen Niels Steensen trehundrede Aar. (*Nordisk tidskrift för vetenskap, konst och industri*, Ny Serie, 3, 1937).

239) The use of isotopes as indicators in biological research. (*Science*, 85, 1937).

240) Osmotic regulation in the frog (*R.esculenta*) by active absorption of chloride ions. (*Skand. Arch. Physiol.*, 76, 1937).

241) Osmotic regulation by active absorption of ions in freshwater animals. Plenarforedrag. (*Skand. Arch. Physiol.*, 77, p. 50, 1937).

242) Rudyard Kipling. Nogle Takkeord. (*Tilskueren*, 54, 1937).

243) Part. I. Natural membranes. Introductory paper: Animal membranes. (*Trans. Faraday Soc.*, 33, 1937).

244) Osmotic regulation in fresh water fishes by active absorption of chloride ions. (*Zeitschr. vergl. Physiol.*, 24, 1937).

1938 245) Extracellular and intracellular fluid. (*Acta Med. Scand. Suppl.*, 90, 1938).

246) A. KROGH & H. H. USSING: Deuterium built into proteins and their amino acids in vivo and in vitro. (*Compt. rend. Lab. Carlsberg, Sér. chim.*, 22, 1938).

247) The use of deuterium in biological work. (*Enzymologia, Haag*, 5, 1938).

248) Myślenie Wzrkowe. *Nauka Polska,* Warsaw, 24, 1938. (Much the same as Nr. 249).

249) Visual thinking. An autobiographical note. (*Organon,* Warsaw, 2, 1938).

250) The salt concentration in the tissues of some marine animals. (*Skand. Arch. Physiol., 80,* 1938).

251) The active absorption of ions in some freshwater animals. (*Zeitschr. vergl. Physiol., 25,* 1938).

252) A. KROGH, K. SCHMIDT-NIELSEN & E. ZEUTHEN: The osmotic behaviour of frogs eggs and young tadpoles. (*Zeitschr. vergl. Physiol., 26,* 1938).

253) RUTH E. CONKLIN & A. KROGH: A note on the osmotic behaviour of *Eriocheir* in concentrated and *Mytilus* in dilute sea water. (*Zeitschr. vergl. Physiol., 26,* 1938).

1939 254) Osmotisk regulering hos vanddyr. Summary of lecture. (*Naturh. Tidende, 3,* 1939, p. 119).

255) *Osmotic regulation in aquatic animals.* The University Press, Cambridge, 1939.

256) Effect of posture on the regulation of circulation. Foredragsreferat. (*Proc. Inst. Med. Chicago, 12,* 1939).

257) The active uptake of ions into cells and organisms. (*Proc. Nat. Acad. Sci. U.S.A., 25,* 1939).

258) The teaching of physiology. (*Science, 89,* 1939).

259) E. HOHWÜ CHRISTENSEN, A. KROGH & V. SAHLSTEDT: Nitrous oxide and nitrogen narcotisation of animals to be slaughtered according to the Jewish ritual. (*Veterinary Rec., 51,* 1939).

1940 260) A micro-climate recorder. (*Ecology, 21,* 1940). Se ogsaa Nr. 290.

261) En norsk undersøgelse af eskimoernes levevis og livsbetingelser i Østgrønland. (*Flensborg Avis,* 7. 10. og 8. 10. 1940).

262) NORBERT CASTERET, en fransk huleforsker og hans gerning. (*Naturens Verden, 24,* 1940).

263) Billedkunst og dens magiske Betydning for 20.000 Aar siden efter Casterets Fremstilling. (*Naturens Verden, 24,* 1940).

264) Mennesket. (Anmeldelse i *Naturens Verden, 24,* p. 381, 1940, and 25, p. 284, 1941).

1941 265) *The comparative physiology of respiratory mechanisms.* University of Pennsylvania Press, Philadelphia, 1941.

266) En nordisk Runesten i Minnesota U.S.A. (*Flensborg Avis* 22. 11. og 24. 11. 1941). See also Nr. 269.

267) A. KROGH & ERIK ZEUTHEN: The mechanism of flight preparation in some insects. (*Journ. Exp. Biol., 18,* 1941).

1942 268) Boligopvarmningsproblemet fra et fysiologisk Synspunkt. (*Beretning om Den første danske Varmekongres. 15.—17. April 1943.*)

269) Runestenen fra Kensington U.S.A. (*Flensborg Avis,* 26. 5. 1942). Answer to critic by Dr. phil. Gudmund Schütte's of Nr. 266, March 14 1942.

270) Dyriske Cellers Permeabilitet og Saltoptagelse. Lecture summary by Dr. phil. H. H. Ussing. (*Naturh. Tidende*, 6, 1942, p. 87).

271) Wetzels teknik til bedømmelse af børns legemlige udvikling prøvet paa et dansk materiale. (*Nordisk Medicin*, 13, 1942).

272) Boligopvarmningsproblemet fra Fysiologisk Synspunkt. (*Varme*, 7, 1942).

1943 273) The exchange of ions between cells and extracellular fluid. I. (*Acta Physiol. Scand.*, 6, 1943).

274) Some experiments on the osmoregulation and respiration of *Eristalis* larvae. (*Entomol. Medd.*, 23 (Jubilæumsbind) 1943).

1944 275) IB HOLM-JENSEN, A. KROGH & VEIJO WARTIOVAARA: Some experiments on the exchange of potassium and sodium between single cells of *Characeae* and the bathing fluid. (*Acta Bot. Fenn.*, 36, 1944).

276) A. KROGH, ANNA-LOUISE LINDBERG & BODIL SCHMIDT-NIELSEN: The exchange of ions between cells and extracellular fluid. II. The exchange of potassium and calcium between the frog heart muscle and the bathing fluid. (*Acta Physiol. Scand.*, 7, 1944).

277) A. KROGH & ANNA-LOUISE LINDBERG: The exchange of ions between cells and extracellular fluid. III. The exchange of sodium with glucose in the frog's heart. (*Acta Physiol. Scand.*, 7, 1944).

278) Bostaduppvärmning ur fysiologisk och hygienisk synpunkt. (*Fläkten*, Sverige, 9, 1944). Same as Nr. 279.

279) Boligopvarmning fra et fysiologisk og hygiejnisk synspunkt. (*Varme*, 9, 1944). Translation of Nr. 278.

280) Respirationsorganernes sammenlignende Fysiologi. (*Videnskaben af i Dag*, København, 1944).

1945 281) A. KROGH, C. G. LUND & K. PEDERSEN-BJERGAARD: The osmotic concentration of human lacrymal fluid. (*Acta Physiol. Scand.*, 10, 1945).

1946 282) On the active and passive exchanges of ions through cell surfaces and membranes in general. (*American Scientist*, 34, 1946).

283) The comparative physiology of respiratory organs. (*Experientia*, 2, 1946).

284) A. KROGH & HANS BURSTRØM: The biochemistry of the development of buds in trees and the bleeding sap. (*K. D. Vid. Selsk. Biol. Medd.*, XX, 2, 1946).

285) The active and passive exchange of inorganic ions through the surface of living cells and through living membranes generally. (*Proc. Roy. Soc. B.*, 133, 1946).

1947 286) V. Frisch's nyeste Undersøgelser over Biernes »Sprog«. (*Naturens Verden*, 31, 1947).

287) The production and ripening of red blood cells. A summary of Danish studies. (*The Scientific Monthly*, 64, 1947).

288) A. KROGH & HANS BURSTRM: Bleeding and bud development in *Carpinus*. (*Svensk Botanisk Tidsskrift*, 41, 1947).

1948 289) Boligopvarmningsudvalgets forhistorie. Engelsk Résumé: The history and setting up of the committee. (*Boligopvarmningsudvalgets Meddelelser,* Nr. 1A, Kbhvn. 1948).

290) En mikroklimatograf. Engelsk Résumé almost as text in Nr. 260. (*Boligopvarmningsudvalgets Meddelelser,* Nr. 5).

291) Måling af textilers varmeisolerende egenskaber. Engelsk Résumé: The heat insulating properties of textiles. (*Boligopvarmningsudvalgets Meddelelser,* Nr. 6).

292) Dammproblemer i museer. (*Fläkten,* Sverige, Nr. 1, 1948).

293) The dust problem in museums and how to solve it. (*The Museums Journal,* 47, 1948).

294) Determination of temperature and heat production in insects. (*Zeitschr. vergl. Physiol.,* 31, 1948).

1949 295) Nogle Erindringer fra min Barndom. (*Grenaa Folketidendes Jubilæumsnummer* 4. 8. 1949).

296) Niels Steensen 1638–1686. (*Store danske Personligheder,* Berlingske Forlag, Kbhvn., 1949, p. 44).

These papers were published after AK's death.

297) Reminiscence of work on capillaries. A lecture to the students in the Harvard Medical School, 1946. (*Isis. Official Quarterly J. of the History of Science Society,* 41, 1950).

298) A. KROGH and T. WEIS-FOGH: The respiratory exchange of the desert locust (*Schistocerca gregaria*) before, during and after flight. (*J. exp. Biol.,* 28, 1951, pp. 344–357).

299) A. KROGH and T. WEIS-FOGH: A roundabout for studying sustained flight of locusts. (*J. exp. Biol.,* 29, 1952, pp. 211–218).

Index

Aakjær, Jeppe, 41
Aarhus, 17, 19, 210
Aarhus Cathedral School, 15, 17
Aarhus University, 207
Abel, John J., 119, 123
academic cabinet, 29
academic citizenship, 62
academic council, 111
Academy of Sciences. *See* Danish Royal Academy of Sciences
acclimatization, 107
Acta Physiologica Scandinavica (physiology journal), 176
actin, 156
advisory panel for natural sciences, recommendation for, 235
aerodynamic sense organ, 230
aglomerular fish, 160
air bladders, 56, 99
air force pilots, respiratory physiology, 181
air sacs, 42, 46, 231
Albrechtsen, Dagmar (Erik Krogh's first wife), 152
alcohol regulation, 134
Alexandrine (queen of Denmark), 157
Alfred Benzon Symposium, 154, 162
Allen, Frederick Madison, 126
Allied troops (WWII), 198, 199
alveolar air, 45
alveolar membrane, 107
Amanita rubescens (fly mushroom), 146
amanuensis (assistant professor), 177
America: 1355–1364 (Holand), 225
American Academy of Arts and Sciences, 164
American Physiological Society, 239

amino acids, 186
Amundsen, Roald, 95
anal papillae of insect larvae, study of, 171
anatomy, 55, 76
    dissections, 32, 46
Andresen, Gad (August Krogh's assistant), 135
Anholt, 15
animal protectionists and Kosher law, 165
anions, exchange across cell membranes, 213
Anschluss (March 1938), 195
Anti-Locust Research Center, 228
anti-Semitism, 204
anti-vivisectionists, opposition to physiological research, 123
apparatus, physiological testing, 45, 54, 74, 99, 118
aquaria, laboratory, 142
aquatic animals, 213
Archbishop of Canterbury, 219
Archiv für Physiologie, 92, 93, 175
Arctic, 96, 100
Arctic Sea, 52
Arctic Station, 84, 85
Armstrong, Wallace, 223
Arnold, Professor, 206
Arrhenius, Svante August (Swedish physicist), 53, 102
arteriolar-capillary junction, 159
arterioles, 112, 113
artium (also *studenter exam*; entrance examination for the university), 21, 29, 62, 152
Asmussen, Erling, 174, 176, 183
Asserbo Castle, 35

assistantship under Christian Bohr, 80
Astrup, Paul, 205
athletic performance, physiological study of, 178
Atlantic City (New Jersey), 222
Atlantis (American research vessel), 168, 169
atmospheric pressure, effect of low, 182
ATP (adenosine triphosphate), 174
Atuagagdliutit (Greenland newspaper), 86
August Krogh Distinguished Lecture, American Physiological Society, 239
August Krogh Institute, 184, 239
August Krogh Lecture, International Congress of Physiological Sciences, 239
August Krogh principle, 167
Austria, 77, 116
Austro-Hungarian Kingdom, 108

bacteria, marine, study of, 169
bacteriological laboratory, 89
Bagger (August Krogh's first student), 19
balance for weighing a person within ± 1 g, 178
ball and ballgowns, 149
ballet, 149
Baltic states, 198
Baltimore, 119, 123, 129
Baly Medal, 215
Bang, Sophus, 133, 134
Banting, Frederick G., 128–130, 136–138
Barcroft, Joseph, 82, 107, 115, 116, 118, 119, 162
 death, 236
barometer, 57
barometric pressure, 57
Battle Creek (Michigan), 128, 129
Battle of Britain, 200
battleaxes, Norse, 222
Bayliss (British physiologist), 119
Beecher, Henry K., 158, 221
beer sales tax, 44
Belgium, 148, 200
Benedict, Francis C., 83, 87, 93, 103, 120, 127, 176
Benedict helmet, 179

Bensley, Robert R., 156, 158
Bergen Biological Station, 95
Bergh, Dr., 39
Berglund, Hilding, 209
Bergstrøm, Hjalmar, 41
Bergsøe, Paul, 225
Berkeley (California), 188, 192
Best, Charles H., 128, 232
Bible, 48, 73
bicycle ergometer, 100, 174, 178
Billedbladet, 235
Biological Society (Biologisk Selskab), 47, 48
Biological Reviews, 168
biological standardization of digitalis, 118
Birck (friend of August Krogh's and fellow student at Aarhus Cathedral School), 18, 19, 26, 27
Birmingham (England), 228
bleeding sap, 215
Blegdams Hospital, 82
Bliss, Michael, 130
blitzkrieg, 200
blood flow, 112, 114; *see also* circulation
blood sugar, 127, 129, 133
board of directors, Nordisk Insulin Laboratory, 194
Board of Governors of the University of Toronto, 132
boatyard (Lynæs), 145
Boaz, J. E. V., 24
Bock, Johannes, 107, 175
body fluids, 213
body temperature, 180
Bohr, Christian (physiologist), 32, 35, 38, 39, 40, 41, 45, 51, 54–57, 59, 74, 77, 79, 82, 88, 93, 108, 167, 189, 190
Bohr, Ellen (*née* Adler; wife of Christian Bohr), 44, 59
Bohr, Harald (mathematician), 59
Bohr, Jenny, 59
Bohr, Niels (nuclear physicist), 59, 111, 185, 187–189, 206
 escapes to Sweden, 204
"Bohr effect," 54
Bohr's institute. *See* Institute for Theoretical Physics
Bohr's laboratory. *See* Physiological Laboratory
Bøje, Ove, 177–179

Index

bomb shelters, 206
bombardment of Copenhagen, 6
Bonn, 46
Boothby, Walter, 123, 128
Bornholm, 15
Bornstein, 101
Boston, 87, 88, 124, 125, 221
botanists, 41, 50
botany, 14, 24, 39
Bøving, Adam, 62, 97, 106, 143, 144, 148
Bøving, Anna, 62, 143, 222
Bøving, Bent, 144, 222
Bøving, Paula, 63, 106; *see also* Brønnum, Paula
Bowman, 116
boycott of the Academy, 234
brain, 213
Brande, 127
Bredgade, 44
Bremen (Germany), 152
brewery, 31, 44, 65, 82, 142
Brick, Marie (Andreas Krogh's wife), 6, 9; *see also* Marie Krogh
Bridge (physiologist), 28
British Research Council, 128
British army, 109
British Council in Stockholm, 215
British Medical Journal, 130
British navy, 109
British Royal Air Force, 205, 206
Brøndsted, Johannes, 140, 225
Brønnum, Paula, 62
Buchtahl, Fritz, 183, 206, 216, 218, 223
Buck, Pearl, 143
Buhl, Valdemar, 8, 15
bulk flow, in osmosis, 186
Burgomaster House, 11
Burmeister (shipbuilder), 8, 9, 168
Burmeister and Wain, 8
Burström, Hans, 215, 216
Busch, Georg, 237

calcium, 203
calcium method, 203
California, 232
"Call for Oxygen," 99
Cambridge (England), 118
Cambridge University Press, 172

Canada, 235
Canary Islands, 152
cancer, 118, 201, 236
candidatus magisterii (cand. mag.; teacher's examination), 26, 164
Cannon, Walter B., 124
Cape Horn, 95
capillaries, 4, 45, 100, 101, 112
 anatomical arrangement, 113
 autoregulated, 162
 book on, 154
 contractility, 158
 dissolved gas, 113
 distribution, 115
 elasticity, 113
 flow rate, 113, 160
 function, 113
 opening and closing, 113
 oxygen tension, 113
 permeability, 162
 wrinkling of wall, 156
carbohydrate, 173–74
 diet for athletes, 174
 failure to metabolize, 126
carbon dioxide (CO_2), 59, 72, 92, 112
 atmospheric, 52, 53, 95
 coal combustion produces, 53
 effect of high percentage of, 182
 effect on climate, 53, 54
 effect on O_2 binding, 54, 72, 112
 in alveolar air, 79
 in arterial blood, 79
 in water and air, 38, 57
 oceanic, 52, 72
 production, 53
 tension, 53, 91
carbon-14, 191
carbon monoxide (CO), diffusion, 74, 92, 93, 106, 107
carbonic acid (as CO_2 was called at the time), 52; *see also* carbon dioxide
cardiac output, 101, 175, 177
Carl, Prince, 121
Carlsberg Brewery, 11
Carlsberg Foundation, 51, 83, 110
Carlsberg Laboratory, 187–188
Carnegie Nutrition Laboratory, 83
carotid artery, 81
Carrier, Beatrice, 124
cation exchange, 213

cell membranes, 213
censor in physiology examinations, 118, 151
Chamberlain, Neville, 195
Chambers, R., 159
channels, 186
Charles de la Bussiere (Hauch), 18
chemical laboratory, 84
chemistry, 14
Chicago, 124, 148, 158, 223, 232
chick embryos, 74
Chievitch, Ole, 205
children, views on, 105
"Children of Zodiac, The" (Kipling), 237
Chile, 106
China, 148
chitin, 102
chloride, 170
    determination, 170
    ions, 191
cholera, 19
Christensen, Erik Hohwü, 165, 176, 177, 179, 180, 182–184, 203
Christensen, Herluf, 37
Christian IX (king of Denmark), 62
Christian X (king of Denmark), 118, 121
Christianity, 36, 37, 72
Christiansen, Johanne (Jonna; Marie Krogh's friend and fellow student), 63, 108
Christmas, 30, 33, 55, 59, 61, 69, 89, 115, 144, 197
chrysalides of butterflies, 74
Church of Our Lady, 6
Churchill, Edward D., 155, 221
Cincinnati (Ohio), 124, 129
circulation of blood, 4, 100; *see also* blood flow
circulatory physiology, 163
Cl^-. *See* chloride ions
Claff, C. L., 222
clerical assistance, 237
Cleveland (Ohio), 129
climatic variations, 230
clinical tool, 118
clinics, 74
CO^2. *See* carbon dioxide
cod liver oil, as dietary supplement, 200
Cohn (British physiologist), 119
Cole, Rufus, 123, 139

Collander, 214
College of Physical Education, 184
Collip, James Bertram, 130, 131, 133–134, 137–138
combustion, 99, 100
    of fat and carbohydrate, 174
commons (Lynæs), 145
comparative physiology, 163; *see also* zoophysiology
Comparative Physiology of Respiratory Mechanisms, The (August Krogh), 172
Comroe, Julius, 107
Conant, Kenneth, 226
Connaught Anti-Toxin Laboratories, 131
consciousness at high altitude, 181
contractile elements, 156
contractility of capillary walls, 157
convulsions following insulin injection, 133
Conway, Edward J., 191
Copenhagen, 15, 39, 145
    coal dust, 147
    film museum, 123
    winter of 1946–47, 227
Copenhagen Medical Society, 132
Corethra larvae, 46, 47
Cossus, 229
Covian, Grande F., 178, 179
creatinine, as a glomerular substance, 159
Croonian Lecture, 190, 209, 215
crustaceans, 212
Curie, Marie, 202
Cushny, Arthur R., 116
cyclotron, 189, 214
Czechoslovakia, 195

D_2O. *See* heavy water
Daladier, 195
Dale, Henry Hallet, 113, 215, 119, 128
Dana (Danish research vessel), 169
Danielli, James Frederick, 212
Danish Commission for the Geological and Geographic Investigation of Greenland, 52
Danish National Museum, 226
Danish Royal Academy of Sciences, 233–235, 236

danske folkekirke (Danish national church), 21, 72
daphnia, 183
Darwin, Charles, 50
Davis Strait, 84
Davson, Hugh, 212
de-to-smaa (the two little ones), 147
Dean, R. B., 213
degenerated gland, 130
dehydration, effect on work performance, 184
Denmark, 105, 110, 138
  government, 108, 235
  neutrality, 196
dentist, 196
Dental School, 118, 233
Department of Culture, 62
Department of Education, 55
Department of Theoretical Gymnastics, 184
deuterium (D), 185, 187
diabetes, 119, 163
diabetic coma, 134
diagnosis, 236
diffusion, 45, 82, 112, 185–191, 213
  coefficient, 229
  constants, 92, 114
  secretion vs., 58, 78, 93, 107
  theory, 82
digestive enzymes, 127, 129
digitalis, 118
Disko (or Disco), 51, 83, 84
dissolved organic substances, 4
  as food for aquatic animals, 168
dissertations, 178, 225, 237
  of August Krogh, 51, 55, 58
  of Marie Krogh, 107
diving seals, 196
Djursland, 24, 29
Djursland Brewery, 11
doctorate, 15, 107
Dogger Bank, 108, 109
Dönitz, Karl, 216
Dotterweich, K., 229
Douglas, C. Gordon, 94, 106, 109
Dr. med. (Doctor medicinae), 107, 237
Dr. phil. (Doctor of Philosophy), 15
drag, elimination of, 231
Dreckmann, Johann (August Krogh's grandfather), 7

Dreckmann, Sine (August Krogh's grandmother), 7, 9, 10, 11
Dreyer, George, 94
Drinker, Cecil, 155, 180, 210, 221, 223
Drinker, Katherine (Cecil Drinker's wife), 164
Duckwitz, Georg F., 204
Duling, Brian, 239
dung beetle, 145
Durig, Arnold, 116
dust-free rooms, 142
Dutch tiles, 145
dyslexia, Claus Munch Plum and, 219

Ebbecke, Ulrich, 113, 154, 155
edema, 127, 200
Edgewood (Pennsylvania), 222
Edinburgh, 124
editor of *Søfartstidende*, 55
eels, 169–170
"Efterlyses" (Guldberg), 237
Ege, Richard, 102, 155, 205
Eli Lilly Company, 131
Elizabeth (Queen of Belgium), 157
Elizabeth Islands, 153
Elsinor. *See* Helsingør
embryos, 75, 186
emphysema, 233
endothelial nuclei, 155
energy, muscular
  source of, 173
  efficiency, 174
England, 50, 74, 113, 118, 196
English language, 26, 47, 50
  reading, 34
  translating, 33, 45, 58
  writing, 7
Ephraim (Wisconsin), 223
Erlang equation, 115
Erlang, K., 114
Esbach method, 87
Esbønderup, 14, 24
escapes to Sweden during WWII, 205
Eskimos, 51, 83, 85
  language, 85, 86
Eslöv, 210, 215
Estonia, 58, 198
Europe, 195

examinations, 151
  of August Krogh 40, 43, 44
  of Marie Krogh, 81
exercise physiology, 3, 100
extracellular fluid, 213

Faber, Knud, 127
Faculty of Medicine, 55, 105, 140
Faculty of Science, 88, 105, 140
failing health, 236
Fair Hill (Scotland), 84
Fascism, Italian, 152
fat, 173–74
  and carbohydrate as fuel for muscular work, 179
  as energy for flight muscles, 231
  in diet, 174
fatigue, 178
Fenger-Eriksen (August Krogh's assistant), 186
Fergus Falls (Minnesota), 223
Fermi, Enrico, 188
Festschrift for the University of Copenhagen, 131
fetal pancreas, 130
Fick principle, 101
Field, Madeleine, 149, 158
Finance Committee (Danish Parliament), 97
Finland, 199, 216
  war with Russia, 198
Finsen Light Institute, 41, 100, 104, 175, 188
fish pancreas, 132
fisherman in Lynæs, 169
fishes, 27, 38, 46, 102
Fitzgerald, J. G., 137
Fladmark, Captain Raider, 225
Fleming, Sir Alexander, 219
Fletcher, Walter M., 173
Flexner, Sigmon, 140
flight, 230; see also insects
  warming up of muscles, 229, 230
  of insects, 210
Florida, 222
fly mushrooms, 146
flywheel, camera modified by August Krogh with, 123

Forbes family, 153
forestry, 147
Forster, Robert, 107
Fram (Amundsen's ship), 95
France, 149, 196
Francis Ferdinand (archduke of Austria), 108
Frederiksberg, 9
Frederiksberg Church, 9, 24
Frederiksberg Park, 9, 12
Frederikshavn, 8, 15, 36
freedom fighters, 207
French language, 23, 26, 33
frogs, 38, 55, 77, 98, 102, 114
  eggs, 186
  metabolism, 40
  respiration, 46
  skin, 46, 186
  webbed foot, 155
fuel shortage, 227
Funchal, Madeira, 96
funeral, August Krogh's plans for, 237
funnel, for making a cast of wasp's tunnel 220
Fure Lake, sampling of water and air, 57, 59
Fyn, 56, 61, 70, 108

gas
  analysis of, 89, 117, 118, 174–75, 183
  diffusion of, 102, 107
  exchange of, 107
  sampling apparatus for, 85
  transport of, 47, 93
gas jet, 83
gas warfare, 116
Gasser, Herbert S., 232
Geiger-Müller counter, 190
gelatin, 114
genetic disease, 196
Gentofte, 194, 210, 211, 216; see also private laboratory
Gentofte Lake, 194, 195
geography, 26, 176
geologists, 41, 97
German language, 13, 26, 33, 40
Germany, 113, 115–116, 188; see also Prussia

Index 283

attacks Russia, 200
invades Denmark, 108, 198, 199
invades Poland, 196
occupies Denmark, 198, 199, 205, 214
scientists, 24, 34, 115, 148
U-boats, 108, 109
Gestapo, 206, 207
headquarters bombed, 216
ghetto, Copenhagen, 204
Gjertsen (*Fram* expedition), 96
glassblowing, 192, 197
Globus arms factory, sabotaged, 206
glomerular capillaries, 159
glomerular filtration rate, 179
glucose injection, 133
glycogen, body's store, 179
Godhavn, 51, 83–85
Godthaab, 52
goldfish, experiments with, 50, 102
governess, 44
Göteborg, 226
Gram, Christian, 117
Grand Canary, 152
grasshoppers, experiments with, 102, 228; see also locusts
Greenland (Grønland), 51–54, 57, 76, 84, 87, 95, 100
Gregersen, Magnus, 223
Grenaa, 5, 10, 12–13, 24–25, 30
Grenaa Harbor, 12
Grollman's acetylene method, 177
Grønland. *See* Greenland
Grueze, Jean-Baptiste, 51
guerilla warfare, 166
Guimar, 152
guinea pigs, experiments with, 114, 182, 209
Guillaume, Charles-Edouard, 121
Guldberg, Hjalmar (Swedish author), 237
Gunn, D. L., 228
gymnasium, 164, 197
gymnastics, 176

Habsburg Monarchy, 108
Haddon, 28
Haemataerometer, 78, 79
hafnium, 187

Hagedorn, Hans Christian, 126–127, 129, 133–134, 193–195, 239
authoritarian nature, 195
Hageman, 101
Haldane, J. Scott, 46, 51, 56, 80, 82, 90, 93–94, 106–107, 109, 119
Haldane, Richard Burdon, 109
Hamsun, Knut, 121
Hannecken, General von, 204
Hans Egede, 84
Hansen, Bjørn Helland, 95, 97
Hansen, Emanuel, 176
Hansen, H. J., 33
Hansen, H. M., 140
Hansen, Jørgen (Marie Krogh's grandfather), 61
Hansen, Mrs. H. M., 177
Hansen, Ove, 178, 179, 183
Hansen, Thyra, 150
Harbor Commission, 9
Harley, Vaughan, 51
Harrop, George A., 124
Hartridge (British physiologist), 119
Harvard University, 113, 161, 222, 223
Harvey Lecture, 123
Hasselbalch, Karl A., 47, 54, 75, 104–105
Harvard Fatigue Laboratory, 184
Hauch (Danish surveying ship), 15
headache, 82
health, August Krogh's, 20, 232
heart disease, 236
heart-gill preparation, 170
heat
  dissipation, 180
  home heating, 181, 203
  loss, 219
heavy water (D_2O), 185–191
Heckscher, Hans, 233
Hedtoft, Hans (head of Danish Social Democratic Party), 204
Heidelberg, 81
Heimdal (school society), 19
Hein, Piet, 161
Heisenberg, Werner, 205, 214
Helsingør (Elsinor), 7, 207
hemoglobin, 90–91, 107, 112
Henderson, Yandell, 106, 123
Henriques, Valdemar, 107, 140–141
Hershel, William, 50
Hevesy, Georg von, 185–191, 206, 209

high altitude, effects of, 184
Highet, Gilbert, 163
Hildebrandt, Mr., 23–24
Hill, Archibald V., 173
Hippocratic oath, 132
histology, thyroid, 151
historical review, 219
Hitler, Adolf, 187, 195, 199
Hjort, Karen, 196; *see also* Karen Krogh.
Hodgkin, Alan L., 191
Hofer, E., 186
Hogben, Lancelot, 228
Højskole Hjemmet, 18, 19
Holand, Hjalmar, 223–224
Holberg, Ludvig (Danish writer), 62
Holland, 109, 118, 200
Holm-Jensen, Ib, 183, 214
Holst, Johannes, 190
Holstein, 7
Holte, 57, 58
home economics, 118
home heating, 181, 203
honorary doctoral degree, 124
Hopkins, Frederick G., 173
Hornbæk House, 233
horses, experiments with, 114
horse and buggy, 69, 106
Houssay, Bernardo A., 232
Hudson Bay, 223
human lungs, 92, 106
human physiology, 164
human teeth, 190
Hundeeiland, 52
Hungary, 187
Husby, 61
hydrostatic regulation, 99
hydrostatic theory, 49
Hyllested, 14
hypercapnia, 91
hyperventilation, 182

Ibsen, Henrik, 38
Imperial Academy of Sciences (Vienna), 71
incubator, 74, 83, 88
India ink, 114
Ingeborg, Princess, 121
Inger, Aunt (August Krogh's cousin once removed), 23

injections for pain, 237
insects, 13, 228
  Cossus larva, 229
  flight of, 210, 229, 230–231
  tethering of, 224
insensible perspiration, 178
Institute for Theoretical Physics (Bohr's institute), 141, 187, 189–191, 205
Institute of Physical Chemistry, 141
instruments, scientific, 45, 51, 98, 227
  construction of, 45, 47, 54, 72, 76, 104
insulin, 4, 126, 163
  "Insulin Leo," 134
  production of, 4, 132–138
  shock from, 134
Insulin Committee, 132
Insulin Foundation, 193, 239
Insulin Laboratory, 239
International Congress of Physiological Sciences
  in Boston, 78, 79, 148, 166
  in Copenhagen, 191, 232, 239
  in Oxford, 231
International Education Board, 140
interviews with August Krogh, 165
intestine, 45, 101
  bacteria in, 74
invasion coefficient, 34
investment in research, August Krogh advocates, 234
ion exchange and transport, 3, 167, 191, 212–215
  active and passive, 215
Irving, Laurence, 196, 222, 224, 228, 232–233
isotopes, 4, 185–192
  as indicators, 187
  in biological research, 189
Issefjord, 16, 145, 146
Italy, 152

Jacksonville (Florida), 222
Jacobaeus, J. C., 137
Japan, scientists and students from, 148
Jean d'Arc School destroyed, 208
Jensen, Martin, 231, 239
Jensen, Norman (pharmacist), 127, 132
Jensen Beach, 222

Index

Jews, in 1930s and '40s
  arrest of, 204
  hostility in Germany toward, 183
  persecution of, 187, 189
  rescue of, 204–205
  rituals of, 165–166
Johansen, W., 39, 88
John B. Pierce Foundation, 184
John Elders and Company, 8
Johns Hopkins University, 123, 159
Joliot-Curie, Frédéric and Irène, 188
Jordbær Kælderen, 150
Jørgensen, Anders Jørgen (Marie Krogh's father), 61
Jørgensen, Anders Vagn (Marie Krogh's nephew), 66
Jørgensen, Ane Margrethe (Marie Krogh's mother), 61, 66, 67–68
Jørgensen, Birthe Marie (Mie). *See* Krogh, Marie 60, 61
Jørgensen, C. Barker, 169
Jørgensen, Emma (Jørgen Jørgensen's wife), 62, 65
  dies in childbirth, 65
Jørgensen, Grethe (Margrethe; Marie Krogh's sister), 61
Jørgensen, Jørgen (Marie Krogh's brother), 66, 108, 125
Jørgensen, Kirsten (Marie Krogh's sister, later named Homsen), 61, 118
Joslin, Elliot Proctor, 126
Journal of Physiology, 136, 215
journalistic polemics, 104
Jungersen, Hector, 42, 59–60, 87, 108
Jungle Book (Kipling), 142
jus practicandi (right to independent practice), 202
Just So Stories (Kipling), 142
Jutland, 64

K. *See* potassium
Kaiserlische Academie der Wissenshaften, 76
kangaroo rats, experiments with, 232
Karolinska Institutionen, 175
kayak, 54, 59
Kempner rice diet, 223
Kennedy, T. S., 230
Kensington Stone, 222–223, 226

Kety, Seymour, 107
Keys, Ancel B., 149, 160, 168, 170
kidneys, 45, 178
  disease of, 199, 207, 209
Killick, Esther, 91
King's College, Cambridge, 82–83, 119
Kipling, Rudyard, 143
Kiruna (Sweden), 200
Klingsley, Miss (August Krogh's landlady), 22, 23, 24, 28
Knisely, Melvin, 222–223, 225
Knutsson, Paal, 223, 224
Koch, Henri, 149, 171
Koefoed-Johnsen, Valborg, 186
Køge Bay, 108
Kommune Hospitalet (communal hospital), 208, 236
Kongsted, August, 132–133
Krabbe, Burgomaster, 11
Krabbe, Mrs., 11
Krebs, Hans, 167
Kristineberg (Marine Biological Station), 175, 197
Krogh, Agnes Helga (August and Marie's daughter), 147, 152–153, 186, 197, 203, 207, 224, 226–227
Krogh, Andreas (August Krogh's great-grandfather), 5, 6
Krogh, Andreas Lauritz (Jacob Krogh's brother), 7
Krogh, Anna (Viggo Krogh's sister), 12
Krogh, August (Schack August Steenberg Krogh)
  Aarhus Cathedral School, mathematics-science artium, 17–21
  ancestry, 5–9
  artificial respiration, 180–181
  attention to accuracy, 186
  attitudes toward
    languages, 33, 40, 47
    decorations and medals, 41
    life, 20, 60, 72
    studying for examinations, 29, 35, 41–43
  Bergen, Helland Hansen, and Amundsen, 95–96
  birth and early childhood, 10–12
  Bøvings as friends, 143–144
  children, 144, 145–150, 152–153, 157, 161, 196–197, 200–203, 206–208
  calling for zoology, 14

Krogh, August *(continued)*
  Christmas tradition with the family, 144
  comparative physiology, 166–167
  courtship and engagement, 60–61, 69
  discussions with J. S. Haldane, 91
  doctoral dissertation, 52, 58
  early education, 13
  final illness and death, 232, 236–238
  finishes *realskolen*, 15
  first lecture, 39
  friendships
    at the university, 27, 28, 35, 38, 43, 54
    during school years, 17–21
  gas transport conflict with Christian Bohr, 78–81, 82–83
  German and Austrian scientists, assistance for, 116–117
  grandchildren, 197, 198, 200, 203, 216, 225, 226
  grandparents, 5–9, 30–31
  Greenland expeditions, 51–54, 83–87, 90
  Hagedorn conflict, 193–195
  home life in Gentofte, 226–228
  instrument construction ability, 99
  laboratory problems, 89, 193–95
  Latin translation, 47, 51
  leaves Academy of Sciences, 233–236
  Lindhard is supported by, 104–105
  London visit, 50–51
  love of Kipling's books, 143
  Lynæshus purchased, 148
  magister conference, 32
  meets Barcroft, 82
  navy apprentice, 15–16
  nervous attacks and mercury poisoning, 48–49, 58, 75
  Nobel Prize, 3–4, 120–121
  Nobel Prize recommendation for Banting and Macloud, 136–138
  Norse archaeology, 221–226
  parents, 7–13, 15, 18–22, 25, 27, 30, 33–34, 36–40, 48, 58, 69–70, 72–73, 77, 82, 121, 146
    permission to study zoology, 25–27
  physics ability, 13, 29, 32, 45
  physiology interest, 32–34
  pilot exam, 59
  position as lecturer in zoophysiology, 87
  position in Bohr's laboratory, 44
  professor in zoophysiology, 110–111
  proposal to Miss Lindberg, 211–214
  protection of the defenseless, 45
  reading to his family, 142–143
  religion and conflict with parents, 21, 36–38, 42, 48, 72–73, 237
  retirement postponed, 196
  return to Denmark, 216
  rigid schedules, 29
  sailing, 59
  scientific work,
    capillary research, 112–115, 117–125, 154–162
    carbon dioxide in atmosphere and water, 51–54, 57, 72
    dissolved organic substances as food for aquatic organisms, 167–169
    exercise physiology with Lindhard and others, 100–102, 173–180
    insect physiology, 34–35, 44, 47–50, 99, 102, 224, 227–238
    insulin and diabetes, 131–138
    isotopes and ion transport, 185–192, 203, 212–215
    osmoregulation and salt transport, 169–172
    oxygen, carbon dioxide, and carbon monoxide transport, 45–47, 54–55, 90–94
    nitrogen excretion, 71–77, 83–87, 90
    sap rising in plants, 215–216
  Seegen Prize, 71–77
  siblings assisted by, 28, 30, 54, 55, 76
  Rockefeller Foundation award for a new institute, 139–142
  solves problem for rabbi, 165–166
  Sørensen's influence, 13–15, 27–28, 33, 41
  statistical treatment of data, 103–104
  teacher Carl Nilsson, 13
  teaching, 164–165
  threats to his life, 206
  United States, travels in, 126–132, 145, 218, 221–224, 232–233
  medical preparatory studies, 22–25
  visitors to his laboratory, 159–162
  well diggers' death, 56–57
  young friends, 219
  Zoophysiological Laboratory becomes reality, 98

Index

Krogh, Bodil Mimi (August and Marie's daughter), 117, 147, 152–153, 190, 194–195, 197, 200–203, 206, 218, 225, 227, 232, 237–238
Krogh, Christen (August Krogh's great-great-grandfather), 5
Krogh, Edel (August Krogh's sister), 11, 29, 67
Krogh, Ellen Rigmor (August and Marie's daughter), 108, 148, 152, 196–197, 210–211, 223, 227
Krogh, Emil (Jacob Emil; August Krogh's brother), 11, 28, 30, 35, 36, 37, 51, 55–56, 59, 66, 76
Krogh, Erik Viggo (August and Marie's son), 88, 89, 118–119, 142, 146, 152, 206–208, 210, 233, 237–238
Krogh, Frida (August Krogh's grandmother), 30
Krogh, Frida (August Krogh's sister), 11, 30, 72, 89, 121, 125
Krogh, Inger Marie (August Krogh's granddaughter), 197
Krogh, Inger Marie (Misse; August Krogh's sister), 11, 30, 76
Krogh, Jacob (Emil); August Krogh's grandfather), 7–9, 29–31
Krogh, Jens, 5, 6
Krogh, Johan (August Krogh's brother), 11, 28, 30, 76, 106
Krogh, Johan (Emil Krogh's son; August Krogh's nephew), 149
Krogh, Karen, 207–208, 223; *see also* Karen Hjort
Krogh, Line (Marenline Petrine; Jacob Krogh's sister), 7
Krogh, Marie (Mie; *née* Birthe Marie Jørgensen), 3, 60, 61
  anatomical dissection in Lund, 71–72
  ancestry, 61
  August becomes her instructor, 60, 63
  Belgian queen, 157
  birth of stillborn son, 106
  birth of twins, 88
  breast cancer, 200–203
  Canary Islands, 152
  caring for family, 142, 144, 146–150, 194
  caring for others, 148, 149
  censor at examinations, 118, 151
  childhood, 61
  children, 88, 105, 108, 117–118, 125, 147, 202
  clinical scientific and health-related work
    biological standardization, 118
    diffusion of oxygen and carbon monoxide, 74, 79, 92–93, 106–108
    medical practice, 105, 117, 149
    mercury poisoning, 182
    metabolic diseases, 117, 118
    metabolic studies in Greenland, 81–82, 90, 106
    nutrition and home economics, 118, 150
    thyroid studies, 151, 209
  courtship and engagement, 60, 63–70
  death, 202
  death of sister-in-law, 65
  decision to study medicine, 62
  diabetes and insulin, 119–120, 126–129, 134, 151
  diplomacy and support of August, 96–97, 104, 113
  doctoral dissertation, 106–108
  entertaining at home, 148, 151
  Erik is kept alive, 88–89, 118
  examinations for medical degree, 76, 81
  family farm, 61
  friendships with fellow students, 62–63, 97, 106
  Greenland expedition, 83–87
  hires Else Nicolaisen, 146
  Italy, travels in, 152
  laboratory, 151, 195
  medical degree and internship, 81–82
  Nielsine Nielsen's example, 62–63
  parents, 61, 72–77
  siblings, 61
  summer houses, 108, 145–146, 153
  Tagea Brandt travel award, 152
  tuberculosis and death of father and siblings, 61
  tuberculosis of Erik Krogh, 118
  view on women's role, 105
  wedding, 72–73
  Zahle's school, 62
Krogh, Marie (*née* Brick; Andreas Krogh's wife), 6
Krogh, Mimi (*née* Marie Magdalene Bolette; August Krogh's mother), 5, 7,

Krogh, Mimi (continued)
  8, 9, 10, 48, 51, 54, 56, 58, 69–70, 72, 77, 80, 87, 121, 146
Krogh, Sofie (née Larsen; August Krogh's sister-in-law), 149
Krogh, Viggo Ditlev (August Krogh's father), 5, 6, 10, 11, 14, 27, 30, 44, 51, 54–56, 58, 69, 77
  death, 146
Kruse (friend of Viggo Krogh), 77
Kulhusrenden, 153
Kullen, 35
Kutchin (member of *Fram* expedition), 96

Laboratory for Theoretical Gymnastics, 176
laboratory instructor, Marie Krogh's, 63
Lagerlöf, Selma, 121
Landis, Eugene, 4, 154, 160, 161, 163, 196, 221
Langfeldt, E., 176
Langley, J. N. (editor of *Journal of Physiology*), 114, 115
Lansdowne (Pennsylvania), 222
Latin, 17, 26
Latin school, 25
Latvia, 198
Lawrence, Ernest, 188
lead, radioactive, 187
League of Nations, 116, 178, 180
leakage of ions, 190
lecturer, 105, 164
  in zoophysiology, 81, 87
Lehrbuch der innere Medicin, 76
Leipzig (Germany), 34, 175
Leshley, Mrs., 24, 58
Levi, Hilde, 189
Lewis, Dr., 128
Liberty ship, 225
Lie, Jonas, 38
Liljestrand, Göran, 175, 176, 216
Lillegade, 12, 31
Lindberg, Anna-Louise, 202, 211–12
Lindberg, Olaf (Olle), 227
Linderstrøm-Lang, Kai, 187, 205
Lindhard, (Jens Peter) Johannes, 99–101, 104–106, 112, 114, 173, 174, 176–181, 184

Lister Institute, 119
Lithuania, 196, 198
liver, 101, 213
  infection of, 236
Liverpool, England, 125
Ljunghusen, Bjørn (later named Krogh; August Krogh's grandson), 201
Ljunghusen, Bodil (later named Krogh; August Krogh's granddaughter), 197, 201
Ljunghusen, Einar (August Krogh's son-in-law), 197
Ljunghusen, Ellen. *See* Ellen Krogh
locusts, experiments with, 235; *see also* grasshoppers
London, 50, 224
London School of Hygiene and Tropical Medicine, 171
Loulou, Mrs. (newspaper reporter), 150
Løven's Chemical Company, 118, 132, 133, 136
Luce, Henry, 226
Lucilia (fly), experiments with, 224
Ludwig, Carl, 34, 46, 78, 116
Lund University's Physiological Institute, 210
Lund (Sweden), 71, 72, 210
Lund (teacher), 23
Lundegårdh, H., 171, 212, 214, 216
Lundsgaard, Einar (professor of physiology, Rockefeller Institute), 220
lungs, 46, 56, 80, 92, 106
  edema of, 182
Lusitania (ocean liner), 109, 110
Lutheran church, 37
Lynæs, 145, 146
Lynæshus, 145, 153, 220

Maar, Vilhelm, 47, 58
Macloud, John James Richard, 128, 129, 136, 137, 138
macrotonometer, 83
Madsen, Christian, 145
Madsen, Victor, 97
magister conference (similar to master's degree), 14, 26, 122, 164
magnets, as brakes for bicycle ergometer, 100

Index

Magnus II Eriksson (king of Sweden and Norway), 223
malnutrition, Agnes Krogh's protein deficiency and, 200
mammals, experiments with, 102
Man's Unconquerable Mind (Highet), 163
Manchester (England), 187
Manhattan Project, 189
manic depression in Krogh family, 196
Many Inventions (Kipling), 236
Marie (princess of Denmark), 16
Marine Biological Station, Kristineberg, 175, 197
Marineland (Florida), 222
Markoff, Müller, and Zuntz, 101
Marshall, E. K. Jr., 159, 160
Märtha, Princess, 121
Martin (physiologist, Lister Institute), 119
Massmanske School, 7
mathematics and science, study of, 21, 24, 26, 28–29, 32
Mayo Clinic, 123
Mayo Foundation, 129, 166
Means, James Howard, 221, 223
Means, Philip, 224
Meddelelser om Grønland (Communications on Greenland), 52
Medicinalco, 219
Meinert, F. V. A., 22
Mellanby, Sir Edward and Lady May, 219, 224, 231, 232, 233
membranes, transport across, 45, 212–215; *see also* ion exchange and transport
Memel (Lithuania), 195
Memphis (Tennessee), 158
mercuric oxide, 75
mercury, 75
  measuring content in air, 183
  poisoning, 48–49, 75, 182
  vapors, 48–49, 75
metabolism, 4, 46, 81, 83, 103, 112, 117, 151, 178, 212
  of carbohydrate, 126, 137, 173–174
  of fat, 129, 173–174
methylene blue dye, 155
mice, experiments with, 133
micro fauna of the sea bottom, 168
microanalysis of gases, 80

microcirculation in capillary physiology, 162
microclimate recorder, 181, 232
microscope, 13, 33
microtonometer, 80, 81, 83
Middle Ages, 224
Miles, Walter R., 127
military service, August Krogh disqualified, 41
Milledge, J. S., 91
mines, 108
Ministry for Church and Education, 96, 110
Ministry for Trade and Shipping, 97
Ministry of Finance, 88
Minneapolis, 129, 222
Minnekahda voyage, 148
Minnesota, 124
Mississippi Delta, 184, 222
Møen, 36, 63
Møller (caretaker, Ny Vestergade), 97
Møller, Eli, 106, 108
Møller, Lars (publisher), 86
Molotov, Vyacheslav Mikhaylovich, 198
Momme, 9, 11
monograph, 195
Moore, Dr. (in Ann Arbor), 232
Mosquito bomber airplanes, 208
mosquito larvae, 50, 171
mouth-to-mouth respiration, 181
movie camera, 123
Mt. Evans (Colorado), 184
Mt. Holyoke College, 160, 222
Müller, Ditlev, 133
Munch, Kai, 206
Munich, 195
Murillo, Bartolomé Esteban, 51
muscles, 4, 112–115
  arteries in, 114
  circulation in, at rest and at work, 115
  work of, 100, 101, 112, 173
Mussolini, Benito, 152
myosin, 156

N_2O. *See* nitrous oxide
Na^+. *See* sodium ion
Nakazawa, Fusakichi, 155
Nansen, Fridjof, 95
Napoleonic Wars, 5

National Gallery (London), 50–51
National Museum (Denmark), 225
natural history, 25, 27, 39, 59
Natural History Society (Naturhistorisk Forening), 24, 48, 220
Nature (English weekly journal), 52, 72, 171
Naturkræfterne (Viggo Krogh), 13
Nazis, 190, 200
Nedergade, 12
Nelson River, 223
neomycin, 236
nerves, sectioning on oxygen uptake, 55
nervous attacks, August Krogh's, 58
neurologist, 58
New Haven (Connecticut), 222
New York, 124
Newport Tower (Newport, R.I.), 223, 225, 226
Newton, Isaac, 50
Nicolaisen, Else. *See* Rahbek, Else
Niels Stensen Hospital, 136, 236
Nielsdatter, Ane Margrethe (Marie Krogh's grandmother), 61
Nielsen, Astrid Tetens, 219, 220
Nielsen, Erik Tetens, 219–221, 228, 230, 233
Nielsen, Helge, 227
Nielsen, Colonel Holger, 181
Nielsen, Holger E., 177, 178
Nielsen, M. B. C., 97
Nielsen, Marius, 177, 178–179, 180, 182, 183, 229
Nielsen, Nielsine (first woman admitted to University of Copenhagen), 62
nightmares, 38
Nilsson, Carl (August Krogh's teacher), 13, 219
Nissen stipend, 20
Nitella (fresh water plant), 214
nitrogen
 used as anaesthetic, 165–66
 excretion of, 47, 74, 75
 Odense well and, 57
nitrous oxide, 166, 177
Nobel Prize, 3, 102, 120, 121, 136, 138, 145, 150, 162, 233
 for chemistry, 189
 for physics, 189
 prize committee, 120, 137, 138

Nordisk Insulin Foundation, 136, 193, 239
Nordisk Insulin Laboratory, 136, 193, 194, 239
Norfolk (Virginia), 225
Nørlund, 226
Normandy, 206
Nørre Alle, 142
Norse archaeological sites, 221
Norse colony, 223
Norsemen, 222
North Africa, 152
North Atlantic, 53
North Pole, 96
North Sea, 109
North Slesvig, 109
Northwest Passage, 95
Norway, 95, 96, 196, 198, 224
 heavy water plant in, 190
Novak and Seegen, 75
Novo Laboratories, 135
Novo Nordisk Pharmaceuticals, Inc., 138
nutrition, Marie Krogh lectures on, 118
Nutrition Laboratory Carnegie Institution, 127
Ny Vestergade (street in Copenhagen), 81, 89, 96, 97, 106, 133, 144
Nybro Street, 6

O_2. *See* Oxygen
occupation of Denmark (WWII), 203–204
ocean, carbon dioxide tension in, 53
oceanarium at Marineland, 222
oceanography, *Fram* expedition and, 96
Odense, 56, 125
Odensjön (Sweden), 35
Ohlman (farmer), 222, 227
oil ration, 227
Okkles, Harald, 151
Oliver, George, 155
øllebrød (alebread), 18
opera, 149
ordner (medals and decorations), 41
organic material, 167
Oslo, 225
osmoregulation, 167
osmosis, 172, 212, 213
Oxford (England), 51
oxygen (O_2), 3, 38, 78, 115, 165
 alveolar air and, 79, 107

arterial blood and, 79
deficiency, 106, 182, 210
diffusion of, 106, 112
reaches flight muscles, 231
secretion of, 79, 91, 92
supplied to tissue, 112
tension, 102, 112, 115
oyster ponds, studies in Norway of, 197
Øresund, 16, 52, 59
Østersø St., 68

P-51 Mustang fighter airplanes, 208
pathology, thyroid, 151
pancreas, 134
　insulin prepared from, 128–130
　canine pancreatectomy in insulin experiments, 130
Panum P. L. (Danish physiologist), 34
Paris, 118
Parliament, Danish, 44, 90, 97, 204
Parsons (British physiologist), 119
pathology, 151
patriotism, August Krogh's, 176
Pearce, Richard M., 139
Pedersen, Harald, 135
Pedersen, P. O., 190
Pedersen, R. (plant physiologist; official opponent at Krogh's doctoral defense), 56
Pedersen, Thorvald, 135
penicillin, 216, 218, 236
Pennsylvania, 195
pension, 145, 152
pericapillary cells, 157
pericytes, 156, 159
periscope, camera modified by August Krogh with, 123
permeability of membranes, 212; *see also* ion exchange and transport
Peary, Robert E., 96
personality, effect of mercury poisoning on, 183
Peru, 52
Peymann, General, 6
Pflüger, Eduard, 46, 78
pharmacology, 76
Phenol Red, 159
Philadelphia, 129, 222

philosophy, 14
physics, 25, 29
Physiol. Zentralblatt (Danish physiological journal), 91
Physiological Laboratory (Bohr's laboratory), 35, 37, 38, 42, 44, 45, 49, 98, 100
Physiological Society, 107
physiologists, 41, 45, 60, 109
Physiology, 33, 34, 47, 76
　anatomy and, 210
　teaching of, 54, 118
　August Krogh writes textbook on, 83
　thyroid, 151
Pico de Teide (mountain, Canary Islands), 116
pigs, insulin from pancreas of, 134
Pikes Peak, 106, 107
Pilehuset (the willow house), 220, 233
pituitary gland, posterior lobe, 155
Pituitrin, 155
plankton, Arctic, 185
plant physiology, 47, 56, 216
plant roots, 212, 215
Plimmer, 109
Plum, Claus Munch, 219–220
pneumonia, 146, 218
Poland, 196, 198
Politiken (Copenhagen newspaper), 236
Pontopidan (professor of neurology), 58, 59
porpoises, 222
Porsild, Morten, 51, 52, 76, 83, 84
portal system, 101
potassium (K), 203
　ion (K^+), 213
Poulesco, N. C., 130
Poulsen, Jacob, 136
Poulsen, Olaf (actor), 23
prelimiær examen (not an entrance examination for the university), 147
private laboratory, August Krogh's, 193, 195, 212, 216; *see also* Gentofte
private practice, Marie Krogh's, 98, 117
Proceedings of the Royal Society, 215
professor of zoophysiology, 110, 111
program declaration, 49
Progress of Physiology, The (August Krogh), 166
propulsion of fishes, 218

prostate, 195
protein, 83
  synthesis of, 186
protozoans, 168
Prussia, 109, 115
Prussian blue stain, 114
psychology, 47
publications, August Krogh's, 110
Puck of Pook's Hill (Kipling), 142
Pütter, August, 167
pulmonary function test, 107
pump for circulating air, 230
pupae, 74

quantum mechanics, 189

R.Q. *See* respiratory quotient
rabbi, August Krogh's help sought by, 165
rabbits, experiments with, 91, 133
radioactivity, 168, 185–192, 214
Ragna (sailing boat purchased by August Krogh et al.), 59, 65
Rahbek, Else (Nic; *née* Else Nicolaisen), 146, 147, 212, 227–228, 236, 237
Rahbek family, 227, 236, 237
railroads, 108
Randers, 66
Raphael-Pedersen, Axel (Raphael; August Krogh's friend), 36, 37, 41, 43
Rasmussen, Knud (Arctic explorer), 85–86, 145
Rasmussen, Ove, 133
realskolen (grade school), 15
Reaumur (measure of temperature), 23
red blood cells, 213, 219
Red Cross, 181, 198, 207
Reenpää, Y., 176
Refnæs, sanatorium at, 119
refugees, Danish (WWII), 210, 216
respiration, regulation of, 100, 101
Rehberg, Paul Brandt, 122, 127, 156–157, 159, 160–161, 164–165, 177, 179, 186, 188, 210
  assigned to Medical Corps, 122
  escapes from Gestapo, 208

Reinhard, Hedvig, 108
religion, August Krogh's views on, 36, 37, 48, 73, 237
  leaves Danish church, 21
reptiles, 24
resistance leaders (WWII), 207
respiration, 46, 55, 82, 102, 163, 229
  artificial, 181
respiration chamber, 83–85
respirator used for polio victims, 180
respiratory center, 180
respiratory quotient (R.Q.), 129, 137, 173–175, 179, 230, 231
retina inflammation, 209
review of Mean and Holand's book rejected, 225
Rhode Island, 223
Ribbentrop, Joachim von, 198
Richards, A. Newton, 113, 159
Riffelsyndikat, 206
Rigshospital, 117, 127
Riukan (Norway), 188
Rochester (Minnesota), 129, 222
Rockefeller Foundation, 139
Rockefeller Institute, 139, 141, 144, 160
Rohman (shipbuilder), 8
Rose, Wickliffe, 140
Rosenow, E. C., 166
Rosenvinge, J. L. A. Kolderup, 86
Roskildefjord, 16
Rouget cells, 157
roundabout, 230
Rowsing, Thorkild, 3
Royal Army Medical College, 109
Royal College of Physicians, 215
Royal Society in London, 190
Rubner, Max, 103
Rungsted, 77
runes (on Kensington Stone), 226
Russia, 41, 108, 198
Rutherford, Ernest, 187

sabotage, 204, 210
Salomonsen, Carl J., 88, 98
Saltholm, 59
Santa Rita Station (Arizona), 232
Sargasso Sea, 169
Scandinavian American Foundation, 226

Schäfer, Edward Albert, 155
Schalburg Corps, 204
Schistocerca gregarius, 230; See also locust
Schlambush, Axel, 23, 88
Schleswig. See Slesvig
Schlieper, Carl, 149, 170
Schmidt-Nielsen, Astrid, 197, 202–203, 216
Schmidt-Nielsen, Bent, 206, 216, 218
Schmidt-Nielsen, Bodil. See Bodil Krogh
Schmidt-Nielsen, Knut, 197, 199, 206, 217, 224–225, 228, 232, 233
Schneider (physiologist), 106
Scholander, Per F., 196, 222, 224, 232
School of Dentistry, 89, 190, 196
School of Home Economics, 150
Schröer, Dr. (German oceanographer), 96
sciopticon, 50
Scotland, 8, 138
Scottl, Robert Falcon, 96
seal meat, 83
secretion theory, 46, 78–80, 92
Seegen and Novak, 75
Seegen Prize, 3, 71, 76–77, 88
Seiling, Caspar, 11
set-point, 180
"seven small devils," 93, 95
sex physiology, 164
Shakespeare, William, 23
shechita (Jewish slaughtering ritual), 165
Shell House, 208
Sidsel (Emil Krogh's girlfriend), 54
Silliman Lectures, 123, 127
Sims, David E., 156, 159
Sjöfart ock Handelstidningen (Göteborg shipping gazette), 225
Skärgården (Stockholm's archipelago), 209
Skandinavishe Archiv für Physiologie (physiology journal), 92, 93, 175
Skaraliden (Sweden), 35
skating, 13
Slesvig (Schleswig), 3, 7
Smith and Haldane, 56, 80, 90–91, 93–95
Smithsonian Institution, 106, 144
Søbredden, 227
Society for the Protection of the Defenseless, 45

sodium ion, 191, 213
Søfartstidende (shipping journal), 55
Sognefjord, 97
Solrød, 108, 118, 125
Sonne, Carl, 175
Sørensen, Ingrid (August Krogh's goddaughter), 34
Sørensen, S. P. L., 187
Sørensen, Valdemar, 27, 29, 35, 37, 54–56
becomes military physician, 56
Sørensen, William (Uncle William), 13–15, 22, 23, 24, 27, 33, 38, 39, 40, 41, 67, 76, 78, 104
South Pole, 96
Spanish flu, 115
Spärck, Ragnar, 167
specific surface, 79–80
sphincters, precapillary, 159
spiders, 14, 17
spiracles, 22, 102
spleen, 101
St. Karlsminde, 153, 196
St. Louis, 129
Stanford University, 232
Starling, Ernest, 82, 84, 127
statistics, 103, 104
Steenberg, Schack August, 10
Steenstrup, Japetus, 41
Steno, Nicholaus (Niels Stensen), 10, 47
Stockholm, 120, 121
Stockholmstidningen (Stockholm newspaper), 121
stomatas in plants, 34, 47
Storegade, 12
strobe light, 231
strophanthin, 118
Strøget (street in Copenhagen), 149
studenter examen. See artium
Studenter Samfundet (Student Society), 38
Studentergården, 177
Studiestræde (street in Copenhagen), 105
Sudetenland, 195
sugar, 129, 215
Sukkertoppen, 52
surface law, 103
swarm of locusts, 230
Swarthmore College, 194, 196
swimbladder, 46

syphilis, 56
syringe pipette, 170
Szent-Györgyi, Albert, 232

Tagea Brandt Award, 152
teaching obligations, 235
Telemark, 59
telescope, 13
Tenerife, 116, 152
Thalbitzer, William, 225
theoretical physics, 111
Theresienstadt, 206
thermostatic box. *See* incubator
thesis, magister conference, 42
Thomsen, Madam, 54, 72, 75
Thoulet, Dr., 81
"Three Musketeers," 183
Thunberg, Torsten, 194
thyroid extract, 209
thyroid gland, 117, 151
thyroxin, 118
Tigerstedt, 92, 101
Tilbury (England), 148
tilting spirometer, 101
tilting table, 181
Tisville, 220
Tolypellopsis stelligera (aquatic weed), 214
tonometer, 76, 78–79, 81, 94
Torm, rector of Copenhagen University, 140
Toronto Insulin Committee, 132
toxic fumes, 75
tracheal sacs, 102
trachea system, 46–47, 102
tracheoles, 102
traitors (WWII), 204
tree buds, 215
Trine (Ane Jørgensen's maid), 70, 149
trioxyhematein, 155
Trissen, 146
Trolle, Carsten, 178
Trondheim, 194
tropomyosin, 156
trypsin, 130
tuberculosis, 10, 61–62, 106, 119
Tuborg, 11

Turner, Abby H., 149, 160
turtles, experiments with, 80

U.S. Army in Korea, 181
Udmærkelse (highest grades), 20, 28
ultra-micro method for chloride, 171
Ultuna-Uppsala, 216
umiak, 51–52
Uncle William. *See* Sørensen, William
United States, visits to, 63, 103, 104, 110, 113, 124, 196, 210
University of Aberdeen, 138
University of Copenhagen, 3, 13, 32, 58, 62, 71, 131
   medical facility, 55, 105
   medical preparatory examination, 14, 22
University of Oslo, 196
Urey, H. C., 185
urine production, 179
Ussing, Hans, 185–191, 197
Uvarov, B. P., 228

vagus nerve, 80
Valdemar (prince of Denmark), 16
van't Hoff, Jacolous Hendricus, 102
Varn, Erik (Jørgen Jørgensen's younger son), 65, 149
vasopressin, 155
ventilation
   of tracheae, 231
   regulation of, 180
Vesterbygden, 223
Vienna, 116
Vienna Academy of Sciences, 71
Vimtrup, Bjowulf, 124, 155, 158
Vincent, George, 139
Vinland, 223
vippe spirometer (tilting spirometer), 101
Vistula River, 198
"visual thinking" of August Krogh, 99
vital forces, 45
vitamins, 150
Volhard titration, 170
von Frisch, Karl, 233

Index 295

Vosegaard (copyhold farm where Marie Krogh was born), 61, 66
Vøtz, Frida (Aunt Frida; Viggo Krogh's sister), 17
Vøtz, Georg (August Krogh's cousin), 17
Vøtz, Johannes Christian (husband of Viggo Krogh's sister Frida), 17
Voxstrup Farm, 7, 8, 14, 24

Wansbeck (Holstein), 7
war minister, 122
Warming, Eugene, 35, 39, 41, 42, 88
Washington, D.C., 124, 127, 129, 222, 232
wasps, solitary digging of, 220
water
  fresh and brackish, 212
  diffusion across cell membranes, 185–191
Watiovaara, Veijo, 214
Webers Street, 28
wedding, 9, 73
Wedell, Count Karl Wilhelm Adam, 61
Weis-Fogh, Torkel, 212, 219, 228, 230–231, 239
well diggers' accidental death, 56
Wellesley, Arthur (later Duke of Wellington), 5
Wernøe, Th. B., 155
Wernstedt, Agnes, 198, 201, 202, 224, 226; see also Agnes Krogh
Wernstedt, Christer, 197, 198, 199, 209, 210, 223, 224, 226
Wernstedt, Lars (Agnes Krogh's son), 197, 226
Wesenberg-Lund, Carl, 221
West Greenland, 223
Westminster Abbey, 50
Westward from Vinland (Holand), 225
White Star Line, 152
wickerwork suitcase, 222
Wiedervelt Street, 68
Wigglesworth, V. B., 171
Wilton, Connecticut, 222
wind tunnel, 224, 227, 228

Woods Hole, Massachusetts, 144, 168, 169
Woods Hole Oceanographic Institution, 169
World War I, 108
World War II, 172, 196
  black market, 206
  resistance fighters, 207–208
wrinkling of capillary wall, 156

X-ray treatments, 195, 201

Yale University, 123, 128
Yale University Press, 123, 124
yeast cells, 213
Young, Robert R. (chairman of Chesapeake and Ohio Railroad), 226

Zahle, Natalie, 62
Zahle's (women's artium-preparatory school), 62, 63
Zealand, 24, 108
Zealand (Danish troop ship), 15
Zeiss dissection microscope, 33
Zerahn, K., 192
Zeuthen, Erik, 42, 229, 230
Zimmerman, K. W., 156
zoological garden, 152
Zoological Museum (Copenhagen), 233
zoologist, 50, 58
zoology, 14, 22, 25, 27, 32, 42, 44, 45, 47
  August Krogh's choice, 25
  departments, 166
  professor, 221
Zoophysiological Laboratory, 88, 98, 135, 142, 157, 177, 180, 191, 197, 205, 211
zoophysiology (comparative physiology), 49, 81
Zotterman, Yngve, 148
Zuntz, Nathan, 82, 101, 173, 174
Zweifach, Benjamin W., 158, 159